ISBN 978-1-330-32867-5
PIBN 10029040

Forgotten Books is a registered trademark of FB &c Ltd.
Copyright © 2017 FB &c Ltd.
FB &c Ltd, Dalton House, 60 Windsor Avenue, London, SW19 2RR.
Company number 08720141. Registered in England and Wales.

For support please visit www.forgottenbooks.com

AMERICAN GOVERNMENT

WITH A CONSIDERATION OF THE

PROBLEMS OF DEMOCRACY

BY

FRANK ABBOTT MAGRUDER, Ph.D.

INSTRUCTOR OF POLITICS IN PRINCETON
UNIVERSITY

———

*" It is the duty of the government to make it easy
for the people to do right, and difficult for the
people to do wrong."* — W. E. GLADSTONE.

———

ALLYN AND BACON

Boston   New York   Chicago

FAN

Norwood Press

J. S. Cushing Co. — Berwick & Smith Co.

Norwood, Mass., U.S.A.

PREFACE

THE aims of *American Government* may be summed up under four heads : —

First, to impress upon the pupil his responsibility, as a future citizen, for the development of better government.

Second, to show how the state has developed from a simple organization for defense to the complex socialized society of to-day ; and to make it clear that government is not operated according to preconceived theories, but is a living organism developed by the people to meet the needs resulting from changing conditions ; to show, for example, that the Constitution of the United States is not a dead contract, but a living agreement which has developed with time and has adapted itself to economic and social conditions.

Third, to explain the actual operation of the National, State, and Local governments, emphasizing the functions of government without neglecting the necessary details of frame-work.

Fourth, to make plain the influence of the judiciary ; and to present the political and social problems of to-day, such as the initiative, referendum, recall, short ballot, woman suffrage, industrial education, and prohibition.

The author has endeavored to make all important facts stand out clearly, by separating details from the main text, by explaining fully in footnotes all necessary technical terms, and by placing interesting collateral material in the questions for discussion. The text is further simplified by brief examples, outlines, diagrams, maps, and illustrations taken from all sections of the country, the details regarding each State being given in their proper setting.

The treatment of the National government precedes that of State and Local governments, because the National government is the general type followed by all of the States; because it is simpler to treat the State governments by showing that they exercise all those powers not delegated to the National government; and because it is easier to arouse the students' interest by approaching the larger subject first. However, if the teacher prefers to commence with Local government, he may begin with Chapters XXIII and XXIV and follow these with Chapters XVIII to XXII, I to XVII, and XXV to XXIX in succession, without loss of sequence.

As special aid to pupils and teachers, questions on the text, and questions for discussion which show the local application of the context, have been placed at the end of each chapter. Attention is called to Appendix II, which gives further suggestions to teachers, and a select list of reference works that may be used in connection with the course.

The author is greatly indebted to Professor **W. W. Willoughby** of the Johns Hopkins University, who read the entire manuscript and offered many valuable suggestions; also to many friends and government officials who have read portions of the text. He also acknowledges the discriminating assistance of his wife in the planning and execution of the work.

FRANK ABBOTT MAGRUDER.

PRINCETON,
    February, 1917.

CONTENTS

ILLUSTRATIONS

FACSIMILES, DIAGRAMS, AND MAPS

AMERICAN GOVERNMENT

CHAPTER I

IMPORTANCE OF GOVERNMENT

1. Creation of a Government. — The Pilgrims found a spot "fit for situation" and landed at Plymouth, Massachusetts, December 22, 1620. No civilized government[1] existed on these new shores,[2] and the Pilgrims, although a religious people, realized that they would be unable to preserve order among themselves and maintain protection against the Indians without government and laws. In fact, dissensions on the Mayflower had already impressed them with the necessity of establishing a government.

Accordingly, while lying off Cape Cod, the forty-one male adults signed the following agreement: "We whose names are under-written . . . doe . . . combine ourselves together into a civill body politick . . . to enact . . . such just and equall laws . . . from time to time as shall be thought most meete and convenient for ye generall good of ye Colonie, unto which we promise all due submission and obedience." Thus a new government came into existence.

2. Why Government is Important. — Government is important because through coöperation we are able to maintain peace, security, justice, and public services more easily than if individuals acted singly.

Each individual may not directly assist in maintaining peace, security, justice, and public services; but every person

---

[1] A government is the agency through which the purposes of a state are formulated and executed.

[2] By "new shores" is meant the New England shores. A government had existed in Virginia since 1607.

who has money to spend contributes his part toward the support of those who are employed to do the work. In general the head of each family contributes annually, directly or indirectly, to the governments of the United States, of his State, and of his local district about as much as he earns in a month.

3. The Cost of Government. — The expenditures of our national government exceed $1,000,000,000 a year; those of our State, county, and district governments are about $1,000,000,-000; and organized villages, towns, and cities spend another $1,000,000,000. Thus our various governments cost us about $3,000,000,000 a year, or an average of about $30 for each man, woman, and child in the United States.[1] (See Secs. 79 and 246.)

4. How the Cost of Government is Borne. — The cost of government is borne by individuals through taxation. Taxes are paid to the respective governments either directly or indirectly. If paid *directly* the owner of property pays the assessed amount of taxes to the collector directly, but if paid *indirectly* he pays it in the form of rent or in the purchase price of articles that he consumes. To illustrate, the owner of a house usually pays a State tax, county tax, township tax (or city tax if he lives in a city) directly to the officers of these governments; but in case a house is rented, although the owner of the house hands over the money to the tax collector, the renter really pays it, for the owner charges more rent than he would if he had no taxes to pay. (See Sec. 44.)

United States taxes are nearly all paid indirectly. The manufacturers of whiskey, tobacco, playing cards, and oleomargarine pay taxes to the United States government and then sell these products at a price high enough to enable them to pay the tax and earn a profit. The person who uses the articles really pays the tax. (See Sec. 45.)

---

[1] It should be understood that the average cost of government for persons living in large cities, where taxes are high, is much more than $30 a year; whereas the average cost for persons living in rural communities, where taxes are low, is much less.

About two thousand articles imported into the United States from foreign countries are also taxed by the United States. The importer pays the tax and then sells the articles at an advanced price; so the consumer is really the man who pays the tax.

5. Increased Cost of Government. — The cost of the national government has increased from an average of $2 per capita for the period before the Civil War to $10 per capita now — fivefold. The cost of our other governments has in like manner increased. But the services rendered the people by these governments have also increased, and the governments have so protected property and encouraged industry that the average estimated wealth per capita in the United States has increased from $300 in 1850 to almost $2000 in 1910 — nearly sevenfold. So it is easier for the people of the United States to pay an average of $10 a person to the support of the national government now than it was to pay $2 in 1850.

6. The Benefits of Government. — Most people feel that they receive little in exchange for the amount of taxes which they pay, but if they would consider the innumerable benefits they derive from government they would support it cheerfully. Let us name and discuss briefly a few of the benefits of government.

(1) Government Enables Us to be Independent of Foreign Countries. — As soon as the thirteen American colonies declared themselves independent of England they established state governments in order to gain their independence. When the separation was acknowledged by the mother country each state was so small that it was in great danger of being seized by one of the European powers, and in order to secure their independence and have the European countries treat them as equals they were obliged to form a strong United States.

To-day if it were not for the United States army and navy your home and billions of dollars worth of property in cities on navigable streams might be blown to destruction by English or German shells. No individual could protect his own property against such attacks because the maintenance of an army and a navy costs hundreds of millions of dollars a year.

Copyright, Underwood & Underwood, N.Y.

FIRING TWELVE-INCH MORTARS AT FORT TOTTEN, NEW YORK.

Of course these nations would not destroy our property without some cause, but the cause might be an unreasonable one.

(2) **Government Protects our Property from Criminals.** — If it were not for the sheriffs, constables, and policemen, persons who are known to carry large amounts of money would never be safe; indeed persons who carry any money would be in constant danger of being robbed. Furthermore, every night one would retire with the dread of being murdered for the few pieces of silver in the house, and on getting up one would seldom find the bottle of milk which the milkman leaves at the door before daylight.

To-day if a crime is committed in your neighborhood, a policeman can be called by telephone, and if the criminal is not caught at once, news of the crime will flash to all nearby towns and cities. In some cities or thickly settled communities a thousand policemen can be notified in ten minutes. For instance, if a crime is committed in Princeton, New Jersey, the police headquarters of Trenton (ten miles away) and other nearby cities are notified. The Trenton headquarters will flash a light in the police box on each policeman's beat, and every policeman will see the signal, go to the box, and learn the nature of the crime by telephone.

(3) **Government Maintains Peace and Order.** — In our early days a fist fight was the most persuasive argument in settling a political dispute, and if the parties involved held a social position which made a fist fight unbecoming a duel answered as well. To-day an officer is at hand to prevent a fight in any public . place, and insults are commonly settled by libel or slander suits. When satisfactory courts exist to enforce the law, people of to-day frown upon those who attempt to settle their differences by physical force instead of resorting to the courts.

(4) **Government Performs Functions Which Would be Unprofitable as Private Ventures.** — Individuals or companies would not find it profitable to perform any of the following functions in the large and accommodating manner in which our governments perform them.

(a) *Protection to Health.* — The United States Public Health Service Bureau employs 2000 persons, of whom there are 150 commissioned surgeons and 250 acting assistant surgeons. This service seeks, so far as it is able, to protect the civilian population of the country from disease.[1] It does this by investigating the causes of such diseases as yellow fever, typhoid fever, malaria, Rocky Mountain spotted fever, hookworm, and pellagra, and the best methods to prevent them. For instance, it regulates the interstate traffic in vaccines, antitoxins, and viruses in order to insure their good quality.

The Public Health Service Bureau maintains numerous quarantine stations in the United States. At Shanghai, Cal-

---

[1] The Army Medical Corps is responsible for the health of the fighting units on land and the Medical Corps of the United States Navy cares for the health of the fighting men while afloat.

cutta, Naples, Havana, and some thirty other important places in different parts of the world highly trained " health scouts " are stationed to watch for contagious diseases and keep the

IMMIGRANTS AT ELLIS ISLAND AWAITING PHYSICAL EXAMINATION.
Immigrants with contagious diseases are put ashore at the quarantine station.

home office informed. American consuls who are stationed in some 500 leading cities of the world make written reports of health conditions to the Public Health Bureau in Washington and see that commodities from infected districts are not shipped to the United States. State and city health officers throughout the United States make like reports to this bureau.

From each week's accumulation of health reports of the world a bulletin is compiled and distributed to these numerous health and consular officers, so that they may know what disease to look for on a ship coming from a port where disease exists. Thus, if plague breaks out at Calcutta to-day the Washington authorities know it at once, and notify our chain of health police to guard the 17,000 miles of American coast line.

A Seventeenth Century English author incidentally mentions the fact that every fourth person in a large representative audience was horribly disfigured by the smallpox. With our modern travel of persons and interchange of commodities in commerce we should never be safe from smallpox, cholera, yellow fever, and other dreaded diseases if it were not for our public health service. Should we begrudge the taxes we pay to insure us against such calamities?

States, counties, and cities also have their health departments to safeguard the health of the community. These departments educate the people in the prevention of diseases, establish quarantines, order general vaccination, and regularly inspect the water, milk, and other food supplies that are most likely to carry disease germs.

(b) *Protection to Life.* — In addition to the protection to life given by police officers and courts, many cities have building regulations limiting the height of buildings in proportion to the local fire protection, requiring fire escapes on high buildings, prescribing rules for sanitary plumbing and fire-proof wiring, and requiring that doors to public buildings open outward. Cities also have traffic regulations, such as limiting the speed of automobiles and prescribing how they shall pass corners, and requiring railroads to have watchmen at crossings.

States employ factory inspectors to see that workmen have fresh air, that boilers and elevators are in proper condition, and that dangerous machinery has safety appliances. The national government provides for the inspection of locomotives and steamboats, requires passenger vessels to have wireless equipment and life-preservers, maintains wireless stations to notify vessels of storms, and maintains lighthouse and life-saving stations. Recently the United States government established mine experiment stations to experiment with life-saving devices in mines.

(c) *Care of Poor and Helpless.* — If it were not for our State governments most of the 188,000 insane persons who are in public asylums would be at large to annoy us and even endanger our lives.   The 84,000 poor who are now cared for in public institutions would have to beg on the streets and at our homes, or steal, or else starve.   (See Chapter XXIX.)

(d) *Free Education.* — In 1913 about $520,000,000 was spent in public free elementary and secondary (high school) education throughout the United States, or an average of $16.17 for each pupil in elementary grades and $56.54 for each high

NEW YORK PUBLIC LIBRARY.
" A t-pe university is a collection of books." — CARLYLE.

school pupil.   The same year the average cost in private elementary schools was $32.00 and in private high schools $94.10. From these figures it can be seen that poor parents with large families could not afford to educate their children if free schools were not provided by the government.   Free libraries, art galleries, and museums are also established by governments, thus providing for all what the rich alone, could otherwise afford. (See Chapter XXVIII.)

(e) *Protection to Public Morals.* — In many ways the national, State, and local governments are seeking to protect public morals. The national government prohibits the bringing of prize-fight films or lottery tickets into any State, and denies the use of the mails for the carrying of fraudulent matter or intoxicating liquors. The national government has not the power to prohibit the sale and use of opium, but in its effort to limit its use as much as possible Congress has imposed a tax of $300 a pound on this drug manufactured for smoking purposes.

State and city governments regulate or prohibit the sale of liquor and prohibit gambling and other recognized forms of vice. Each State maintains one or more reformatories for incorrigible boys and girls, where they are trained to better citizenship. Cities commonly have censors to visit theaters, moving picture shows; and such public places, to prevent immoral performances.

(f) *The Census.* The United States census of 1910 was taken by 75,000 census collectors within four weeks, but four years were required to tabulate the facts in detail although electric tabulating machines were used for the purpose. The facts filled eleven large volumes and cost the government $15,000,000. Not only does this census give the number of persons of each race, color, sex, age, occupation, whether married or single, and whether able to write, but three of the eleven volumes give detailed information regarding manufactures and three give the same regarding agriculture.

The census is especially valuable because it shows the condition of industry in each locality of the United States and thus assists legislators in remedying bad conditions. From these tabulated facts the general tendency of the country can be observed. For instance, it shows that 46.3 per cent of the population of the United States lived in cities in 1910 as compared with 40.5 in 1900, and that the total number of illiterates is becoming less though population is rapidly increasing.[1] It also shows that in 1880 only 25 per cent of our farms were operated by tenants as compared to 37 per cent in 1910.

The volumes on manufactures and agriculture are especially valuable to persons interested in these industries. For in-

A FIFTEEN MILLION DOLLAR SET OF BOOKS.
These books are compiled by the United States Government for your use.

stance, if a manufacturer of corn cutters, milk cans, or poultry food wants to know where there is a demand for his products he can learn the production of corn and the approximate number of cows and of chickens in each county in the United States.

(g) *Aids to Commerce.* — The national government maintains lighthouses, beacons, and buoys, builds dams, digs canals, and dredges rivers and harbors. It coöperates with the States in building levees. States and counties build roads and bridges. Cities construct streets, bridges, and wharves.

---

[1] From 1900 to 1910 the degree of illiteracy among negroes was reduced from 45 per cent to 30 per cent.

WEAVING TREECLOTH MATTRESSES.

These mattresses are used to protect the banks of the Mississippi River.

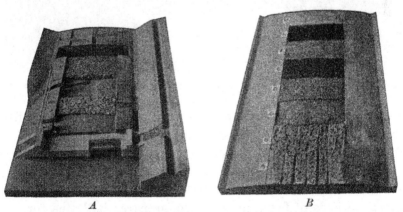

A   B

THE GOVERNMENT TEACHING THE ART OF ROAD MAKING.

Models prepared by the Department of Agriculture showing the proper drainage (A) and construction (B) of roads.

(h) *Aids to Agriculture.* — The national, State, and county governments all give aid to agricultural industry. For instance, the Federal Department of Agriculture has a division of plant introduction, with scientists to introduce valuable plants into the United States — *e.g.*, hardy wheat from northern Russia which resists wheat rust and thrives in dry climates, a variety of alfalfa from the plains of Turkestan which

Courtesy, Virginia State Highway Department.

A Road in Spottsylvania County, Virginia, before Improvement.

resists droughts, Smyrna figs in California after twenty-five years of experimentation, and dates which are now successfully grown in the Southwest.

The Agricultural Department prepares numerous bulletins for free distribution, which keep farmers informed as to the latest methods of farming. It also prepares bulletins for the wives of farmers, so many of whom are thin and old at thirty because they work fifteen hours a day without mechanical helps while the husband buys machinery for the fields, but none for the household. These bulletins give the housewife such information as how to have running water in the house, how to can fruits, and how to operate a community laundry by the waste steam from the creamery.

Roads are built by State or local governments, but the national government contributes money to aid the State or local governments [1] and encourages these to have good roads.

Courtesy, Virginia State Highway Department.

THE SAME ROAD AFTER IMPROVEMENT BY THE GOVERNMENT.

---

[1] In 1916 Congress appropriated $75,000,000 to aid the States in the construction of rural post roads — the first appropriated by the National Government for this purpose for nearly a century. Of this sum $5,000,000 is to be expended in 1917, $10,000,000 in 1918, $15,000,000 in 1919, $20,000,000 in 1920, and $25,000,000 in 1921. The National Government's share in road work in coöperation with the States is limited to 50 % of the cost of the road. The National aid is apportioned among the States in the following manner:

" One third in the ratio which the area of each State bears to the total area of all the States;

" One third in the ratio which the population of each State bears to the total population of all the States; and

" One third in the ratio which the mileage of rural delivery routes and star routes in each State bears to the total mileage of rural delivery routes and star routes in all the States."

Not many years ago it was found that the average cost of hauling one ton one mile in Europe was 10 cents; in the United States, 23 cents. Upon the number of tons hauled in this country the difference in cost between 10 cents and 23 cents a mile was about $250,000,000. The Agricultural Department of the United States organized the Office of Public Roads. This office

ARROW ROCK DAM, IDAHO, UNDER CONSTRUCTION.
This dam is 67 feet higher than the Roosevelt Dam.

has collected information from all parts of the world. It has also constructed sections of experimental road in various States. Any county or city building new roads can have the results of all this investigation free for the asking.

Since the national government began constructing irrigation plants, during the presidency of Roosevelt, it has constructed or is now constructing plants which water an area about equal in size to the State of Connecticut, thus bringing barren lands into a high state of cultivation. One irrigation tunnel in Colorado is six miles long. The Roosevelt dam in Arizona, 280 feet high, sells electric power to Phoenix and Mesa and to large copper mines. The Elephant Butte dam in New Mexico holds enough water to cover 3,000,000 acres a foot deep. The Huntley project in Montana gives a demonstration of a canal which lifts itself by its own boot-straps. A waterfall furnishes power to raise a portion of the water to a plateau above and thus water it as well as the plains below.

Congress also aids animal industry by investigations. For instance, in 1914 it appropriated $600,000 for the investigation, treatment, and eradication of the hog cholera and other diseases of animals. The Agricultural Department protects this industry by preventing the shipment of stock from States in which a certain animal disease is prevalent to other States where it does not exist.

(5) **Government Protects the Poor against the Oppression of the Wealthy.** — Among the wealthy, business can be conducted on a large scale, and this tends to drive the smaller dealers out of business, especially when unfair means of competition are used. Until prohibited by law large organizations commonly sold their product at or below the cost of production, in regions where there was much competition, in order to drive the smaller dealers out of the business. The loss thus caused was covered by profits in the regions where there was little or no competition, because there the large organizations could raise the prices unreasonably. For example, on October 1, 1904, the Standard Oil Trust earned more than six cents a gallon on oil sold in Spokane, where there was no competition, and in New Mexico, where there was but little competition, while at the same time it was selling oil at a loss of more than a cent a gallon in New Orleans and more than three cents a gallon in Los Angeles, where it had determined to drive the smaller dealers from the field. But a law passed by Congress, under the influence of President Wilson, expressly made this practice illegal. Many similar practices have been prohibited by national and State laws.

(6) Government Performs Functions in the Interest of the Many Which as Private Ventures Would be Performed in the Interest of the Few. — If the national government had not built the Panama Canal it would likely have been built as a private venture. Much of the western land irrigated by the national government would have been irrigated by private companies. If the national government were not to build the Alaskan railroad, private capital would do so; and if the United States had not established a postal system, private capital certainly would have organized such a system. All of these enterprises are now conducted in the interest of the people, whereas private companies would have conducted them in their own interest.

Of these national ventures the postal system is the most interesting. Originally such systems were maintained by governments of the Old World to carry messages for the king and ministers of state. The carrying of letters for the public was added later, and as late as 1860 the sole business of the United States post office was to carry letters, papers, and small packages from one office to another, where they were distributed from a window. Now it supplies city and rural carriers, special delivery messengers, street boxes, registry, postal cards, stamped paper, stamp books, and cancelling machines. It maintains a money-order system, a parcel post system, and a savings-bank system.

BIBLIOGRAPHY

DUPUY, W. A. Uncle Sam's Modern Miracles. 1914.

QUESTIONS ON THE TEXT

1. Why is government important?

2. How much is spent by our national government each year? By our State, county, and other local governments?

3. What is the average cost of government per capita in the United States?

4. How is the cost of government borne, and by whom? *[handwritten]*

5. Is the cost of government becoming more or less of a burden? *[handwritten]*

6. Name and explain the benefits of government discussed in the text. *[handwritten] Independence, ... peace, protect poor, equal ...*

7. How much was spent on public free education in the United States in the year 1913? *[handwritten] 520 million*

8. How is the health of citizens of the United States protected from contagious diseases prevalent in foreign countries? *[handwritten]*

9. What great services have been rendered the American people by the United States Public Health Service? *[handwritten] Quarantines, ...*

10. In what way are the public morals of your community regulated? *[handwritten] Liquors cannot ...*

11. What is the census of the United States? What did the census of 1910 cost, and what are its benefits? *[handwritten] 15 million ...*

12. What service has the Agricultural Department of the United States performed for American farmers? *[handwritten]*

13. How do governments protect the poor against the oppression of the wealthy? *[handwritten] The large corporations ...*

14. Why is it better to have some lines of business conducted by the government instead of by individuals? *[handwritten] Because the government ... the interference in ... hands would ...*

QUESTIONS FOR DISCUSSION

1. In the United States about 400,000 persons are incapacitated and about 30,000 are killed by typhoid fever each year. This disease is only one fifth as prevalent in some of the European countries as it is in the United States, the improvement having been brought about by better sanitary regulations by the governments. Would you favor a State law for compulsory vaccination against typhoid fever? Or would you favor having your local government spend enough money to prevent the spread of this disease? *[handwritten marginal notes] late the law ...*

2. What connection is there between free public schools and government by the people? *[handwritten] People support the free schools ...*

3. Is it cheaper to send articles by mail or by express? How many pounds may be sent by mail? How does the parcel post encourage commerce? *[handwritten] Quickness of delivery. ...*

4. What would be the effect upon the stock-raising industry if there were no cattle quarantine regulations? *[handwritten] It would perhaps ...*

5. It has been said that society would drift into barbarism in a generation if it were not for religion and public opinion. What would be the effect upon society if all governments ceased to exist? *[handwritten] There would be absolutely no rest and ...*

6. Why are taxes lower in China than in the United States? Give arguments in favor of high taxes. *[handwritten]*

7. Do you think that only taxpayers should be permitted to vote? Who are the taxpayers? *[handwritten]*

8. In 1910 there were 8,000,000 single men and 5,000,000 single women above twenty years of age in the United States. Where could you verify this fact? What practical use could a manufacturing firm make of the fact that there are 90 men to every 100 women in the District of Columbia and 187 men to every 100 women in Montana?

In the census. The manufacturer knows where he may obtain help easily.

CHAPTER II

DEVELOPMENT OF THE STATE

7. Introduction. — In living organisms there is a continual tendency for the simple to develop into the complex, and so it has been with organized society — the state. In the beginning very few functions were performed by the state, but new discoveries and inventions created new social and economic conditions which could be solved only through the united action of society; so the state has developed to its present

A PRIMITIVE FISHERMAN.

position along with these various social and economic changes.

At some time in the history of the world the ancestors of every race of people lived in a rude, uncivilized manner. The want of food and of other material comforts brought suffering; superstition brought fear; and lack of wisdom brought misunderstanding, quarreling, fighting, war. From this rude condition some peoples have advanced through many stages of social and economic development in the upward trend of the human race. The most highly developed nations have gradually advanced through the following stages: hunting and fishing, pastoral, agricultural, commercial, and capitalistic. Each social or economic stage demanded a more extensive organization:

19

and in turn, each extension of political organization made possible the advance to a more complex social or economic stage.

8. Hunting and Fishing Stage. — During the hunting and fishing stage of each race the mode of living was but little above that of beasts. Men lived from hand to mouth in the struggle for existence. Ownership in land was unknown, but each savage horde had temporary hunting grounds beyond which their members went at their peril. They had little need and less capacity for political organization.

A Shepherd with his Flock.

9. Pastoral Stage. — When an ingenious horde saved alive the young of wild animals and domesticated them, an epoch-making step was taken. By a little foresight and self-denial food was on hand for times of scarcity. The abundance of flesh foods gradually banished cannibalism, especially when it was perceived that a muscle of a captive was worth more for labor than for food. Permanent food supplies and slaves gave leisure and opportunity for meditation. Wandering hordes became family tribes bound together by the common possession of flocks and herds. These possessions brought the envy of neighboring bands, and organization for defense became necessary. The patriarch of a family became leader of this organization and developed absolute authority to the extent of life and death over his wives, sons, daughters, sons' wives and children, and slaves. In reality he was an absolute ruler over a "family state."

10. Agricultural Stage. — The possession of flocks made the habitation of man sufficiently permanent to make possible the planting of seeds with the thought of ultimately reaping the harvest. Slavery became more profitable, the possession of land became necessary, and ownership desirable. As family tribes gradually sent out clans to establish

PRIMITIVE AGRICULTURE.

new village communities, common blood, common religion, and common economic interests held them together into loose confederations for social and commercial intercourse and for self-defense. In short, the necessary elements of a modern state existed : law and authority, definiteness and permanence of organization, and a consciousness of political unity.

AN EARLY TYPE OF MERCHANT VESSELS.

11. Commercial Stage. — Wealth in flocks; herds, and agriculture multiplied man's needs. Commerce met the demand. Yoked beasts of burden, sailboats, and forms of money as a medium of exchange gave the merchant a place in civilization. Cities developed at convenient locations on

A Primitive Hand Loom.

trade routes. Coöperation against pirates and robbers and regulation of city populations made city states necessary.

12. Manufacturing Stage. — The establishment of cities and commercial routes encouraged manufacturing, and in turn manufacturing gave a further contribution to commerce. During the manufacturing stage hand implements slowly gave way to machines. For example, the hand spindle of prehistoric times was replaced by the spinning wheel in 1530; and late in the eighteenth century steam power was applied to the manufacture of cloth. This process brought people from scattered farms into growing towns and cities. City life brought experience and education to the people, and enabled them to wrest their rights from absolute monarchs or privileged nobles.

13. Capitalistic Stage. — The present capitalistic stage that the advanced nations have attained grew out of the development of expensive factory machines, which makes large scale production profitable, but requires the concentration of capital. The appli-

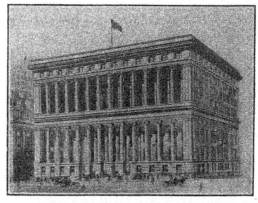

The National City Bank of New York.

cation of steam to boats and railroads, which bring raw material and food supplies to the manufacturing plants and distribute the output to the distant consumers, makes possible the concentration of capital. The development of banking systems has also aided in the concentration of capital. The result is the downfall of business competition and the formation of nation-wide and even world-wide monopolies. Thus most persons must work for wages, and if monopolies were not controlled by the state the wages of the workmen could be determined by the capitalists. The condition of employees then would be no better than that of slaves.

14. Socialistic Stage. — In reviewing the above stages of social, economic, and political development it should be noted that the first duty of politically organized society, or the state, was the protection of life and of movable

THE GOVERNMENT IN THE EXPRESS BUSINESS.

property; then the regulation of land was added; commerce and manufacturing in turn had to be regulated. The question now facing the people is whether capital can be regulated. If a group of millionaires or bankers combine their capital to control the entire production of certain commodities or services and advance the prices, the masses of people will naturally use their power, the state, to prevent this. If regulation fails, what then ? — the socialistic stage.

By a socialistic stage is meant a stage when the state will own and operate large industries which would be operated by the people or private corporations if left to their own initiative. The indications are that the United States will merely regulate most monopolies unless regulation ceases properly to protect the masses. Should regulation cease to be effective, state ownership would be necessary; and it is possible that in the near future the United States will conduct other large businesses as it now conducts the postal and parcel post business, or as many European states conduct express, telegraph, and railroad businesses. (See Sec. 148.)

15. How a State Exercises Its Powers. — A *state*[1] is an organized body of people living within a limited territory and having power to make and enforce laws without the consent of any

Courtesy, World's Work, Vol. 23.
REPUBLICAN GOVERNMENT FIFTY YEARS AGO.

higher authority.[2] A *government* is the agency through which a state's purposes are formulated and executed. If the agents who run the machinery of government are under the absolute control of one person, such as the Sultan of Turkey, an *absolute monarchy* is said to exist; but if the monarch is restricted in his powers, as in Italy, the government is known as a *limited*

---

[1] Throughout this volume the word *state* printed with a small "s" denotes an independent state belonging to the family of nations, as England, France, the United States; the word *State* printed with a capital "S" refers to one of the members of the United States of America, as Maine, Pennsylvania, Virginia.

[2] A state is the sum total of all its citizens — men, women, and children.

monarchy. If the people select their own agents to run the government without a monarch, a *republic* exists.[1]

If the citizens of a state are uneducated and incapable of choosing representatives or unwilling to abide by laws which their representatives make, an absolute monarchy may be the only form of government able to hold the state together. At one time England was an absolute monarchy, but in 1215 the nobles compelled the king to sign the Magna Charta and thereby to yield certain of his powers; in 1689 the king signed the Bill of Rights, in which he transferred many powers to the

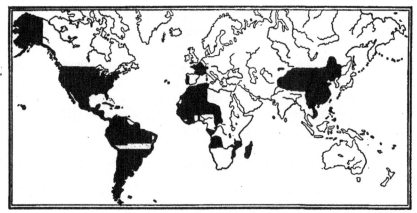

Courtesy, World's Work, Vol. 23

REPUBLICAN GOVERNMENT TO-DAY.

representatives of the people in Parliament; and from time to time powers have been transferred until to-day the King of England is much less powerful than the President of the United States.

The people of England now rule through their representatives in Parliament as truly as the American people rule through their representatives in Congress. Thus we see that an absolute monarchy is limited in proportion to the enlightenment of

---

[1] If any state were small enough for the people to assemble and make their laws directly, a *democratic government* would exist.

the citizens and in time naturally gives way to a limited monarchy, as in England, or to a republic, as in France.

BIBLIOGRAPHY

DEALEY, J. Q. The Development of the State. Its Governmental Organization and Its Activities. 1909.

HOBSON, J. A. The Evolution of Modern Capitalism. New and revised edition. 1912.

WILLOUGHBY, W. W. The Nature of the State.

QUESTIONS ON THE TEXT

1. Name six stages of social and economic development.

2. Describe these six stages and explain how each developed into the other.

3. How have economic development and political development depended upon each other?

4. What stages of economic and political development have been attained by the following nations: American Indians when America was discovered?   The Jews at the time of the patriarchs Abraham, Isaac, and Jacob?   France during the days of feudalism?   The Phœnicians about 1000 B.C.?   England about 1800 A.D.?   The United States to-day?

5. Under what conditions may the socialistic stage develop in the United States?

6. What is a *state?* What is a *government?* Distinguish clearly between a state and a government.

7. Distinguish between *state* and *State* as used in this text.

QUESTIONS FOR DISCUSSION

1. The first function of the state was to protect life and property; now it provides conveniences and comforts. In the future do you think it should further encourage our sense of the esthetic or beautiful? Do you think it should prohibit billboards on a person's vacant lot if they mar the beauty of the town or landscape?

2. In 1914 Congress provided for a railroad in Alaska to be built and owned by the United States. Do you believe that the United States or your State should develop further into the socialistic stage by owning and operating railroads? Express systems? Telegraphs?

Telephones? Wireless? Forests? Water power plants? Coal mines? Banks? Insurance companies? *No,*

3. Do you think your county should establish a jitney bus system? What would be the advantages of such a system? *Making a better place*

4. Do you think your town should install a water system? Electric power system? Gas system? Jitney bus system? *Yes if possible*

5. Do you think your city should establish an ice plant? Heating plant? *Yes if the town & population can afford the support,*

6. There was no great need of laws governing copyrights until long after the printing press began its work. The invention of the steam engine created a need for what character of laws? The automobile? The moving pictures?

Bill of rights etc,

CHAPTER III

ORIGIN OF THE FEDERAL CONSTITUTION

16. Colonial Government. — In the year 1607 the first permanent English settlement in America was made at Jamestown, Virginia, by colonists whom a commercial corporation, known as The London Company, sent out from England. The Company placed a council with a president over the colonists until 1609, when a governor replaced the president. In 1619 the Company permitted the addition of a general assembly composed of burgesses[1] elected by the inhabitants of each settlement.

This assembly, the first representative legislature that ever sat in America, met on the 30th day of July, 1619, in the chancel of the church at Jamestown. In 1624 the London Company surrendered its charter, and henceforth Virginia was known as a Royal Colony until it declared itself independent of England in the year 1776. The other twelve colonies were established in various ways and from time to time enjoyed different rights or degrees of self-government. According to the mode of government the colonies were divided into three classes: Royal, Proprietary, and Charter.

The Royal Colonies. — At the time of the Revolution, 1776, there were seven Royal colonies: New Hampshire, New York,

---

[1] The term "burgesses" was used because it was expected that the settlements would develop into boroughs (towns). After 1634 the "burgesses" represented counties, and in 1776 the name was changed to "assemblymen." Virginia called its colonial representatives "House of Burgesses"; South Carolina, "House of Commons"; Massachusetts, "House of Representatives."

New Jersey, Virginia, North Carolina, South Carolina, and
Georgia. For each of these colonies a governor and a council,
"upper house," were appointed by the King, and a popular
assembly, "lower house," was elected by the people. The
governor in conjunction with his council and assembly ruled
the colony in conformity with written instructions issued from
time to time by the Crown. There was no written charter between the colony and the King, nevertheless various concessions
that the Crown made to the people and the customary mode of
government formed a traditionary charter or constitution.

The Proprietary Colonies. — In 1776 there were three Proprietary colonies: Pennsylvania, Delaware, and Maryland.
These colonies got their name, "Proprietary," from the term
proprietor, which was applied to a "petty king" to whom the
King of England had granted the land. For each of these
colonies a governor and a council were appointed by the proprietor and a popular assembly was elected by the people.
Hence we may think of a Proprietary colony as very similar
to a Royal colony, the only material difference being that the
proprietor, or "petty king," was obliged to concede more rights
and privileges to the people than the King would grant. As in
the case of the Royal colonies, the concessions and precedents
of government formed a traditionary charter or constitution.

The Charter Colonies. — In 1776 there were three Charter
colonies: Massachusetts, Rhode Island, and Connecticut. Unlike the other two classes of colonies, a real charter existed
between each of these colonies and the King. This charter
was a written document outlining certain rights of self-government which could be withdrawn by the King at any time he
saw fit to do so. In each of these colonies, except Massachusetts, the governor was elected by the people; in each the
council was elected by the assembly; and in each the assembly
was elected by the people. The charters of Connecticut and
Rhode Island were so liberal that by substituting the word
"people" for "King" these colonial charters served as State
constitutions until 1818 and 1842 respectively.

17. Legislative Powers. — In all of the colonies, except Pennsylvania where the council had no legislative power, there were two branches of the legislature and a governor with the power of vetoing measures passed by the two branches. Legislation was enacted on purely colonial affairs. In matters of general interest to the whole British Kingdom the British Parliament or the King exercised control. It was often a disputed question whether a particular affair was purely colonial or a matter of general interest to the whole Kingdom; and the question whether or not a stamp tax to support a standing army in America was a tax which the British Parliament had a right to impose upon the colonies was decided only by the Revolutionary War.

CARPENTERS' HALL, PHILADELPHIA.
The First Continental Congress met here.

18. Continental Congresses. — In 1774 the Virginia House of Burgesses issued an invitation to all of these colonial assemblies, calling a meeting of delegates at Philadelphia to consider what could be done to meet their common grievances. This Congress, in which all the colonies except Georgia were represented, is known as the First Continental Congress. It adopted a declaration of rights and grievances to be presented to the King, and adjourned.

In 1775, after the battle of Lexington, the Second Continental Congress met at Philadelphia, with representatives from all thirteen colonies. Schouler, the great historian, has concisely described the work performed by this body in the following words: "The Continental Congress . . . with its periodical sessions and frequent changes of membership bore for fifteen years the symbols of federal power in America; which, as a single house of deputies acting by colonies or States, and blending with legislative authority imperfect executive and judicial functions, raised armies, laid taxes, contracted a common debt, negotiated foreign treaties, made war and peace; which, in the name and with the assured warrant of the thirteen colonies, declared their independence of Great Britain, and by God's blessing accomplished it; which, having framed and promulgated a plan of general confederation, persuaded these same thirteen republics to adopt it."

19. The Articles of Confederation. —The authority for the acts of the Second Continental Congress rested upon no definite grant of powers by the colonies, but was assumed by it to meet the crisis of war. However, a plan of perpetual league and a statement of the powers which the Continental Congress might exercise was framed and proclaimed by the Second Continental Congress in 1777.

This scheme of union was set forth in a paper termed "The Articles of Confederation." These articles did not go into effect until 1781 because it was necessary for them to be ratified by all the States of the Confederation before they could become the law of the land, and it was not until that year that the ratification of Maryland was secured.

These articles provided that each State should be represented in this Confederate (Continental) Congress by not less than two nor more than seven members, to be elected annually and to be subject to recall by the legislatures of the respective States; but each State should have only one vote. This body had power to declare war, enter into certain treaties and alliances with foreign nations, borrow money, coin money, establish post offices, regulate the affairs of all Indians not members of the States, together with a few less important duties.

The expenses of this government were to be paid by taxes raised through the respective State legislatures, the amount to be paid by each State being in proportion to the value of all real property within its boundaries. The compensation of the delegates was paid directly by the State which they represented.

The distinctive features, which also proved to be the greatest defects, of the Articles of Confederation were:

(1) One vote for each state, to which the larger States naturally objected.

(2) Want of power by the central government to act directly on individuals. The articles bestowed upon Congress no direct power to raise revenue other than to borrow money. The States retained this power and they frequently refused to collect the amount of taxes demanded of them by Congress.

(3) Want of means for enforcing obedience to the Acts of Congress. They provided neither for an executive, except committees, nor for permanent courts. A single State could disregard any law, or treaty, which fact was soon recognized by foreign countries, and clearly expressed by Washington, who said: "We are one nation to-day and thirteen to-morrow. Who will treat with us on such terms?"

(4) Want of power by the central government to regulate commerce with foreign countries and between the several States.

(5) Unanimous consent of the thirteen States for amendment of the Articles of Confederation. The consent of nine of the States was required for all important ordinary laws. To obtain these unusual majorities was practically impossible.

20. The Critical Period. — The independence of the thirteen States was recognized in 1783, but a large national debt remained unpaid, upon which the interest was not met, because only about one fourth of the revenue which Congress asked of the States was collected. Under these circumstances even the existence of Congress was threatened. For example, some eighty drunken soldiers of the Pennsylvania line mutinied from want of pay and forced Congress to flee from Philadelphia to Princeton, where the college afforded it shelter.

In 1785 Congress made a final attempt to raise the neces-

A. Connecticut's Western Reserve
B. Virginia's Military Reserve

THE UNITED STATES IN 1783 — STATE CLAIMS AND CESSIONS

sary revenue by endeavoring to add an amendment to the Articles of Confederation levying a tax on imports. New York reaped the benefit of a State tax on imports and refused to agree to this amendment, so the measure failed. To save expense some States failed to send delegates to this Congress, and unfortunately many of those that attended were not the leading statesmen who were present during the period of the war. The condition was so bad that the French minister was prompted to write to his country thus : " There is now no general government in America, no head, no Congress, no administrative department."

In colonial days there had been little communication between the colonies, and as soon as peace was restored the States began to fall apart, and to manifest their sectional hatred by commercial discrimination.

The following quotation from Fiske well illustrates the existing conditions :

"The city of New York with a population of 30,000 souls had long been supplied with firewood from Connecticut, and with butter and cheese, chickens and garden vegetables from the thrifty farms of New Jersey. This trade, it was observed, carried thousands of dollars out of the city and into the pockets of the detested Yankees and despised Jerseymen. ' It was ruinous to domestic industry,' said the men of New York. ' It must be stopped by . . . a navigation act and a protective tariff.' Acts were accordingly passed, obliging every Yankee sloop which came down through Hell Gate and every Jersey market boat which was rowed across from Paulus Hook to Cortlandt Street to pay entrance fees and obtain clearances at the custom house, just as was done by ships from London and Hamburg; and not a cart-load of Connecticut firewood could be delivered at the back door of a country house in Beekman Street until it should have paid a heavy duty. Great and just was the wrath of the farmers and lumbermen. The New Jersey legislature made up its mind to retaliate. The city of New York had lately bought a small patch of ground on Sandy Hook, and had built a light-house there. This lighthouse was the one weak spot in the heel of Achilles where a hostile arrow could strike, and New Jersey gave vent to her indignation by laying a tax of $1800 a year on it. Connecticut was equally prompt. At a great meeting of business men, held at New London, it was unanimously agreed to suspend all commercial intercourse with New York. Every merchant signed an agreement, under a penalty of $250 for the first offence, not to send any goods whatever into the hated State for twelve months." [1]

The tariff system of Virginia imposed higher duties upon imports than those imposed by the system of Maryland, and naturally all articles which could be distributed from Maryland as well as from Virginia were brought to Maryland instead of to Virginia. Virginia retaliated by imposing a toll upon vessels entering Chesapeake Bay between the Virginia capes. Maryland disputed the right of Virginia to impose these tolls. To settle this dispute, as well as to reach an agreement upon other uniform rules governing the Chesapeake Bay and Potomac River, commissioners from Maryland and Virginia met at Alexandria, but upon the invitation of Washington moved to Mount Vernon.

Through discussion the commercial difficulties were found to extend beyond the two States, and the commissioners recommended that Delaware and Pennsylvania be invited to meet with them the following year, 1786. Maryland did better; she invited *all* the States to meet at Annapolis. However, only five States sent delegates, and these, after concluding that it was necessary to amend the Articles of Confederation before any real commercial progress could be made, adjourned to meet at Philadelphia in 1787.

21. The Constitutional Convention. — Virginia was the first State to announce her delegates for the Philadelphia Convention. They were Washington, Madison, and Edmund Randolph. The name of Washington inspired confidence. In May, 1787, delegates from all the States except Rhode Island assembled, fifty-five able delegates being present. Washington was chosen President of the Convention, and it was agreed that each State should have one vote, and that the sessions should be secret.

Drafting the Federal Constitution. — Immediately the Convention divided into two factions — the one representing the

---

[1] "The Critical Period of American History," p. 146.

smaller States and the other the larger States.   Randolph of Virginia presented the Large State Plan, or the so-called "Virginia Plan," which proposed a Congress of two houses with power to legislate on all national matters and to compel obedience on the part of the States.   Representation in both houses was to be based on population, thus giving the larger and more populous States the control of both branches of the legislature; furthermore, since by this scheme the President, executive officers, and judges were to be appointed by Congress, supervision of the whole administration of the new government would be under the control of the larger States.

INDEPENDENCE HALL.

Pennsylvania's Old State House in Philadelphia, where the Declaration of Independence was signed, and where the Federal Constitutional Convention met.

Patterson of New Jersey introduced the Small State Plan, or the so-called "New Jersey Plan," which provided for a Congress consisting of one house.   According to this plan each State was to have equal representation.

The result was a compromise.   It was agreed that there should be a legislature of two houses: a Senate, the less numerous branch, and a House of Representatives, the more numerous branch.   In the Senate each State was to have an equal representation, thus putting the small States on an equal footing with the large ones; but in the House of Representatives the representation was to be according to population, thus favoring the larger States.

It was also decided by the Convention that the Constitution should be considered ratified and should go into effect as soon as accepted by nine of the thirteen States. Persons favoring the adoption of the Constitution by their respective States were called Federalists, and those opposing it were called Anti-Federalists. From this contest rose the first political parties in the United States.

The Convention adjourned in September, having been in session a little over four months. Gladstone, the famous English statesman, considered this constitution the greatest work ever struck off at one time by the hand of man.

The fundamental difference between the new Constitution and the old Articles was that the Constitution provided an adequate executive and judiciary to enforce the federal laws directly upon the individual instead of depending upon the indirect enforcement by the State governments, which had enforced only such as they individually approved.

Arguments For and Against Adoption. — The Federalist Party with such leaders as Hamilton, Washington, and Marshall favored the proposed Constitution because it established a strong national government. This party was especially strong in commercial New England, where the weakness of the old Confederation and the tariff discriminations of the States were brought forcibly home. The arguments used by the Federalists appeared in a collection of eighty-five essays, called "The Federalist," written by Alexander Hamilton, John Jay, and James Madison. These essays contain an excellent exposition of the Constitution.

The Anti-Federalists, such as Patrick Henry and George Clinton, favored strong State governments and a comparatively weak national government. They felt that too much power was given to the central government and that State liberty would be crushed out. Patriotism at that time was devotion to the State. A citizen of Virginia abroad called himself a

" Virginian " and not an " American." The Anti-Federalists compared a strong national government to the English government, by which they had so recently felt oppressed, and they declared that it would be a government founded upon the destruction of the governments of the several States.

A further objection was that the Constitution contained no definite " bill .of rights " guaranteeing to individuals such fundamental liberties as freedom of speech, liberty of the press, assurance against unjust arrest, and trial by jury. The Federalists practically agreed to add these guarantees, which promise was fulfilled by the adoption of the first ten constitutional amendments in 1791. It was feared that a President might become so popular as to obtain life tenure of office, and thus the government might degenerate into a monarchy. Patrick Henry cried, "We shall have a King; the army will salute him monarch."

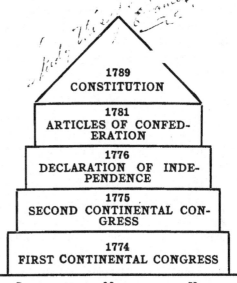

1789
CONSTITUTION

1781
ARTICLES OF CONFED-
ERATION

1776
DECLARATION OF INDE-
PENDENCE

1775
SECOND CONTINENTAL CON-
GRESS

1774
FIRST CONTINENTAL CONGRESS

STONES IN THE MONUMENT TO UNION
Adapted from Forman's " Advanced Civics "

By June, 1788, the Federalists prevailed. New Hampshire,[1] the ninth State, ratified. The Continental Congress provided for the election of a President and his inauguration on March

[1] The Constitution was ratified by the several States in the following order: Delaware, December 7, 1787; Pennsylvania, December 12, 1787; New Jersey, December 18, 1787; Georgia, January 2, 1788; Connecticut, January 9, 1788; Massachusetts, February 6, 1788; Maryland, April 28, 1788; South Carolina, May 23, 1788; New Hampshire, June 21, 1788; Virginia, June 26, 1788; New York, July 26, 1788; North Carolina, November 21, 1789; and Rhode Island, May 29, 1790.

4, which day has since been observed as the beginning of a
new term of office. Owing to a delay in the assembling of the
new Congress, which Congress had to count the electoral vote,
Washington was not inaugurated or our new government put
into actual operation until April 30, 1789.

BIBLIOGRAPHY

BEARD, CHARLES A. An Economic Interpretation of the Constitution of the United States. 1913.

FISKE, JOHN. The Critical Period of American History. 1888.

MACDONALD, WILLIAM. Select Documents of United States History,
1776–1861. 1901.

QUESTIONS ON THE TEXT

1. Name the three kinds of colonies and describe the characteristics of each. *Royal, Proprietary, and Charter.*

2. When did the First Continental Congress meet? Where? *1774*

3. What was done by the First Continental Congress? *Declaration of rights*

4. When did the Second Continental Congress meet? Where? *1775*

5. What was accomplished by the Second Continental Congress?

6. What were the Articles of Confederation? When were they
framed? When ratified? Why the delay? *Laws of the land. 1781, Delay*

7. What were the powers of the Confederate Congress? *meager*

8. Name five distinctive features of the Articles of Confederation
which proved to be their greatest defects.

9. Describe the unsatisfactory conditions existing during the
Critical Period. What dispute arose between New York and New
Jersey? New York and Connecticut? Maryland and Virginia?

10. When and where was the Constitution drafted?

11. What was the "Virginia Plan"? The "New Jersey Plan"?
What was the compromise?

12. How many States were required for the ratification of the Constitution?

13. What was the fundamental difference between the Constitution
and the Articles of Confederation?

14. Who favored the adoption of the Constitution and what argument did they use for its adoption? Who opposed it and what were
their arguments?

15. In what year was the required number of ratifications obtained?

16. When was Washington inaugurated as first President of the United States?

QUESTIONS FOR DISCUSSION

1. Let five pupils report on the experiences commemorated by the five stones of the pyramid.

2. Prepare a five-minute paper on "The Critical Period of the American Confederation (1781–1789)." Consult Fiske's "Critical Period of American History."

3. What did the individual State gain by entering the federal union? What did it lose?

4. What advantages would result if the fifty-odd states of the world should form a World State as the forty-eight States now form the United States of America? What powers should be granted to such a World State?

E.J.

CHAPTER IV

THE FEDERAL SYSTEM OF GOVERNMENT

22. Confederate and Federal Government Distinguished. — The Constitution of the United States provides a federal combination of States as distinguished from the loose leagues or confederations of the ancient Greeks and as distinguished from the unitary state of the present-day French. In 1787, when our Constitution makers changed the thirteen *confederate* States into thirteen *federated* States, they showed to the world a type of government never before tried.

Greek confederations, the Holy Roman Empire (800–1806), the Swiss Confederation (1291–1848), and the American Confederation (1781–1788) depended upon the governments of the States composing them to enforce all laws. In fact, this old type, known as *confederations,* was, at best, scarcely more than an arrangement for offensive and defensive alliances. On the other hand the new type, known as *federations,* is a close union which enforces its laws directly upon the people, and, with few exceptions, through its own officers.

23. Advantages of Federal Government in the United States. — The system of federal government in the United States retains the advantages of local self-government for the States as well as secures the strength which results from union. This system of state-making is the most complicated of all methods, but is at the same time the most stable. Not only are the American people enabled to protect their liberties through representation in Congress, but in such matters as religion, suffrage, and the liquor problem, which produce determined sentiments, the American federal system gives consideration to the wishes of the people of each State.

The State of Texas can tax church property or not as it thinks best; Colorado can have woman's suffrage; South Carolina can have the educational test to exclude negroes from voting; Maine can have state-wide prohibition, etc., etc. And further, if the peace of Texas should be disturbed by Mexican invaders, Texas could depend upon the assistance of the remaining forty-seven States for defence; and should yellow fever in Cuba threaten the United States the united effort of the States would be exerted to prevent it.

24. Division of Powers between Nation and States. — The Constitution of the United States is a written agreement entered into by the people of the thirteen original States, and agreed to by the people of the thirty-five States which have since entered the Union.

The general principle governing the division of powers between the National government on the one hand and the State governments on the other is thus laid down in the Tenth Amendment: "The powers not delegated to the United States by the Constitution, nor prohibited by it to the States, are reserved to the States." The National government is said to have "delegated" or "enumerated" powers,[1] while the State governments have "residual" or "unenumerated" powers; that is, the State governments may do all things other than those provided for by the Constitution.[2] In other words, the National

---

[1] Most of these powers are enumerated in the eighteen clauses of Article I, Section 8.

[2] There are many powers delegated to the National government but not expressly denied to the States. Some of these powers are concurrent in that they may be exercised by either the Nation or the States. The Supreme Court has decided that those powers which are of such a character that the exercise of them by the States would be, under any circumstances, inconsistent with the general theory of National government may be exercised only by the United States.

Those delegated powers not of this character may be exercised by the States until the United States sees fit to exercise them. To illustrate, the Constitution delegates to Congress the power to enact bankruptcy laws. From 1878 to 1898 Congress did not desire a national bankruptcy law. All States enacted them. When a new National bankruptcy law was enacted in

government must show some specific or implied grant of power for everything it does; a State government need only show that the Constitution does not prohibit it from doing whatever it sees fit to do.

The National government has power to

> Maintain an army and navy. (Art. I, Sec. 8; Art. II, Sec. 2.)
>
> Declare war and make peace. (Art. I, Sec. 8; Art. II, Sec. 2.)
>
> Make treaties and other foreign relations. (Art. II, Sec. 2.)
>
> Regulate immigration and naturalization. (Art. I, Sec. 8.)
>
> Regulate foreign and interstate commerce. (Art. I, Sec. 8.)
>
> Maintain post offices and post roads. (Art. I, Sec. 8.)
>
> Issue coins and paper money. (Art. I, Sec. 8.)
>
> Grant copyrights and patents. (Art. I, Sec. 8.)
>
> Maintain federal courts of justice. (Art. I, Sec. 8; Art. III, Sec. 1.)
>
> Collect taxes for the above purposes and for the general welfare. (Art. I, Sec. 8.)
>
> Do anything "necessary and proper[1] for carrying into execution the foregoing powers." (Art. I, Sec. 8.)

By way of illustration, let us enumerate a few powers which the State of Alabama could exercise. She could make laws requiring the consent of police officers to hold a church service; could pay the salaries of Catholic priests; could require all news items to be approved by a State censor before being published; could prohibit the carrying, or even owning, of fire-arms; and could try without a jury persons accused of crime.

Alabama could do all these things because there is no provision

---

1898 any details of the State laws inconsistent therewith became void. Therefore, while the States have a certain amount of power, the National government in reality is supreme in the sphere of concurrent power.

[1] The Supreme Court has construed "necessary and proper" to mean "expedient" or "appropriate."

in the Constitution of the United States prohibiting her.[1] The Congress of the United States, as we have just seen, could not make any of these things lawful because it has not been delegated the power to pass any of these laws. A State can legislate concerning marriage, divorce, insurance, regulation of cities, saloons, factories, and innumerable things which affect only the one State; but the United States cannot legislate concerning these matters because there are no clauses in the Constitution permitting it either specifically or by implication.

25. Supremacy of Federal Law. — In our federal system of government some powers granted to the National government are almost certain to conflict with others which were apparently reserved for the State governments. The following passage from the Constitution shows that State laws which conflict with such National laws as Congress has constitutional authority for enacting must yield to the National laws:

"This Constitution and the laws of the United States which shall be made in pursuance thereof, and all treaties made or which shall be made under the authority of the United States shall be the supreme law of the land." This means that California could not prohibit Japanese born in the United States from voting at regular elections, as this would violate the fifteenth amendment to the Constitution of the United States. Further, this also means that California could not hold regular elections for Congressmen in June because a law of the United States prescribes the month of November. Or, if the United States should make a treaty with China agreeing to guarantee to all Chinese residing in the United States all privileges of citizens of the United States, California could not place a higher license upon laundries run by alien Chinese than upon similar laundries conducted by Americans.

---

[1] It is barely possible but not probable that the courts would declare some of these laws contrary to the Fourteenth Amendment of the Constitution of the United States. For instance, they might hold that the State censorship would deprive a person of his liberty without due process of law.

26. Supremacy of the Federal Judiciary. — Not only is the federal law supreme but the federal courts decide whether a State or an individual has violated this law. If Virginia should pass a law conflicting with the Constitution, laws, or treaties of the United States, any individual who feels aggrieved thereby might go to court, and if the case is finally appealed to the Supreme Court of the United States this court would decide whether the State law really conflicts. The decisions of the Supreme Court are binding not only on private persons, but on States, and even on the Congress of the United States, if the latter passes a law contrary to the Constitution.

27. Interstate Relations. — In the preceding sections of this chapter the relations that exist between the United States on the one hand and the States composing it on the other have been considered. In this section the relations that exist among the forty-eight States will be discussed.

States Independent of One Another. — "Except as otherwise specifically provided by the federal Constitution, the States of the American Union, when acting within the spheres of government reserved to them, stand toward one another as independent and wholly separated States. The laws of the State have no force, and their officials have no public authority, outside of their own territorial boundaries. As to all these matters their relations *inter se* (among themselves) are governed by the general principles of private International Law."[1]

Full Faith and Credit Clause. — The Constitution specifically provides that "full faith and credit shall be given in each State to the public acts, records, and judicial proceedings of every other State, and Congress may by general laws prescribe the manner in which such acts, records, and proceedings shall be proved and the effect thereof." (Art. IV, Sec. I.)

Suppose A brings suit against B in a court of New York, of which State both parties are residents, and the court decides that B owes A $1000 and gives A judgment. B moves to

---

[1] Willoughby on the Constitution, p. 194.

New Jersey taking all of his property with him before it can be attached for the debt. A follows him and shows in the New Jersey court of proper jurisdiction the judgment of the New York court with the certificate of the New York judge, the signature of the clerk of the court, and the seal of the court. The New Jersey court, without reëxamining the merits of the original claim, will give "faith and merit" to the judgment and will have its officer collect the debt for A.

Privileges and Immunities. — The Constitution specifically provides that "the citizens of each State shall be entitled to all privileges and immunities of citizens in the several States." (Art. IV, Sec. 2.) This means that a citizen of one State may go to another State and there enjoy the same civil rights[1] that citizens of the latter State enjoy, and likewise be subject to the same restrictions.

As an example of the rights a citizen of one State may enjoy in another State, the legislature of Maryland passed a law (1868) imposing a license on the privilege of selling articles not manufactured in Maryland. For citizens of Maryland the license was not to exceed $150, but for citizens of other States the license was to be $300. Mr. Ward of New Jersey refused to pay more than $150, and the Supreme Court of the United States decided that Mr. Ward could not be required to pay more than citizens of Maryland.

As an illustration of a restriction upon a citizen of one State while in another State, A has the right to sell cigarettes in Illinois. In Indiana the sale of cigarettes is forbidden by law, hence if A moves to Indiana he cannot sell cigarettes there.

The courts have never given a complete list of privileges and immunities, but the following are some of them: The right to pass through, or reside in any other State for the purpose of trade, agriculture, professional pursuits, or otherwise; to demand the writ of *habeas corpus* (see Sec. 135); to bring suit in the courts of the State; to make contracts; to buy, sell, and

---

[1] *Civil rights* are those of person and property. .

own property ; to pay no higher taxes than the citizens of the State ; to marry.

Extradition. — The Constitution specifically provides that "a person charged in any State with treason, felony, or other crime, who shall flee from justice and be found in another State, shall on demand of the executive authority of the State from which he fled be delivered up to be removed to the State having jurisdiction of the crime." (Art. IV, Sec. 2.)

Occasionally a governor has refused to surrender an accused person and neither the United States Courts nor the President of the United States have compelled him to do so. For instance, about ten years ago ex-Governor Taylor of Kentucky was indicted as having been implicated in the murder of Governor Goebel, and fled to Indiana. The governor of Indiana, feeling that Taylor, a republican, would not receive a fair trial by the excited Democrats who were then in control in Kentucky, refused to extradite him.

28. Separation of the Powers of the National Government. — The division of the powers between the National government and the State governments has been discussed. The powers of the National government are further separated into three grand departments — the legislative, the executive, and the judicial.

Legislative Department. — The Constitution of the United States provides that all legislative (lawmaking) powers of the National government shall be vested in a Congress. This body cannot authorize any other persons to legislate in its stead, but it can lay down rules and authorize others to put them into effect conditionally. For instance, it can direct the Interstate Commerce Commission (see Sec. 117) to prescribe reasonable railroad rates. Thereupon the Commission can prescribe a two-cent passenger fare on condition that this low rate will allow the railroad companies to earn reasonable profits.

Executive Department. — The Constitution of the United States provides that the executive (law-enforcing) powers shall be vested in a President, whose duty it is to see that the laws that have been made by Congress are executed.

Judicial Department. — The Constitution of the United States provides that the judicial (law-interpreting and law-applying) powers shall be vested in one Supreme Court and such inferior courts as Congress shall from time to time ordain and establish.

29. Check and Balance System. — The legislative, executive, and judicial functions of government were vested in three separate bodies of public servants in order that each might be a check upon or balance to the other. The Constitution makers greatly feared the tyranny of a king after they had succeeded in throwing off the yoke of George III, and considered the principle of the separation of powers essential to the protection of individual liberty. Therefore, the President was given the veto power over legislation passed by Congress; Congress was given the right to impeach the President, judges, and other civil officers; and the courts were allowed to declare unconstitutional, and hence of no force, laws enacted by Congress.

30. Criticism of the Check and Balance System. — The principle of checks and balances in government is not held in such high esteem to-day as it was a century ago. The people no longer fear the officers whom they elect every few years. They admit that mistakes or evil designs of one department might be checked by another, but they have also come to realize that well-planned, honest policies of one department can be checked by the officers of another department if the latter are unfavorable to them.

Moreover, many laws passed by the legislative department which are theoretically good work badly when enforced by the executive department; while, conversely, the executive department is always in need of practical laws which the legislative department refuses to enact. In England, where the same persons are heads of executive departments and leaders in Parliament, this check on efficient government does not exist.

There are times when our government comes to a standstill because the departments cannot agree upon a certain policy. The ideas of any one of the departments might work well if vigorously pushed forward; but when there is a difference of opinion between the legislative and executive departments, a political "boss," good or bad, must mount the vehicle of state and keep it moving. Since it has become necessary to have a boss it would seem well to be bossed by the President, who is elected by all of the people and is responsible to all of the people — at least every fourth year.

31. Constitutional Amendments. — The legal methods of amending the Constitution of the United States are more difficult than those of any other nation. There are four ways of amending it.[1]

First, an amendment may be proposed by a two-thirds vote of each House of Congress and ratified by the legislatures of three fourths of the States. All of the seventeen amendments have been adopted in this manner.

Second, an amendment may be proposed by a two-thirds vote of each House of Congress and ratified by Conventions in three fourths of the States. Representative Hobson of Alabama recently offered an amendment providing for nation-wide prohibition, which would have been submitted to State Conventions if it had received a two-third vote of each House of Congress.

Third, an amendment may be proposed by a National Convention, called by Congress when requested by the legislatures of two thirds of the States, and ratified by the legislatures of three fourths of the States.

Fourth, an amendment may be proposed by a National Convention, called by Congress when requested by the legislatures of two thirds of the States, and ratified by Conventions in three fourths of the States. The Constitution was originally adopted in this manner. The Committee on the Constitution, an unofficial organization, now advocates a number of changes in the Constitution and urges that a National Convention be called for this purpose.

---

[1] See Art. V of the Constitution, p. 443.

FOUR WAYS OF AMENDING THE CONSTITUTION OF THE UNITED STATES

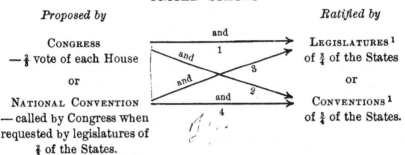

Proposed by   *Ratified by*

CONGRESS — ⅔ vote of each House

or

NATIONAL CONVENTION — called by Congress when requested by legislatures of ⅔ of the States.

LEGISLATURES[1] of ¾ of the States

or

CONVENTIONS[1] of ¾ of the States.

As soon as the government of the United States was established the first ten amendments were added to the Constitution; the eleventh amendment was added in 1798; the twelfth, in 1804. For sixty-one years no other amendment was added until the Civil War resulted in the ratification of the thirteenth (1865), the fourteenth (1868), and the fifteenth (1870). Since then hundreds of proposals have been introduced, but only two have been submitted to the States; the sixteenth, providing for a federal income tax, and the seventeenth, for the popular election of Senators, were both ratified in 1913.[2]

Thus is the Constitution formally amended. Owing to the difficulty of persuading two thirds of the members of Congress to propose an amendment and three fourths of the States to ratify it, the Supreme Court has been led to give an elastic construction to the Constitution.

32. Constitution Adaptable to Economic Changes. — While we have referred to the Constitution as an agreement, it is not an agreement in the sense of a contract which must be interpreted exactly as the parties to the contract understood it when it was entered into. When the Constitution was drafted in 1787 there

---

[1] Congress determines whether an amendment is to be ratified by State Legislatures or by State Conventions.

[2] A State might ratify an amendment any time after Congress has submitted it, but after voting in favor of it a subsequent legislature of that State may not change its vote so long as the proposed amendment is pending.

were only 4,000,000 scattered people in the United States, no large cities, few factories, no steamboats or railroads, no telegraphs, telephones, automobiles, no great monopolies ("trusts").

Things which concerned one State then now concern the entire Union, and as it has been almost impossible to amend the Constitution, the Courts have allowed Congress to read a new meaning into the words which the framers of the Constitution used. So the Constitution instead of being a dead contract is a living agreement which changes with time and adapts itself to economic and social changes. One might say that the Elastic Clause of the Constitution, which gives Congress power to legislate on all matters "necessary and proper for carrying into execution" the enumerated powers, has kept the Constitution alive for more than a century of eventful years. (See Sec. 48.)

BIBLIOGRAPHY

WILLOUGHBY, W. W. The American Constitutional System. (American State Series) 1904.

QUESTIONS ON THE TEXT

1. Distinguish the meaning of confederate government from that of federal government.

2. What are the advantages of federal government in the United States?

3. What is meant by "local self-government"?

4. What is the Constitution of the United States?

5. Mention some powers which the national government may exercise.

6. What powers are reserved to the States? What amendment of the Constitution provides for this reservation?

7. Distinguish "delegated" or "enumerated" powers from "residual" or "reserved" powers.

8. If a State law conflicts with a national law which must yield to the other?

9. With whom does the final interpretation of the federal law rest?

10. What relation do States bear to one another except as specifically provided by the Constitution?

11. What is meant by the requirement that each State give full faith and credit to the public acts, records, and judicial proceedings of every other State?

12. Name some privileges and immunities which a citizen of one State is entitled to enjoy in every other State.

13. What is meant by *extradition*?

14. The powers of the national government are divided among what three grand departments? What powers has each?

15. What is meant by the check and balance system? What are the arguments in favor of and against the system?

16. What Article of the Constitution explains the manner in which the Constitution may be amended? Explain in what four combinations of ways it may be amended.

17. How many amendments to the Constitution of the United States are there?

18. Is the Constitution a "dead contract" or a "living document"?

QUESTIONS FOR DISCUSSION

1. The United States is a representative, constitutional, federal republic. Consult unabridged dictionaries and explain fully the meaning of each of these words.

2. Let each pupil prepare a large chart showing the powers of government under our federal system. The accompanying figure adapted from Tiedman's "Unwritten Constitution" can be enlarged. Let the outer circle represent all the powers of government. In section *A* write all the powers exclusively delegated to the National government; in section *B*, all the powers reserved to the States; in section *C*, the concurrent powers, those which may be exercised by either the National or State governments; in 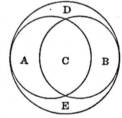 section *D*, those denied to the National government; in section *E*, those denied to the State governments. Space may be economized by the use of figures. I.8.3. in section *A* would mean Article I, Section 8, Clause 3; Am. X in section *B* would mean Amendment X.

3. Give reasons why each power granted exclusively to the National Government was so granted.

4. What legal complication would arise if the federal law and system of courts were not supreme?

5. Wisconsin recently enacted a law making a doctor's certificate a prerequisite for obtaining a marriage license. Couples crossed into neighboring States and there married without a doctor's certificate and returned to Wisconsin to live. Could Wisconsin enact a law declaring such marriages illegal and prohibit the parties in question from living together within her boundaries?

6. In the government of one's self an individual is actuated by conscience, judgment, and will. Which of these is legislative, which executive, and which judicial?

7. Do you believe in the check and balance idea in government? To bring the problem close to home let us suppose your father the legislative department, your mother the judicial, and you the executive.

8. Power has a tendency to concentrate in the President if he becomes the party leader, in the Supreme Court, which may declare laws unconstitutional, or in Congress, which holds the purse strings. In which of the three would you consider the concentration of power the least objectionable? Give reasons for your decision.

9. Representative Hobson's resolution provided that Congress submit the amendment for nation-wide prohibition of the liquor traffic to Conventions in the States for ratification instead of to the Legislatures. Why to Conventions instead of to Legislatures?

CHAPTER V

THE LEGISLATIVE DEPARTMENT

33. Congress. — The Legislature of the United States is called the Congress. It consists of a House of Representatives and a Senate. The House represents the national principle, because its members represent the people directly in proportion to population; and the Senate represents the federal principle, because its members represent the States, each State having equal representation. Article V of the Constitution provides that "no State, without its consent, shall be deprived of equal suffrage in the Senate." Without equal representation in the Senate such small States as Rhode Island, Delaware, and Maryland would not willingly have become members of the United States.

The advantages derived from a Congress composed of two houses are: (1) The minority is protected against the majority. (2) The one acts as a check upon the other. Through this check system a bill passed in the heat of passion by one house can be submitted to the cool judgment of the other. (3) One large house elected for a short term can express the wishes of the people, while the other house elected for a long term and small enough for deliberate debate can carefully weigh and consider them. (4) The press of our country has a better opportunity to point out the defects of a bill before it is acted upon by the second house.

Thomas Jefferson, who possessed great faith in "the voice of the people," was in France when the Constitution was framed. Upon his return, while taking breakfast with Washington, he opposed the two-body form of legislature, and was disposed to twit Washington about it. At this time Jefferson poured his coffee from his cup into his saucer. Washington asked him why he did so. "To cool it," he replied. "So," said Washington, "we will pour legislation into the Senatorial saucer to cool it."

Recently it has been argued that it is not in keeping with democratic institutions for Nevada, for instance, with 81,875 inhabitants to have as much legislative power in the Senate as New York with more than one hundred times as many

THE UNITED STATES CAPITOL.

(9,113,614). If New York were represented in the Senate proportionately with Nevada there would be 223 New York senators. To this argument Woodrow Wilson replied:

"These critics are entirely wrong in assuming . . . that the newer, weaker, or more sparsely settled parts of the country have less of an economic stake in its general policy and development than the older States and those which have had a great industrial development. Their stake may not be equal in dollars and cents — that, of course —

but it is probably greater in all that concerns opportunity and the chances of life. There is a sense in which the interest of the poor man in the prosperity of the country is greater than that of the rich man: he has no reserve, and his very life may depend upon it. The very life of an undeveloped community may depend upon what will cause a rich community mere temporary inconvenience or negligible distress."

A country so extensive as ours, and representing such a great variety of social, economic, and political conditions, would not have held together without equal representation of the States in the Senate.

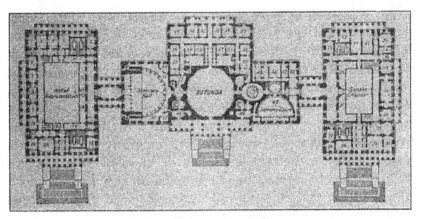

PRINCIPAL FLOOR OF THE CAPITOL.

Each number indicates a room, e.g., rooms 1, 2, 3, and 4 are occupied by the Committee on Appropriations, and number 40 is the room of the President.

34. Sessions of Congress. — Each Congress is numbered consecutively from the first term, which began March 4, 1789. The Sixty-third Congress began March 4, 1913, and ended March 4, 1915.

There are two regular sessions of each Congress, which are commonly designated as the "long" and the "short" session. The long session begins on the first Monday in December of the odd-numbered years and lasts until some time in the following spring or summer. The short session begins on the same date in the even-numbered years and lasts until March 4 following, when the term of all representatives expires. Prior to 1853 the short session ended at midnight, March 3, but at the the present time all business transacted between midnight of the third and noon of the fourth is dated the 3d of March. Also, if business is pressing at noon of March 4, the clock is turned back.

The President may call extra sessions, such as President Wilson called for April 4, 1913, which session was called primarily for the purpose of enacting a low tariff law and a currency law.

35. The House of Representatives.— *Membership.*—The House of Representatives is the more numerous body of Congress. The membership is determined by Congress after each census, but the number allotted to each State must be in proportion to its total population.[1] With a single exception (1842) the number of representatives has regularly increased with each new apportionment. A representative from a State which has increased very little in population will naturally not consent to a reduction in the representation of his own State, as this would possibly mean the destruction of his own district. His only alternative is to vote to increase the representation of the States that have increased in population.

The number of representatives for the decade 1910–1920 is 435, which is one for every 211,877 of population or fraction thereof greater than half. Even with this large membership the average number of inhabitants to a member has increased from 33,000 in 1793 to 211,877 for the present decade. A State is entitled to at least one member, regardless of population. Nevada, which has a population of only 81,875, and Arizona, New Mexico, Wyoming, and Delaware have one

---

[1] The Fourteenth Amendment declares that whenever a State shall limit the right of its adult male citizens to vote, except for crime, its representation in Congress shall be proportionately reduced. This provision has never been enforced, and some statesmen claim that it has been superseded by the Fifteenth Amendment.

representative each.   The largest number from any one State is forty-three, the number from New York State.[1]

Election of Representatives. — The time, place, and manner of electing representatives are determined by Congress, but the Constitution provides for two-year terms of office and that any person may vote for them whom the State permits to vote for members of the most numerous branch of the State legislature. Since 1871 Congress has required the States to use ballots and since 1872 to hold congressional elections uniformly on the Tuesday following the first Monday of November every even-

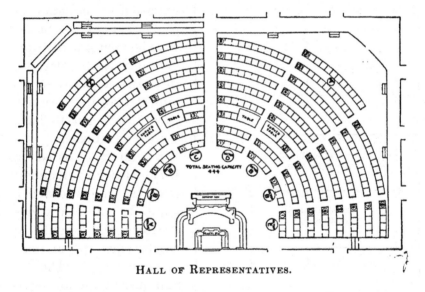

HALL OF REPRESENTATIVES.

numbered year.[2]   But in case of a vacancy in any State the Governor thereof may call a special election.

During the first fifty years of our Union the States were permitted to elect their representatives as they chose.   The method of electing them by districts early became popular, but

[1] A territory is represented in Congress by one delegate, the Philippine Islands by two Resident Commissioners, and Porto Rico by one.   Any one of these may take part in debate, but none of them can vote.

[2] By a special provision of Congress Maine is permitted to hold her congressional election in September.

some States elected all members at large,[1] which made it possible for a State with a small Democratic majority to elect all Democratic members. This was clearly unrepresentative, and in 1842 Congress prescribed that thenceforth all members should be chosen by districts. The district system tends to give representation to the minority party, but, as the States were laid out into districts by the State legislatures, the districts were so arranged that the majority party continued to have a great advantage.

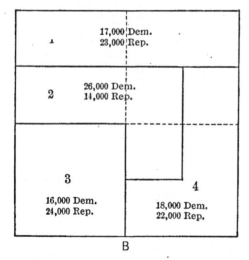

By an act passed in 1872, Congress required that the congressional districts be of contiguous territory and contain as nearly equal populations as practicable. The requirement that all territory of a district be contiguous has been observed to the letter but not always in spirit. For instance, in South Carolina the first district of the 1890 apportionment was shaped like two arrow heads which merely touched at the points.

---

[1] *At large* means from the entire State. Each voter expresses as many preferences as there are congressmen to elect from the State.

The requirement that population be as nearly equal as practicable has been frequently violated. Recently one of the Republican districts in New York State contained 165,701 inhabitants while one of the Democratic districts had a population of 450,000 inhabitants.

Gerrymandering. — The scheme resorted to by an unfair legislative body to lay out congressional or other districts so

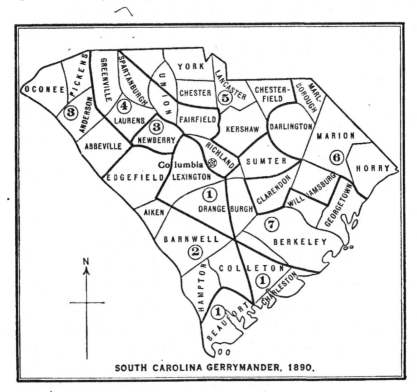

SOUTH CAROLINA GERRYMANDER, 1890.

as to secure a majority of voters for the party in power in the greatest possible number of them is known as gerrymandering. This can sometimes be done by collecting as many voters of the minority party as possible into one district so as to make other bordering districts safe for the majority party.

For instance, the accompanying figure A represents a State with four congressional districts, each consisting of 40,000 voters. In districts 1 and 4 the Democrats have a majority whereas in districts 2 and 3 the Republicans have a majority, but in the entire State the Republicans have a majority of voters and therefore elect the majority of the members of the State legislature. This Republican State legislature redistricts the State as shown in figure B, having gerrymandered it so that the Republicans have a majority of voters in districts 1, 3, and 4 and the Democrats a majority in district 2 only.

The map on page 59 shows how the districts of South Carolina were skilfully arranged in 1890 so as to throw large blocks of the Republican negro vote together, the populations varying from 134,000 in the first district to 217,000 in the seventh.

THE ORIGINAL GERRYMANDER.

The scheme of unfair apportionment of districts is called "gerrymandering" from Elbridge Gerry of Massachusetts. In 1812, when Gerry was governor of Massachusetts, the Republican legislature re-districted the State in such a manner that one district had a dragon-like appearance. It was indicated on a map of Massachusetts which hung over the desk of a Federalist editor. A celebrated painter added with his pencil a head, wings, and claws, and exclaimed, "That will do for a salamander!" "Better say Gerrymander," growled the editor.

Qualifications of Representatives. — A member of the House must be a man or woman twenty-five years of age, at least seven years a citizen of the United States, and an inhabitant of the State from which he is chosen, but not necessarily of the particular district. In practice, members are inhabitants of their districts, though in New York City a member of Congress has been elected by a district in which he did not live. If this practice should become general there would be many more able men from whom to select congressmen.

The House is judge of the elections, returns, and qualifications of its members and has excluded persons for various reasons. For instance, in 1900 a majority of the House excluded Brigham H. Roberts of Utah on the ground that he was practicing polygamy and thus violating the laws of his State. Two thirds of the House may expel one of its members for any reason it may think fit.

36. The Senate. — *Membership.* — The Senate is the smaller body of Congress, and is composed of two members from each State. As there are now forty-eight States there are ninety-six senators.

Term of Senators. — Senators are chosen for a term of six years, one third retiring every second year. By thus dividing senators into three classes the presence of too many new and inexperienced members is avoided.

Election of Senators. — Until the Seventeenth Amendment was ratified in 1913 senators were elected by State legislatures. Now at the regular November election of every even-numbered year one third of the senators are elected directly by the people, and are sworn into office when the new Congress assembles.[1] Each senator is elected from his State at large. All persons qualified to vote for members of the House of Representatives may vote for senators.

Qualifications of Senators. — A senator must be a man or woman, at least thirty years of age, nine years a citizen of the United States, and an inhabitant of the State from which he is elected. The Senate, like the House, is judge of the qualifications of its members. In 1912 Mr. Lorimer of Illinois was excluded by a majority vote, being elected as a result of

---

[1] Only one senator is elected from a State in any one year. Though when a vacancy occurs in the Senate the Governor of the respective State must call a special election unless the legislature empowers him to make a temporary appointment.

bribes paid to Illinois legislators in behalf of his election. He had been seated, although under protest, and had voted on many measures before the committee on elections could investigate. Also, like the House, the Senate can expel a member for any cause by a two-thirds vote.

Special Functions of the Senate. — The Senate performs three special or non-legislative functions, two of which are executive and the third judicial. They are as follows:

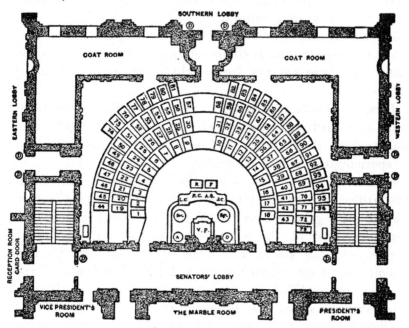

SENATE CHAMBER.

(1) The Constitution makes the approval of the Senate necessary to the validity of all appointments made by the President, unless otherwise provided. The reason for requiring the approval of the Senate was to prevent any errors or abuses of the chief executive, but in practice the senators claim the right of dictating to the President regarding appointments to such federal offices in the States as postmasters, federal judges, federal attorneys, and revenue collectors.

Under the custom known as "senatorial courtesy" the Senate will usually ratify or refuse to ratify an appointment according to the recommendation of the senators from the State in which the appointee resides. If the senators from that State are not members of the party in power the President will confer with a representative or some politician from the State. Appointments are always considered in secret sessions, called "executive sessions."

(2) All treaties are made by the President with the "advice and consent" of the Senate. For a short period after the adoption of the Constitution the advice of the Senate was asked before the President prepared a treaty, but now he merely consults with the Senate Committee on Foreign Relations and with influential members of both parties. The Senate may reject a treaty in full or may suggest amendments to it. Treaties are considered in "executive session."

(3) The Senate acts as a court of impeachment to try the President, Vice-President, or any other high civil officer.[1] A two-thirds vote of the Senate is necessary to sustain an impeachment. This removes the guilty person from office, and may deprive him of holding any other federal office if the Senate so desires.

37. Compensation of Congressmen. — Congressmen, unlike other officers or employees of the government, fix their own salary, and the only limit upon the amount is the President's veto and the fear of not being reëlected. Senators and representatives have always received the same salary. Each senator and representative now receives: (1) a salary of $7500 per annum;[2] (2) twenty cents a mile going and coming by the shortest route

---

[1] Senators and representatives are not impeached, since either house can expel a member by a two-thirds vote. Military officers are removed by court-martial.

[2] The salaries of congressmen from time to time have been as follows:

1789–1815, $6 per diem while in attendance.   1866–1871, $5000 per annum.
1815–1817, $1500 per annum.   1871–1874, $7500 per annum.
1817–1855, $8 per diem.   1874–1907, $5000 per annum.
1855–1866, $3000 per annum.   1907– $7500 per annum.

for each regular or special session; (3) publication and free distribution of speeches ;[1] (4) free postage, called the "franking privilege"; (5) free offices and $125 per annum for stationery; (6) $1500 per annum clerk hire for representatives, $1800 clerk hire for senators, and an additional amount ranging as high as $5000 clerk hire for the chairman of each of the fifty-eight House and seventy-five Senate committees.

In 1816 nearly all congressmen lost their seats because they increased the salary to $1500 a year, including the term partly served. In 1873, upon the last day of the session, Congress passed a bill increasing the compensation of its members from $5000 to $7500 per annum, and made it apply to the two years past. The next Congress repealed the measure. In 1907, during the last session of the term, Congress, by a standing vote, increased the salary from $5000 to $7500 — *after it had been defeated by a yea and nay vote.* This did not take effect until the next session, but the members of this session had already been elected, so the voters were powerless for two years. It was recognized, however, that the increase was just.

38. Privileges of Congressmen. — Congressmen are free from arrest during their attendance, and in going to and returning from the sessions, in all cases except treason, felony, and breach of the peace. As persons are no longer imprisoned for debts the privilege is of little value. "Treason, felony, and breach of the peace," include all indictable crimes.

Another privilege of congressmen is freedom of speech during debate in Congress. That is, they may not be sued for any statement made on the floor of Congress. This privilege includes the right to circulate copies of their speeches delivered in Congress. But a congressman is not privileged to defame any person in a newspaper article.

---

[1] Many speeches which are not actually delivered on the floor of Congress are published in the Congressional Record, of which each congressman receives sixty copies free. However, a congressman may obtain any number of reprints of his speech by paying the Government Printing Office the actual cost of the same.

REVIEW
OUTLINE OF CONGRESS

MEMBERS	HOUSE OF REPRESENTATIVES 435	SENATE 96
Qualifications . .	25 years of age, 7 years a citizen of the United States, inhabitant of State where elected. Other qualifications determined by the House.	30 years of age, 9 years a citizen of the United States, inhabitant of State where elected. Other qualifications determined by the Senate.
Elected by . .	Votes of Congressional Districts.	Votes of State.
Term	Two years.	Six years.
Salary	$7500 plus allowances.	$7500 plus allowances.
Sole Powers . .	(1) Impeachment. (2) To originate revenue bills.	(1) Court of impeachment. (2) Confirmation of appointments made by the President. (3) Ratification of all treaties.
Convene (in regular session) .	First Monday in every December.	First Monday in every December.

PRESIDING OFFICER	SPEAKER	VICE-PRESIDENT[1] OF THE UNITED STATES CALLED "PRESIDENT OF THE SENATE"
Qualifications . .	Member of House.	The same as for President.
Elected by . . .	Members of the House.	Presidential electors or Senate.
Term	Two years (often re-elected).	Four years.
Salary	$12,000.	$12,000.
Vote	The same as any other member of the House.	Only in case of tie.

[1] A president *pro tem* of the Senate is elected by the Senate to preside in the absence of the Vice-President.

BIBLIOGRAPHY

ALEXANDER, D. A. S. History and Procedure of the House of Representatives, 1916.
McCALL, SAMUEL W. The Business of Congress. 1911.
REINSCH, PAUL S. Readings on American Federal Government. 1909.

QUESTIONS ON THE TEXT

1. What Article of the Constitution treats of Congress?
2. Congress consists of what two houses? What does each house represent?
3. What are the advantages of a two-body legislature?
4. Do you favor equal representation in the Senate?
5. When does the long session of Congress begin? When does the short session end?
6. How is the membership of the House of Representatives determined? Of how many members does it now consist? Each represents how many people?
7. Do any States have more senators in the Senate than representatives in the House?
8. When are congressional elections held? How long is it after the election until the members take their seats? What is the term of office?
9. Explain *gerrymandering*.
10. What are the qualifications of membership in the House of Representatives?
11. Of how many members does the Senate consist? What is the term of office?
12. When are senators elected? Who may vote for them? What are the qualifications for office?
13. What special functions are performed by the Senate?
14. What salary do congressmen receive? What other compensation do they receive?
15. What special privileges have congressmen? May a congressman defame the character of a person in a newspaper article?

QUESTIONS FOR DISCUSSION

1. Do you favor equal representation of States in the Senate?
2. The number of any Congress can be determined by subtracting 1789 (the year the 1st Congress met) from the year in which the Con-

gress of which the number is desired ends, and dividing the remainder by 2, because a Congress lasts two years. As a Congress always ends upon an odd-numbered year the number from which 1789 is subtracted is necessarily an odd number. By what number is the Congress now in session known?

3. The first woman representative, Miss Rankin, was elected from Montana in 1916. Give arguments for and against electing women to Congress.

4. How are the political parties represented at present in the Senate and in the House of Representatives?

5. Is your State gerrymandered?

6. To how many representatives is your State entitled?

7. In what congressional district do you live? Who is your representative? How long has he been in Congress? What party does he represent? What stand has he taken in regard to tariff legislation, woman suffrage, national prohibition, or any matter in which you are interested? (You can learn how congressmen vote from the Congressional Record or by writing to the National Voters' League, Washington, D. C.)

8. Discuss in regard to your senators the same matters that you have considered in regard to your representative.

9. Do you believe that popular election of senators will make them more responsive to popular opinion? Do you think they should respond as readily as representatives do, or should they decide measures according to their own individual opinions?

10. In 1913 President Wilson's special session of Congress merged into the regular session, and a mileage allowance was not voted by Congress because the President opposed it. A few years previous thereto, under similar conditions, mileage was voted with the approval of President Roosevelt. This is known as "constructive mileage," because it is not actually travelled. Do you favor or oppose constructive mileage? Why?

11. Members of the House of Commons in England receive a salary of $2000 a year; those of the House of Representatives in the United States, $7500. Which members are more likely to voice the will of the people?

12. Men of eminent ability in the United States engaged in other professions and commercial pursuits earn much more than we pay the members of the House of Representatives. What are the advantages and disadvantages of a high salary for a legislator?

13. Do you believe in the unrestricted use of the "franking privilege"? In 1914 Senator Root franked 715,062 copies of his speech opposing tolls exemption of American coastwise vessels. This speech advocated an honorable compliance with our treaty obligations with England, but the frank is also used by congressmen representing special interests.

CHAPTER VI

THE POWERS OF CONGRESS

39. Interpretation of the Constitution. — When our thirteen States united to form the United States of America they limited Congress to certain expressed powers enumerated in the Constitution and those "necessary and proper" to carry the expressed powers into execution. Persons who favor strong State governments and a weak National government would restrict the powers of Congress to the bare letter of the Constitution, while those who favor a strong National government would interpret these powers liberally, thus increasing the legislative powers of Congress.

Fortunately for the National government Chief Justice Marshall, who dominated the Supreme Court during the formative period of our government (1800–1835), gave a *liberal construction* to the Constitution, thereby permitting Congress to do many things which Jefferson and other *strict constructionists* would have reserved for the States. Such men as Washington, Hamilton, Lincoln, and Roosevelt have favored a liberal construction, believing that the government of the United States can govern more efficiently and with less annoyance to the people than the numerous States whose different laws often conflict.

I. Expressed Powers

40. Expressed Powers Interpreted. — The expressed powers of Congress are enumerated very briefly; and without courts to decide exactly what they mean and what they include, Congress would often be tempted to exceed its authority. To illustrate, the Constitution (Art. I, Sec. 8, Cl. 3) provides that " Congress shall have power to regulate commerce with foreign nations and among the several States."[1]   These words are very general, and federal courts have decided more than 2000 cases in explanation of them, and several hundred of these cases have been appealed and decided and supported by lengthy opinions of the Supreme Court of the United States.

41. Foreign Commerce. — Congress has "power to regulate commerce with foreign nations." Under this power Congress regulates shipping; determines numerous conditions under which vessels may fly the American flag, such as requiring a wireless equipment, life-preservers, life-boats, a definite limit to the number of passengers, and inspection of the ships; prescribes how ships must enter and leave ports — *e.g.*, stop at quarantine stations for health inspection and have proper entry or clearance papers; and imposes other requirements too numerous to mention.

Under this power Congress has prohibited the importation of numerous articles — *e.g.*, diseased animals or vegetables, opium except for medical purposes, obscene books, lottery tickets, adulterated and misbranded foods, articles having names or emblems simulating domestic trade marks, aigrettes, convict-made articles, white or yellow phosphorus matches, and prize-fight films.

Under this power Congress has prohibited the exportation of white or yellow phosphorus matches and has authorized the President at his discretion to prohibit the exportation of contraband of war.

42. Interstate Commerce. — Congress has power to regulate commerce among the several States. The strongest motive that led to the formation of our Union was the annoying taxes which each State placed upon the commerce of the others, hence the Constitutional Convention was prepared to give a liberal regulation of commerce to the central government.

---

[1] Congress also has power to regulate commerce within the Indian Tribes. For example, Congress prohibits the sale or gift of liquor to Indians or even the introduction of it into Indian country.

When the Constitution was framed wagons or stage coaches naturally needed very little regulation, and slow sail boats did not present many interstate problems. The chief and perhaps the only purpose of this clause in the minds of the Constitution-makers was to prevent the States from interfering with the freedom of commercial intercourse among themselves; it referred to the articles to be transported rather than to the means of transporting them.

However, the Supreme Court decided that the power of Congress to regulate commerce could not be confined to the

FULTON'S FIRST STEAMBOAT.
The *Clermont.*

instrumentalities in use at the time of the adoption of the Constitution, but kept pace with inventions and with the growth of the country. Thus, by this liberal and progressive attitude of the court, Congress has been able to do many things through its "power to regulate commerce . . . among the several States." *Commerce Includes Navigation.*—Thirty-five years after our government was established the Supreme Court was called upon to explain this commerce clause. Robert Fulton invented the steam-boat in 1807, and the legislature of the State of New York granted to Fulton and Livingston the exclusive right to run steam-boats on the Hudson River. Another person, Gibbons by name, disputed the right, and in 1824 the Supreme Court decided, in an opinion prepared by Chief Justice Marshall, that "commerce" is not only the purchase, sale, and exchange of commodities, or "traffic," but is also "intercourse," which includes the means of traffic, at least on water, and hence includes "navigation." So the legislature of the State of New York did not have the right to grant an exclusive privilege to any person to "navigate" her rivers, as Congress alone had been given authority to regulate commerce among the States.

Under the right "to regulate . . . commerce among the States" the Courts have allowed Congress to extend its control

THE FIRST RAILROAD TRAIN.

over "navigation" until it now controls all navigable waters within States as well as between States. For example, between New York City and Albany, the United States Government deepens the channel, lights the river, inspects the boats, requires them to carry life-preservers, limits the number of passengers; and further, a bridge could not be built across the Hudson River where navigable without permission from the federal authorities.

Commerce Includes Transportation. — The first railroads were built about 1830. Until the Civil War they were short lines, usually within the limits of one State. Just after the War they rapidly consolidated into through trunk lines, at which time Congress began to control them. In 1887 the "Interstate Commerce Act" created the "Interstate Commerce Commission." The courts justified the regulation of interstate railroads under the commerce clause, saying that commerce means "traffic," "intercourse," and also "transportation."

INTERSTATE TELEGRAPH LINES.

· Under this power to control interstate "transportation" the Federal Government regulates rates for articles or persons carried from one State to another, limits the number of hours that employees are permitted to work, requires safety appliances, compels roads to pay damages to employees actually engaged in carrying on interstate commerce, or their assignees, if any employee is injured or killed from the negligence of any of the railroad's officers, agents, or employees.

Commerce Includes the Communication of Ideas. — The first telegraph line was built in 1842 and the first telephone was ex-

THE WIRELESS STATION AT ARLINGTON, VIRGINIA.

hibited at the Centennial Exposition in the year 1876. Both, when extending from one State to another, are regulated by the Federal Government inasmuch, as the courts have said, "commerce includes the transmission of messages." It likewise regulates the wireless, because by means of this device messages are transmitted.

The Right to Regulate Commerce Includes the Right to Prohibit Commerce. — The right of Congress to regulate commerce includes the right to exclude commodities — at least under some circumstances. Diseased cattle, dangerous explosives, goods and persons infected with disease, lottery tickets, C.O.D. shipments of liquor, impure or misbranded foods, products owned by railroads except for their own consumption, and liquor shipped into a prohibition State contrary to the law of the State, are examples of articles which Congress has excluded from interstate commerce.

The Child Labor Law enacted by Congress in 1916 makes it unlawful to ship from one State to another or to a foreign state products of mines or quarries in which children under sixteen years of age are employed. It also makes it unlawful to so ship products of mills, canneries, or factories in which children under fourteen years of age are employed, or in which those between fourteen and sixteen years of age are worked more than eight hours a day, or more than six days a week, or before six o'clock A.M., or after seven o'clock P.M.

The Right to Regulate Commerce Includes the Right to Protect Commerce. — The Sherman Anti-Trust Law of 1890 was enacted under the power to regulate commerce. It prohibits "every contract, combination in the form of a trust[1] or otherwise, or

---

[1] The *trust* was originally a device by which several corporations engaged in the same line of business would combine to eliminate competition and regulate prices. This was done by creating a central board composed of the presidents or general managers of the different corporations and the transfer to them of a majority of stock from each of the corporations to be held "in trust" for the stockholders who thus assigned their stock. The stockholders received in return "trust certificates" showing that they were entitled to receive dividends on their assigned stock, though the voting power of it had

conspiracy in restraint of trade or commerce among the several
States, or with foreign nations." Under this act railroads are
prohibited from forming combinations or "pools" for the
maintenance of freight or passenger rates. Also, it was under
this act that the Supreme Court ordered the Standard Oil
Trust and the Tobacco Trust to dissolve.

Another violation of the Anti-Trust law is quite interesting.
Hat makers in Danbury, Connecticut, organized as a labor
union, could not agree with their employer as to wages, so
"scabs" (non-union men) were employed by the manufacturer.
Thereupon the union endeavored to prevent the "scabs" from
laboring for the manufacturer in question and at the same time
persuaded merchants in other States not to buy hats made in
Danbury. This was done by having their fellow labor union
men in other States refuse to deal at stores handling these hats.
The United States Supreme Court declared this boycott to be a
conspiracy in restraint of commerce among the States, and the
United Hatters of North America were ordered to pay the sum
of $272,000 to the manufacturer whom they had thus injured.

43. Taxation. — The power conferred upon Congress to levy
and collect its own revenues is almost absolute, except (1) that
no duties may be levied upon exports; (2) that excises[1] and
import duties must be uniform throughout the United States;
and (3) that direct taxes except income taxes, if levied, must
be apportioned among the States on the basis of population.

---

been passed to the trustees. This enabled the trustees to elect all the directors
of all the corporations, and thus prevent competition and insure better prices.
Though the "trust" has been superseded by "holding corporations" and
other devices, any monopolistic combination is called a "trust."

A "holding corporation" is a corporation which purchases a controlling
portion of stock in the various competing corporations, and controls those
various corporations as trustees would, except that the holding corporation
actually owns the stock. In case of the "Standard Oil Trust," the Standard
Oil Company of New Jersey gradually exchanged its stock for that of the
numerous different corporations. This, too, was considered in restraint of
trade and the Supreme Court of the United States ordered that the stock be
returned to the respective companies.

[1] See Sec. 45.

Export Taxes Prohibited. — The reason for the Constitutional prohibition against the export tax is plain. Suppose Congress could levy an export tax on cotton amounting to five cents a pound. The English buyers of cotton would pay to the American growers no more than to those of other countries. Therefore, in order to compete, the American grower would have the tax to pay. As all cotton is grown in a few of the Southern States the South would have the entire tax to pay.

Excises and Import Taxes Must be Uniform. — The Constitutional requirement that excise taxes and import duties must be uniform throughout the United States means that these taxes must be the same on the same commodities in all parts of the country. To illustrate, the federal excise tax on the manufacture of whiskey, which is now $1.10 a gallon, must be the same in New York as it is in New Mexico. The import duty on diamonds, which is now ten per cent *ad valorem*, must be the same at the port of New York as it is at the port of New Orleans.

Direct Taxes Must Be Apportioned. — Without the Constitutional provision that all direct taxes must be apportioned among the States on the basis of population, a tax of so much an acre on land would have worked a hardship on States with much cheap land but little population. When the Constitution was framed wealth was distributed among the States very nearly in proportion to population, and a tax in proportion to population was just; but since then wealth has concentrated in a few large cities and a direct tax which must be levied in proportion to population would be very unjust to rural States.

Power to Tax is Power to Destroy. — With the three exceptions just considered the power of taxation is so absolute that it may be used even to destroy an industry so long as Congress professes to be exercising its power of taxation, for the courts will not consider the motives of Congress. As an illustration, in 1914 Congress laid a tax of $300 a pound upon the manufacture of opium to be used for smoking and in this way destroyed the industry by taxation.

The white or yellow phosphorus used in the manufacture of the old-fashioned match is very poisonous. Workmen in match factories often had their teeth fall out or their jaw bones decay, and many died from the poison. Matches made from other materials were a little more expensive. The Constitution does not give Congress power to regulate labor conditions directly; therefore in 1912 Congress imposed a stamp tax of two cents a hundred on matches made of white or yellow phosphorus. As matches retail for one cent a hundred the phosphorus match industry was of course destroyed.

Taxation, in the form of tariff, has long been used to restrict or hinder the importation of various products in order to protect manufacturers in the United States from the competition of foreign manufacturers.

The only redress against high taxes on certain articles is the right of the voters to elect new congressmen who might repeal an objectionable tax law.

44. Direct Taxes. —Taxes which are actually borne by the person upon whom they are imposed, such as capitation taxes and taxes on land and buildings, are direct taxes. Such taxes have been levied by the United States government only in case of war emergency — five times in all. No direct tax has been levied since the Civil War, except an income tax which need not be in proportion to population since the adoption of Amendment XVI to the Constitution of the United States.

45. Indirect Taxes are those that can be shifted from the person who pays them to other persons, and are therefore indirectly paid by the people generally. To illustrate, such taxes are those which are levied on commodities before the commodities reach the persons who consume them but are ultimately paid by the consumers as a part of the market price. Indirect taxes are of two kinds — *excises* and *customs*.

Excises, popularly known as internal revenue duties, are taxes on commodities produced in the United States, such as the stamp tax on liquor, tobacco, playing cards, and oleomargarine. (See Sec. 77.) The manufacturer pays the tax to the government when he buys internal revenue stamps to stick on each barrel or package, but ultimately the consumer pays the tax, since the manufacturer adds the cost of the stamp to his selling price.

Customs, popularly known as tariff duties, are taxes on commodities imported from foreign countries. (See Sec. 77.) The tariff rate is frequently changed, recent changes having been made in the years 1894, 1897, 1909, and 1913, and it varies on different articles, now being as high as sixty per cent on some. Articles entering the United States without tariff are said to be on the " free list " — *e.g.,* coffee, raw wool, agricultural implements ; articles taxed at a low rate are said to be taxed " for revenue only " — *e.g.,* diamonds, chamois skins, pineapples ; while articles taxed at a high rate are said to be taxed " for protection " — *e.g.,* automobiles, silks, jewelry.

UNITED STATES CUSTOM HOUSE AT PHILADELPHIA.

The tax is often so high that certain articles are not shipped into this country at all. Then, of course, no revenue is collected, but the manufacturer ·of the articles in this country can charge more for these articles than otherwise, since foreign competition is removed. The tax is " for protection " to home industry.

The Corporation Tax, first enacted by Congress in 1909, is·a tax on most kinds of corporations, joint-stock companies, or associations. It is a tax equivalent to two per cent of the net income of such organizations. It is an indirect excise tax, or license, upon the special privilege of operating as a corporation.

The Inheritance Tax was levied by the National Government during the Civil War and during the Spanish American War. The United States Revenue Act of 1916 again imposed an inheritance tax. The rate of the present tax varies from one to ten per cent, the rate increasing according to the amount inherited; but estates worth less than $50,000 are exempt from this national tax. (See Sec. 248.)

This tax is classed as an indirect tax because it is a tax on the privilege of inheriting rather than upon the property inherited. It is therefore in the nature of an excise tax.

46. The Income Tax. — This tax is now practicable as a result of the Sixteenth Amendment (1913). The United States Revenue Act of 1916 provides for a progressive income tax on all incomes in excess of $3000,[1] varying in rate from two per cent on incomes between $3000 and $20,000 to fourteen per cent on incomes of more than $2,000,000.

47. Other Expressed Powers of Congress. — The two expressed powers of Congress just discussed — the power to regulate commerce and the power of taxation — have been so liberally construed by the courts as to give rise to other powers not necessarily associated with taxation or commerce, and because of their far-reaching importance we have discussed them at some length. The following expressed powers of Congress need not be discussed in such detail.

Power to Make Money. — Congress has power to coin money and issue paper money, but the States are forbidden to do either.

Power to Borrow Money. — The Constitution gives Congress power to "borrow money on the credit of the United States." When there are unusual undertakings, like the Civil War or the construction of the Panama Canal, the usual revenues are

---

[1] A married man living with his wife or a married woman living with her husband is taxed on all income in excess of $4000 ; but in case each has an income in excess of $4000 only one is exempt from the tax on $4000.

not adequate and Congress borrows money. The ordinary method employed by the government for borrowing money is the sale of bonds.[1] Bonds which are used by governments and corporations when they borrow money are like promissory notes given by individuals when they borrow money — a promise to pay a certain sum at a specified time. The United States has been able to borrow money at a rate of interest as low as two per cent.

Bankruptcy. — Both Congress and the State legislatures have the power to regulate bankruptcy, but since the national law enacted in 1898 covers the entire domain of bankruptcy it supersedes all State bankruptcy laws.[2]

Naturalization is the process by which citizens of one country become citizens of another, and Congress has the power "to establish a uniform rule of naturalization." Under the immigration laws certain persons are not allowed to enter the United States, and naturally such persons are not permitted to become naturalized. This applies to Orientals; and the Chinese, the Japanese, the Burmese, and the East Indians have been refused naturalization.

Postal Service. — Congress has power to establish post offices and post roads.[3] The government may condemn land for post-office sites and could condemn it for post roads should it become necessary. Of course a fair price must be paid the owner for his property. A State is not permitted to establish a postal system, nor is an individual. For instance, express companies could not make a business of carrying first-class mail.

---

[1] There are two forms of bonds — coupon and registered. A twenty-year coupon bond has attached to the bottom, like stamps, forty small engraved coupons, and every six months the owner cuts one coupon which represents his semi-annual interest, and has it cashed at bank as he would an ordinary check. Holders of registered bonds receive their interest by checks. A registered bond can be replaced if lost but a coupon bond cannot.

[2] For meaning of "bankruptcy" see U. S. Constitution, Act I, Sec. 8, note.

[3] "Post roads" are all letter carrier routes in towns and cities, railroads and canals, and all the waters of the United States during the time that mail is carried thereon.

Copyrights and Patents. — Congress has the power " to promote the progress of science and of useful arts, by securing for limited times to authors and inventors the exclusive right to their respective writings and discoveries."

A copyright is the exclusive right of an author or his assignee to print and publish his literary or artistic work. The protection is granted by the government for a period of twenty-eight years; renewable for another twenty-eight years. The right extends to maps, charts, engravings, sculpture, dramatic or musical compositions, and pictures, as well as books. In 1912 the Supreme Court decided that moving pictures of *Ben Hur*, a copyrighted book, was a dramatization, and hence an infringement of the copyright. (See Sec. 120, note.)

A patent is a grant of the exclusive right to manufacture, use, or sell a new and useful invention for a period of years. At present the number of years is seventeen, which term may be extended only by special act of Congress. (See Sec. 99.)

Weights and Measures. — Congress has power to regulate weights and measures. By a recent act of Congress fruit and vegetable barrels packed for interstate commerce must be of a prescribed uniform size. Congress could establish the metric system throughout the United States if it chose to do so.

Judicial Powers. — Congress has power to establish federal courts, to define and punish piracy on the high seas, to define and punish offences against the law of nations, and to punish counterfeiters of federal money and securities.

Power over Federal Districts. — Congress has power to legislate for territories of the United States, the District of Columbia, forts, dockyards, national parks, federal buildings, etc.

War Powers. — Congress has power to declare war, to grant letters of marque and reprisal, to make rules concerning captures on land and water, to raise and support armies, to provide and maintain a navy, to make laws governing land and naval forces, to provide for calling out the militia, and to provide for organizing, arming, and disciplining the militia.

II. Implied Powers

48. The Elastic Clause. — The last clause of Article I, Section 8, of the Constitution, known as the "elastic clause," or the "necessary and proper clause," gives Congress power "to make all laws which shall be necessary and proper for carrying into execution the foregoing (expressed) powers." Chief Justice Marshall decided that "necessary and proper" means "convenient or useful." Therefore, Marshall concluded that this "necessary and proper" clause *implies* that Congress might pass any laws which are "convenient or useful" in carrying into execution those laws which Congress has a specific, undisputed right to enact.

Subsequent Supreme Court judges have construed the "necessary and proper clause" very liberally; they have practically changed the "and" in "necessary and proper" to "or," so that the Constitution really reads "necessary or proper." With this clause thus interpreted Congress has been able to exercise wider and wider powers.

The Constitution gives the United States express power to punish only four crimes — counterfeiting, felonies committed on the high seas, offences against the law of nations, and treason; but other laws that Congress has express power to enact would be worthless if it could not punish the breaking of them, therefore Congress has the *implied* right to punish all crimes against the United States.

The Constitution does not specifically allow Congress to charter a National bank, but the great Chief Justice Marshall decided that the right is *implied* in the power to collect taxes and to borrow money. State banks were not carefully managed and a National bank was "convenient and useful" for the safe-keeping of the taxes collected.

The Constitution does not expressly provide for river and harbor improvements or the building of canals, but the power is *implied* from the express power to maintain a navy and regulate commerce.

The power of eminent domain is not expressly granted to the United States, but the express powers to establish post-offices and to establish courts *implies* the necessity of post-office buildings and court houses, therefore the United States can condemn land for these purposes by the right of eminent domain.[1]

If our Constitution could be more easily amended the meaning of its clauses need not be "stretched" to meet new conditions, but most of the *implied* powers would become *enumerated* powers through Constitutional amendments.

OUTLINE OF THE EIGHTEEN POWERS VESTED IN CONGRESS BY ARTICLE I, SECTION 8

49. Expressed Powers :

I. PEACE POWERS :
  1. To lay taxes.
      a. Direct (not used since the Civil War, except income tax).
      b. Indirect.
          Customs = Tariff.
          Excises = Internal revenue.
  2. To borrow money.
  3. To regulate foreign and interstate commerce.
  4. To establish naturalization and bankruptcy laws.
  5. To coin money and regulate its value ; to regulate weights and measures.
  6. To punish counterfeiters of federal money and securities.
  7. To establish post offices and post roads.
  8. To grant patents and copyrights.
  9. To create courts inferior to the Supreme Court.
  10. To define and punish piracies and felonies on the high seas; to define and punish offences against the law of nations.
  11. To exercise exclusive jurisdiction over the District of Columbia ; to exercise exclusive jurisdiction over forts, dockyards, national parks, federal buildings, etc.

---

[1] The right of eminent domain is the right that a government exercises in taking private property for a public purpose by paying the owner a fair price for it.

II. WAR POWERS:
12. To declare war; to grant letters of marque and reprisal; to make rules concerning captures on land and water.
13. To raise and support armies.
14. To provide and maintain a navy.
15. To make laws governing land and naval forces.
16. To provide for calling out the militia.
17. To provide for organizing, arming, and disciplining the militia.

50. Implied Powers:

18. To make all laws necessary and proper for carrying into execution the foregoing powers.
   For example — To punish the breaking of any federal law.
   To establish National banks.
   To improve rivers and harbors.
   To dig canals.
   To condemn property by eminent domain.

BIBLIOGRAPHY

McCLAIN, EMLIN. Constitutional Law in the United States. (American Citizen Series.) Second edition. 1910.
HALL, J. P. Constitutional Law. 1910.
WILLOUGHBY, W. W. The Constitutional Law of the United States. Students edition. 1912.
WILLOUGHBY, W. W. The Constitutional Law of the United States. 2 vols. 1910.

QUESTIONS ON THE TEXT

1. In what Article and Section of the Constitution are most of the *expressed* powers of Congress enumerated?
2. Upon what clause of this Section is the theory of *implied* powers based?
3. What two general views are there as to the proper method of construing the Constitution?
4. Should a congressman refuse to vote for a law which he thinks a desirable law but unconstitutional?

5. Name some statesmen who have favored a liberal construction of the Constitution.

6. Name one or more strict constructionists.

7. What three restrictions are placed upon Congress as to the power of taxation?

8. What is the reason for prohibiting export taxes?

9. What is the meaning of import taxes? Why must they be uniform throughout the United States?

10. Explain how Congress has used the power of taxation for the purpose of regulating or destroying certain industries.

11. What is the only redress against unreasonably high taxes?

12. What are *direct* taxes? Has the United States levied any direct taxes since the Civil War?

13. What are *indirect* taxes? What two kinds of indirect taxes are there? By what other name are customs duties known? Give an example of a customs tax. Of an excise tax.

14. There are what two kinds of tariff? What is meant by *ad valorem* tariff? By specific tariff? By tariff for revenue? By tariff for protection?

15. What is meant by the corporation tax?

16. What is meant by an income tax? How much federal income tax would a single man whose income is $5000 have to pay?

17. What is meant by foreign commerce?

18. Under its powers to regulate foreign commerce Congress has excluded what articles from the United States?

19. What is meant by interstate commerce?

20. Explain how the power of Congress to regulate commerce has expanded? Does commerce include navigation? Transportation? Wireless telegraphy?

21. What interstate commerce has been prohibited by Congress?

22. How has commerce been protected by Congress under its power to regulate interstate commerce?

23. What is a trust or monopoly?

24. What are the two most important expressed powers of Congress?

25. May a State coin money or issue paper money?

26. What does *naturalization* mean? Who may not be naturalized in the United States?

27. What is meant by post roads?

28. What is a copyright? A patent? For how many years does each protect the author or inventor?

29. What war power has Congress?

30. What is meant by *implied* powers? Give examples.

31. What is meant by the *elastic clause?* What other name is given this clause? In what Article and Section of the Constitution is it found?

QUESTIONS FOR DISCUSSION

1. The English Parliament has power to do "anything but make a man a woman or a woman a man." Why has Congress only about eighteen enumerated powers and those necessary and proper to carry the enumerated powers into execution?

2. Do you favor a "liberal construction" or a "strict construction" of the Constitution? Why?

3. Are direct taxes or indirect taxes more just? Which are easier to collect?

4. When a high internal revenue tax was placed on tobacco the people of Virginia, who manufactured large quantities of tobacco, felt that they were being unjustly taxed. The tax has not been reduced, but complaints are no longer heard. Why?

5. How could Congress destroy the manufacture and sale of liquor in the United States?

6. Why is the tariff on champagne $3.00 a gallon and that on vinegar only four cents?

7. Does the American manufacturer or the American laborer receive more benefit from a protective tariff when cheap labor from Europe can come to this country for a few dollars and compete with American laborers?

8. Is a protective tariff a tax in proportion to ability to pay or does it unfairly tax the poor?

9. When the tariff on luxuries, *e.g.*, 46 per cent *ad valorem* on silk fabrics, is so high that scarcely any are imported is it a tax on luxuries or merely a bounty to those who produce it in this country?

10. The patriarchs of old were blessed with many children, and their private property immediately benefited a large number. The multi-millionaires to-day are blessed with few children, and property from generation to generation tends to concentrate in a few hands. Does this condition make a high progressive income or inheritance tax more reasonable and expedient to-day than formerly?

11. Why is an inheritance tax easy to collect? Why is it a just tax? Should inheritances of less than $50,000 be taxed? Should one of $50,000 be taxed at the same rate as one of $100,000?

12. A congressman has recently proposed that the National government borrow a billion dollars and lend it to States or counties for road-building under certain restrictions including provision for the permanent maintenance of the road. States and counties have to pay about six per cent interest on money that they borrow; the United States can borrow money at about four per cent. If the States and counties pay an average of six per cent interest to the National government, how long would it be before the debt would be entirely wiped out if the difference of four per cent and six per cent is applied to the principal? The National government has been an honest borrower; some States have not been honest. How much would the United States' reputation be worth in fifty years?

13. In 1913 Congress enacted a law providing for the physical valuation of all railroads that carry interstate commerce. Why does Congress desire to know what it costs to construct or reconstruct these roads?

14. Under the pure food act of 1906 the labels on bottles of patent medicines must name the ingredients of the medicine. Do you favor this "prying into a man's business" or do you favor the old theory, "Let the purchaser beware"? What other articles should the government require the manufacturers to label correctly?

15. Does the federal Interstate Commerce Commission or the Virginia Corporation Commission regulate the rate of carfare between Norfolk and Richmond, Virginia? Between Norfolk, Virginia, and Baltimore, Maryland?

16. A Brooklyn boy was fined fifty dollars for setting up a wireless apparatus on the roof of his house without first securing a federal license. The instrument could pick up messages from ships and from other States. Why can the Federal government require a license for such an apparatus?

17. The independent press agencies claim that the Associated Press violates the anti-trust law by monopolizing the agencies for the distribution of news. If this accusation is true is the Associated Press a very dangerous monopoly?

18. Of more than a million immigrants who came to this country annually before the European war more than 300,000 could neither

read nor write any language. Do you favor the law of 1917 which excludes aliens who cannot read any language?

19. At present a patent gives a person a monopoly. The Socialists claim that this is bad policy, and that anybody should be permitted to manufacture a patented article who will pay the patentee a uniform royalty, the amount to be determined by the government. What argument can you advance for and against the contention of the Socialists?

CHAPTER VII

CONGRESS IN ACTION

51. Organization of the House of Representatives. — *Officers.* — Before a new Congress assembles it is known which party will control the House; and the members of the majority party hold a caucus (see Sec. 57) to nominate the Speaker, who is the presiding officer of the House; a clerk; a chaplain, who opens each daily session with a short prayer; a sergeant-at-arms, who preserves order;[1] a door-keeper; a postmaster; and other less important officers. As the action of this caucus is considered binding upon the majority members, the final election after the House convenes is a mere formality.

Opening of a New Congress. — Representatives who are elected in November of the even-numbered year succeed their predecessors the following March, when the previous Congress officially ends; but unless a special session is called between March 4 and the first Monday in December they will not be sworn in until the latter date — thirteen months after election. Immediately after the expiration of a Congress at noon on the 4th of March of every odd-numbered year the House is without a Speaker and committees. It has no rules, no sworn membership, and no actual existence as an organized body. All un-

---

[1] The sergeant-at-arms also has charge of the halls and pays members their salaries, but his most interesting function is that of custodian of the mace, a representation of the Roman *fasces* surmounted by a globe and an eagle of silver, which is the symbol of authority. When the House is in session the mace is always in a stand to the right of the Speaker. If the Speaker cannot maintain order he instructs the sergeant-at-arms to approach the unruly member with the mace and demand order in the name of the House. If the display of the mace does not restore order the House may authorize the sergeant-at-arms to arrest the unruly member.

passed bills of the old Congress are dead and must be reintro-
duced when the new Congress organizes.

When a new Congress assembles in December the members-
elect are called to order by the clerk of the preceding House.
The clerk reads a roll of members-elect whose credentials are
in due form; the members-elect select a Speaker, who takes his

THE SENATE BUILDING.

This building contains committee rooms, a caucus room, and offices for
each senator. It is connected with the Capitol by a tunnel. There is a
building of the same kind for the representatives, called the House Building.

oath of office from the oldest member-elect in point of service — called "the Father of the House"; the Speaker, in
turn, administers the oath to members-elect against whom no
objections are raised by fellow members; the Democrats seat
themselves to the right of the centre aisle, the Republicans
to the left; and, finally, the new clerk is chosen. The rules,
usually those of the preceding House, are adopted. Thus the
House is organized.

The Senate, a continuous body, is notified that the House is organized and ready to proceed to business. A joint committee of the two houses notify the President that they are ready to receive any communications. The following day the President's message, outlining desired legislation, is sent to the houses and read, or delivered by the President himself if he desires, as Washington, Adams, and Wilson did.

52. Rules of Procedure. — According to the Constitution each house may make its own rules of procedure, but must keep a public journal showing how motions are disposed of and the vote for and against bills and resolutions. It also requires the votes of each member to be recorded if one fifth of the members present demand it. This requirement enables a small number of members to put all the members on record, and thus their constituents may know how their representatives have voted on important bills.

Senate Rules are not so drastic as those of the House because the body is smaller and can proceed in a somewhat less formal manner. The President of the Senate recognizes members in the order in which they rise, and a member may speak as long as he chooses, unless the Senate resorts to the closure rule, which was adopted in 1917. According to this rule, on petition of sixteen senators, supported two days later by a two thirds vote of the Senate, no senator can speak on the measure under discussion more than one hour. Thus the old abuse of "talking a bill to death," which is known as *filibustering*, may be prevented if two thirds of the members desire to do so.

House Rules are changed oftener than Senate rules, and are more drastic, otherwise the large house would make no progress. A member may not speak more than an hour without unanimous consent; the Speaker is not obliged to recognize members in the order in which they rise; and a majority, by means of the "previous question,"[1] may end a debate at any time.

---

[1] "The previous question" means, "Shall the main question now be put?"

Though the rules prescribe a regular order of business for each day in the week — *e.g.*, Friday is "private bill day" — most bills are considered when the regular order of business is departed from. The regular order of business may be departed from by the unanimous consent of the members or by the adoption of a "special order" recommended by the committee on rules. On two Mondays in every month, and during the last six days of the session, rules may be suspended by a two-thirds vote, and therefore popular bills may be taken up out of their regular order.

The House Committee on Rules was originally intended to report upon desirable changes in the rules of the House. Gradually it obtained the power to determine the order of procedure and practically what measures should be considered. Until 1910 it was composed of five members, the Speaker and four others appointed by him — two of the majority party and two of the minority. This allowed the Speaker to dominate legislation to such an extent that he spoke of the committee as consisting of "myself and two assistants," the two assistants being members of his own party whom he could control. By 1910 Speaker Cannon, "stand-patter of stand-patters," so offended the "insurgent" or "progressive" Republicans that, with the aid of the Democrats, they passed a rule depriving the Speaker of membership on the committee and increased the size of the committee to ten members.[1] The appointment of this committee and of all other committees was finally taken from him.

53. Committees. — The House of Representatives has become too large for free debate and neither the House nor the Senate could work out the details of important legislation upon the floors of the houses. Therefore each house is divided into numerous standing committees, which are permanent throughout a term of Congress (two years), and into other temporary committees. The Sixty-fourth Congress had fifty-eight stand-

---

[1] This Committee has since been increased to eleven members.

ing committees in the House and seventy-five in the Senate. The committees vary in size from two to twenty-two members. Each member of the House serves on one or two committees, each senator on from five to ten.

These committees investigate proposed legislation and recommend for passage the bills which they approve. In each house there are only twenty-odd active committees, and though

DEMOCRATIC MEMBERS OF THE WAYS AND MEANS COMMITTEE OF THE SIXTY-SECOND CONGRESS.

The majority members frequently meet alone in the consideration of a bill.

these vary in importance from time to time the following ten are of first importance:

House of Representatives	*Senate*
Rules	Rules
Ways and Means	Finance
Appropriations	Appropriations
Rivers and Harbors	Public Expenditures
Military Affairs	Military Affairs
Naval Affairs	Naval Affairs
Foreign Affairs	Foreign Relations
Interstate and Foreign Commerce	Interstate Commerce
Judiciary	Judiciary
Banking and Currency	Commerce

Until the year 1910 all members of House committees were
selected by the Speaker, but under the new rules they are
elected by the members of the House.[1] Senate committees are
also elected by members of the Senate.[2] The majority party of
each house gives the minority party representation on each
committee.

The names of committees indicate the class of bills which
the Speaker of the House and the President of the Senate
refer to them; for instance, the Speaker refers bills for raising
revenue to the Ways and Means Committee of the House and
the President of the Senate refers them to the Finance Committee of the Senate.

54. Bills. — Any member of either house of Congress may
introduce bills, except that a bill for raising revenue must be
introduced in the House by a representative. During the
second session of the Sixty-second Congress senators introduced
9077 bills and resolutions; representatives, 29,713; total 38,790.
Of these, 530 public bills and resolutions and 186 private bills
— a total of 716 — passed. Less than two per cent of those
introduced became law. However, most of them were not
intended to become law, but were merely introduced " to please
the voters back home."

---

[1] Though the committees are formally elected by the members of the House
they are practically chosen in a very different manner. The dominant party
of the House meets in caucus some time before the House is organized and
selects the majority members of the Ways and Means Committee, who act as
a committee on committees to nominate majority members of all standing
committees. The minority members of the House also meet in caucus and
delegate to their leader the duty of nominating members. For instance, in
the winter of 1914–1915 the Democrats decided that Mr. Kitchin of North
Carolina should be their floor leader as well as chairman of the Ways and
Means Committee. The Republicans decided that Mr. Mann of Illinois should
be their floor leader. So, practically, the members of the standing committees
of the House were chosen by these two men. When the Sixty-fourth Congress
met in December, 1915, Mr. Kitchin nominated all members of the standing
committees and they were promptly elected without a word of debate.

[2] Committees of the Senate are in reality chosen by two committees on committees selected by the caucuses of the two leading parties. The nominees of
these committees are usually elected by the Senate without debate.

A bill may become law by a majority vote of each house of Congress and the signature of the President.   If the President takes no action within ten days, Sundays excluded, the bill becomes a law without his signature.   Or, if he vetoes a bill, it may still become law if again passed by a two-thirds vote of each House.

55. The Underwood-Simmons[1] Tariff Bill Traced. — In 1912, when a Democratic President and Congress who favored tariff reduction were elected, the party leaders conferred and prepared a tariff bill during the winter months.   President Wilson was inaugurated March 4, 1913, and on March 17 called a special session of Congress, which convened on the 7th of April.

The bill "to reduce the tariff duties and to provide revenue for the government, and for other purposes," having been prepared to the satisfaction of the President and the Democratic members of the Ways and Means Committee, Representative Underwood of Alabama, Chairman of the Committee, introduced it on April 21 by placing it in the "hopper" of the House.[2]   The parliamentary clerk at the Speaker's table, acting for the Speaker, numbered the bill H. R. 3321, there having been 3320 other bills introduced by members of the House of Representatives since the 7th of April.   He referred it to the Committee on Ways and Means.   The bill was recorded by its title in the Journal of the House[3] and in the Congressional Record[4] for that day and thus brought to the attention of the members.

---

[1] A law commonly takes its name from the chairman of the House committee and the chairman of the Senate committee to which the bill has been referred.

[2] The "hopper" is a large basket in which new bills are deposited.

[3] The Journal of the House contains the minutes of the proceedings from day to day, which are read at the opening of each daily session.

[4] The Congressional Record reports the debates of congressmen, the motions, the votes, and the disposition of bills.   Each morning a copy of it is furnished to each member of Congress.   The official reporters always correct the English of speeches and often give them a more elegant finish without changing the meaning.

As the Committee had already considered the bill, Mr. Underwood, acting for the Committee, reported it back to the House the following day, April 22, without amendment and with recommendation that it be passed. It was listed upon the proper calendar, announced by title to the House, and reported to the Committee of the Whole.[1] The House resolved itself into Committee of the Whole day after day for the consideration of this bill, and here only was it read and considered section by section. On May 7 the Committee of the Whole reported the bill back to the House with amendments. The bill was ordered "engrossed," that is, printed upon paper of a fine texture under the direction of the clerk. The next day it was read by title and passed by a vote of 281 yeas to 139 nays.

The clerk of the House carried a certified copy of the bill to the Senate and announced that it had been passed by the House. After debate for several days as to whether the Finance Committee should hold public hearings upon the bill, it was referred to the Finance Committee on the 16th of May. (It should be noted that there is no Ways and Means Com-

[1] After revenue or appropriation bills have been reported from one of the standing committees, the House always resolves itself into the Committee of the Whole in order that these bills may be discussed freely. This committee is composed of all the members of the House, but only 100 are required for a quorum, therefore members who are not interested in the bill under consideration need not attend. It operates with less formal rules than the regular sessions of the House and no individual votes are recorded — only the totals. The Speaker does not preside when the House is in Committee of the Whole but calls another member to the chair. There is no reason for his vacating the chair except that we follow the old English custom whereby the Speaker of the House of Commons was excluded from the Committee of the Whole of Parliament for fear he would report to the King what was being discussed in committee. The mace is also removed from its high pedestal at the right of the Speaker. In Committee of the Whole the bill is discussed in detail, and amendments are usually recommended when it is reported back to the House (regular session) for a final vote.

In the Senate all bills are debated *as in Committee of the Whole*. The Senate "Committee of the Whole" differs very little from the Senate proper. The President of the Senate remains in the chair and a full majority of the whole body is necessary for a quorum.

mittee in the Senate, as all bills for raising revenue originate in the House.)   On July 11 Senator Simmons of North Carolina, Chairman of the Finance Committee, reported the bill back to the Senate with numerous amendments.   It was freely debated by the Senate "as in Committee of the Whole" and passed with amendments on the 9th of September.

As the bill had been amended by the Senate it was necessary to have a conference committee of the two houses to reconcile the differences, therefore the Speaker appointed seven representatives and the President of the Senate appointed seven senators. This committee brought the houses to an agreement and the amended bill was accepted by the respective houses.   After the presiding officers of the houses had signified this agreement the bill was sent to the President, who signed it on the 3d of October.   Thus did bill H. R. 3321 become Public Law No. 16, this being the sixteenth bill of a public character enacted into law by the Sixty-third Congress.

56. **Making the National "Budget."** — Nearly every civilized state has a finance minister who prepares a statement of the estimated cost of conducting the government and indicates how the necessary money is to be raised.   The legislative body of such a state accepts the proposal or rejects it, or may decrease certain items, but it may not increase them.   This method of raising money and expending it creates a true budget.

The United States government does not have a finance minister who is responsible for raising and expending its revenues, hence it has not a true budget.   However, Congress devotes a large portion of its time to the creation and consideration of a so-called budget.   The Ways and Means Committee of the House of Representatives prepares bills for raising all revenue, and nine other distinct committees of the House prepare bills appropriating the revenue.

The head of each of the ten administrative departments prepares an estimate of its needs for the succeeding year and transmits it to the Secretary of the Treasury.   When the Secretary has collected these ten estimates, he sends them to the Speaker of the House as he received them.   The Speaker, in turn, separates these estimates into eight groups, referring one group to each of the eight committees [1] having power to prepare appropriation bills.

Each congressman, through these various appropriating committees, endeavors to get as much money as possible out of the treasury to be spent in his home district — to use the congressional phrase, " to get pork out of the public pork-barrel."

These " pork-barrel " appropriations are commonly obtained for pensions, private claims, federal officers, post offices in small towns where they are not needed, for a new army post or naval station where the committee chairman's district happens to be, and for river and harbor improvements where there is no commerce.   Some years ago Senator Tillman of South Carolina openly declared that when general stealing is going on it is his business to see that his State gets its share. During a Senate debate he declared: "The whole scheme of river improvement is a humbug and a steal; but if you are going to steal, let us divide it out, and not go on complaining."   Upon another occasion when the naval appropriation bill was before the Senate, he remarked: "We have a little orphan of a naval station down in South Carolina, for which I am trying to get a few crumbs of this money which is being wasted."

---

[1] These eight committees having power to prepare appropriation bills are :
1. Committee on Appropriations. This committee prepares bills for the legislative, executive, and judicial expenses ; for sundry civil expenses ; for fortifications and coast defences ; for the District of Columbia ; for pensions; and for all deficiencies.
2. Committee on Military Affairs.
3. Committee on Naval Affairs.
4. Committee on Indian Affairs.
5. Committee on Foreign Affairs.
6. Committee on Post Offices and Post Roads.
7. Committee on Rivers and Harbors.
8. Committee on Agriculture.
The Committee on Claims and the Committee on War Claims prepare special appropriation bills from time to time.

Each congressman is able to get "pork" for his district because·he helps every other one to get it for his own. This practice of working together in securing appropriations is known as "log-rolling"—a term drawn from pioneer life where neighbors lent a hand in rolling logs when a settler was building his cabin.

This pork-barrel-log-rolling practice is a natural result of the present irresponsible system of budget-making in the United States, and shows the great need of a true budget system to prevent waste. In 1909 the late Senator Aldrich of Rhode Island, Chairman of the Committee on Finance, said: "I am myself satisfied that the appropriations made last year could have been reduced at least $50,000,000 without impairing the efficiency of the public service."

Representative Fitzgerald of New York, Chairman of the Committee on Appropriations, thinks that no money should be appropriated from the treasury except by a vote of two thirds of each House of Congress, unless it is requested by one of the department heads and submitted to Congress by the President.[1] In 1910 the Commission of Efficiency and Economy recommended the creation of a national budget prepared by the Executive, not by Congress. The plan reverts to that originally devised by Alexander Hamilton.[2]

---

[1] This idea is practically the provision found in the Constitution of the southern Confederate States, paragraph nine of Section IX.

[2] The law creating the office of Secretary of the Treasury provided that the Secretary should be a true finance minister. His duty was " to prepare and report estimates of the public revenue and the public expenditures." Alexander Hamilton, the first Secretary of the Treasury, prepared a true budget, which provided for raising the revenue as well as appropriating it.

In the early part of the nineteenth century the House created a Committee on Ways and Means to provide revenue and to make all appropriations, thus taking from the Secretary of the Treasury the responsibility of creating a true budget.

For many years one annual bill provided for raising all revenue and also for its expenditure. Gradually more and more appropriation bills were passed each year, but all were prepared by the Ways and Means Committee.

As a result of the Civil War a new committee, known as the Committee on

57. The Party Caucus. — Each party in the House of Representatives has a secret conference of its members, known as the party caucus, for the purpose of securing unanimous party action on any important question. The important question may be the nomination of the speaker, the floor leader, or the whips[1] of the party. More often the work of the caucus is to determine the party attitude on pending legislation.

When important legislation is under consideration the majority caucus meets and decides whether or not the bill will be made a party measure. In the caucus each member may speak freely; but if the majority decide to make the bill a party measure every member of the party is expected to vote for it in the House. For instance, when the Underwood-Simmons Tariff Bill was under consideration in 1913 the Democratic caucus decided that the bill should pass the House, and that it should not be amended by the House unless Mr. Underwood himself, chairman of the Ways and Means Committee, should offer the amendment. If any member fails to vote as directed by the caucus he is likely to lose all influence in the party.

The minority party of the House also has a caucus for the selection of its leaders and to determine whether it will act solidly as a party in opposing a bill favored by the majority party.

The Democratic caucus is held in secret. In 1913 the caucus of the Republican party in the House was thrown open to the public, but a majority of its members may hold a special secret caucus; and on the most important matters it is yet held in secret.

The political parties in the Senate also have their caucuses. In fact, there is a special caucus room in the Senate Building as well as one in the House Building.

Appropriations, was created to prepare all appropriation bills, the Committee on Ways and Means continuing to prepare all bills for raising revenue.

In 1885 the House began to divide the work of creating appropriation bills among various committees, and to-day there are eight such committees.

[1] A "whip" is a member of a party who looks after the interest of the party and secures the attendance of as many members as possible when an important vote is to be taken.

BIBLIOGRAPHY

FORD, HENRY JONES. The Cost of Our National Government. 1910.
HAINES, LYNN. Your Congress. 1915.
REINSCH, PAUL S. Readings on American Federal Government. 1909.
The Congressional Directory.
House and Senate Rules.
The Congressional Record.
The Searchlight on Congress. A monthly bulletin published by The
   National Voters' League of Washington, D. C., to acquaint the
   people with the methods and votes of their lawmakers.

QUESTIONS ON THE TEXT

1. What is a *caucus?*

2. When are Representatives elected? How many months later
do they succeed their predecessors? How many months later do they
ordinarily take their seats?

3. Who calls a new Congress to order?

4. How is the Speaker of the House chosen?

5. A term of Congress extends over how many years? Does the
Senate ever have to reorganize?

6. Who makes the rules of procedure for each house?

7. How many members of each house are necessary to demand that
all votes on any measure be recorded?

8. How long may a member of the Senate speak? What is meant
by a *filibuster?*

9. How long may a member of the House speak? How may a
debate be brought to a close in the House?

10. Under what conditions may a bill be taken up out of its regular
order?

11. What committee recommends changes in the rules of the
House?

12. What duties are performed by the committees of the House
and of the Senate? About how many committees are there? Name
some of the more important ones.

13. How are House committees chosen?

14. Who may introduce bills? About what proportion of the bills
introduced become law?

15. Name the steps through which a bill must pass to become law?

16. When a term of Congress comes to an end what becomes of all the bills which have been introduced during that term?

17. Trace the course of the Underwood-Simmons Tariff Bill.

18. What is the Journal of the House? How often read?

19. What is the Congressional Record? How often issued?

20. What is the Committee of the Whole? How many members are necessary for a quorum? Who presides?

21. Does the United States have a true budget? How is the "budget" of the United States prepared? How should it be prepared?

QUESTIONS FOR DISCUSSION

1. Why cannot a bill be defeated in the House of Representatives by filibustering as well as in the Senate?

2. Around every legislative body are numerous lobbyists, or persons whose business it is to influence legislation. Capitalistic organizations, labor organizations, liquor associations, the Anti-Saloon League, and similar bodies keep lobbyists in Washington. Some lobbyists are kept there purely for selfish or corrupt purposes, and some to educate Congress concerning the needs of the country. Do you think it would be wise to require all lobbyists to register with the clerk of the House in order that it might be publicly known how much and what kind of influence is being brought to bear on Congress? (See Sec. 167.)

3. A roll call of 435 members requires much time and a representative recently introduced a bill providing for an electric voting machine with which each member could record his vote "yes," "no," or "paired," by pressing one of three buttons attached to his seat. At the clerk's desk the machine would puncture a hole in one of three columns opposite the names of the members, and give the total at the bottom of each column. That each member may know how the others are voting it is also proposed that the names of all members be posted on the wall back of the Speaker with a red, blue, and white small electric bulb opposite his name, the color of the light indicating the nature of his vote. What arguments are there for and against this scheme?

4. The fate of all important bills is determined in the majority party caucus. Our laws are really not enacted by a majority of Congress but by a majority of the majority party in each house. As a result of this custom a bill might conceivably become a law when only one fourth plus one of the members favor it. This is party

QUESTIONS

the custom.

5. Unless an extra session is called, a congressman does not take
his seat until 13 months after his election. In the meantime the
members of the old Congress who have been reëlected to the new
make all arrangements for the organization of the new Congress, the
newly elected members merely ratifying the work of the old organization. What are the advantages and disadvantages accruing from
this custom?

6. In the spring of 1914 Representative Hobson introduced in the
House a resolution to amend the Constitution, giving Congress power
to regulate the manufacture of liquors. The resolution was referred
to the Judiciary Committee. Congressmen who were unwilling to
vote upon the question before the November election hoped that the
Judiciary Committee would live up to its reputation of being a
"legislative morgue." But the committee members, aroused by criticism against them, refused to "hold the bag," and on May 5 reported
the resolution to the House without recommendation. Explain the
words "legislative morgue."

7. Is the wastefulness of our system of appropriating money due
to the character of congressmen elected or to the system which they
find when they enter Congress? How might the system be improved?

8. Prepare a bill on some subject in which you are interested. All
bills must begin with the following enacting clause:

*Be it enacted by the Senate and House of Representatives of the United
States of America in Congress assembled, that, etc.*

CHAPTER VIII

THE EXECUTIVE DEPARTMENT

I. THE PRESIDENT

58. Qualifications of the President. — The President of the United States must be a natural born citizen of the United States, must be at least thirty-five years of age, and must have been for fourteen years a resident within the United States.

59. Election of the President. — The framers of the Constitution intended to remove the office of chief magistrate as far as possible from the passions of the masses. Accordingly they arranged that the President should be chosen indirectly by a "college of electors" composed of as many members as there are representatives and senators in Congress. These electors were expected to use their own judgment and to select the fittest person for the presidency. This system of electing the President continues, but since Washington's two terms (1789–1797), *i.e.* since political parties became well defined, these electors have been merely honorary mouth-pieces to vote as their political party directs.

Each State is entitled to as many electors as it has representatives and senators in Congress, and may select them in any manner that the State legislature desires. At first the legislatures themselves chose the electors, and chose those who were known to favor certain candidates. This method was considered undemocratic, and gradually the legislatures transferred the choice of the electors from themselves to the voters of the respective States.

In some States two electors were chosen by the voters of the State-at-large, and the remaining electors were chosen by congressional districts. The result was that some districts chose Democratic electors, while others chose Republican electors. But the majority party of each State saw that all its electors could be elected if they were chosen at large, and naturally the majority party abandoned the district system in favor of the State-wide system.

To-day all States choose their quota of electors by a general State-wide ticket; thus a State whose Democratic voters are in the majority will select all Democratic electors, and a State whose Republican voters are in the majority will select all Republican electors.[1] For instance, in 1884 the Democratic party in New York had a majority of only about 1000 in a total vote of more than 1,000,000; but all of the thirty-six Democratic electors were chosen and cast their votes for the Democratic candidate, Mr. Cleveland. On the other hand, the Republican party in Pennsylvania had a majority of 81,000 in a total vote of 866,000, and hence all of the Republican electors were chosen. In other words, in these two States Blaine received 80,000 more popular votes than Cleveland, but Cleveland received six more electoral votes than Blaine. If the Democrats had not carried New York State Blaine would have been elected President of the United States instead of Cleveland.

On several occasions the presidential candidate who received the most popular votes throughout the country did not receive the most electoral votes, and was therefore not elected. For instance, in 1888 Harrison received 233 electoral votes against Cleveland's 166 and was elected, though Cleveland received about 100,000 more popular votes than Harrison. This was due to the fact that Cleveland's electors piled up votes in the Southern States, whereas the Harrison electors carried Northern States by small majorities. The accompanying table shows exactly how the popular vote and electoral vote were cast for each candidate at this election.

---

[1] There are several instances where the electoral vote of a State has been divided, even with the State-wide ticket. In 1908 Maryland gave two electoral votes to Taft and six to Bryan, although a small majority of the voters of the State thought they were casting their full vote for Taft. The election was so close that the few voters who blundered by marking their ballots for the first-named Taft electors only, believing that they were thereby voting for all of the Taft electors, caused six votes to go to Bryan.

STATES	POPULAR VOTE		ELECTORAL VOTE	
	Harrison	Cleveland	Harrison	Cleveland
Alabama	56,197	117,320	—	10
Arkansas	58,752	85,962	—	7
California	124,816	117,729	8	—
Colorado	50,774	37,567	3	—
Connecticut	74,584	74,920	—	6
Delaware	12,973	16,414	—	3
Florida	26,657	39,561	—	4
Georgia	40,496	100,499	—	12
Illinois	370,473	348,278	22	—
Indiana	263,361	261,013	15	—
Iowa	211,598	179,887	13	—
Kansas	182,934	103,744	9	—
Kentucky	155,134	183,800	—	13
Louisiana	30,484	85,032	—	8
Maine	73,734	50,481	6	—
Maryland	99,986	106,168	—	8
Massachusetts . . .	183,892	151,856	14	—
Michigan	236,370	213,459	13	—
Minnesota	142,492	104,385	7	—
Mississippi	30,096	85,471	—	9
Missouri	236,257	261,974	—	16
Nebraska	108,425	80,552	5	—
Nevada	7,229	5,362	3	—
New Hampshire . . .	45,728	43,458	4	—
New Jersey	144,344	151,493	—	9
New York	648,759	635,757	36	—
North Carolina . . .	134,784	147,902	—	11
Ohio	416,054	396,455	23	—
Oregon	33,291	26,522	3	—
Pennsylvania	526,091	446,633	30	—
Rhode Island	21,968	17,530	4	—
South Carolina . . .	13,736	65,825	—	9
Tennessee	138,988	158,779	—	12
Texas	88,422	234,883	—	13
Vermont	45,192	16,785	4	—
Virginia	150,438	151,977	—	12
West Virginia . . .	77,791	79,664	—	6
Wisconsin	176,553	155,232	11	—
Total	5,439,853	5,540,329	233	168

In brief, the President is to-day elected as follows: Each political party nominates a candidate for the presidency at a national convention (see Sec. 149) held in June or July of the "presidential year." About the same time the various parties in each State nominate in any manner the State legislature permits the quota of electors to which the State is entitled. These nominees are voted for in the various States on the Tuesday following the first Monday of November in each "leap year." To illustrate, a Democrat in New Jersey votes for the fourteen Democratic electors as shown on the ballot on the following page.

If, after the State election board has received all of the returns of the election from the various local election boards, it is found that the Democratic electors have received more votes than any other set of electors, they assemble at the capital city, Trenton, and cast their votes the second Monday of the January next following. These votes are signed by each elector, certified by the Governor, sealed and sent to the president of the United States Senate. Each of the other States follows the same method.

On the second Wednesday in February the president of the Senate opens these returns and, in the presence of the two houses, counts them and declares the candidate elected who has received the majority of electoral votes (now 531). If no candidate has a majority (266) of all the electoral votes, the House of Representatives elects one of the three leading candidates, the representatives from each of the 48 States casting one vote. If no candidate receives a majority (25) of these votes by the fourth of March next following, the Vice-President is inaugurated as President.

The uselessness of our Electoral College is expressed in an interesting way by Elbert Hubbard in the following sentences: "The original argument [in favor of the Electoral College] was that the people should not vote directly for President, because the candidate might live a long way off, and the voter could not know whether he was fit or not. So they let the

OFFICIAL BALLOT

G. A. Robbins
County Clerk.

Princeton Borough, County of Mercer, Election District No. 6, November 7, 1916.

Column 1

X. To Vote for All the Electors of Any Party, Mark a Cross ✗ or Plus ✚ In Black Ink or Black Lead Pencil in the SQUARE at the Left of the Surnames of the Candidates for President and Vice-President for Whom You Desire to Vote.

To Vote for Part of the Electors of Any Party, Mark a Cross ✗ or Plus ✚ In Black Ink or Black Lead Pencil in the SQUARE at the Left of the Name of Each Elector for Whom You Desire to Vote. VOTE FOR FOURTEEN ELECTORS.

PRESIDENT AND VICE-PRESIDENT
OF THE UNITED STATES

REPUBLICAN.
HUGHES AND FAIRBANKS.
ELECTORS.

- [ ] F WAYLAND AYER.
- [ ] AUSTEN COLGATE.
- [ ] NORMAN GREY
- [ ] F WALLIS ARMSTRONG.
- [ ] LEWIS S. THOMPSON.
- [ ] MOSES TAYLOR PYNE.
- [ ] RICHARD B. WILLIAMS.
- [ ] DANIEL E POMEROY.
- [ ] PETER QUACKENBUSH.
- [ ] DeWITT VAN BUSKIRK.
- [ ] MANTON B. METCALF.
- [ ] W I LINCOLN ADAMS.
- [ ] GEORGE L. RECORD
- [ ] GEORGE C WARREN, JR

SOCIALIST.
BENSON AND KIRKPATRICK.
ELECTORS.

- [ ] CHARLES BUICKEROOD.
- [ ] ARCHIBALD O CRAIG.
- [ ] WALTER KRUSEN
- [ ] FRANK A. RINEHART
- [ ] SAM W ROKE.
- [ ] WILLIAM H. DERRICK
- [ ] CHARLES DE YONKER
- [ ] ORRIE W FLAVELLE.
- [ ] FREDK C FINCH.
- [ ] JOHN FRACKENPOEL
- [ ] EMANUEL HARTIG.
- [ ] FLORENCE D. GREINER.
- [ ] HENRY PETZOLT.
- [ ] WILLIAM KAMPR.

NATIONAL PROHIBITION.
HANLY AND LANDRITH.
ELECTORS.

- [ ] THEODORE F CRANE.
- [ ] ROBERT BRUCE CROWELL.
- [ ] GRAFTON E DAY
- [ ] CHARLES C. DEMPSEY.
- [ ] AUGUSTUS J SMITH
- [ ] JAMES GILBERT MASON.
- [ ] SILVANUS GORDON.
- [ ] HENRY M. DUTT
- [ ] JAMES O PATTON.
- [ ] ALFRED B EDGERLEY.
- [ ] WILLIAM L. JONES.
- [ ] STEPHEN D. RIDDLE
- [ ] ULYSSES S. KNOX.
- [ ] JAMES PARKER

X. To Vote for a Person, Mark a Cross ✗ or Plus Mark ✚ In Black Ink or Black Lead Pencil in the SQUARE at the Left of the Name of the Person for Whom You Desire to Vote.

For United States Senator. Vote for one.

- [ ] LIVINGSTON BARBOUR — National Prohibition.
- [ ] WILLIAM O. DOUGHTY — Socialist.
- [ ] JOSEPH S FRELINGHUYSEN — Republican
- [ ] RUDOLPH KATZ — Socialist Labor
- [ ] JAMES E. MARTINE — Democrat.

For Member of Congress. Vote for one.

- [ ] AZARIAH M. BEEKMAN — Democrat
- [ ] ELIJAH C BUTCHINSON — Republican
- [ ] WILLIAM LUNGER — National Prohibition
- [ ] J LINDSAY VAN WEST — Socialist

Column 2

X. To Vote for All the Electors of Any Party, Mark a Cross ✗ or Plus ✚ In Black Ink or Black Lead Pencil in the SQUARE at the Left of the Surnames of the Candidates for President and Vice-President for Whom You Desire to Vote.

To Vote for Part of the Electors of Any Party, Mark a Cross ✗ or Plus ✚ In Black Ink or Black Lead Pencil in the SQUARE at the Left of the Name of Each Elector for Whom You Desire to Vote. VOTE FOR FOURTEEN ELECTORS.

PRESIDENT AND VICE-PRESIDENT
OF THE UNITED STATES

DEMOCRAT.
WILSON AND MARSHALL.
ELECTORS.

- [ ] JAMES F FIELDER
- [ ] JOHN W. WESCOTT
- [ ] JOSEPH E. NOWREY.
- [ ] JOHN S. WARE
- [ ] LAURANCE RUNYON.
- [ ] RICHARD STOCKTON.
- [ ] DENNIS F COLLINS
- [ ] JOHN A. WILDRICK.
- [ ] NATHAN BARNERT.
- [ ] GEORGE H. LAMBERT
- [ ] FREDERICK SEYMOUR.
- [ ] T ALBEUS ADAMS.
- [ ] FRANK B. ECKERT.
- [ ] THOMAS J. MALONEY

SOCIALIST LABOR.
REIMER AND HARRISON.
ELECTORS.

- [ ] HERMAN LANDGRAF
- [ ] JOHN ERNST.
- [ ] PAUL EBERDING.
- [ ] MICHAEL D. FITZ GERALD.
- [ ] JOHN REESE.
- [ ] JAMES THOMAS PHILLIPS.
- [ ] WILLIAM J CARROLL.
- [ ] BERNARD BURGHOLZ
- [ ] CHARLES G. SANDBERG
- [ ] RUDOLPH KATZ
- [ ] ANDERS H. LYZELL.
- [ ] RUSSELL PALMER.
- [ ] GEORGE T. LEWIS.
- [ ] HARRY OAKES

X. To Vote for a Person, Mark a Cross ✗ or Plus Mark ✚ In Black Ink or Black Lead Pencil in the SQUARE at the Left of the Name of the Person for Whom You Desire to Vote.

For Members General Assembly. Vote for three.

- [ ] JOSIAH T. ALLINSON — Republican
- [ ] A. DAYTON OLIPHANT — Republican
- [ ] CLINTON H. READ — Republican.
- [ ] JAMES BAILEY — Socialist.
- [ ] KENNETH BUCK — Socialist
- [ ] ANTHONY SPAIR — Socialist
- [ ] MAGNUS BREDENBEK — Democrat
- [ ] RUDOLPH L. MARSHALL. — Democrat.
- [ ] JOHN B. PHILLIPS, JR — Democrat
- [ ] W. CLIFFORD CASE — National Prohibition.
- [ ] RICHARD WARNER COOK. — National Prohibition
- [ ] WILLIAM B. HOUSEL. — National Prohibition

Column 3

X. To Vote for a Person, Mark a Cross ✗ or Plus ✚ In Black Ink or Black Lead Pencil in the SQUARE at the Left of the Name of the Person for Whom You Desire to Vote.

For Senator. Vote for one.

- [ ] GEORGE W. CASE — National Prohibition
- [ ] JAMES HAMMOND. — Republican.
- [ ] S ROY HEATH. — Democrat.
- [ ] WILLIAM H YOUNG. — Socialist

For Freeholder, Three year term. Vote for three.

- [ ] ARTHUR BRAY, JR. — Republican.
- [ ] WILLIAM F. CONARD. — Republican.
- [ ] JOHN McCULLOUGH — Republican
- [ ] JOHN M BURGNER — Democrat
- [ ] JOHN J. DONNELLY. — Democrat.
- [ ] GEORGE O WOOD — Democrat
- [ ] DAVID H COLEMAN — Socialist.
- [ ] MORIS HOROWITZ. — Socialist.
- [ ] S FRANK URBANIAK — Socialist

For Freeholder, Two year term. Vote for two.

- [ ] GEORGE R. HUTCHINSON — Republican
- [ ] GEORGE H. ROYLE. — Republican.
- [ ] JOHN J. O'DONNELL — Democrat
- [ ] CHARLES R. RANDALL. — Democrat
- [ ] JOHN H. RICHARDS. — Democrat
- [ ] ROMAN SOSENKO — Socialist.
- [ ] FREDERICK H. UDY — National Prohibition.

For Freeholder, One year term. Vote for two.

- [ ] BARTON T. FELL. — Republican.
- [ ] ELMER E. MARGERUM — Republican
- [ ] HARRY GREINER — Democrat
- [ ] WILLIAM F. McGOVERN. — Democrat.
- [ ] ROBERT B HUSSEY. — National Prohibition
- [ ] CARL F SHAFFER. — National Prohibition
- [ ] J. VERN JOHNSTON. — Socialist
- [ ] ANTHONY ROBERTON — Socialist.

For Member of Council. Vote for two.

- [ ] HENRY G. DUFFIELD — Republican.
- [ ] WILLIAM HENRY SAYEN, JR — Republican.
- [ ] CHRISTIAN GAUSS — Democrat
- [ ] LESLIE L ZAPF. — Democrat

For Assessor. Vote for one.

- [ ] VAN BUREN COOK. — Democrat
- [ ] WALTER M RIGGS — Republican.

For Collector. Vote for one.

- [ ] HOWARD D. ELDRIDGE — Republican
- [ ] WILLIAM D. HILL — Democrat

For Justice of the Peace. Vote for one.

citizen vote for a wise and honest elector he knew. The result is that we all now know the candidates for President, but we do not know the electors. The Electoral College in America is just about as useful as the two buttons on the back of a man's coat, put there originally to support a sword belt. We have discarded the sword, yet we cling to our buttons."

However, it would not be practical to elect the President by a direct popular vote of the people, because a State with unrestricted equal suffrage casts five times as many votes as a Southern State with merely manhood suffrage restricted by educational qualifications. But presidential electors should be dispensed with, each state retaining its apportioned number of electoral votes. Then the voters would cast their ballots directly for the presidential candidate of their preference, and the candidate receiving the most popular votes in each State would be entitled to all the electoral votes of the State. This method of electing the President would save the trouble of nominating presidential electors, the cost of printing their names on the ballots, the expense of having them assemble to cast their votes, and would avoid the difficulties arising from the death of electors before their votes are cast.

60. Term of the President. — The President-elect is inducted into office on March fourth following his election, and serves until the fourth of March four years later. There is no legal limit to the number of terms he may serve, though in practice no President has been elected oftener than twice.

61. Succession to the Presidency. — The Constitution provides that in case the President is removed by impeachment, death, resignation, or inability, his duties shall devolve upon the Vice-President; and by the Presidential Succession Act of 1886 it is provided that in case of the inability of both the President and Vice-President to perform the duties of the office, the cabinet officers shall succeed in the following order: (1) Secretary of State; (2) Secretary of the Treasury; (3) Secretary of War; (4) Attorney-General; (5) Postmaster-General; (6) Secretary of the Navy; (7) Secretary of the Interior.

62. Compensation of the President. — The President's salary is determined by Congress, but the amount may be neither increased nor diminished during the period for which he is elected. From 1789 until 1873, the beginning of Grant's second term, the salary of the President was $25,000; from the latter date until 1909, $50,000; since 1909 his salary has been

THE EXECUTIVE OFFICES, SHOWING THE WHITE HOUSE TO THE RIGHT.

The room with the bay window is the President's office; the rooms to the left are occupied by the Secretary to the President, and those to the right are the cabinet rooms.

$75,000 a year, plus $25,000 or as much thereof as needed for travelling expenses, and the use of the Executive Mansion, commouly called "The White House."[1]

---

[1] Other appropriations made in connection with the presidential office for 1912–1913 were: For Executive Mansion (1) care, repair, horses, vehicles, etc., $35,000; (2) fuel for Mansion, greenhouses, and stables, $6000; (3) lighting, $8600; (4) grounds, $5000; (5) greenhouses, $12,000; oil portrait of Taft for Mansion, $4000. For Executive Office (1) secretary, clerks, stenographers, etc., $72,056; (2) contingent expenses, $25,000. For the President's protection, an indefinite amount.

63. **Duties and Powers of the President.** — In order that the President may perform the various duties which the Constitution, acts of Congress, treaties, and customs place upon him, he has to have corresponding powers. As the head of the executive branch of government it is his duty to see that the Constitution, laws and treaties, and decisions of the federal courts are enforced. To perform this duty he has been given power to appoint and dismiss thousands of officers; command the army and navy; call extra sessions of Congress, recommend proper legislation, and veto improper bills. The sum total of his powers is much greater than that of many constitutional monarchs.

An aggressive President who becomes party leader or a national hero can greatly increase his powers by a loose construction of the Constitution. During the Civil War Congress permitted Lincoln to become practically a dictator. He issued a proclamation suspending the writ of *habeas corpus,* which Congress subsequently legalized. He also issued the emancipation proclamations of 1862 and 1863, declaring all slaves in the insurgent States to be thenceforth free; and he forced through the thirteenth amendment in 1865 legalizing the same. Though the President cannot declare war he can at any time bring on war by ordering the army into foreign territory, or by managing foreign affairs in such a manner that a foreign nation will become the aggressor.

64. **Power of Appointment.** — The Constitution provides that the President " shall nominate, and by and with the advice and consent of the Senate, shall appoint ambassadors, other public ministers and consuls, judges of the Supreme Court, and all other officers of the United States whose appointments are not herein otherwise provided for,[1] and which shall be established by law; but the Congress may by law vest the appointment of such inferior officers as they think proper in the

---

[1] The officers whose appointments are "otherwise provided for" are the President, Vice-President, Electors, Senators, Representatives, and Officers of the Senate and House of Representatives.

President alone, in the courts of law,[1] or in the heads of the departments."

The United States has on its pay-roll more than half a million persons. Excluding those in the military and naval service, there remain nearly 500,000 in the executive civil service of the United States. Of these the President unaided appoints very few ; the President and the Senate appoint about 10,000 of the most important; about 300,000 are selected by civil service competitive examinations ; and the remainder, many of whom are laborers, are appointed directly or indirectly by cabinet officers. But because the cabinet officers are themselves dependent upon the President, he can influence many of these appointments if he desires.

The President alone appoints his private secretary, who in turn appoints his subordinates ; and with a few unimportant exceptions, *e.g.* during the administrations of Johnson and Grant, the Senate has always approved cabinet officers appointed by a President. For special reasons Congress has from time to time provided that certain officers, such as the Librarian of Congress, shall be appointed by the President alone.

The President with the consent of the Senate appoints the most important officers.[2] For the positions to be filled within a congressional district, the President usually confers with the representative from that district if he is of the same party ; for the more important, the senators will be consulted. When the Senate receives the names of persons selected for positions,

---

[1] Courts of law appoint clerks, reporters, and other minor ministerial officers.

[2] This class includes such officers as ambassadors, ministers, and consuls; federal judges; most military and naval officers; cabinet officers and their immediate subordinates; the Treasurer of the United States; the Comptroller of the Currency; superintendents of mints; commissioners of internal revenue; collectors of customs and internal revenue; interstate commerce commissioners; commissioners of patents; commissioners of pensions; pension agents; Indian agents; district attorneys and marshals; territorial governors; and postmasters of the first, second, and third classes (any postmaster whose salary is $1000 or more). See footnote to Sec. 90.

it refers them to the appropriate standing committee; and the committee confers with the senators of the State from which the nominee comes, provided the senators are of the President's party. Under the practice known as "senatorial courtesy" the Senate will ratify only those appointments which are approved by the senators (of the President's party) from the State in which the offices in question are to be filled.

The Civil Service Commission examines for the President or other appointing officials more than 300,000 persons from whom appointments are made according to civil service rules.[1]

Heads of Departments directly or indirectly appoint about 150,000 employees without civil service examinations. The greater number of these are skilled or unskilled laborers.

Term of Officers. — Most of the important officials are appointed for four years.[2] The cabinet officers are appointed to serve during the pleasure of the President, and in practice always resign when a new President enters office. The terms of minor officers and laborers vary, and persons who enter the civil service through competitive examinations hold office for an indefinite term.

Power of Removal. — The President may remove without the consent of the Senate any officer whom he appoints alone or in conjunction with the Senate, except judges, who may be removed by impeachment only, and military and naval officers in time of peace, when they may be removed by court-martial only. His power to remove officers may not be restricted by Congress[3] and may be employed for

---

[1] This class includes most of the clerks in Washington, fourth-class postmasters, first and second class post-office clerks, railway mail clerks, letter carriers, rural free-delivery men, and employees in the Indian service, custom houses, revenue service, and the government printing office.

[2] Four years is the term for territorial judges and governors, marshals, district attorneys, customs collectors, pension agents; Indian agents, chiefs of many bureaus, and postmasters of the first, second, and third classes.

[3] The Tenure of Office Act of 1867 required the consent of the Senate for the removal of an officer whose appointment had to be approved by the Senate. This act was aimed at President Johnson and was finally repealed in

political purposes as well as for ridding the service of incompetent and unfit persons.	Those who have entered office through competitive examinations may be removed or reduced for any cause which will promote the efficiency of the service; but like penalties are imposed for like offences, and no political or religious discrimination is shown.

65. Receiving Diplomatic Representatives. — The President receives ambassadors and ministers sent to the United States. Upon an appointed day the Secretary of State escorts a new minister or ambassador to the White House, where the latter delivers a short ceremonial address to which the President responds.	The minister or ambassador is then recognized as the official organ of communication between the United States government and the government represented.	When the independence of a country is in doubt, or the representative is personally objectionable to the United States government, the President may refuse to receive him; and the President may request a foreign country to recall a representative, or dismiss one for conduct offensive to the government.

66. Treaty Power. — If the United States desires to enter into commercial compacts, define its boundaries, make peace, or enter into any other compacts appropriate for international agreements, the President, with the assistance of the State Department, may negotiate a treaty with the other state or states concerned.	Because a treaty becomes law, the Constitution provides that a vote of two thirds of the Senate present is necessary before the treaty may be signed by the representatives of the United States government.[1]

1886.	Though the Supreme Court has never passed upon this law it is considered to have been unconstitutional.

[1] As a treaty is merely a law, Congress may repeal it by passing a law contrary to its provisions; or an existing law may be repealed by the terms of a treaty.	In other words, when a treaty and a law of Congress conflict a court will consider the one last enacted to be the law.	A treaty which is contrary to the Constitution is void, but the courts have, as yet, never declared one to be contrary to the Constitution.

Money cannot be appropriated by a treaty, but in practice whenever the

67. Military Powers of the President. — As the Constitution makes the President commander-in-chief of the army and navy, he has complete control over their movements.   For instance, when Mr. Roosevelt was President, he sent the navy around the world in order that the men might gain experience and that other nations might be impressed with its strength.   Some congressmen objected to the cost and threatened to withhold the necessary appropriation.   Mr. Roosevelt is said to have replied : " Very well, the existing appropriation will carry the navy halfway around the world and if Congress chooses to leave it on the other side, all right."   President Polk

Copyright, Underwood & Underwood, N. Y.

PRESIDENT WILSON REVIEWING THE WEST POINT CADETS.

brought on the Mexican War by ordering the troops across the Nueces River, and President Wilson narrowly averted another war with Mexico in 1914 when he sent the navy to Vera Cruz.

The President directs campaigns and could take personal command of the army or navy if he wished.   So long as he acts within the rules of international law he may do anything to weaken the power of the enemy.   For instance, he may order the confiscation of property used by the enemy for warlike purposes.   In the exercise of this power President Lincoln

Senate has agreed to a treaty providing for the payment of money the House has concurred on a bill appropriating it.

issued the emancipation proclamation during the Civil War, freeing the slaves in certain Southern States.

Whenever the enforcement of federal laws is prevented by combinations too strong to be suppressed by the courts with their marshals, the President may send United States regular troops to protect the mails and interstate commerce, as Cleveland did in 1894 during the Pullman strike at Chicago; or he may call out State militia, as Lincoln did in 1861. When the army occupies the enemy's territory, the President, as commander-in-chief, may assume control of the government, as Lincoln did in certain Southern States during the Civil War, or as McKinley did in Porto Rico and the Philippines during the Spanish-American War.

In case of domestic violence the legislature of a State, or the governor if the legislature is not in session, may request the President to send regular troops into the State to restore order.

68. President's Part in Legislation. — The President is primarily an executive officer, but the Constitution bestows upon him many powers which enable him to influence legislation.

Presidential Messages. — When Congress meets in December the President sends his annual message to Congress, and from time to time during the term he sends special messages. In these messages he recommends the enactment of certain laws. They may be laws which the party platform pledged to enact, laws recommended by heads of the departments of administration, or possibly a personal hobby. The messages are usually read in each house by a clerk; but Washington, John Adams, and Wilson read their messages to the two houses assembled in one of the chambers. Different parts of the messages are referred to appropriate committees. Full reports from the heads of departments usually accompany the annual message. The consideration of the recommendations depends upon the influence of the President. They are at least valuable to form public opinion, because the daily papers publish the messages and comment freely upon them.

Extraordinary Sessions. — A President may call an extra session of Congress whenever he deems it proper. In 1913 Wilson called an extra session to consider the tariff and currency questions. The session continued from April 7 until the regular session convened on the first Monday of December, during which time Congress passed the Underwood-Simmons tariff law and thoroughly debated the Glass-Owens

PRESIDENT WILSON ADDRESSING CONGRESS IN JOINT SESSION.
He is here urging the enactment of an eight hour law for railroad employees in order to avoid a general strike.

currency bill, which was enacted into law before the end of the year.

Issue of Ordinances. — When the President must execute a law which does not specify means for its enforcement it is necessary for him to issue an ordinance prescribing uniform means for the enforcement of the same. Inasmuch as the Constitution makes the President commander-in-chief of the army and navy he may issue ordinances for their regulation. Congress frequently authorizes the President to issue ordinances for specific purposes. For instance, Congress has authorized the President to govern the Panama

Canal Zone, and in so doing he has the power to issue legislative ordinances.[1]

The Veto — The President, for any reason, may veto any bill or joint resolution[2] passed by Congress. This veto power enables the President, who is the only representative of *all* the people, to act as a check upon the legislative branch. Unfortunately the President must sign or veto a bill in its entirety. If he could veto certain items in appropriation bills, as the governors of many States may do, a bold President could save much revenue by preventing appropriations for such purposes as dredging rivers where there is little navigation or building post offices where government buildings are not needed.

Inasmuch as the President can introduce a bill into Congress only through some congressman, he seldom prepares one; but as party leader he coöperates with any committee of Congress that is preparing an important bill. For instance, when the Currency Bill was being prepared during the summer of 1913, Congressman Glass, Chairman of the Banking and Currency

---

[1] The following proclamation issued by President Taft, as governor of the Canal Zone, is an example of ordinances issued by the President:

"I, William Howard Taft, President of the United States of America, by virtue of the power and authority vested in me by the Act of Congress, approved August 24, 1912, to provide for the opening, maintenance, protection, and operation of the Panama Canal and the sanitation and government of the Canal Zone, do hereby prescribe and proclaim the following rates of toll to be paid by vessels using the Panama Canal:

1. On merchant vessels carrying passengers or cargo, one dollar and twenty cents ($1.20) per net vessel ton — each one hundred (100) cubic feet of actual earning capacity.

2. On vessels in ballast without passengers or cargo forty (40) per cent less than the rate of tolls for vessels with passengers or cargo.

3. Upon naval vessels other than transports, colliers, hospital ships, and supply ships, one dollar and twenty cents ($1.20) per net ton, the vessels to be measured by the same rules as are employed in determining the net tonnage of merchant vessels.

The Secretary of War will prepare and prescribe such rules for the measurement of vessels and such regulations as may be necessary and proper to carry this proclamation into full force and effect."

[2] Joint resolutions proposing amendments to the Constitution are not sent to the President. This is the only exception.

Committee, was continually conferring with President Wilson, and relying upon his influence as party leader to secure the passage of the measure.

Extra-Legal Methods. — There are many indirect methods by which a President can persuade congressmen to support his measures, although he has no part directly in legislation. Roosevelt threatened to "take the stump" against congressmen who would not support his measures, and Lincoln allowed a congressman to name the appointee to a $20,000 position in the Custom House of New York in consideration of a vote which was necessary to admit Nevada into the Union, for without Nevada's vote Amendment XIII to the Constitution of the United States could not have been ratified.

69. Pardoning Power. — The pardoning power of the President is absolute for all offences against the United States, except in cases of impeachment, where a pardon may never be granted. Of course he cannot pardon offences against State law ; but for crimes committed in territories or the District of Columbia, or offences against federal laws such as the postal, revenue, or banking laws, the accused may be pardoned either before or after conviction.

If an individual is involved, a pardon is seldom granted before conviction. But in 1889 President Harrison issued a proclamation known as *amnesty*, which pardoned the Mormons who had violated the anti-polygamy laws applying to the territories of the United States. The President may pardon conditionally provided the condition is reasonable, or he may *commute* a sentence by decreasing the penalty. He may reduce a fine or remit it entirely. By a law of 1910 a board of parole was created at each of the three federal prisons.[1] This board hears applications for release on parole and makes recommendations to the Attorney-General, who grants or refuses the parole.

70. Independence of the President. — The President, as head of one of the three branches of government, must have a degree

---

[1] At Leavenworth, Kan., Atlanta, Ga., and McNeil Island, Wash.

of independence of the other two branches, else he would not remain a check upon them. So long as the President is in office — and he may be removed only by impeachment — he may not be arrested. But as soon as he is out of office he may be punished for any crime committed by him while in office. The courts can neither restrain him nor compel him to perform any act. When Aaron Burr was being tried for treason Chief Justice Marshall issued a subpœna requiring President Jefferson to produce a certain paper relating to Burr's acts. Jefferson refused to obey. He reasoned that the duties of a President could not be performed if he could be compelled to obey court writs.

II. The Vice-President

71. The Vice-President is elected by the same electors and in the same manner as the President, except that when no Vice-Presidential candidate receives a majority of the electoral votes the Vice-President is chosen by the Senate from the two candidates receiving the highest number of electoral votes.

The qualifications for the Vice-President are the same as for the President. His salary is $12,000 and his only duty, unless he succeeds to the presidency, is to preside over the Senate. As he is not a member of the Senate, does not appoint committees, and has no vote except in case of a tie, he has little influence. A candidate for the Vice-Presidency is seldom nominated because of his fitness to become President, but to help carry a doubtful State, to appease a defeated faction in the national nominating convention, or to replenish the party treasury.

III. The Cabinet

72. In order that the President may have assistants in executing the laws Congress has authorized him to appoint ten chiefs.[1] Washington was authorized to appoint only three: a Secretary of State, a Secretary of the Treasury, and a Secre-

---

[1] The statutes creating these offices provide for the assent of the Senate, but in practice the Senate never interferes with the President's choice.

tary of War.[1]   As governmental duties increased, however, the work of administration was further divided and new secretaries were added.   There are now ten chief assistants.

	NAME OF OFFICE	OFFICE CREATED IN
1.	The Secretary of State	1789
2.	The Secretary of the Treasury	1789
3.	The Secretary of War	1789
4.	The Attorney-General	1789
5.	The Postmaster-General	1794
6.	The Secretary of the Navy	1798
7.	The Secretary of the Interior	1849
8.	The Secretary of Agriculture	1889
9.	The Secretary of Commerce	1903
10.	The Secretary of Labor	1913

These ten secretaries are appointed by the President for indefinite terms, and as he alone is responsible for the official action of any secretary he may dismiss him at any time.   A new President always selects some new Cabinet officers, and a President of a different party from his predecessor selects an entirely new Cabinet.   The Cabinet meets twice a week, or as often as the President desires, in the executive offices, which adjoin the White House.   The meetings are secret and only the weightier matters are discussed, as the President meets the chiefs of each executive department alone to discuss the less important affairs.

There is no provision for the Cabinet either in the Constitution or in the Statutes of Congress.   The Constitution says, " The President may require the opinion in writing of the principal officers in each of the executive departments upon any subject relating to the duties of their respective offices." (Art. II, Sec. 2.)   At first Washington requested written opinions, but by his second term he held secret meetings, which were called " cabinet meetings."

---

[1] The Attorney-General was also considered a member of Washington's Cabinet, but he was not the head of a department until 1870, when the Department of Justice was created.

It is the President's privilege to invite persons other than departmental heads to attend the cabinet meetings, but he does not do so; and he is not compelled to take the advice of the Cabinet contrary to his own judgment. This is illustrated by an incident told of President Lincoln. He brought before his Cabinet a proposition which he favored, but every member of

PRESIDENT WILSON AND HIS CABINET.

his cabinet voted against it. He announced the vote, "Seven nays, one aye; the ayes have it."

OUTLINE FOR REVIEW

The Executive Department

I. PRESIDENT.
    (A) Qualifications:
        (1) Natural born citizen of the United States.
        (2) Thirty-five years of age.
        (3) Fourteen years a resident of the United States.

(B) Elected: (1) By Electoral College, or
(2) By the House of Representatives.

(C) Oath taken when inaugurated.

(D) Term: Four years.

(E) Vacancy: (1) Filled by Vice-President, or
(2) By Cabinet Officer, according to law of Presidential succession.

(F) Salary: $75,000 plus travelling expenses, house rent, etc.

(G) Powers and Duties: (1) Executes the laws of the nation.
(2) Appoints ministers, consuls, judges, postmasters, and other officers.
(3) May remove officers and fill vacancies.
(4) Receives foreign ministers.
(5) May make treaties with consent of two thirds of Senate.
(6) Commander-in-Chief of the army and navy.
(7) Delivers a message to Congress each December and at other times.
(8) May call special session of Congress or of either House.
(9) Signs or vetoes bills passed by Congress.
(10) May grant reprieves and pardons.

(H) Removal: (1) May be impeached by bare majority of House.
(2) May be tried and convicted by two thirds of Senate.

II. VICE-PRESIDENT.

(A) Qualifications: The same as required for the President.

(B) Elected: (1) By the Electoral College, or
(2) By the Senate.

(C) Term: Four years.

(D) Vacancy :   Not filled until next presiden-
                           tial election.

(E) Salary : $12,000.

(F) Duty :   Presides over Senate and votes
                           only in case of tie.   Becomes
                           President if President dies or
                           is in any way disqualified.

III. TEN CABINET MEMBERS (non-official).

   (A) Qualifications :   None prescribed.

   (B) Appointed :   ' By President.

   (C) Term :   Indefinite.

   (D) Salary : $12,000.

   (E) Duty :   To advise President and admin-
                           ister their respective depart-
                           ments according to the will
                           of the President.

BIBLIOGRAPHY

DOUGHERTY, J. HAMPTON. The Electoral System of the United
   States. 1906.

FAIRLIE, J. A. The National Administration of the United States
   of America. 1905.

HASKIN, F. J. The American Government. 1912.

HILL, JOHN PHILIP. The Federal Executive. 1916.

LEARNED, HENRY BARRETT. The President's Cabinet. 1912.

REINSCH, PAUL S. Readings on American Federal Government.
   1909.

STANWOOD, EDWARD. A History of the Presidency from 1788 to
   1897. 1898.

TAFT, WILLIAM H. The Presidency. 1916.

WILSON, WOODROW. The President of the United States. 1916.

The Congressional Directory.

QUESTIONS ON THE TEXT

Q: What are the qualifications for the presidency?

A Explain in detail how a President is elected.

3. For what term is a President chosen?   May he succeed
himself?

4. Who succeeds to the presidency in case the President does not complete his term?

5. What is the annual salary of the President?

6. What are the powers of the President?

7. What officers are appointed by the President alone? President and Senate? President and Civil Service Commission?

8. How are other officers chosen?

9. For what term are the various officers chosen?

10. What officers may be removed by the President?

11. Who appoints diplomatic officers? Who receives those from foreign countries?

12. Who makes treaties? If a treaty and law of Congress conflict which will the courts enforce?

13. What powers has the President as commander-in-chief of the army and navy?

14. Explain the President's power over legislation by means of (1) messages, (2) extraordinary sessions, (3) the issuance of ordinances, (4) the veto, and (5) extra-legal methods.

15. What persons may be pardoned by the President? May he pardon such persons conditionally? May he return a fine? May he commute a sentence? What is meant by *amnesty*?

16. Can a court compel the President to perform a duty? Can he be punished after he is out of office for a crime committed while in office?

17. How is the Vice-President chosen? Term? Qualifications? Salary? Duties?

18. How many members are there in the President's cabinet? Name the ten secretaries? For what term are they appointed? Salary? Need the President accept their advice?

QUESTIONS FOR DISCUSSION

1. What Article of the Constitution treats of the President?

2. Explain how Mr. Harrison was elected President in 1888 although Mr. Cleveland received more popular votes.

3. The indirect method of electing the President of the United States is no longer of value. Discuss a better method.

4. The Southern Confederacy provided that its president should hold office for six years and not be re-eligible. Give reasons why you favor or oppose a like term for the President of the United States. How could this change be made?

5. President Taft travelled 125,000 miles during his four-year term. How much per mile was he allowed by the government?

6. What federal officers or employees reside or have duties in your city or county? How are they appointed?

7. Why is it proper for the President to be left practically unrestricted in selecting and dismissing the members of his Cabinet?

8. The veto power has, in times past, been considered an instrument of kingship, but no king or queen of England has dared to use it for two centuries. Yet, Andrew Jackson, the "Father of Democracy," was the President who used this power most extensively. Explain why this apparent inconsistency is really not inconsistent.

9. The President of France may veto a bill and state his reasons, but a bare majority of the House of Deputies and the Senate may override it. Do you prefer the French or the American veto?

10. The President has absolute pardoning power for all offences committed against the United States, except in cases of impeachment. Under what circumstances do you think this power should be used?

11. Why is the vice-presidential office one of the worst features of our government?

12. Who are the members of the present cabinet?

13. Congress provided for the building of a government railroad in Alaska. The President was authorized to select the route, determine other details, and have the road built. What other similar undertaking was so successfully carried out by the President?

CHAPTER IX

THE DEPARTMENT OF STATE

73. The Secretary of State[1] ranks first among the Cabinet officers. At cabinet meetings he sits at the right of the President, and on all ceremonial occasions he is given precedence over his colleagues. In case of death or removal of both the President and Vice-President the Secretary of State is the first in line for the presidency. The duties of the Secretary of State are partly connected with domestic affairs, but to a much greater extent with foreign affairs.

Domestic Duties of the Secretary. — The Secretary attends to all correspondence between the President and the governors of the several States. Thus, if the President calls for a State's national guard for war, or if a governor requests the extradition[2] of a criminal who has taken refuge in a foreign country, the correspondence takes place through the Secretary of State.

---

[1] There are three assistant secretaries of State who, with the advice and consent of the Senate, are appointed by the President. The Second Assistant Secretary is by custom a permanent occupant of the office. The present incumbent has held the office for thirty years, and has been connected with the diplomatic service and the department since 1870. He has charge of the diplomatic business, and his knowledge of precedents makes him almost indispensable. His predecessor held the office for twenty years.

[2] Extradition means the handing over by one State to another of fugitives from justice. The United States has extradition treaties with the leading nations of the world. When a person accused of crime flees from an American State to a foreign state the governor of the State applies to the Secretary of State for the return of the fugitive, furnishing evidence of probable guilt. The governor also names a person who will go for the fugitive. The proper papers are sent to our diplomatic representative, and he is instructed to request the extradition of the fugitive. The "President's Warrant" is given the agent whom the governor has designated to bring back the accused. Frequently an application is made by telegraph for the provisional arrest and detention of the fugitive in advance of the presentation of formal proof.

When a State ratifies an amendment to the Constitution of the United States the Secretary of State is notified, and when three fourths of the States notify him he must certify that the amendment has been adopted. Also, when Congress admits a new State into the Union the Secretary of State

Copyright, Underwood & Underwood, N. Y.

STATE, WAR, AND NAVY BUILDING.

issues a proclamation declaring the fact. He is custodian of the original copies of the Constitution, treaties, and all laws enacted by Congress.

The Secretary of State also has charge of the Great Seal[1] of

---

[1] As distinguished from the Great Seal there is another seal of each of the ten administrative departments and one for each court.

the United States, which he affixes to all executive proclamations, to various commissions, such as civil appointments made by the President, and to warrants for the extradition of fugitives from justice.

Foreign Duties of the Secretary. — In most other governments the officer corresponding to our Secretary of State is called "Secretary of Foreign Affairs." Our Secretary of State is the head of the diplomatic service and of the consular service, grants passports for the protection of American citizens who travel or reside in foreign countries, and is the "head of a great clearing house of international claims." These several duties require a detailed treatment.

74. Diplomatic Service. — Diplomatic correspondence with foreign governments is carried on by the State Department through diplomatic representatives. We send these representatives to the governments of practically all independent states, and most of these governments have diplomatic representatives at Washington. We send ambassadors to the important countries, ministers-plenipotentiary [1] to most countries, ministers-resident to several, and commissioners for special purposes. In the absence of the permanent diplomatic representative the first secretary or some other person takes charge temporarily and is known as the *chargé d'affaires ad interim.*

Ambassadors, appointed by the President with the consent of the Senate, are sent to the most important countries, that is, to Great Britain, Germany, France, Spain, Austria-Hungary, Russia, Italy, Turkey,[2] Japan, Argentina, Brazil, Chile, and Mexico. The term of office is not prescribed by law, hence there are numerous changes whenever a new party comes into

---

[1] The official title of the minister-plenipotentiary is "envoy extraordinary and minister-plenipotentiary."

[2] One would hardly expect to find an ambassador in Turkey, but at Constantinople a minister may wait hours or even until the next day for an important affair, while ambassadors from much less important countries are given an audience at once. Only ambassadors are allowed access to the Sultan to discuss official matters. Thus Congress, in 1906, felt obliged to send an ambassador to Turkey.

power. There are no prescribed qualifications, but the ruler to whom the ambassador is accredited may refuse to receive in a diplomatic way any person who is for any reason objectionable (*persona non grata*). Any country may demand the recall of an ambassador who has made himself obnoxious to its government, and in extreme cases may dismiss him.

The duties of an ambassador are to transmit official communications; make reports to the Secretary of State; promote

WINDSOR CASTLE, ENGLAND.

American interests in every way; protect American citizens; and negotiate treaties and other agreements.

To perform the above duties efficiently the ambassador must be on terms of friendly intimacy with leading men in the country to which he is sent. Newspaper editors may be most useful acquaintances because the ambassador can both learn from them and impress upon them the good intentions of our government, and so reach the public through the press. The salary is $17,500, and as the social affairs of the official set at a European capital call for heavy expenditures few ambassadors can live upon their salaries. It is said that a recent ambassador, in maintaining the American embassy at London, spent $250,000 a year.

Ambassadors, and their families and servants to a great extent, are exempt from arrest and from taxation of personal belongings. Within their embassies (official residences) they may do anything not prohibited by the laws of the nation which has sent them. Of course noises, or anything which proves a nuisance outside of the embassy, are not permitted. These privileges are associated with a legal fiction known as *exterritoriality*, which term means that the ambassador has, as it were, carried a portion of the territory of his home country with its laws to the foreign country.

Ministers are sent to the governments of all independent countries of any importance except the thirteen to which ambassadors are sent. Everything that has been said concerning ambassadors applies to ministers except the honor or rank, salary, and the name of their residences. The salaries of ministers range from $10,000 to $12,000 and their official residences are called " legations."

75. Consular Service. — In addition to diplomatic agents, the President, with the consent of the Senate, appoints about 700 consular officers. The full consuls are appointed from those who have passed the civil service examination. They are commercial agents, or "America's lookouts on the watchtowers of .international trade," and one is stationed at every important commercial city. One is sent even to the inaccessible town of Chung King, far back in the interior of China, six weeks' travel by river from Shanghai.

A consul, being primarily a commercial representative, must certify the invoices of goods exported to the United States, and is thus required to be familiar with the character and value of commodities and with every detail of our tariff system. He must also " spy out new promised lands of commercial opportunity." A few years ago this service secured an order amounting to $23,000,000 for battleships and armament from Argentina, and recently a New England manufacturer of knives asked the Consular Service for a list of English retail dealers in cutlery. He got the list and is now "carrying coals to Newcastle" by shipping knives to Sheffield.[1]

Consular Jurisdiction. — The consul has some jurisdiction over whatever relates to the internal economy of American vessels. For instance, he settles disputes among masters, officers, and men; and in China, Siam, Borneo, Persia, Morocco, Tripoli, and Turkey, the American consuls have jurisdiction over American citizens in both civil and criminal cases by virtue of treaty arrangements. They try Americans who commit criminal offences within their districts and try all civil disputes between citizens of the United States residing therein.

For American citizens the consul also administers oaths, takes depositions, and acts as a witness to marriages. In brief, he is a friend and counselor to every American citizen. Any consul whose pay is less than $1000 a year may transact a private business. A few years ago the Stars and Stripes marking the office of a consular agent floated over a laundry in a South American city. —

Consuls' Compensation. — The salaries of regular consuls range from $2000 to $8000, but those of consuls-general, who are ordinarily sent to foreign capitals and have supervisory authority over the other consuls sent to the country, range from $3000 to $12,000. They are not entitled to the immunities of diplomatic representatives, but most countries by treaty exempt them from arrest in civil cases and guarantee

---

[1] The daily Commerce Report, published by the Bureau of Foreign and Domestic Commerce, is sent to about 10,000 American manufacturers who subscribe for it. Items like the following are published in it:

No. 2547. *Souvenir button machines.* — A letter has been received by the Bureau of Manufacturers in which the names of makers of hand machines for making souvenir buttons are asked for.

No. 2548. *American breeding cattle and horses.* — An American consular officer reports that a business man has written to him that it is his intention to import American breeding cattle and horses into one of the Latin American countries, and he desires that breeders communicate with him.

The names of prospective buyers are not published for fear foreign manufacturers might get the information gathered by our consuls.

the protection of their archives. A consulate of the United States in a weak state is a fairly safe place in times of disturbances, and an embassy or legation is almost invariably a place of safety.

Passports. — A passport is a certificate used to identify a citizen of one state when travelling or residing in a foreign country in order that the citizen may enjoy all the privileges that international law, treaties, or the prestige of his native state can insure. The Bureau of Citizenship controls matters relating to the issuance of passports, and determines questions relating to the citizenship of Americans in foreign countries.

An American citizen[1] who desires to travel abroad may make a written application to the Secretary of State for a passport. The application blank contains a detailed description of the person and information as to his age, residence, and occupation. It must be signed by the person applying, and an affidavit must be attested by an officer qualified to administer oaths; also it must be accompanied by a certificate from a credible witness that the applicant is the person he represents himself to be, and by a fee of one dollar. The passport is authenticated by the Great Seal of the United States and is good for two years. A diplomatic officer may renew a passport for two additional years. A diplomatic officer and certain consular officers may issue emergency passports for six months.

The Emergency Fund for this department, which is about $100,000 a year, is the only fund in the administration of which no original accounts or vouchers to the Treasury Department are required. The Secretary of State gives a " certificate " of such expenditure. This fund enables him to keep a watch on affairs in other countries. The costs of entertaining

---

[1] A passport may be issued to any person who has declared his intention to become an American citizen if he has resided in the United States three years. This does not entitle the holder to protection against the government of the country of which he was last a citizen, is good for only six months, and may not be renewed.

guests of the Nation, such as Admiral Togo, are paid from this fund.

BIBLIOGRAPHY

FAIRLIE, J. A. The National Administration of the United States of America. 1905.

HASKIN, F. J. The American Government. 1912.

VAN DYNE, FREDERICK. Our Foreign Service: the "A B C" of American Diplomacy. 1909.

The Congressional Directory.

Annual Report of the Secretary of State.

QUESTIONS ON THE TEXT

1. Who is considered the most important cabinet officer?

2. What are the domestic duties of the Secretary of State? The foreign duties?

3. What are the duties of ambassadors and ministers? What special privileges do they enjoy? .

4. What is meant by *exterritoriality* ?

5. How do ambassadors differ from ministers?

6. What is a *chargé d'affaires* (pronounced shär-zhä'däf-fâr')?

7. What are consuls, and how does the consular service differ from the diplomatic service?

8. How do consuls serve manufacturers?

9. What is meant by consular jurisdiction?

10. What salaries are paid to ambassadors? Ministers? Consuls?

11. How is a passport obtained and what is its value? Is it of equal value in all countries and at all times?

12. What is the *emergency fund* ? How does it differ from all other funds?

QUESTIONS FOR DISCUSSION

1. Explain the following simile: " The State Department may be likened to an artificial person, whose head is in Washington and whose body lies abroad."

2. In Japan the United States had consular jurisdiction until 1899, when it was abolished by treaty. Why do you suppose it was abolished?

3. A mediæval ambassador has been defined as "a person sent to lie abroad for the good of his country." Washington thus instructed

John Jay, special minister to Great Britain, in 1794: "It is the President's wish that the characteristics of an American minister should be marked on the one hand by a firmness against improper compliances, and on the other hand by sincerity, candor, truth, and prudence, and by a horror of finesse and chicane." This standard set by Washington has almost invariably been followed by the United States. Aside from moral right and wrong, which policy is the wiser, the mediæval policy of deception or the modern policy of sincerity?

4. In 1892 an attaché of the Swiss Legation at Washington was suspected of theft and arrested at Bay Shore Park, Maryland. When examined at Annapolis he was discharged. The Swiss government asked for the punishment of the officer making the arrest. The State Department requested the Governor of Maryland to investigate. The police officer was dismissed and an apology tendered by the Governor. A diplomatic officer cannot be arrested for exceeding the speed limit in an automobile, but he can be warned, and if he habitually violates the law in this respect complaint may be made to his government. Why is this courtesy to foreign countries necessary?

5. The position of American Ambassador to Great Britain with a salary of $17,500 a year "went begging" for some months in 1913. What was the cause of this condition?

6. Should we have a United States academy for training diplomats as well as academies for training army and navy officers? Our diplomatic agents are not so well trained in foreign languages and international law as those of other countries. The diplomatic service would then be taken out of politics, as are the army and navy. Is it not as important to train men to prevent war as to train men to make war?

CHAPTER X

THE TREASURY DEPARTMENT [1]

76. The Secretary of the Treasury supervises the collection, safe-keeping, and disbursement of all moneys of the United

Copyright, Underwood & Underwood, N.Y.

SOUTH FRONT OF THE UNITED STATES TREASURY BUILDING.

States government, and maintains the stability of its monetary system. In doing this he is aided by three assistant secre-

---

[1] One would hardly expect to find the three following services in this department: (1) The United States Public Health Service has charge of marine hospitals, controls the national quarantine service, and supervises the medical examination of immigrants. (2) The Coast Guard Service maintains

taries and some thirty bureau chiefs who have immediate
charge of the several bureaus and divisions of the department.

77. The Collection of the Revenues. — For the fiscal year
ending June 30, 1916, the receipts of the United States were
from the following sources:

Internal Revenue:

Distilled Spirits	$153,457,996.76
Tobacco (manufactured)	85,324,094.46
Fermented Liquors	87,875,672.22
Corporation Income Tax	56,993,657.98
Individual Income Tax	67,943,594.63
Special Taxes	16,580,480.38
Oleomargarine	924,699.91
Playing Cards	819,654.20
Schedule A (Documentary stamps)	38,110,282.49
Schedule B (Perfumery, Cosmetics, etc.)	4,086,160.99
Miscellaneous	606,993.75
Total Internal Revenue	$512,723,287.77
Internal Revenue	$512,723,287.77
Customs	213,185,845.63
Sales of Public Lands	1,887,661.80
Miscellaneous [1]	51,889,016.28
Total Ordinary Receipts	$779,685,811.48
Panama Canal Receipts	2,369,995.28
Public Debt Receipts	58,452,402.50
Postal Revenues	312,057,688.83
Total Receipts	$1,153,065,898.09

several hundred stations at dangerous points on the coasts of the oceans and
great lakes, etc. (see page 140, note). (3) A supervising architect has charge
of the selection of sites and the construction and maintenance of buildings
belonging to the United States.

[1] *Miscellaneous* includes such items as the following (in round numbers):
profit on coinage, bullion deposits, etc., $4,000,000; receipts from the District
of Columbia, $8,000,000; judicial fees, fines, etc., $1,000,000; immigration
fund, $5,000,000; forest reserve fund, $2,000,000; fees on letters patent,
$2,000,000; tax on circulation of national bank notes, $3,000,000; customs
fees, fines, penalties, etc., $1,000,000; land fees, $1,000,000; and consular
fees, $1,000,000.

Internal Revenue is taxes derived from the sources indicated in the table on the preceding page, *e.g.*, $1.10 a gallon on distilled spirits (50 % alcohol), ten cents a pound on oleomargarine artificially colored to look like butter, and two cents a deck on playing cards.[1] The internal revenue commissioner and his three deputy commissioners collect most of these taxes by means of stamps, which are pasted upon packages in such a way that the stamp will be broken when the package is opened.[2]

Copyright, Underwood & Underwood, N.Y.
UNITED STATES CUSTOMS OFFICER EXAMINING DIAMONDS FOR APPRAISEMENT.

The country is divided into internal revenue districts; and in each district there are a collector of internal revenue, deputy collectors, gaugers who determine the amount of liquor produced, storekeepers who are in charge of storehouses where distilled spirits are kept before being marketed, and detectives to prevent such frauds as "moonshining."

Customs are taxes (tariff) on imported goods. These taxes are collected by the Secretary of the Treasury through one of his assistant secretaries. The country is divided into forty-eight customs districts. In each one of these districts there

---

[1] There are also federal license taxes on the manufacturer, wholesaler, and retailer of certain articles listed above under the head of internal revenue, *e.g.*, $25.00 for retail liquor dealers. The license certificate must be exposed in one's place of business.

[2] The corporation tax, income tax, and inheritance tax are internal revenue taxes not collected by means of stamps. (See Secs. 45 and 46.)

is a collector who is assisted by a surveyor, appraiser, examiners, inspectors, store-keepers, and clerks. ▬

All articles brought into the country must enter at specified points where there are custom-houses. At the principal point in each district the collector resides ; at subordinate places a deputy collector. Along the two oceans and the Canadian and Mexican borders are numerous " ports of entry "; and numerous

UNITED STATES CUSTOM HOUSE, NEW YORK.

interior cities, such as Chicago and St. Louis, are " ports of entry." [1]

Customs on about 2000 taxable articles are of three kinds — *specific*, *ad valorem*, and *mixed*. *Specific* means so much per unit, as four .cents a gallon on vinegar or $3.00 a gallon on champagne. *Ad valorem* means in " proportion to value," as 10 per cent of the value of diamonds (in the rough) or 60 per ⟋

[1] Two thirds of all custom dues are collected at New York

cent of the value of laces. *Mixed* means that both a *specific* duty and an *ad valorem* duty are imposed upon the same article.

As the determination of values is very difficult, persons exporting to the United States articles valued at over $100 are required to have invoices certified by an American consul; when valued at $100 or less an oral statement is accepted. If the consul is not certain of the value he may demand three samples, one for himself, one for the board of general appraisers in New York, and one for the appraiser at the port to which the merchandise is sent.

A CUSTOMS EXAMINER, NEW YORK.
The Examiner is searching the trunk of a fair arrival for dutiable goods.

To prevent fraud when merchandise is received at a port, ten per cent of the packages, taken at random, are opened and examined; and all personal baggage is examined. To prevent smuggling, detectives are at work here and abroad. The Treasury Department, independent of the navy, maintains a number of revenue cutters to prevent the smuggling of goods to this country.[1]

---

[1] The Coast Guard Service performs many other functions. It enforces immigration laws, neutrality laws, quarantine laws, and fisheries laws including seal fisheries; it also enforces rules to ensure the safety of passengers and crews on excursion steamers and yachts. It operates the life-saving stations, assists vessels in distress, and when directed by the President it coöperates with the navy.

78. The Safe-Keeping of the Revenues. — *The Treasurer* of the United States may keep the revenues in the Treasury at Washington; in the sub-treasuries located at Baltimore, Boston, Chicago, Cincinnati, New Orleans, New York, Philadelphia, St. Louis, and San Francisco; in the Federal reserve banks; in the Federal farm loan banks; and in National banks under direction of the Secretary of the Treasury.

79. The Disbursement of the Revenue is regulated by acts of Congress. For the fiscal year ending June 30, 1916, the disbursements from the Treasury of the United States were as follows:

Civil Establishment (including foreign intercourse, public buildings, collection of revenue, District of Columbia, and miscellaneous)	$204,038,737.91
Military Establishment (including rivers and harbors, forts, arsenals, sea-coast defences, and miscellaneous).	164,635,576.67
Naval Establishment (including new vessels, machinery, armament, equipment, navy yards, and miscellaneous)	155,029,425.78
Pensions	159,302,351.20
Interest on Public Debt	22,900,313.03
Indian Service	17,570,283.81
Panama Canal	17,503,728.07
Public Debt	24,668,913.50
Postal Service (payable from postal revenue) . .	306,228,452.76
Total Disbursements	$1,371,877,782.73

No money is paid out of the Treasury unless authorized by an act of Congress. The money is paid by the *Treasurer* upon the presentation of a warrant drawn by the Secretary of the Treasury and approved by the Comptroller of the Treasury. In 1895 Comptroller Bowles refused to authorize the payment of a bounty on beet sugar under an act of 1890, on the ground that the law creating the bounty was unconstitutional, whereupon suit was brought. The Supreme Court issued a man-

damus[1] compelling the payment of the money. More recently
the comptroller had to decide whether a "tip" is a legitimate
expense for an official whose expenses are paid. His opinion
was that a tip of twenty-five cents to a Pullman porter for a
day's ride is a legitimate part of travelling expenses.

80. United States Currency. — Currency, a term which includes all money authorized by the government, is of two
kinds — metallic and paper.

UNITED STATES MINT AT PHILADELPHIA.

Metallic Currency. — Gold, silver, nickel, and bronze coins are
stamped at the mints in Philadelphia, Denver, and San Francisco.[2] At present these mints issue the double eagle ($20),
eagle ($10), half eagle ($5), and quarter eagle ($2.50) in gold.
Gold is coined free for any person bringing the metal to the
mints; but as ten per cent of the coin must be alloy (copper, or

---

[1] A *mandamus* is an order issued by a court compelling an inferior court or
an officer of the government to perform a legal duty.

[2] At the head of the Bureau of the Mint is a director of the mint. Subordinate to him is a superintendent for each mint.

nine parts copper and one part silver) to make it durable, there is a small charge for the alloy. If one desires to store the gold in bank vaults or to export it, the mint will mould it into bars containing the government stamp to indicate its fineness and weight.

The United States Treasury will not receive gold coins which have been reduced in weight more than one half of one per cent, and then only in case they have been in circulation twenty years. If in circulation a shorter period the abrasion must be only in proportion. As the government makes no profit in coining gold it will not bear the cost of wear. When banks receive any quantity of gold coins they weigh them, and the last party that accepts a light weight gold coin is the loser.

The mints now issue the dollar, half dollar, quarter, and dime in silver. Silver is purchased at its market value by the superintendent of the mint under the supervision of the "Director of the Mint." A silver dollar weighs 412.5 grains, of which one tenth is alloy (copper), and as the cost of an ounce (480 grains) of silver is now only $49\frac{3}{8}$ cents (Oct. 30, 1915), the cost of the silver in a dollar is 38 cents.[1] The treasurer, assistant treasurers, and depositories of the United States will redeem half dollars, quarters, and dimes in lawful money if they are not mutilated. Smooth coins are re-coined at the expense of the government.

The five-cent piece is made of three parts copper and one part nickel, and the cent is made of bronze (95 % copper and 5 % tin or zinc). Metal for these coins is purchased from the lowest bidder by the superintendent of the mint, with the approval of the Director of the Mint. The profit on these coins is even greater than that on silver coins. The Treasurer, assistant treasurers, and depositories of the United States will redeem these minor coins in lawful money provided they are

---

[1] The cost of silver changes like that of other commodities. On October 30, 1916, an ounce of silver cost $67\frac{3}{4}$ cents.

not mutilated. Coins worn smooth are re-coined at the expense of the government.

Money which the law requires a creditor to receive in payment of a debt (unless otherwise agreed) when tendered by a debtor is known as *legal tender.* Besides United States notes, gold dollars and silver dollars are legal tender in any amount; half dollars, quarters, and dimes, known as *subsidiary coins,* are legal tender to the amount of ten dollars; nickels and cents, known as *minor coins,* are legal tender to the amount of twenty-five cents.

The only practical value of a legal tender law to-day is to prevent the payment of debts in coins which would be inconvenient to carry. The United States is on the gold standard, which means that the value of all United States money will be kept on a parity with gold.

Paper Currency consists of gold certificates, silver certificates, United States notes, National bank notes, Federal reserve notes and Federal reserve bank notes. It is printed in Washington by the Bureau of Engraving and Printing.[1]

Gold certificates are receipts given any person who deposits gold coin or bars of gold with the Treasurer of the United States. The gold is kept in the government vaults until certificates are presented for the return of the same. Silver certificates certify the same in regard to silver dollars. United States notes ("greenbacks") were issued during the Civil War with nothing to secure them except the promise of the government to pay.

In 1864 when Maryland was invaded by General Lee's army these greenbacks were worth only 39 per cent in gold. As we now have the gold standard they can be presented to the Treasurer of the United States and exchanged for gold. For this purpose the Treasurer is required to keep in reserve at least $150,000,000 in gold coins or bullion.

---

[1] The average life of paper money in the United States is less than three years; the average life of silver certificates, the paper money in most common use, is only about one year. When the old is exchanged for the new the old is either laundered and reissued or ground into pulp.

National bank notes have been issued by National banks under the direction and control of the Comptroller of the Currency. They have been issued in amounts equal to the par value of United States bonds deposited with the Comptroller of the Currency as security. They are redeemed in lawful money of the United States whenever presented to the Treasurer of the United States, and for this purpose each bank is

MONEY LAUNDERING MACHINES.
These machines are in the Treasury at Washington.

required to keep on deposit with the Treasurer an amount of gold equal to five per cent of the amount of notes the bank has in circulation. The National bank notes now in circulation will doubtless be gradually retired through operation of the Federal Reserve Act.

Under the Federal Reserve Act, approved December 23, 1913, Federal reserve notes, which are prepared by the Comptroller of the Currency under the authority of the Federal Reserve Board, may be issued by the twelve Federal reserve

banks.   In addition, these banks may issue Federal reserve
bank notes in much the same way as the National bank notes
are issued.   The purpose of these notes is to give elasticity
to our currency, *i.e.* to allow the government to increase the
volume of money when money becomes scarce, and thereby
prevent a money panic.   (See Sec. 118.)

These notes may be issued upon the security of short term
commercial paper (*e.g.*, private notes, drafts, etc.), and the only
limit which the law places upon the amount of Federal reserve
notes which may be issued is that arising from the requirement
for collateral and reserve, and the provision that interest may
be charged upon them in the discretion of the Federal Reserve
Board.   Federal reserve notes are receivable for taxes, customs
and other public dues and are redeemable in gold on demand at
the Treasury Department in Washington, or in gold or lawful
money at any Federal reserve bank.   The gold reserve required against Federal reserve notes is 40%.

Mutilated paper currency may be redeemed if its condition
permits its identification by the Government experts.

81.   The Gold Standard. — The United States formally adopted
the gold standard by the Act of March 4, 1900, but had actually
been on a gold standing since 1879.   The act provides, "That
the dollar consisting of twenty-five and eight tenths grains of
gold nine tenths fine . . . shall be the standard unit of value,
and all forms of money issued or coined by the United States
shall be maintained at a parity of value with this standard and
it shall be the duty of the Secretary of the Treasury to maintain
such parity."

In the above sections the reader must have observed that one
can exchange gold certificates, United States notes, Federal
reserve notes, Federal reserve bank notes, and National bank
notes for gold coins.   This paper money which can be exchanged
directly for gold, plus actual gold coins, forms four fifths of all
our money.   The other fifth, composed of silver coins, silver
certificates, nickels, and pennies, can easily be exchanged for the
above-mentioned forms of money, hence all of our money can be

converted into gold. This means that a dollar of any kind of United States money is worth the same as 23.22 grains of pure gold (25.8 grains of gold containing one tenth alloy).

The basic cause for the recent advance of prices is the increased supply of gold. Since 1896 the supply of gold in the world has increased more rapidly than the demand for it at the former prices of commodities. Therefore gold has become cheaper and it naturally requires more of it to buy a given amount of other commodities. The value of all United States money is based on that of gold; so you now give more money for other commodities. In 1910 in the United States you gave on the average, at wholesale prices, 45.6 per cent more money for commodities than in 1896.[1]

[1] PRICES IN 1910 AS COMPARED WITH 1896 AND THE PERIOD 1890–1899

KIND OF COMMODITIES	NUMBER	PERCENTAGE INCREASE IN 1910 OVER 1896	PERCENTAGE INCREASE IN 1910 ON AVERAGE FOR 1890–1899
Farm products	20	110.2	64.6
Foods, etc.	57	53.6	28.7
Cloths and clothing	65	35.5	23.7
Fuel and lighting	13	20.2	25.4
Metals and implements	38	37.1	28.5
Lumber and building material . .	28	64.0	53.2
Drugs and chemicals	9	26.3	17.0
House-furnishing goods	14	18.7	11.6
Miscellaneous.	13	45.6	33.1
All commodities	257	45.6	31.6

EXTENT TO WHICH GENERAL PRICES IN LEADING COUNTRIES OF THE WORLD WERE HIGHER IN 1910 THAN IN 1896

COUNTRY	PERCENTAGE INCREASE IN 1910 OVER 1896
Belgium	27
Canada	35
England	28
France	31
Germany	42
India	37
Italy	21
United States	46
Average for all eight countries	33

Why It Costs You More To Live. — KEMMERER.

BIBLIOGRAPHY

DEWEY, D. R. Financial History of the United States. Third Edition. 1907.

FAIRLIE, J. A. The National Administration of the United States of America. 1905.

HASKIN, F. J. The American Government. 1912.

The Congressional Directory.

Annual Report of the Secretary of the Treasury.

. QUESTIONS ON THE TEXT

1. What are the duties of the Secretary of the Treasury?

2. How much revenue does the United States government receive annually? From what sources does this money come?

3. What is meant by *internal revenue?*

4. What is meant by *customs?*

5. Upon how many articles are tariff duties imposed?

6. How does the United States prevent fraud by importers of articles upon which a tariff is imposed?

7. Where does the United States government keep its money?

8. For what purposes does the United States expend its money?

9. What body must authorize the expenditure of all government money?

10. What officer sees that no money is expended except such as is authorized by Congress?

11. What is meant by *currency?*

12. What metallic currency does the United States now make? Where is it made?

13. On what kinds of metallic money is a profit made?

14. What is meant by *legal tender* money? *Subsidiary* coins? *Minor* coins?

15. What kinds of coins are *legal tender* money?

16. Where is paper currency printed?

17. What are gold certificates? Silver certificates?

18. How much gold does the Treasury keep in reserve and for what purpose?

19. What are Federal reserve notes? How many may be issued? How may the Reserve Board prevent the issuance of too many? How are these notes secured?

20. If you have mutilated paper money that can be recognized, how would you exchange it for good money?

21. In 1900 the United States adopted the gold standard. What is meant by the *gold standard?*

22. How do you explain the recent advance in prices?

QUESTIONS FOR DISCUSSION

1. During the past twenty years the average annual production of gold has been three times that of the previous twenty years, and there is now twice as much pure gold in the world as there was twenty years ago. Explain what effect this has had on prices of commodities.

.2. If a man is saving money during a period when prices are rising, should he buy a farm which will yield him 6 per cent net interest upon the amount invested, or should he lend it on a good security at 6 per cent?

3. Buying stocks is buying shares in actual property. Buying bonds is lending money. Which would you buy when prices are rising?

4. In 1896 President Cleveland received a salary of $50,000. In 1916 President Wilson received a salary of $75,000. Can Wilson buy any more commodities with his salary than Cleveland could with his?

5. Previous to 1896, when prices were falling, a very large number of people were without work and marched with Coxey's Army to Washington to petition the government to provide work, but as soon as prices began to rise labor was in great demand. Explain the reason for these conditions.

6. Since 1896 the volume of bank notes in the United States has increased from about $200,000,000 to $700,000,000. What effect would you expect this increase to have upon prices?

7. Why do banks encourage their depositors to use checks instead of money?

8. If some chemist should discover a cheap means of extracting gold from sea water and, as a result, gold should become extremely cheap, what effect would it have upon the wealth of a person who has all his money in United States notes? In State bonds? In land or houses?

9. So long as the National government is financially sound why does it not make any material difference whether certain kinds of paper money are or are not legal tender?

10. During the Civil War the United States paper money was worth much less than gold money. Why? Confederate paper money was worth even less than United States paper money; and at the end of the war Confederate paper money had no value. Why?

11. Bring to class as many kinds of paper money as possible and examine the various kinds carefully. If you should happen to burn your paper money beyond recognition who would gain thereby? If a mouse should tear it to shreds could you exchange the pieces for new money?

CHAPTER XI

WAR, NAVY, JUSTICE, AND POST-OFFICE DEPARTMENTS

WAR DEPARTMENT

82. The Secretary of War directs the army, including the Military Academy,[1] Service Schools, and War College. He also has charge of fortifications, river and harbor improvements, bridges over navigable streams, and the administration of the Philippine Islands and Porto Rico. All estimates of appropriations for the above functions of the department must be examined by him and referred to the President and to Congress. The war department is especially subject to the President because the Constitution makes him commander-in-chief of the army.

83. Military Administration is distributed as follows: The *adjutant-general* transmits to the the troops and individuals the orders that go out from the central administration and

---

[1] For the United States Military Academy at West Point the President appoints 60 cadets from the United States at large, 4 from each State at large (recommended by senators), 2 from each congressional district (recommended by representatives), 4 each from the District of Columbia and the Philippines, and 2 each from Hawaii, Alaska, and Porto Rico (recommended by local officials), 20 honor graduates of schools having officers of the Regular Army detailed as professors of military science and tactics (recommended by heads of schools), and not exceeding 180 enlisted men of the Regular Army and National Guard (recommended by commanding generals and State governors respectively). Appointees must be between 17 and 22 years of age, except those from the Regular Army and National Guard, who must be between 19 and 22. All must pass a physical examination and a mental examination equivalent to a college entrance examination unless they come from accredited schools. During the four years of attendance each cadet is allowed about $700 a year for expenses; and upon graduation he is commissioned as second lieutenant in the Regular Army on a salary of $1700.

keeps records and statistics of the army. The *inspector-general*
supervises the inspection of all branches of the army. The
quartermaster-general has charge of transportation, buildings,
subsistence, and other supplies. The *surgeon-general* supervises the medical department. The *paymaster-general* is
charged with the payment of soldiers and employees of the department. The *chief of engineers* is head of the corps of engi-

COAST DEFENCE DRILL BY WEST POINT CADETS.

neers which looks after the construction and maintenance of
forts, military roads, bridges, and river and harbor improvements. The *chief of ordnance* provides and distributes the
implements of war. The *judge-advocate-general* records the
proceedings of courts-martial, and is legal adviser to the Secretary of War.

84. The General Staff. — During the Spanish-American War
(1898) President McKinley, the Secretary of War, and the

Secretary of the Navy sat in the War Room at the White
House and sent out general instructions to the army and navy,
leaving the details to the commanding officers. At this time
it was seen that these civil administrators lacked practical
experience for this duty and, in 1903, a supervising military
bureau of the War Department, known as the General Staff,
was created.

This staff is composed of certain generals, colonels, majors.
and captains, selected by the President; and the Chief of Staff
is military adviser of the Secretary of War and the President.
The members of the General Staff do not serve for more than
four consecutive years, and thus the body is kept in constant
touch with the practical problems of warfare.

The duties of the General Staff are to prepare plans for national defence and for the movement of the standing army and
State militia in time of war, to investigate the needs of the
army, and to carry out orders of the President. Under the
supervision of this bureau is the Army War College at
Washington, where selected officers study special war problems.

85. The Army War College was established in 1901, when
Elihu Root was Secretary of War. It is a school for twenty-
three commissioned officers — colonels, lieutenant-colonels,
majors, and captains. Those who have proved their ability in
active service or at army service schools are usually chosen for
this college, and those who succeed there have a chance for
appointment on the General Staff, upon which there are about
fifty of the ablest army men of the nation.

The War College is not only a school of training but also a
place where the secret military information is kept. It gathers
maps, plans, drawings, photographs, and written descriptions
of countries, of their armies and their guns.

86. The Army. — The army of the United States is composed of regulars, national guards, reserves, and in time of
war, volunteers.

Enlistments in the regular army are for a term of seven
years. The first three years are spent in the regular organi-

zations and the remaining four are spent in civil life as members of the regular army reserve corps, who are subject to call; however men may reënlist for the regular organizations at the end of three years. According to the law of 1916. the size of the regular army is being gradually increased, and by 1920 there should be not exceeding 175,000 combatant and 40,000 noncombatant troops.

Enlistments in the national guard are for a term of six years,[1]

ARMY WAR COLLEGE, WASHINGTON, D. C.

the first three years being spent in the active organizations and the remaining three in the national guard reserve. According to the law of 1916 the number of national guards should increase to nearly half a million men by 1920. In time of peace the national guard of any State is subject to the order of the governor, and is commonly called the "organized militia."[2]

---

[1] No person under eighteen years of age may enlist without the consent of his parents or guardian.

[2] The unorganized milita includes all male citizens between 18 and 45 years of age.

In time of war it can be ordered anywhere the President needs it. It receives its equipment from the national government, and since 1916 the guardsmen have received a small regular salary from the national government. .

Volunteers may be called by the President in such numbers as Congress authorizes.

In times of peace the army is often used at the discretion of the President for various purposes. For instance, it has frequently been used to hold the Indians in subjection. In 1894,

THE FIRST ARMORED CAR COMPLETED FOR THE UNITED STATES ARMY.
It carries a field gun and a number of machine guns.

when the strikers of the Pullman Car Company interfered with trains carrying mail near Chicago, President Cleveland sent United States troops to prevent any delay of the mails. At the time of the San Francisco earthquake United States troops were. used to guard the property, and recently when the Mississippi River overflowed its banks troops were used to rescue persons in peril. In 1915 troops were used in Colorado to guard property and maintain order in the strike region. Army officers are also often used for various engineering projects of the government, such as making surveys and the building of the Panama Canal.

87. Cost of War in Time of Peace. — The average annual army appropriations for the eight years just preceding the Spanish-American War amounted to $24,000,000; those for the navy $27,500,000. In 1914 the military establishment (including river and harbor improvements) amounted to $173,500,000; naval establishment, $139,600,000; pensions $173,400,000; and interest on public debt, $22,800,000. Thus more than

AUTOMOBILE MACHINE GUN.
It is leaving New York for the military training camp at Plattsburg.

half a billion dollars is spent annually because of wars past and future. This is more than two-thirds of the total revenue of the National government exclusive of postal receipts.

NAVY DEPARTMENT

88. The Secretary of the Navy has the administration of his department distributed among the following seven bureaus: navigation, yards and docks, ordnance, construction and repair, steam engineering, medicine and surgery, and supplies and accounts. The United States Naval Academy at Annapolis educates officers for the navy.[1] The navy consists of several hundred vessels and about 50,000 men, plus a marine corps of 10,000. Enlistments for the navy are for four years. The vessels are distributed between the Atlantic fleet and the Pacific fleet, each under the command of a Rear Admiral.

Copyright, Underwood & Underwood, N. Y.

ATLANTIC FLEET.

Viewed from U. S. S. Wyoming by the Conference of Governors.

---

[1] Midshipmen are recommended by representatives, senators, and delegates of the territories, and appointed by the Secretary of the Navy; each representative, senator, and delegate being allowed three. In addition to these, the President appoints two for the District of Columbia and one for Porto Rico, and he also annually appoints ten at large from the United States. Fifteen enlisted men of the Navy or Marine Corps who pass highest on competitive examination are appointed by the Secretary of the Navy each year.

Appointees must be between sixteen and twenty years of age, and must pass entrance examinations similar to those required for West Point. The course is four years. Midshipmen are paid $600 annually from the date of admission, and at graduation they are commissioned as ensigns.

NUMBER OF VESSELS IN THE UNITED STATES NAVY

TYPE	FIT FOR SERVICE JANUARY 1, 1916	UNDER CONSTRUC- TION JANUARY 1, 1916	AUTHOR- IZED BY ACT OF AUGUST 29, 1916	TOTAL
Battleships, first line . . .	8	9	10	27
Battleships, second line . .	25			25
Battle Cruisers			6	6
Armored Cruisers	10			10
Cruisers, first class . . .	5			5
Cruisers, second class . .	4		10	14
Cruisers, third class . . .	16			16
Monitors	7			7
Destroyers	41	17	50	108
Coast torpedo vessels . .	16			16
Torpedo boats	19			19
Submarines	35	38	70[1]	143
Tenders to torpedo vessels .	8		3	11
Gunboats	29		2	31
Transports	4	1	1	6
Supply ships	4	1		5
Hospital ships	1		1	2
Fuel ships	20	2	3	25
Converted yachts	14			14
Tugs	48	2		50
Special type	8		3	11
Unserviceable for war pur- poses	21			21
Total	343	70	159	572

The President is commander-in-chief of the navy, as of the army. The Secretary of the Navy, like the Secretary of War, is usually taken from civil life. Strategical and tactical matters are under the control of a General Board, corresponding to the General Staff of the Army. The Naval War College at Newport prepares officers for the General Board as the Army War College prepares them for the General Staff.

[1] Including two authorized previous to January 1, 1916.

DEPARTMENT OF JUSTICE

89. The Attorney-General, head of the Department of Justice, has been a member of the President's Cabinet since 1789, but the department was not established until 1870. Besides giving legal advice to the President and heads of the other departments he is prosecuting attorney for the government, directs the administration of the federal court system, and supervises federal prisons.

THE FEDERAL PRISON AT FORT LEAVENWORTH, KANSAS.

As Prosecuting Attorney the Attorney-General seldom appears in court in person. His numerous assistants prepare cases and represent him in court. One, known as the "chief trust buster," prosecutes those accused of violating the anti-trust laws of the United States; another represents the government in all suits brought against the United States in the Court of Claims; another has charge of cases arising out of the administration of our customs laws; and so the work is divided.

As Director of the Federal Court System the Attorney-General is consulted by the President in the appointment of federal district attorneys and federal district marshals. After these officers are appointed by the President they are under the direction of the Attorney-General.

As Director of Federal Prisons the Attorney-General not only provides for the detention and support of federal prisoners,[1] but supervises the paroling of prisoners, examines petitions for pardons, except those of military prisoners, and makes recommendations to the President.

The Secret Service of the Department investigates such breaches of the federal law as violations of the national banking laws, anti-trust laws, bucket-shop laws, Chinese smuggling, customs and internal revenue frauds, and post-office frauds.

POST-OFFICE DEPARTMENT

90. The Postmaster-General is the head of the Post-Office Department, which was advanced from a bureau of the treasury

WASHINGTON CITY POST-OFFICE, WITH UNION STATION ADJOINING.
The location of this building obviates the necessity of hauling the mail to and from the station.

---

[1] See Sec. 69, note.

department to an independent department in 1829. He awards contracts for the transportation of mails, appoints departmental employees and fourth-class postmasters subject to the civil service rules, and sends the name of the person passing the highest civil service examination for first-, second-, and third-class post-masters [1] to the President, who, with the consent of the Senate, appoints them. The work of the department is divided among four bureaus with an assistant postmaster-general over each.

The department is approximately self-sustaining; but it works at a great disadvantage because Congress controls postage rates and salaries of employees, and it is often governed more by political expediency than by economy and efficiency.

Copyright, Underwood & Underwood, N. Y.

CLERKS ASSORTING MAIL IN RAILWAY MAIL CAR.

The Franking Privilege. — The privilege extended to congressmen and officials in the administrative departments whereby they may mail official letters and other articles such as the Congressional Record, reports, documents, and packages of seed free of postage is known as the "franking privilege." This privilege is much abused, especially in campaign years. Campaign literature is printed for congressmen in the government printing office at actual cost

---

[1] Postmasters are graded into classes according to the receipts of the office. First-class postmasters receive an annual salary of $3000 or more ; second class, between $2000 and $3000 ; third class, between $1000 and $2000 ; and fourth-class postmasters receive less than $1000 a year, the amount being graded according to stamp cancellation.

and then sent broadcast to voters at the expense of the government. During the fiscal year 1912 more than 300,000,000 pieces of mail, weighing about 61,000,000 pounds, were carried by the postal service free of charge under the franks of congressmen and of the various government establishments. If postage at the usual rates had been paid on this matter, the postal revenues would have been increased by more than $20,000,000. If the government should issue special stamps in limited quantities to congressmen this abuse would be ended.

Copyright, Underwood & Underwood, N. Y.

STAMP PRINTING MACHINE.

These machines are located in the Bureau of Printing and Engraving, and each prints, gums, perforates, and coils 350,000 stamps daily.

91. Improvements in the Service. — Among the improvements made in our postal service during the past half century the following might be mentioned : registration of letters with insurance not exceeding $50, free delivery, money orders, one-cent post cards, two-cent postage at home and to many distant countries, special delivery, rural free delivery, postal-savings banks, and parcel post. It is advocated that the telegraph and express business be monopolized by the United States government as has already been done by the governments of England and many other countries.

92. Prohibited Articles. — Lottery tickets, whiskey, obscene literature, and all things which are likely to injure other mail are excluded from the mails ; and further, when any person or firm attempts to procure money or property through the mails by fraudulent schemes, the privileges of the mails are withdrawn from the offender.

If the Postmaster-General decides that a business is fraudulent he issues a " fraud order " to the local postmaster and to the person accused, whereupon the postmaster stamps the word " fraudulent " upon all letters addressed to the accused and returns them to the writers if there are return addresses upon the envelopes ; if not, they are sent to the Dead Letter Office in Washington, where all unclaimed letters are sent to be opened and forwarded to the address found inside.

Recently a fraudulent firm, under the name of the National Mail Order Brokerage Exchange, mailed letters from Minneapolis offering a $ 4.50 silk petticoat for ten cents in silver on condition that the purchaser notify five friends of the offer, and request each one of them to do likewise.   More than 500,000 orders were received at the Minneapolis office, but the promoters received comparatively few of them, as an investigation by the postal authorities frightened the swindlers away.   It has cost the government thousands of dollars to handle and return these letters.   If these fakers are ever captured a term awaits them in the federal prison.

BIBLIOGRAPHY

FAIRLIE, J. A.   The National Administration of the United States of America.   1905.
HASKIN, F. J.   The American Government.   1912.
The Congressional Directory.
Annual Report of the Secretary of War.
Annual Report of the Secretary of the Navy.
Annual Report of the Attorney-General.
Annual Report of the Postmaster-General.

QUESTIONS ON THE TEXT

1. What are the duties of the Secretary of War?

2. What are the duties of the Adjutant-General? Inspector-General? Surgeon-General? Paymaster-General? Chief of Engineers? Chief of Ordnance? Judge-Advocate-General?

3. Why was the General Staff created? Of whom does it consist? What are its duties?

4. What is the Army War College? Of whom does it consist?

5. What information is kept by this college?

6. Of what forces is the United States army composed? Is your father a member?

7. For what purposes may the President use the army in times of peace?

8. What is the cost of war in times of peace?

9. What are the duties of the Secretary of the Navy?

10. How are naval cadets appointed? What pay do they receive while they are being educated?

11. What officer commands a fleet?

12. Who is commander-in-chief of the navy?

13. What is the purpose of the General Board?

14. What are the duties of the Attorney-General?

15. How is the work of the Department of Justice divided?

16. What are the duties of the Secret Service of the Department of Justice?

17. What are the duties of the Postmaster-General? What salaries are paid postmasters?

18. What is meant by the *franking privilege?*

19. What improvements have been made in the postal service during the past fifty years?

20. What articles are excluded from the mails?

21. What is a *fraud order*, and by whom is it issued?

QUESTIONS FOR DISCUSSION

1. Mention some purposes for which you think the army could be used other than those for which it is now used.

2. The Secretary of the Navy reported that seventeen cruisers and some other vessels (not "battleships") could be used in time of peace to carry mail and commerce to South America. Do you favor the recommendation? Why?

3. Until shortly before the Civil War every private in the navy received his grog ration. Later, privates were forbidden to bring intoxicants on board. In 1914 the restriction was made to include officers. Explain why the dangers from intoxicants became more apparent with our more complex machinery.

4. A single war vessel of the super-dreadnaught type costs about $20,000,000, or enough to pave a thousand miles of road which would last about twice as long as the vessel. Is not the fact that nations seem to find it necessary to waste such large amounts a great reflection upon civilization and Christianity? How do you think the need of so many war vessels might be avoided? Do you favor building vessels in private shipbuilding yards, as most of them are built at present, or in government yards where the Secretary of the Navy thinks they can be built more cheaply?

5. The best corporation lawyers in the Department of Justice are frequently offered higher salaries by commercial corporations who have been prosecuted by lawyers of said department. This means that the private corporations have better attorneys to represent them in court than the people of the United States have to represent them. How would you meet this situation?

6. Name some crimes the perpetrators of which would be prosecuted by the Department of Justice.

7. The National Advisory Board, composed of scientists and inventors who are to give the Navy Department expert advice, unanimously passed a resolution that the government establish a large laboratory to test the many plans that inventors suggest. The cost of such a laboratory would be about $5,000,000, and half that sum additional annually to keep it going. Mr. Edison proposes that it be enclosed in a walled city in order to secure secrecy. Are you in favor of such a plan?

8. In 1897 rural free deliverymen received a salary of $300 a year. In 1898 they received $400; 1900, $500; 1902, $600; 1904, $720; 1907, $900; 1911, $1000; 1912, $1100; and 1914, $1200. Why do you suppose Congress has increased the salary of these rural free deliverymen more rapidly than that of other government employees?

9. When a new post-office building is erected in a small town the janitor for the new building often costs as much as the rent of the former quarters. This appears extravagant. On the other hand, a new well-ventilated and lighted building of pleasing architecture may inspire the people of the town with respect for the government and

for other civic improvements. Do you favor a government-owned post-office even if it costs more than a rented one ?

10. Learn from your postmaster what is included in first-, second-, and third-class mail, and the rates on each. What articles can be sent by parcel post? Can you insure a parcel? Send it by special delivery? Send it C. O. D.?

11. If it were not that newspapers and magazines are carried for less than cost, penny postage on letters could be introduced. Do you think this change would be wise?

12. On R. F. D. routes each home has a letter box. In the city a box is not required. Do you think it should be? Have you any other suggestions as to the more economical handling of the mail?

13. It has been discovered that the farmers who produce much of the food consumed in New York City get for their products only 40 per cent as much as the consumer pays for them. How can the National Government help to remedy this situation?

CHAPTER XII

INTERIOR, AGRICULTURE, COMMERCE, AND LABOR DEPARTMENTS

DEPARTMENT OF THE INTERIOR

93. The Secretary of the Interior is the head of the Department of the Interior, which department grew out of the large accession of territory following the Mexican War. In 1849 various functions were withdrawn from the other departments to form this new department of unrelated governmental bureaus and divisions, of which the following now exist: government lands, geological survey, reclamation, mines, Indians, education, patents, and pensions.

A recent Secretary of the Interior, realizing the difficulty of supervising such unrelated bureaus, recommended that *patents* be placed under the department then known as the Department of Commerce and Labor; *pensions* under the War and Navy Departments; and that the remaining functions be consolidated with the Agricultural Department. This, however, has not as yet been done.

94. The General Land Office, the most important bureau of the department, has charge of the patrolling, surveying, and sale of several hundred million acres of public lands of the United States. In the past large tracts have been sold to land speculation companies, given to railroad corporations in order to promote the construction of railroads and thus develop the country, given to States for public schools, agricultural colleges, and internal improvements; but gradually the practice of giving a 160-acre homestead free, or for a small fee, to any person who will live on it has gained favor. The

167

present policy is to preserve government lands containing minerals, timber, or water-power, and to give title to the surface of the land only.

95. The Geological Survey, during the past thirty years, has made topographic and geologic maps of more than one-third of the surface of the United States; and because of this work

we not only know the height of hills and the volume of water which flows in streams, but we know where valuable minerals occur below the surface.

· As an illustration of the value of this work, a few years ago when the Lackawanna Railroad relocated thirty-four miles of its main line the engineer of construction sat comfortably at his office desk and ran all the preliminary surveys, and even made the final location for the $12,000,000 improvement from the data contained on the topographic sheet.

UNITED STATES GEOLOGICAL SURVEYOR AT WORK.

· **96. The Reclamation Bureau's** most important work is irrigating the desert places of the Western States. By an act of Congress passed in 1902 a fund received from the sale of public lands in certain Western States, except five per cent set aside for educational purposes, is to be used permanently for the reclamation of arid lands. In 1913 the fund was about $82,000,000. Some idea of the vastness of this work can be gathered from the fact that in one Colorado plant a tunnel six miles long had to be dug through a mountain. The reclaimed land is sold to farmers in forty-acre tracts on easy terms, and the money derived therefrom is used in the furtherance of this work.

97. The Commissioner of Indian Affairs has charge of the lands, moneys, schools, and general welfare of 300,000 Indians now living on reservations in the United States. As soon as Indians become able to perform the social, political, and legal duties of citizens they are given tracts of land and made responsible as other citizens ; but the land which is assigned them may not be sold for a certain number of years, at the end of which time it is hoped they will not squander the proceeds. After that, each will have to " hoe his own row " as any other citizen of the State in which he lives.

98. The Bureau of Education is " a national clearing house " for educational information. The annual report of the Commissioner of Education contains extensive statistics of colleges, and of common and high schools. This report also contains accounts of experiments made in some one State. For example, if a certain community makes an exceptional success in the transportation of pupils to rural schools, the bureau will have experts investigate the details, and print the findings for educators all over the country.

99. The Bureau of Patents, with a Commissioner of Patents at its head, issues patents and registers trade-marks, prints, labels, and the like. More than a million patents have been granted by the United States, including 8000 by women and 500 by colored persons.

Among the early important patents are Eli Whitney's cotton gin (1793) and Robert Fulton's steam-boat (1809). When the Wright Brothers invented the biplane air-ship they took out numerous patents, one covering every variety of the invention, so that no one else could manufacture a biplane similar to their invention without paying a royalty. Thomas A. Edison has more than three hundred patents. He spends about $ 300,000 annually on experiments carried on in his laboratories. Some corporations purchase all promising patents offered them, using those which will save them money and keeping the others so that competing corporations may not be able to use them.

Any American, and any foreigner whose native country protects American inventions, by the payment of a $35 fee, is given the exclusive right to manufacture the patented article for seventeen years.[1]   On filing an application for a patent $15 must be paid, and the additional $20 is paid if the patent is granted.   The applicant for the patent must declare to the Commissioner of Patents that he is the real inventor of the article described by drawings, or by a model if the commissioner demands it.

When a new patent is applied for, it requires considerable research to know whether a prior patent is being infringed. To facilitate this research the bureau is divided into a number of divisions.   If, for example, application is made for a patent upon a trap of any kind it is referred to the division which examines nothing but traps.   In obtaining a patent a patent-attorney is not essential, but a good one is valuable for the reason that if one's claims are rejected, an attorney can often suggest other claims which will persuade the patent clerks that the invention really contains a new idea.   However, if by error the patent office grants a second patent for the same invention the owner of the first patent can have the Commissioner of Patents or the Federal Courts declare the second patent void.

The United States reciprocates with all the principal nations of the world for copyrights and patents by treaty or other agreement.   A copyright attorney or patent attorney can obtain copyrights or patents for an author or inventor simultaneously in the various countries.   A fee must be paid to each country.

100. The Pension Office examines applications for pensions and makes recommendations to Congress, which body votes all money for pensions.   Of the more than 800,000 pensioners,

---

[1] Rights are secured to heirs and assignees of inventors.

half a million are federal veterans of the Civil War. Others fought in the Spanish War, Mexican War, or served in the army or navy in times of peace. In 1913, there were on the list 199 widows of veterans of the War of 1812. Because of the Civil War alone the National government has paid between $4,000,- 000,000 and $5,000,000,000 in pensions through this office.

DEPARTMENT OF AGRICULTURE

101. The Secretary of Agriculture is the head of the Department of Agriculture, which, until 1889, was the Bureau of

Copyright, Underwood & Underwood, N. Y.

ONE WING OF THE AGRICULTURAL DEPARTMENT BUILDING, WASHINGTON, D. C.

The main building is not yet erected, the entire appropriation having been spent upon the two wings.

Agriculture in the Department of the Interior. The functions of the department are divided among the following bureaus and divisions: animal industry, plant industry, weather, forest service, soils, chemistry, entomology, biological survey, crop estimates, state relations, roads and rural engineering, markets and rural organization, insecticide and fungicide, horticulture, publications, library.

102. The Bureau of Animal Industry regulates the national quarantine for live stock, studies animal diseases, inspects animals before slaughter and the meat after they have been slaughtered. By experiments in the breeding and feeding of live stock and poultry it has discovered that about one fourth of the dairy cows of the United States do not pay for their feed, and if the bureau's directions were followed as to the best breeds of chickens to keep and how to feed them it is estimated that the increased annual value of eggs would be $50,000,000.

103. The Bureau of Plant Industry among its various discoveries has shown us that the fungus which causes cedar rust upon apples must have each alternate generation on the red cedar; thus, by destroying all red cedars fruit growers are able to keep their orchards clean of this once dreaded disease. This bureau also ransacks the world for new crops suitable to the American soils.

104. The Weather Bureau receives reports from stations all over the United States, from hundreds of vessels, and from foreign countries. Storm warnings save millions of dollars invested in vessels besides many lives; frost warnings serve the growers of fruit and vegetables; flood forecasts, often a week in advance, enable farmers to save live stock and other property. Freezing forecasts enable railroads to save perishables in transit, greenhouses to fire their boilers, gasoline engines to be drained, concrete work to be stopped, coal dealers to supply partial orders to all instead of full orders to a few, ice factories to reduce their output, and merchants to curtail their advertising. Rain forecasts protect the raisin crop, enable fruit growers and farmers to harvest and shelter crops, protect the manufacturer of lime, cement, and brick, as well as photographers. Humidity forecasts are useful to silk and candy manufacturers.

105. The Forest Service has charge of national forest reserves — now about 200,000,000 acres. The forests are constantly patroled by forest-service rangers, who prevent destructive fires and the stealing of timber. Large areas are planted with trees suitable to the climate and soil of the particular regions.

106. The Entomology Division combats insects which are a menace to crops, animals, and persons. It imports harmless insects which prey upon harmful insects.

The Biological Survey is carried on under the Entomology Division and investigates the relations of birds and mammals to the work of farmers and stockmen.

107. The Bureau of Chemistry has an important duty in connection with the pure food laws. It determines which foods are adulterated with poisonous elements and with ingredients that give little or no nourishment. When Dr. H. W. Wiley was chief of this bureau he had a " poison squad " who tested the effects of foods by eating large quantities and studying the effects upon their own systems.

DEPARTMENT OF COMMERCE

108. The Secretary of Commerce is the head of the Department of Commerce. This department gathers census statistics; regulates standards and measures; propagates and distributes fishes; maintains light-houses; supervises navigable waters, coast and geodetic survey work, and steam-boat inspection. One bureau of this department, the census bureau, demands further mention.

The Census Bureau enumerates the population of the United States every ten years in order to apportion representation in the House of Representatives and presidential electors among the States. In 1910 more than 70,000 enumerators counted the people according to race, sex, and age, and collected many other facts, such as agricultural statistics. Several years are required to tabulate the statistics gathered each decade. Between the periods for the decennial censuses various other special reports are made on agricultural, vital, and other statistics. Every fifth year an investigation of all manufacturing industries is made. (See Sec. 6, 4 *f.*)

DEPARTMENT OF LABOR

109. The Secretary of Labor has a portion of the functions performed by the Secretary of Commerce and Labor until 1913, when the Department of Commerce and Labor was divided, with a few new functions added. The purpose of the new department is to foster, promote, and develop the welfare

Copyright, Underwood & Underwood, N. Y.
ELLIS ISLAND.

of wage earners in the United States, to improve their working conditions, and to advance their opportunities for profitable employment. The department has a bureau of immigration, a bureau of naturalization, a bureau of labor statistics, and a children's bureau.

110. The Bureau of Immigration. — The Commissioner-General of Immigration is charged with the reception of all immigrants, three-fourths of whom enter at the port of New York (Ellis Island). Adults, with a few exceptions, are required to read forty words of some language; a head tax of $8.00 is collected, and all steerage passengers must undergo a physical examination and comply with various other regulations.

Our immigration law excludes persons mentally defective or those likely to become public charges, such as children without parents, persons with contagious diseases or physical defects, criminals, polygamists, anarchists, immoral women, and laborers brought to this country by contractors. All Chinese and other Orientals are excluded unless they are citizens of the United States, merchants, travellers, or students. We aim merely to exclude the coolie class of Chinese, and many of these get in secretly from Canada and Mexico. The steamboat companies must take back without charge any passengers that are excluded.

111. Bureau of Naturalization. — In order that immigrants to this country may become citizens of the United States in the prescribed manner only, the government maintains a bureau of naturalization. This bureau keeps records of immigrants and sees that they become naturalized according to law.

Whites, American Indians, and Africans may become naturalized in the following manner:[1] (1) The applicant for citizenship appears before a court of record (federal or State) at least two years before admission to citizenship and declares on oath his or her intention to become a citizen and renounces allegiance to any other government. This application is recorded and the applicant is furnished a copy of the record.

---

[1] The Texans were naturalized *en masse* by a joint resolution of Congress. In 1848 the President and the Senate, by means of a treaty with Mexico, naturalized the citizens of the ceded territory, except those who chose to remain citizens of Mexico. Inhabitants of Louisiana (1803) and of a portion of Maine (1842) and Indians have been admitted by treaty. Indians remaining in States when their tribes moved West have also been naturalized *en masse* by statute.

The wife and minor children of a naturalized male citizen become citizens through his naturalization. If a mother becomes naturalized her minor children likewise become citizens. Children born abroad to citizens of the United States, whether native born or naturalized, are American citizens.

(2) Two years later the applicant must appear in court, show proof that he has resided in the United States for five years, and in the State where he is appearing before the court for at least one year, and that he is a person of good moral character. (3) He must take an oath to support the Constitution of the

FUTURE CITIZENS OF AMERICA.

Armenians rescued from Turkish massacres arriving at Ellis Island.

United States and renounce allegiance to any foreign government. In case he, has any title of nobility it must be renounced. These facts are recorded by the clerk of the court and a certificate of naturalization is granted.

112. The Children's Bureau investigates the labor conditions under which children work; also the care and training of infants and children. This bureau is the first United States bureau to have a woman at its head.

BIBLIOGRAPHY

FAIRLIE, J. A.   The National Administration of the United States of
America.   1905.
HASKIN, F. J.   The American Government.   1912.
The Congressional Directory.
The Yearbook of the Department of Agriculture.
Annual Report of the Secretary of the Interior.
Annual Report of the Secretary of Agriculture.
Annual Report of the Secretary of Commerce.
Annual Report of the Secretary of Labor.
Annual Report of the Commissioner of Education.
Bulletins of the Bureau of Education.   A list of such bulletins can
be obtained from the Commissioner of Education, Washington,
D. C., and most of the bulletins will be furnished free.

QUESTIONS ON THE TEXT

1. When was the Department of the Interior created?   What
bureaus are under this department?

2. What are the duties of the General Land Office?   The Geo-
logical Survey?   The Reclamation Bureau?   The Commissioner of
Indian Affairs?   The Bureau of Education?   The Bureau of Patents?
The Pension Office?

3. How may a patent be obtained?

4. Into what bureaus and divisions is the Agricultural Department divided?

5. What are the duties of the Bureau of Animal Industry?
Bureau of Plant Industry?   The Weather Bureau?   Forest Service?
The Entomology Division?   Bureau of Chemistry?

6. What are the different bureaus of the Department of
Commerce?

7. What functions are performed by the Census Bureau of the
Department of Commerce?

8. What are the duties of the Secretary of Labor?

9. What are the duties of the Bureau of Immigration?

10. What tax is imposed upon immigrants entering the United
States?

11. What classes of persons are excluded from the United States?

12. What persons may become naturalized?   How?

13. How did the Texans become naturalized? The inhabitants of Louisiana in 1803? Certain Indians?

14. What is the purpose of the Children's Bureau?

15. In what respect does the administration of the Children's Bureau differ from that of any other?

QUESTIONS FOR DISCUSSION

1. If you desired to construct an electric power plant along some river how would you learn how much power you could produce during the different months?

2. Great irrigation plants are being constructed in the West. Would it be possible for you to irrigate your farm, orchard, or garden?

3. Last year the United States paid $175,000,000 in pensions to 820,200 persons, principally to Union Civil War veterans and their widows. The number of such pensions will gradually decrease. Should we follow the example of England and give a small pension to all persons above seventy years of age?

4. What use do you make of the government weather report?

5. If you live on a farm do you get government bulletins giving experiments on growing the crops that you grow and the cattle that you raise?

6. Why is a knowledge of the habits of birds — e.g., food supply — so important to farmers?

7. For centuries it was believed that there was no practical limit to the number of fish in the lakes and bays. To-day countries find it necessary to restrict the catching of fish and to hatch fish to replenish the lakes and bays. If there were no governments to replenish this great source of food could private individuals be depended upon to do it? Where can you get a supply of minnows for your lake or stream?

8. In 1914 there reached our shores 1,197,892 immigrants, together with about 140,000 persons who were not classed as immigrants. Why is the immigration bureau under the Department of Labor?

CHAPTER XIII

BOARDS AND COMMISSIONS

113. Why Boards and Commissions are Created. — In addition to the ten administrative departments, whose heads are members of the President's cabinet, various independent boards and commissions have been created to relieve the pressure of business on the President and Congress. Boards and commissions have been created instead of additional administrative departments (1) because the duties to be performed require experts whose terms of office should not depend upon the political fortune of the President, and (2) because their duties require the deliberation of a board rather than the opinion of one individual.

The following boards and commissions are discussed in the order in which they were created.

114. Commissioners for the District of Columbia. — The Constitution of the United States gives Congress power to exercise exclusive legislation over the District of Columbia in all cases whatsoever. Previous to 1874 Congress permitted the District to be governed by elective officials, elections being held there the same as in the States. Elections became so corrupt — a fact partly due to the vote of inexperienced negroes — that Congress abolished the council form of government and provided for its government by Congress and commissioners.[1]

Since 1874 the District has been administered by three commissioners, two of whom are appointed for terms of three years

---

[1] Since 1874 the inhabitants of the District of Columbia have been excluded from all suffrage, not even being permitted to vote for presidential electors. However, a large proportion of the population consists of government employees who may return to their home States to vote.

by the President and Senate of the United States, and one engineer detailed by the President from the United States army to serve for an indefinite period. Other officers are likewise appointed by the President. These three commissioners administer the municipal departments, such as schools, police,

MUNICIPAL BUILDING, WASHINGTON, D. C.

In this building the offices of the District of Columbia Government are located.

and public health. They recommend needed legislation, but Congress is the only legislative body of the District.

All bills relating to the governing of the District are considered by committees, usually by the House Committee and the Senate Committee on the District of Columbia, or by the House Committee and the Senate Committee on Appropriations. It is at public hearings of these committees that the people of the District make their wishes known. Congress appropriates one half of the expenses of the District from the Treasury of the

United States on the assumption that about one half of the property within the District belongs to the United States, but the other half of the expenses is paid by taxing the inhabitants.

115. The Civil Service. — The Constitution of the United States provides that Congress may by law vest the appointment of such inferior officers as they think proper in the President alone, in the courts of law, or in the heads of departments. (See Sec. 64.) Congress vested the appointment of most inferior officers in the President or in the heads of departments. From the time of Andrew Jackson's administration until the past few decades, the President and heads of departments appointed members of their own political parties, giving little consideration to qualifications, and turning out of office those of the opposing party. This practice was known as the "spoils system."[1]

The Civil Service Act of 1883, subsequent laws of Congress, and executive orders of the President have gradually increased the number of persons securing permanent positions by competitive examinations, until to-day about a quarter of a million employees of the government secure their appointments in this manner. A President may issue orders providing that certain classes of employees shall be appointed in accordance with civil service examinations. For instance, President Taft issued such an order covering all fourth-class postmasters, Roosevelt having issued one applying to those of fourteen States.

The President can do this because the right to make appointments belongs either to him or else to the heads of departments, whom he can remove; hence they are practically compelled to make appointments according to civil service examinations if the President so orders. If a President should be opposed to the civil service plan he could revoke the orders of former Presidents and again bring most of the civil service positions under the spoils system.

---

[1] In 1832 when President Jackson was criticized for removing political opponents from office, William L. Marcy in defending the action of the President said, "to the victors belong the spoils of the enemy."

Even employees who have entered the service of the government as a result of civil service examinations may be dismissed for incompetency, but because there is no pension for civil employees they are usually kept long after their efficiency is gone, some being wheeled to their desks in roller chairs. It is estimated that one out of every fourteen government employees in Washington is over 65 years of age. It has been suggested that one and a half per cent of the salaries of government employees be deducted for a retirement fund, thus enabling the officials to retire the aged upon pensions.

116. The Civil Service Commission, which was created in 1883, consists of three commissioners appointed by the President and Senate, only two of whom may be of the same political party. The duty of this commission is to prepare examination questions for approximately five hundred kinds of positions and to have examinations conducted at convenient places throughout the Union by government employees of the respective localities. The commission recommends those making the highest grades to appointing officers of the various branches of government which make appointments in accordance with civil service examinations.

When a federal official has a vacancy to be filled the commission sends him the names of the three eligibles for appointment having the highest ratings upon their examination papers, except that military veterans have preference over all others, and that an effort is made to distribute the appointments among the States in proportion to population. If one of the three is selected the two remaining names will again appear among the next three names sent to the appointing officer, and he may not reject a name in order to reach a name further down the list unless he thinks those heading the list are mentally, morally, or physically unfit for the position to be filled.

No senator or representative may recommend any applicant to the commission, though he may show the appointing officer why the person making the highest grade should not be appointed. A period of probation always precedes final appointment. No appointee may be required to contribute to a political fund or to perform political services. The President of the United States may amend or make exceptions to the Civil Service Rules.

117. The Interstate Commerce Commission, created in 1887, consists of nine members appointed by the President and Senate. It has supervision over all common carriers engaged in interstate commerce, such as railroads, steamboats, express companies, sleeping-car companies, telegraph, cable, telephone, wireless-telegraph companies, and pipe lines carrying other commodities than water and gas.

This commission, unlike a court, will interpret interstate commerce laws for shippers or carriers before an actual case has arisen. If any individual has been overcharged for a ticket, or if a railroad is not properly hauling his products, he can complain to this commission, and an investigation will be made involving no expense to the individual who complains. Or large commercial corporations, cities, and towns may make formal complaints of poor service or discrimination in rates.

All interstate freight and passenger rates must be submitted to this commission before going into effect. That it may know what rate will give these interstate companies a fair profit on the money invested, each company is required to have uniform bookkeeping; and in this way the commission may account for all money received, where it comes from, and where it goes.

These companies cannot charge less to some persons than to others for similar service; cannot give any preference to any person, company, or city; nor may they make agreements with other roads or lines for pooling freights and thereby destroying competition. When the commission discovers that any of the foregoing crimes has been committed, the fact is reported to the Attorney-General of the United States, whose duty it is to prosecute the offenders.

118. National Banks, the Federal Reserve Board, and the Federal Farm Loan Board. — *National Banks.* — With the approval of the

Comptroller of the Currency any five or more persons may receive from him a charter of incorporation for a National bank if they can raise the required amount of capital. The minimum capital depends upon the size of the city and varies from $25,000 in places of less than 3000 inhabitants to $200,000 in cities of more than 50,000 inhabitants.

These banks receive deposits from individuals and lend money to individuals. They must be examined by a United States examiner at least twice a year, must make reports to the Comptroller of the Currency at least five times a year — whenever called for — and are required to keep a certain per cent of their deposits always on hand in lawful money and a prescribed per cent in federal reserve banks as a reserve.

Every National bank is a member of the federal reserve bank of the district in which it is located.[1]

Federal Reserve Banks. — The United States is divided into twelve federal reserve districts, and there is one federal reserve bank located in the federal reserve city [2] of each district. These banks were created by Congress in 1913 to put more money into circulation when honest business men need it, and thus prevent "hard times" caused by a lack of money to carry on the business of the country. The Federal Reserve Board authorizes the issue of federal reserve notes [3] to the federal reserve banks, accepting as security certain private notes, drafts, etc., which the federal reserve banks have rediscounted for the member banks.

A federal reserve bank must have at least $4,000,000 capital, and this capital must be subscribed by all member banks. Each reserve bank has a board of nine directors, of whom six are elected by the member banks, each bank having one vote, and three by the federal reserve board. The officers of each reserve bank are chosen by the directors thereof.

---

[1] State banks and trust companies may become members of a federal reserve bank if they conform to most of the regulations governing National banks.

[2] The twelve federal reserve cities are Boston, New York, Philadelphia, Richmond, Atlanta, Cleveland, Minneapolis, Chicago, St. Louis, Dallas, Kansas City, and San Francisco.   [3] See Sec. 80.

The board of directors of each federal reserve bank elects one of its members as a member of the Federal Advisory Council, a body composed of one member from each reserve bank, which meets in Washington at least four times a year to consult, advise, and question the Federal Reserve Board in regard to the business of the reserve banking system.

At the head of our federal reserve banking system is the Federal Reserve Board. This board was created in 1913 by

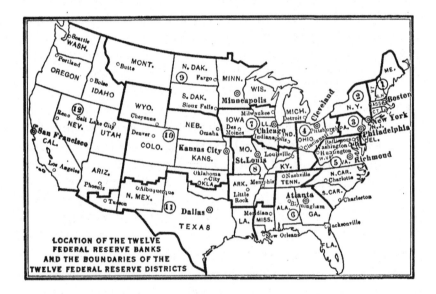

LOCATION OF THE TWELVE
FEDERAL RESERVE BANKS
AND THE BOUNDARIES OF THE
TWELVE FEDERAL RESERVE DISTRICTS

the same act of Congress which provided for the federal reserve banks. It is composed of seven members, five of whom are appointed by the President and Senate for a term of ten years. The Secretary of the Treasury and the Comptroller of the Currency are *ex officio* members, the Secretary of the Treasury being *ex officio* chairman of the board. The salary for each of the appointed members is $12,000 per annum and expenses, and the Comptroller of the Currency receives $7000 in addition to his salary as Comptroller.

The Federal Reserve Board has general supervision of our federal reserve banking system. For instance, it may examine any bank in the system; it regulates, through the Comptroller of the Currency, the issue and retirement of reserve notes, and determines the rate of interest to be paid the government for these notes; it suspends or removes federal reserve bank officers, taking possession of such bank if necessary; and it publishes a weekly statement of the reserve banks. This board has its offices in the Treasury Building at Washington.

Farm Loan Banks. — The federal land bank system, which was created by Congress in 1916, does for the farmer, to some extent, what the federal reserve system does for the commercial man. The farmer is given an opportunity to secure money on his most available commodity — his land — just as the merchant or the manufacturer is able through the federal reserve system to obtain money on paper based on commercial transactions.

The United States is divided into twelve land bank districts[1] with a federal land bank located in each. These twelve banks are supervised by the Federal Farm Loan Board consisting of four members appointed by the President and Senate for terms of eight years and the Secretary of the Treasury, who is a member and *ex-officio* chairman of the board. Each of the four members appointed receives an annual salary of $10,000.

These twelve banks will not, except in special cases, lend money directly to farmers; but there are three ways through which a farmer may borrow money by giving a first mortgage on his farm property. First, any ten owners of farm land who desire to borrow at least $20,000 may form a National Farm Loan Association, and receive the amount desired from the land bank of their district through this agency. Second, the Federal Farm Loan Board may authorize federal land banks to make loans to farmers through local agents, such as State

---

[1] 1. Me., N. H., Vt., Mass., R. I., Conn., N. Y., N. J. (Springfield). 2. Pa., Del., Md., Va., W. Va., D. C. (Baltimore). 3. N. C., S. C., Ga., Fla. (Columbia). 4. Tenn., Ky., Ind., O. (Louisville). 5. Ala., Miss., La. (N. Orleans). 6. Ill., Mo., Ark. (St. Louis). 7. Mich., Minn., Wis., N. D. (St. Paul). 8. Neb., S. D., Wy., Ia. (Omaha). 9. Okla., Kan., Col., N. M. (Wichita). 10. Tex. (Houston). 11. Cal., Nev., Utah, Ariz. (Berkeley). 12. Wash., Ore., Mont., Idaho (Spokane).

banks. Third, joint stock land banks may be created under the supervision of the Federal Farm Loan Board to lend money secured by first mortgages on farm lands.

. The money to be lent to farmers is obtained principally from the sale of bonds which may not bear more than five per cent interest. The money thus obtained is lent through the above agencies at a rate not to exceed six per cent.

Loans are made only for the purchase of land, for its improvement, or for purchase of live stock, equipment, fertilizers, or to provide buildings on a farm, or to liquidate indebtedness existing when the first association was formed in the county where the land is located. No loan is made of more than $10,000 or less than $100. The loan itself is reduced by annual or semi-annual payments on the principal. No mortgage shall run for more than forty years nor less than five.

. **119. The Federal Trade Commission.** — In 1914 Congress created a Federal Trade Commission composed of five commissioners, who are appointed by the President and Senate. Not more than three of the commissioners may be of the same political party. The salary of each commissioner is $10,000 a year.

The powers of the commission are twofold. First, it is empowered to prevent persons, partnerships, or corporations, except banks and common carriers (*e.g.*, railroads),[1] from using unfair methods of competition in commerce among the States or with foreign nations. In performing this duty the Commission has access to the books and documents of a commercial firm whenever there is reason to believe that such a concern is using unfair methods of competition. If any irregularity is discovered the Commission may order the concern to cease using such unfair methods.

The second power of the Commission is to gather and compile information from such commercial corporations as are under its control and require them to furnish the Commission

---

[1] Federal banks are under the control of the Federal Reserve Board and the Comptroller of the Currency. Common carriers are under the control of the Interstate Commerce Commission.

with detailed reports of their transactions.   It also makes investigations for the Attorney-General, the President, or Congress, concerning violations of the anti-trust laws ; it classifies corporations and makes rules and regulations to assist the commission in the performance of its duties; it investigates trade conditions in and with foreign countries ; and it submits to Congress recommendations for additional legislation.

As an illustration of the Commission's investigation of trade conditions, it has just investigated how manufacturers of European countries combine in order to capture foreign trade. As a result of this investigation it was found that manufacturers of these countries form selling agencies which send representatives to foreign countries to advertise and to obtain orders. The orders are distributed among the manufacturers in proportion to the amount paid toward the maintenance of the agency. By thus coöperating, orders can be obtained on a large scale at much less cost than if each manufacturer attempted to maintain his own agents in foreign countries.

120. United States Shipping Board. — In 1916 Congress established the United States Shipping Board. This board consists of five commissioners appointed by the President and Senate for terms of six years, and each member receives a salary of $7500 per annum.

The board has three general lines of duty:

(1) It investigates and reports to Congress means by which American shipping can be developed.

(2) It regulates carriers by water engaged in the foreign and interstate commerce of the United States. For instance, it prevents discriminatory rates; and it sees that no "fighting ships" (ships run at a loss to destroy a competitor) are operated for the purpose of driving a competing line out of business.

(3) It has authority, with the approval of the President, to charter, lease, purchase, or have constructed vessels suitable for commerce and for naval and military purposes. These ships may be rechartered, re-leased, or resold to American citizens

under such conditions as the board prescribes.[1] For example, the President may at any time make use of these vessels for naval and military purposes by compensating the persons who hold them.

For the purpose of carrying into effect this shipping program; the board may issue United States bonds to an amount not exceeding $50,000,000.

Copyright, Underwood & Underwood, N. Y.

THE LIBRARY OF CONGRESS, WASHINGTON, D. C.
It has the most beautiful interior of any American building.

The United States Tariff Commission. — In 1916 the United States Tariff Commission was established by Congress. It is composed of six members, not more than three of whom shall

---

[1] If these vessels cannot be rechartered, re-leased, or resold the board may form corporations, in which the United States must take a majority of the capital stock, to operate these or other vessels. The total stock of such corporations may not exceed $50,000,000 and the corporations will cease to exist five years after the end of the European War.

be of the same political party, appointed by the President and Senate for terms of twelve years. Each member receives a salary of $7500 per annum.

The commission is given wide powers to investigate the administration and financial and industrial effects of the customs laws of the United States, various tariff relations between the United States and foreign countries, and international tariff agreements in Europe. This information is collected for the benefit of the President, the Ways and Means Committee of the House, and the Finance Committee of the Senate in order that Congress may legislate more wisely upon the tariff problem, and thus remove it as far as possible from politics.

Other Institutions Administered by Executive Officials. — The following institutions are administered by executive officials independently of the ten administrative departments or of the eight boards and commissions just described: Government Printing Office, Library of Congress,[1] Smithsonian Institution, National Museum, and International Bureau of American Republics.

BIBLIOGRAPHY

DODD, W. F. Government of the District of Columbia. 1909.
FAIRLIE, J. A. The National Administration of the United States of America. 1905.
HASKIN, F. J. The American Government. 1912.
The Congressional Directory.
Annual Report of the United States Civil Service Commission.
Proceedings of the National Civil Service Reform League.

---

[1] Subordinate to the Librarian of Congress is the Register of Copyrights, whose office is in the Library of Congress building in Washington. When a book is published the notice of copyright should be printed on the title page or the page following. Promptly after publication two copies of the best edition must be sent to the register with an application for registration and a money order for one dollar payable to the Register of Copyrights. Application forms will be furnished upon request. For a work of art a photograph is sent. For photographs the fee is only 50 cents if a certificate of registration is not desired; for anything else the fee is one dollar. Only one copy of lectures and dramatic or musical compositions not to be published need be sent. (See Sec. 47.)

Questions on the Text

1. Why have boards and commissions been created independent of administrative departments?

2. By whom is the District of Columbia administered? Who legislates for the district? Do the inhabitants of the district have any right of suffrage?

3. About how many employees of the United States secure their employment through competitive examinations?

4. What is the *spoils system?*

5. When was the Civil Service Commission created? Composed of how many members? By whom appointed?

6. What are the duties of the Civil Service Commission? Through what local agents do they conduct examinations?

7. What are the more important civil service rules?

8. May civil service employees be dismissed?

9. When was the Interstate Commerce Commission created? Of how many members does it consist? By whom are they appointed? What are the duties of the commission?

10. When the commission discovers that a corporation has violated a law to what United States officer is the fact reported?

11. When was the Federal Reserve Act passed? How many federal reserve banks are there? Where is the one nearest you?

12. From whom do the federal reserve banks receive deposits? When they lend money to member banks, what security must be given?

13. What banks are members of a federal reserve bank? How may a bank become a member?

14. When was the Federal Farm Loan Board created? How many federal farm loan banks are there? How do they differ from the federal reserve banks?

15. What is the Federal Trade Commission? When was it created? Of how many members is it composed? By whom are they appointed? What are the duties of the commission?

16. What are the duties of the United States Shipping Board?

17. What are the duties of the United States Tariff Commission?

18. Name some institutions administered independently of the administrative departments, boards, and commissions just described.

19. How may a copyright be obtained?

QUESTIONS FOR DISCUSSION

1. The District of Columbia is perhaps the only civilized capital in the world whose inhabitants have absolutely no rights of suffrage, yet Washington is well governed. Do you consider that Congress acted wisely in depriving the inhabitants of suffrage?

2. In our civil service should promotion be based upon length of service, efficiency of service, or examination?

3. Each State has a commission to regulate railroads within its own borders. The Interstate Commerce Commission regulates railroads extending from one State into another. Would you favor the control of all railroads by the Interstate Commerce Commission alone?

4. Should the Trade Commission have power to permit agreements in restraint of trade if it thinks such agreements beneficial to the public?

5. Of what federal reserve bank are the National banks in your town members?

6. How will the Federal Reserve Act of 1913 prevent "panics" like that of 1907, which resulted from a scarcity or rather hoarding of money?

7. How much money would be necessary to establish a member National bank in your town or city?

Know difference between state & federal courts.

CHAPTER XIV

THE JUDICIAL DEPARTMENT

121. The System of Federal Courts. — The Constitution declares that the judicial power of the United States shall be vested in one Supreme Court and in such inferior courts as Congress may from time to time ordain and establish. Congress has established, and later abolished, various inferior courts, but at present the following federal courts exist:

Regular Courts

One Supreme Court
Nine Circuit Courts of Appeals
Eighty-one District Courts

Special Courts

One Court of Claims
One Court of Customs Appeals

122. The Jurisdiction[1] of Federal Courts. — Cases are tried by federal courts either because of the character of the subject matter of the suit or because of the character of the parties to the suit. Depending upon the subject matter of the suit, the following cases may be tried in federal courts: (1) cases in law or equity[2] arising under the Constitution or statutes of the United States, or treaties made under their authority; (2) cases of admiralty and maritime[3] jurisdiction. Depending upon the

[1] Jurisdiction means the legal right to hear and determine cases. A court is said to have jurisdiction over those cases which it has authority to try.

[2] For meaning of "equity," see Sec. 182, note.

[3] For meaning of "admiralty and maritime," see U. S. Constitution, Art III, Sec. 2, note.

parties to the suit, the following cases may be tried in federal courts: (1) cases affecting ambassadors, other public ministers, and consuls; (2) controversies to which the United States is a party; (3) controversies between two or more States; (4) controversies between a State and citizens of another State;[1] (5) controversies between citizens of different

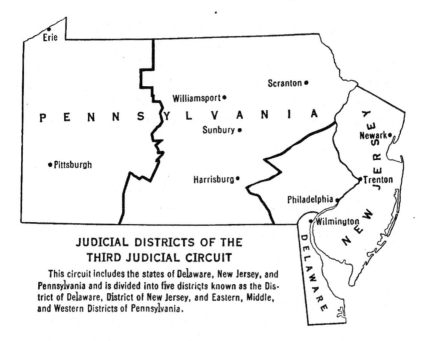

**JUDICIAL DISTRICTS OF THE
THIRD JUDICIAL CIRCUIT**

This circuit includes the states of Delaware, New Jersey, and Pennsylvania and is divided into five districts known as the District of Delaware, District of New Jersey, and Eastern, Middle, and Western Districts of Pennsylvania.

States; and (6) controversies between a State, or citizens thereof, and foreign states, citizens or subjects. ·

123. Regular Courts. — In order to show the proper relation of the different regular courts and how cases may be appealed from the lowest to the highest, the District Courts will be dis-

---

[1] In 1793 in the case of Chisholm *vs.* Georgia the Supreme Court construed this passage to mean that an individual may sue a State without the consent of the latter. The States had not so understood this clause, and immediately the Eleventh Amendment was added to the Constitution, which provides that a State may not be sued in a federal court by citizens of another State. However, a State may still bring suit in a federal court against a citizen of another State or against an alien.

cussed first, the Circuit Courts of Appeals second, and third the Supreme Court, which is the highest court, or the court of final jurisdiction.

The District Courts. — The lowest regular federal courts are known as District Courts. There are eighty-one districts in forty-eight States, each State forming at least one district.[1] As a rule there is one judge for each district, but in several States where there are few federal cases to be tried there is but one judge for two districts, whereas a few important districts require more than one judge each.[2] There are ninety-odd judges for eighty-one districts; and inasmuch as district court cases are conducted by a single judge, several cases can be heard at the same time where there are several judges for one district.

A District Court has original jurisdiction[3] of all civil and criminal cases which come under the jurisdiction of the federal courts,[4] except cases between two States, suits involving rep-

---

[1] Pennsylvania, for example, forms three districts — Eastern, Middle, and Western. The two judges of the Eastern District hold court in Philadelphia; the one of the Middle District holds court at Harrisburg, Sunbury, Williamsport, and Scranton; and the two of the Western District hold court at Pittsburgh and at Erie.

[2] The Northern and Southern districts of Mississippi have but one judge, whereas the Southern District of New York has four judges.

[3] By " original jurisdiction " of a District Court is meant that a case is first brought in that court.

[4] The District Court has jurisdiction of (1) all civil suits brought by the United States or one of its officers authorized to sue; (2) cases arising under the Constitution, statutes, or treaties of the United States where the sum or value in controversy exceeds $3000; (3) cases between citizens of different States, or between a citizen of a State and a foreign state or citizen thereof, where the sum or value in controversy exceeds $3000; (4) all crimes and offences recognized by the laws of the United States; (5) admiralty and maritime cases; (6) revenue cases, except tariff classifications which come before the Court of Customs Appeals; (7) postal cases; (8) all suits arising under the patent, copyright, and trade-mark laws; (9) suits arising under the federal laws regulating commerce (10) damage suits brought by an officer against a person injuring him while protecting or collecting revenues of the United States; (11) suits against consuls and vice-consuls; (12) proceedings in bankruptcy; (13) claims not exceeding $10,000 against the United States (concur-

resentatives of foreign governments, customs cases, and claims against the United States. In most cases appeals may be taken from the decision of a District Court to a Circuit Court of Appeals, but in a few cases may be taken directly to the Supreme Court.[1]

The Circuit Courts of Appeals. — In 1891 there were nine Circuit Courts of Appeals [2] established to relieve the Supreme Court of a large class of cases appealed from the District Courts.[3] These cases had become too numerous for one court to hear, and as a result the Supreme Court was then about three years in arrears with its business.

The judges for each Circuit Court of Appeals include one justice of the Supreme Court assigned to the circuit, two or more circuit judges appointed for the circuit,[4] and all the district judges within the circuit. The Supreme Court justice supervises his circuit, but seldom finds time to sit in the court. Normally the court is held by three regular circuit judges, but any district judge within the circuit may be assigned to sit on

rent jurisdiction with Court of Claims); (14) immigration and contract labor cases; (15) suits against monopolies (trusts); (16) suits brought by any person to redress the deprivation of any right, privilege, or immunity secured by the Constitution or statutes of the United States. But note that if the sum or value involved in cases enumerated under (2) and (3) is less than $3000 the action must be brought in a State court.

[1] Appeals may be taken directly to the Supreme Court (1) when the jurisdiction of the court is at issue; (2) when a federal law or treaty or a State law is claimed to be repugnant to the Constitution of the United States; (3) cases growing out of prizes captured at sea; and (4) certain kinds of injunctions. The first and second classes of cases referred to are allowed to go directly because they are practically sure to reach the Supreme Court sooner or later. The third class goes directly because there is great danger of complications with foreign nations. The fourth class goes directly because of the urgent need for an immediate final decision.

[2] Previous to the establishment of the Circuit Courts of Appeals there existed nine Circuit Courts, but these courts have since been abolished (1909) and their jurisdiction transferred to the District Courts and to the Court of Customs Appeals.

[3] The First Circuit comprises Rhode Island, Massachusetts, New Hampshire, and Maine. The judges hold court at least once a year at Boston.

[4] There are now thirty-nine circuit judges.

any case except those which have been appealed from his own district.

These Circuit Courts of Appeals have no original jurisdiction, but hear all cases appealed from the District Courts except the special classes of cases which may be appealed directly to the Supreme Court of the United States. These courts have final jurisdiction[1] in some classes of cases, while in others appeals may be taken to the Supreme Court of the United States.

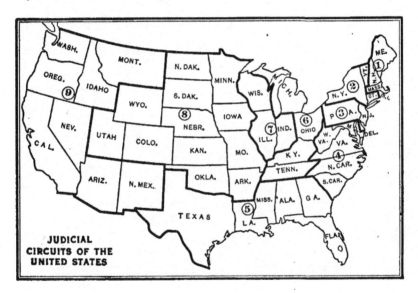

JUDICIAL
CIRCUITS OF THE
UNITED STATES

The Supreme Court is composed of one Chief Justice and eight associate justices. It sits in the Capitol at Washington from October to May of each year, and has both original and appellate jurisdiction. Suits between States and cases in which ambassadors, other public ministers, and consuls are parties originate in this court. Such cases are few, but very important, because States have tempers differing from individuals, and the failure to handle with care cases involving foreign diplomats might involve the United States in war. Nearly all of its cases are appealed from inferior courts, *i.e.* from the

---

[1] By "final jurisdiction" is meant that a case may not be appealed to any higher court.

District Courts, the Circuit Courts of Appeals, the Court of Customs Appeals, the Court of Claims, and the highest court of each State, the District of Columbia, and a territory or island possession.

The most important duty of the Supreme Court is to give a final interpretation to the Constitution of the United States.

THE UNITED STATES SUPREME COURT ROOM.

This view shows the court attendants, counsel, and visitors awaiting the arrival of the judges.

Whenever any person thinks that a clause of the Constitution has been violated by a law of Congress, a treaty, a provision of a State constitution, or a State statute, he can raise the question in any State or federal court from the local justice of the peace to the highest judge, and may appeal until he obtains the final opinion of the Supreme Court of the United States.

Concurrent Jurisdiction. Congress gives federal and State courts concurrent jurisdiction in many cases, that is, it permits certain cases to be tried either in a federal court or in a State court. Often a federal question and a State question are included in the same controversy. Owing to the difficulty and expense of dividing a case for separate trials in different courts, both State and federal questions are decided in the federal court, or in some cases both questions may be tried in a State court. But if a plaintiff[1] brings a suit in a State court, over which the United States District Courts are given jurisdiction, the defendant[2] may have it transferred to the District Court.

124. Special Courts. — There are two special federal courts, the Court of Claims and the Court of Customs Appeals.. The former was established as a sort of investigating commission to advise Congress concerning claims against the United States government, and the latter to insure a uniform interpretation of technical tariff laws.

The Court of Claims. — The Court of Claims, established in 1855, consists of five judges who sit in Washington. It is a well-established principle of public law that a sovereign state cannot be sued against its will, and before the establishment of this court a person having claims against the United States government could get no redress except by an act of Congress.

Now the government allows itself to be sued in this court on all claims, except pensions and certain " war claims," founded upon the Constitution of the United States or any laws of Congress, or upon any regulation of an administrative department, or upon any contract, expressed or implied, with the government of the United States, but it will not permit itself to be sued for the wrongful acts of its officers.

The awards of this court, unlike those of all other courts, cannot be paid until Congress appropriates the money to pay them. Upon the first day of each regular session of Congress the findings of the court for the year are sent to Congress, and the money is appropriated almost as a matter of course.

The attorneys of the United States may appeal any case

---

[1] A "plaintiff " is the person who commences a suit in law against another.
[2] A " defendant " is a person accused or summoned into court who defends himself against the charge.

decided against the government from this court to the Supreme Court, and the plaintiff may appeal if the amount in controversy exceeds $3000.

Congress or any administrative department may refer claims to this court. The court will investigate the claims and report to Congress or to the department whether they ought to be paid. For instance, Congress will refer " war claims " which cannot be sued for in the courts ; or a department will wish an opinion of the court which will enable it to settle claims in a practical and amicable way without the necessity of suit. No court other than the Court of Claims will give an opinion unless suit is actually brought.

The Court of Customs Appeals. — The Court of Customs Appeals was established by the tariff law of 1909 and is composed of five judges who sit in Washington or at any other convenient place. Most of its cases arise in New York City, as its jurisdiction extends only to tariff cases concerning the classification of merchandise and the rates of duty imposed thereon.[1]

The Court of Customs Appeals has such questions as the following to decide : Does the term " Corinthian Currants " mean currants grown and cured in the locality of Corinth, or does it mean all currants like those grown there ? This is important, because upon " Corinthian Currants " is paid a different tariff duty from that paid upon other currants. Also, does " manufactured furs " include fur skins whose holes have been sewed ? This was decided affirmatively, hence the same rate had to be paid upon them as upon furs manufactured into garments. Upon these matters the decisions of this court are final. If a constitutional question is raised an appeal may be taken directly to the Supreme Court.

125. Judges. — All federal judges are appointed by the President of the United States and confirmed by the Senate.

---

[1] All cases coming under the jurisdiction of this court are appealed from the Board of General Appraisers.

The salaries of these judges vary from $6000 to $15,000 a year, and they hold their office during good behavior,[1] which means that they cannot be removed except through impeachment by Congress. However, removal by impeachment has occurred only three times.[2]

At the age of seventy any federal judge may retire on full salary, provided he has served for ten years.

As all federal courts, except the Supreme Court, are mere creations of Congress, they may be abolished by Congress at any time. In 1911 nine Circuit Courts were abolished but the judges were retained for service in the Circuit Courts of Appeals, the Court of Customs Appeals, and the Commerce Court. In 1913 the Commerce Court, which had been created a few years before, was abolished, but its judges were made " circuit " judges of the Circuit Courts of Appeals.[3]

126. Court Officials. — *District Attorneys* are appointed by the President and Senate for a term of four years. There is usually one attorney for each judicial district. It is the attorney's duty to bring suit against all persons violating the federal laws within the district, and to prosecute them — in short, to represent the Federal Government in any case arising within the district to which the government is a party.

In addition to these district attorneys there are numerous attorneys assigned to special classes of cases — *e.g.*, anti-trust, claims, and customs attorneys.

United States Marshals are appointed in the same manner as

---

[1] Judges for the territories and island possessions are appointed for only four years.

[2] Judge Pickering of the District Court for New Hampshire was removed for drunkenness in 1803; Judge Humphreys of a Tennessee District Court, for disloyalty in 1862; and Judge Archbald of the Commerce Court, for improper business relations with persons having cases in court in 1913. Three other judges have been impeached by the House but acquitted by the Senate, the most famous one of whom was Associate Justice Chase of the Supreme Court, who was accused of expressing himself too freely in regard to politics.

[3] Inasmuch as federal judges are appointed to hold their offices during good behavior, President Wilson felt that judges could not be deprived of office by the abolition of a certain court, but should be transferred to other courts.

the district attorneys, one for each district. It is the marshal's[1] duty to make arrests and execute various court orders. If he meets with resistance in the performance of his duties, he may call upon the citizens for assistance; and if necessary, the President will send United States troops to assist him.

In the appointment of district attorneys and marshals the President consults with the Attorney-General, as the latter officer exercises general supervision over them.

Clerks are appointed by the courts, each court appointing one. The clerk has custody of the seal of the court and keeps a record of its proceedings, orders, judgments, etc.

District Court Commissioners are appointed in sufficient number by each district court. A commissioner issues warrants of arrest on criminal proceedings, takes bail, and inquires whether there is probable cause to hold the accused to answer to the charge in court.[2]

OUTLINE REVIEW OF FEDERAL COURTS

Name	Established	Number of Courts	Number of Judges	Term of Judges	Judges Appointed by	Salary of Judges
District Court	1789	81	93	Life	President and Senate	$6,000
Circuit Court of Appeals	1891	9	39	"	"	7,000
Supreme Court	1789	1	9	"	"	14,500[3]
Court of Claims	1855	1	5	"	"	6,000[3]
Court of Customs Appeals	1909	1	5	"	"	7,000

[1] A United States marshal bears the same relation to the federal court that a sheriff bears to the State court.

[2] A federal district court commissioner discharges for the United States government such functions as are performed for a State government by a justice of the peace.

[3] The Chief Justice receives $500 extra.

BIBLIOGRAPHY

BALDWIN, SIMEON E.   The American Judiciary.   (American State
Series.)   1905.
The Judicial Code of the United States.   Washington.   1913.

QUESTIONS ON THE TEXT

1. Name the regular courts of the United States.   The special courts.

2. The federal courts have jurisdiction of what two classes of cases because of the character of the subject matter?   Of what six classes because of the character of the parties?

3. How many District Courts are there and how many judges for each court?

4. The District Courts have jurisdiction of what kind of cases?

5. To what higher courts may appeals be taken from the District Courts?

6. How many Circuit Courts of Appeals are there?   Who supervises each of the circuits?

7. How many judges has each of the Circuit Courts of Appeals?

8. From what court are cases appealed to the Circuit Courts of Appeals?   To what court are certain cases appealed from them?

9. Of how many judges does the Supreme Court of the United States consist?   When and where does the court sit?

10. From what courts are cases appealed to the Supreme Court of the United States?

11. In what two classes of cases does the Supreme Court have original jurisdiction?

12. May a question involving the interpretation of the Constitution of the United States be taken to the Supreme Court?

13. Of how many judges does the Court of Appeals consist? What cases are decided by this court?   In what respect does the Court of Claims differ from all other courts?

14. Of how many judges does the Court of Customs Appeals consist?   Where does it sit?   Of what cases does it have jurisdiction?

15. Who appoints all federal judges?   For what term?   How may they be removed?   Under what condition may they retire on full salary?

16. May Congress abolish federal courts?

17. What is the duty of district attorneys? By whom are they appointed?

18. What is the duty of the United States marshals?

19. What is the duty of court clerks? By whom are they appointed?

20. What are the duties of district court commissioners? By whom are they appointed?

QUESTIONS FOR DISCUSSION

1. A woman attempted to pass a fifty-dollar note at Gimbel's store in New York City, but the clerk detected something peculiar about it. The floor detective discovered it to be a twenty-dollar bill with each figure two changed to five. The woman was arrested on the charge of attempting to pass counterfeit money. She was believed to be a "shover" for a band of counterfeiters. In what court was she tried?

2. At a "port of entry" along the Canadian border frog legs were appraised as dressed poultry, there being a tariff duty on poultry but not on frogs. Naturally the importer was dissatisfied with the decision of the appraiser. To what court could he carry the case?

3. The penalty for defacing a letter box is a fine not exceeding one thousand dollars or imprisonment for not more than three years, or both. In what court would a party accused of this offence be tried?

4. If Virginia should pass a law prohibiting farm hands from working more than six hours a day, the law would be unconstitutional. However, if a sheriff or constable should arrest a farmer for violating the State law and bring him before a justice of the peace for trial, he could claim that the law is unreasonable and contrary to the Fourteenth Amendment of the Constitution of the United States. If the lower courts should decide against the contention how high could the farmer appeal the case?

5. In 1913 the legislature of California passed the alien land bill, which provided that only those persons eligible to citizenship might own land in that State. Japan claimed that this provision violated a treaty between the United States and Japan. President Wilson suggested that Japan sue the State of California. If the treaty was violated the California law was void, as a treaty is the supreme law of the land. In what court could the state of Japan bring suit?

6. When the Chicago Canal was dug, connecting Lake Michigan with the Illinois River, the sewage of Chicago was emptied into this

Canal. The outlet of the Canal is through the Illinois River into the Mississippi. St. Louis obtains its drinking water from the Mississippi; hence the State of Missouri sued the State of Illinois, demanding that Chicago be prohibited from polluting the accustomed supply of water of St. Louis. The counsel for Illinois had several hundred barrels of harmless bacteria emptied into the stream at Chicago and found that none survived until the water reached St. Louis. In what court did Missouri lose the suit?

7. The United States built a dam across a river in South Carolina to aid navigation, and thereby destroyed the value of rice lands. Mr. Hayward, the owner, claimed damages and won the suit. In what court?

8. During the Civil War some colored Union soldiers destroyed a home in Alabama which they had been sent to protect. After the war a congressman from Alabama asked Congress to pay the owner for the loss of his property. Congress referred the matter to the proper court, which decided that there was no legal claim against the United States, only against the soldiers, but recommended the appropriation of $17,500 as an honorable obligation upon the principles of right and justice. To what court was the matter referred?

127. Civil Rights Defined. — The civil rights of an individual are all the legal rights he has except the right to vote and to hold office, which two rights are known as political rights. An individual has a right to do anything which is not prohibited by the laws of the land ; but inasmuch as the laws of the land are continually changing, the individual's rights are also continually changing.

However, there has always existed a feeling that one should not be deprived of certain rights without exceptional consideration. These more precious rights are listed in the Constitution of the United States and in the constitutions of the States, and are therefore beyond the control of Congress and the State legislatures. (See Sec. 159.)

128. Civil Rights Beyond the Control of Congress and the States. — The Constitution of the United States provides that neither the United States nor the States may

(1) Deprive any person of the right to be free. (Amend. XIII.)

(2) Punish any person by a bill of attainder or *ex post facto* law. (Art. I, Secs. 9 and 10.) A *bill of attainder* is a legislative act which inflicts punishment without a judicial trial. An *ex post facto law* is a law that makes criminal an act which was innocent when done, or an *ex post facto* law is a law which operates to the detriment of one accused of a crime committed prior to the enactment of such law. It applies to criminal cases only.

206

(3) Deprive any person of life, liberty,[1] or property,[2] without due process of law. (Amend. V and Amend. XIV.) *Due process of law* means a legal procedure which hears before it condemns and which renders judgment only after a fair trial. For instance, to deprive a person of his life, liberty, or property without giving him and his witnesses a chance to testify in court would be to deprive him of his life, liberty, or property without due process of law, hence deprive him of his constitutional rights.

Due process of law also means *reasonable law.* Therefore, if Congress or a State legislature enacts a law which, in the opinion of the United States Supreme Court, deprives a person of his life, liberty, or property unreasonably, such a law cannot be enforced.

It is impossible for the court to enumerate all laws which it would declare reasonable, because what is reasonable under one set of circumstances may be unreasonable under another. This can be illustrated by the three following decisions of the Supreme Court of the United States:

(1) It is reasonable for Utah to prohibit coal miners from working more than eight hours a day, because working long hours in mines is injurious to health.

(2) It is reasonable for Oregon to prohibit women from working in factories or laundries more than ten hours a day, because woman is the mother of the family and the general welfare of the race depends in an especial manner upon her physical condition.

(3) It is unreasonable for New York to restrict bakers to a ten-hour working day, because the court does not consider working in a bakery to be especially injurious to the health; hence it is unreasonable to interfere with the baker's liberty to

---

[1] *Liberty* means not only the right of freedom from imprisonment, but the right of one to use his faculties in all lawful ways, and to pursue any lawful trade or diversion.

[2] *Property* means more than mere physical property. It includes stocks, bonds, good will, professional knowledge, and the income therefrom.

contract with his employer to work a greater number of hours. In other words, a person has a right to enter into any contracts which are consistent with the general welfare. To deprive him of this is to deprive him of his liberty unreasonably, hence contrary to the rights guaranteed in the Fifth and the Fourteenth Amendments.

By going through the decisions of the Supreme Court interpreting the Fifth or Fourteenth Amendment [1] we can get some idea as to whether or not the court will consider that a certain law deprives one unreasonably of life, liberty, or property; but we cannot be certain that an Act passed by Congress or a State legislature is a good, valid law until the Supreme Court of the United States has upheld the law after hearing an actual case in which the constitutionality of the law was questioned. [2]

129. Civil Rights Beyond the Control of Congress. — The first ten amendments to the Constitution of the United States are

---

[1] Within the last decade the Supreme Court has delivered nearly four hundred opinions interpreting the "due process clause" of the Fourteenth Amendment. Fifty of these decisions declared State laws unconstitutional. For example, a State legislature enacted a law requiring railroads to carry passengers within the State at two cents a mile. The railroads showed that they would lose money carrying passengers at this rate, and the Supreme Court declared the law unconstitutional because its enforcement would be taking property unreasonably — "without due process of law."

Among the other three hundred and fifty laws which were tested in the Supreme Court but held to be constitutional were the following: (1) A Boston ordinance prohibiting the holding of meetings on the Boston Common. (2) A woman was denied the privilege of practicing law in Virginia courts because of her sex. (3) Tennessee prohibited the sale of cigarettes. (4) A Boston ordinance restricted the height of buildings. (5) Texas compelled railroads to cut wild (Johnson) grass from their right of way. (6) Massachusetts compelled people to be vaccinated.

[2] Courts will not tell one whether a certain Act will be lawful. The court never acts until an individual or corporation accuses another of breaking the law and brings an actual case for its decision. This practice is necessary for two reasons: First, a judge could not possibly foresee all of the effects of a certain legislative act. Second, when an actual case comes to court, attorneys collect the law and arguments for each side of the contention and the judge acts somewhat as a referee. If the judge did not have these arguments collected for him it would be necessary for him to investigate the law as well as decide it, and for this he has not the time.

known as the Bill of Rights because they contain so many
guarantees of liberty that are set forth in the English Bill of
Rights.[1] These amendments restrict Congress alone. This
fact cannot be too strongly emphasized, because most people
think that these restrictions apply to the States as well as to
the United States. Congress may not take away any of the
liberties set forth in these amendments, but through legislation
the States may deprive their citizens of many of these liberties
without violating the Constitution of the United States.

130. Civil Rights Beyond the Control of States. — The Constitution of the United States places upon the States three important restrictions involving civil rights which it does not
place upon Congress.

(1) *No State may pass any law impairing the obligation of
contracts.* (Art. I, Sec. 10.) This restriction means that a law
enacted after a lawful contract has been made shall not affect
the provisions of such contract. For example, Crowninshield
of New York gave his note to Sturges of the same State on
March 22, 1811. Shortly thereafter the State of New York
passed a bankruptcy law[2] under which Crowninshield became
a bankrupt. Paying Sturges a certain per cent of the debt,
Crowninshield claimed that he was exempt from payment of
the remainder. Application of this bankruptcy law of New
York State to debts contracted before its passage was declared
unconstitutional by the Supreme Court of the United States as
impairing obligations of contract.

(2) *No State may make anything but gold and silver coin a
tender in payment of debts.* (Art. I, Sec. 10.) This restriction
means that no State may enact a law requiring a creditor to
accept anything but gold or silver when tendered in payment
of a debt.

---

[1] The English Bill of Rights is an act of Parliament enumerating various
liberties guaranteed to the subjects to which King William assented in 1688.

[2] For meaning of "bankruptcy law" see U. S. Constitution, Art. I, Sec. 8,
note.

(3) *No State may deny to any person within its jurisdiction the equal protection of its laws.*[1] (Amend. XIV.) This means that no State may enact laws which discriminate unreasonably between persons or classes of persons. For instance, Illinois could not prohibit all combinations to fix prices or restrict competition "except farmers and stock raisers." A State could not require railroads "alone" to pay court costs when defeated in a suit. In 1914 Arizona provided that any company or individual that employs more than five persons must employ not less than 80 per cent qualified voters or native-born citizens of the United States. This law was declared unconstitutional because its enforcement would have discriminated against aliens and thus would have deprived them of the equal protection of the State's laws.

131. Civil Rights Beyond the Control of State Legislatures. — Each State constitution contains a Bill of Rights placing restrictions upon the State legislature just as the Bill of Rights in the Constitution of the United States places restrictions upon Congress. The Bills of Rights of State constitutions contain such provisions as the following: guarantee of trial by jury, religious freedom, freedom of the press, writ of habeas corpus; prohibition of excessive bail, excessive fines, cruel and unusual punishment; .and the guarantee that no person shall be deprived of life, liberty, or property without due process of law.

132. Religious Liberty. — Congress may not make any law respecting the establishment of a religion, nor may it interfere with the freedom of religious worship. (Amend. I.) The Constitution of Virginia provides that "all men are equally entitled to the free exercise of religion, according to the dictates of conscience." (Art. I, Sec. 16.) However, "Holy

---

[1] Though this *equal protection of the laws* clause is a restriction upon the States only, a law of Congress depriving persons of equal protection might be declared unconstitutional as being in conflict with Amendment V, which prohibits Congress from depriving any person of life, liberty, or property without due process of law.

Rollers " may not conduct their worship in such a manner as to disturb the peace of a neighborhood ; Mormons may not marry two wives ; and Christian Scientists may not deny medical attention to their children. A person may believe whatever he pleases, but in the name of religious liberty he must not violate a statute enacted for the general welfare of society.

133. The Freedom of Speech and of the Press. — Congress can make no law abridging the freedom of speech and of the press (Amend. I); and the Constitution of Virginia provides that " any citizen may freely speak, write, and publish his sentiments on all subjects, being responsible for the use of that right." (Art. I, Sec. 12.)

A person has the right to speak or publish what he chooses so long as he does not violate a statute law, injure some one's reputation or business, or violate public morality. Officers of government and candidates for office may be criticised if the critic speaks of what he knows or believes, has only the public interest in view, and speaks without malice.

To illustrate, if John Smith is a candidate for the city treasurership one could publish the fact that he had stolen city funds in New York back in the sixties when the Tweed Ring governed the city. But publishing the same fact against Smith simply because one dislikes him would make such person subject to damage suit; or, if the publication results in a feud or a breach of the peace, such publication is also a crime[1] which the State can punish, and proof that the statement is true will be no defence. If a person has lived as a good citizen for a number of years he has a right not to have his past record made public by a person prompted by a spiteful or malicious motive.

The prohibiting of addresses in public parks or thoroughfares and of profane language in certain places is not considered an abridgment of freedom of speech.

134. The Right to Assemble and to Petition. — Congress may not prevent any peaceable assembling or any governmental peti-

---

[1] For the meaning of " crime " see Section 183.

tion, and a State may prevent neither a petition to the National Government nor a peaceful meeting for the purpose of preparing a petition to the National Government, but a State may prescribe where and when meetings may be held. To illustrate, a State could not prevent the meeting of suffragists for the purpose of petitioning the National Government to propose a constitutional amendment extending suffrage to women; but if street meetings interfere with traffic the city authorities may require the suffragists to meet in halls or in the suburbs.

135. The Writ of Habeas Corpus. — The Constitution of the United States (Art. I, Sec. 9) provides that "the privilege of the writ of *habeas corpus* shall not be suspended, unless when, in cases of rebellion or invasion, the public safety may require it." All State constitutions have similar provisions. This writ secures to any person who claims to be unlawfully detained the right to have an immediate preliminary hearing before a civil court that he may learn the reason for his detention.

136. Inequalities Before the Law. — In theory all men are equal before the law; in practice they are not.

(1) A poor man cannot afford able lawyers "to outwit and baffle the judge and jury." If a poor man is accused of having committed a crime, and is tried, the State furnishes an attorney to defend him; but the fee allowed is small and an able lawyer is seldom secured. When a poor man has to sue a man of means for civil damages he is often obliged to offer an attorney half the amount involved.

(2) When a poor man is arrested he is often unable to give bail, and must remain in jail until his case is finally disposed of; whereas a "well-to-do" man gives bail and is released to await trial. This condition can be remedied only by giving speedier justice, and by releasing on parole persons who have committed minor offences.

(3) When a fine is imposed, the rich man pays the fine — perhaps with no inconvenience; the poor man serves his time in jail. If the offence is petty why not give the poor man credit, release him, and allow him to pay the fine by instalments?

(4) A rich man may appeal to the higher courts if the lower court decides against him and thus may drag out the case until the poor man is obliged to abandon his right for lack of lawyers' fees and court fees; or if it is a criminal case the rich man can raise and contest one technical point after another until the prosecutors and judges are so worn out that they are glad to dismiss the case.   Here again is a demand for speedier justice. And should not the State furnish free legal advice just as free medical advice is given in most cities?   If a poor man has not a good case he should know it; if he has a good case should not the State get justice for him just as it would get justice for society by punishing him as a criminal if he were in the wrong?

BIBLIOGRAPHY

See Bibliography for Chapter VI.

QUESTIONS ON THE TEXT

1. What are *civil* rights?   What are *political* rights?

2. In what documents are the more precious civil rights preserved?

3. What three civil rights are beyond the control of Congress or the States?

4. What is a *bill of attainder?*

5. What is an *ex post facto* law?

6. Explain fully the meaning of "due process of law."   Give one illustration of a law which would be contrary to "due process of law" because of improper procedure.   Because of unreasonableness.

7. Will courts consider a moot point of law, or must actual cases be brought before them before they will explain the law?

8. What is a Bill of Rights?   Why are the first ten amendments to the Constitution of the United States known as the Bill of Rights?

9. Do these amendments restrict State legislatures or only Congress?

10. Amendment II provides that the right of the people to keep and bear arms shall not be infringed.   Could your State legislature pass a law restricting the carrying of arms?

11. What three important civil-right restrictions are placed upon the States which are not imposed upon Congress?   Illustrate.

12. State Bills of Rights commonly prohibit State legislatures from interfering with what rights of the people?

13. May a person *believe* whatever he pleases regarding religious matters? May he *do* what he pleases, pretending his deeds to be a part of his religion?

14. May one person say what he chooses regarding another? May he publish it?

15. May the right to assemble and petition be denied?

16. What is the privilege of the writ of *habeas corpus?* Under what conditions may it be denied?

17. *In theory* all men are equal before the law. *Practically* are they?

QUESTIONS FOR DISCUSSION

1. If the President's daughter should be slapped by a disreputable character while attending a session of Congress, the offender could not be sent to the penitentiary. Could Congress enact a law providing that he should be sent to the penitentiary for five years?

2. Why could not the legislature of your State enact a law providing that no farm hand may work more than five hours a day?

3. If an inmate of an insane asylum claims to be sane how could he proceed to have himself released if the superintendent of the asylum would not permit him to leave?

4. Mr. Dicey says, "Freedom of discussion is in England little else than the right to write or say anything which the jury, consisting of twelve shopkeepers, think it expedient should be said or written." Is this practically true in your State?

5. "We have learned that it is pent-up feelings that are dangerous, whispered purposes that are revolutionary, covert follies that warp and poison the mind; that the wisest thing to do with a fool is to encourage him to hire a hall and discourse to his fellow citizens. Nothing chills folly like exposure to the air; nothing dispels folly like its publication; nothing so eases the machine as the safety valve." — Woodrow Wilson. Do you agree or disagree with Mr. Wilson? Why?

6. In 1798, after a series of most exasperating attacks upon the government, Congress passed the sedition act providing a "fine and imprisonment for anyone uttering or publishing false, scandalous and malicious statements against the government." A Jerseyman named Baldwin violated the sedition law and was fined $100 for expressing

the wish that the wad of a cannon discharged as a salute to President Adams had hit the broadest part of the President's breeches. Again, Matthew Lyon, of Vermont, also violated this law while canvassing for reëlection to Congress. He charged the President with "unbounded thirst for ridiculous pomp, foolish adulation, and a selfish avarice." This expression cost Mr. Lyon four months in jail and a fine of $1000. Do you think this sedition law was unconstitutional? (Constitution, Amendment I.)

7. In January, 1913, more than a thousand men and a thousand women marched to the Capitol to present to Congress, through Senator Sheppard of Texas and Representative Hobson of Alabama, a bill for the submission to the States of an amendment to the Constitution of the United States prohibiting the manufacture or sale of intoxicating liquors to be used as a beverage in the United States. Could the Washington police have compelled this assemblage to disband? (Constitution, Amendment I.)

8. In 1913 Buffalo, New York, put 759 prisoners on probation, allowing them to pay by instalments their fines, amounting to a total of $12,500. The Juvenile Court of Cleveland imposes fines upon youthful gamblers, allowing them to pay these fines by instalments from their own earnings of the week. Tell why this method is better than having parents pay the fines of their children.

CHAPTER XVI

TERRITORIES AND FOREIGN POSSESSIONS

137. Hawaii. — Upon the outbreak of hostilities with Spain in 1898 the value of island possessions as coaling stations and for other strategic purposes became very apparent. There-

HAWAII.

fore, the same year, the Hawaiian Republic, which had previously desired to become annexed to the United States, was admitted as the Territory of Hawaii.

The Hawaiian islands are in the mid-Pacific between California and the Philippine Islands, and have a total area of 6449 square miles. According to the United States Census of 1910 their population was 191,909, of whom 38,547 were native Hawaiians, 21,674 Chinese, 79,674 Japanese, and the remainder Caucasians, including more than 10,000 Americans. Immigration from China, Japan, and Korea to Hawaii is now prohibited in the same manner that immigration from these countries to the United States is prohibited; but Filipino immigration is unrestricted, and in 1912 about 3000 Filipinos entered the Territory.

In 1900 Congress framed laws for the government of Hawaii. These laws were very largely copied from those for the government of Oklahoma, New Mexico, and Arizona, which were then territories of the United States and hence governed

216

according to the wishes of Congress.[1] All of the provisions of
the Constitution and laws of the United States, except where
special exception was made or where they are locally inappli-
cable, were extended to Hawaii. Under this government
American citizenship was extended to all Hawaiian citizens
and Hawaiian citizenship to all resident American citizens.

The Hawaiian government is divided into three branches —
the executive, the legislative, and the judicial. Members of
both houses of the legislature are popularly elected, and because of this fact Hawaii is known as a *fully organized territory*
of the United States.

The Chief Executive of the Territory of Hawaii is the *governor*.
He is appointed by the President and Senate of the United
States for a term of four years, and must be a citizen of the territory. He, in turn, appoints the chief administrative officers with
the advice and consent of the territorial senate, and exercises
the usual powers of a governor, including the veto of bills
in their entirety or of separate.items in appropriation bills.

The Legislature of the territory consists of a *senate* with
fifteen members elected for the term of four years, and a
house of representatives with thirty members elected for the
term of two years. Regular sessions of the legislature are
held biennially and are limited to sixty days. The legislature
may enact any law which does not conflict with the Constitution, statutes, or treaties of the United States. Congress, however, has by statutes imposed restrictions upon the power of
the legislature, especially in regard to financial matters.

The Judiciary of the territory consists of a Supreme Court
with three judges, residents of the territory, appointed by the
President and Senate for a term of four years, a United States
District Court with two judges appointed by the President and
Senate for a term of six years, and inferior courts created
by the territorial legislature.

---

[1] All of our forty-eight States were Territories before becoming States, except the thirteen original States and Maine, Vermont, Kentucky, West Virginia,
Texas, and California.

A Territorial Delegate to the government of the United States is elected by the people of the territory for each term of Congress. He is allowed a seat in the House of Representatives with a right to debate and serve on committees, but he cannot vote. His salary is $7500 a year.

138. Alaska. — In 1867 Alaska was purchased from Russia, and its inhabitants became citizens of the United States, but

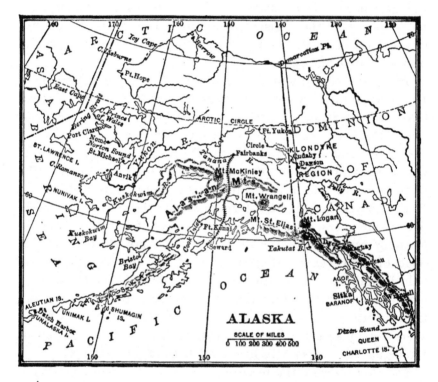

Congress did not create a *fully organized* territorial government for it until 1912. Its area is 590,884 square miles, but its population in 1910 was only 64,356 including 25,331 Indians (Eskimos). To-day the Territory of Alaska is governed in very much the same manner as the Territory of Hawaii.

The Governor is appointed by the President and Senate of the United States for a term of four years and has the usual powers.

The Legislature consists of a *senate* with eight members popularly elected and a *house of representatives* with sixteen members popularly elected. It meets biennially for a period not exceeding sixty days and its powers are general except where specifically restricted. All Alaskan laws are valid until disapproved by an act of Congress if they are originally passed within the limits of the organic act.

As an example of the restrictions imposed by Congress, neither the Hawaiian nor the Alaskan government may grant divorces to persons who have resided in the country less than two years.

It is interesting to note that one of the first acts passed by the legislature of Alaska extended full suffrage to women, and that in 1916 the people voted for territory-wide pro-

UNITED STATES GOVERNMENT RAILROAD.

This is a construction scene on the government railroad from Seward to Fairbanks, Alaska, a distance of 471 miles. Cost $35,000,000.

hibition by a large majority, carrying every incorporated town but Engle, which cast a tie vote.

The Judiciary of Alaska consists of four United States district courts with judges appointed by the President and Senate for a term of four years. The Alaskan legislature creates inferior courts.

A Territorial Delegate is elected every second November to represent Alaska in the Congress of the United States. Like the territorial delegate from Hawaii he has a seat in the House of Representatives, debates, and serves on committees, but may not vote. His salary is $7500 a year.

139. Porto Rico. — The United States took possession of the island of Porto Rico in 1898 during the Spanish-American

War, and acquired it by treaty the following year. Its area is 3606 square miles and its population in 1910 was 1,118,012, including 732,555 whites, 50,245 blacks, 335,192 mulattoes, and 20 mongolians.

Congress provides for the government of Porto Rico, and did not extend complete American citizenship to its inhabitants until 1917. However, between 1898 and 1917 Porto Ricans owed allegiance to the United States, could enter the country unrestricted by immigration laws, and were protected by the United States when travelling abroad. Most of the civil rights guaranteed to American citizens were extended to them. The law of Congress, signed March 2, 1917, gives Porto Ricans full American citizenship and provides for universal manhood suffrage.

The Executive branch of the Porto Rican government consists of a governor and an executive council of eleven members, all of whom are appointed by the President, with the advice and consent of the Senate. At least five of the members of the executive council must be Porto Ricans.

The executive council grants franchises, ratifies important nominations to public office, determines salaries, and approves municipal ordinances.

Seven members of the executive council act as heads of the administrative departments: secretary, attorney general, treasurer, auditor, commissioner of the interior, commissioner of education, and commissioner of public health, charities, and corrections.

The governor has the usual powers, except that he does not appoint the heads of administrative departments. His veto may be overridden by a two-thirds vote of the legislature. In some cases where the veto is overridden, the bill may be referred to the President of the United States, who has an absolute veto.

The, Legislature of the Island is composed of two houses, a senate and a house of delegates. The *senate* consists of nineteen members, fourteen elected from seven districts and five elected at large. The *house of delegates* consists of thirty-nine members, thirty-five elected from seven districts and four elected at large.

The Judiciary of Porto Rico has been almost completely Americanized in form, law, and procedure. The supreme court consists of five judges appointed for life by the President — three Porto Ricans and two Americans in practice. Below this court are seven local district courts, each having one judge appointed by the governor of the territory with the consent of the council for four years. Below the district courts are twenty-four municipal courts with justices of the peace elected by the voters of the territory for terms of two years.

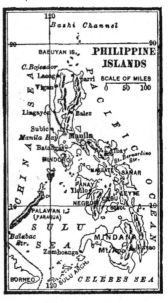

A Commissioner, elected by the voters every two years, represents the island in Washington. Unlike the territorial delegate, he has no statute right to a seat in the House, but by courtesy the House has given him the privilege of speaking and of serving on committees. He receives a salary of $7500 per annum.

140. The Philippines. — The United States took possession of the Philippine Islands in 1898 during the Spanish-American War, and they were ceded to the United States the following year. This archipelago consists of about 3141 islands with a total area of 127,853 square miles, and a population estimated at 8,600,000. There are about 25,000 Americans and Europeans and about 40,000 Chinese in the islands. The Chinese are now excluded.

Originally Congress provided a government for the Philippine Islands in which the natives played a very minor part, but in order to test their ability for self-government Congress and the President have gradually entrusted more offices to them.

The present government of the Philippines is provided for by a law enacted by Congress in 1916. This Act provides that the laws of Congress hereafter enacted shall not apply to the Philippine Islands except when they specifically so provide, and extends general legislative power to the Philippine Legislature with certain fundamental restrictions enumerated therein.

THE FIRST PHILIPPINE ASSEMBLY, 1907.

The Executive department consists of the Governor General, the Vice Governor, the heads of the executive departments, and an auditor. The Governor General is appointed by the President and Senate of the United States. His position in the Philippine government is very similar to the President's position in the government of the United States. The Vice Governor is also appointed by the President and Senate, and acts as governor in case of the latter's inability to act. He is head of the executive department of public instruction, which consists of the bureaus of education and health. The other executive departments are created by the Philippine Legislature and their heads are appointed by the Governor General. The Auditor, who is appointed by the President, safeguards the revenues of the central and local Philippine governments.

The Legislature consists of a senate and a house of representatives. The senate is composed of twenty-four members chosen in twelve districts for terms of six years. The house of representatives is composed of ninety members chosen in ninety districts[1] for terms of three years. Sessions are held annually. All legislative acts are subject to the approval of the Governor General or the President of the United States.

The Judiciary consists of a supreme court of seven judges appointed by the President and Senate, twenty-six courts of first instance with judges appointed by the Governor General and the Philippine Senate, and numerous justices of the peace.

Appeals may be taken from the Philippine supreme court to the Supreme Court of the United States if the Constitution, a statute, or treaty of the United States is involved, or if an amount exceeding $25,000 is in question.

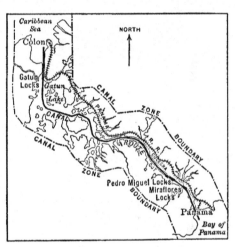

PANAMA CANAL ZONE.

Two Commissioners, elected by the Philippine legislature for terms of three years, represent the archipelago in Washington. These representatives have no seats in Congress, but by courtesy of the House they have the privilege of debating, and receive a salary of $7500 per annum.

141. Panama. — The occupation, use, and control of a zone five miles wide on each side of the Panama Canal was granted by Panama to the United States by treaty in 1904. The present permanent government for this zone was provided for by an act of Congress in 1912. The government is placed in the hands of the President of the United States. With the con-

---

[1] Two senators and nine representatives are appointed by the Governor General for indefinite terms to represent the non-Christian tribes, which were unrepresented before 1916; all other members of the legislature are elected by a restricted suffrage.

THE PANAMA CANAL.

This scene shows the first ship through the canal after the great Culebra slide.

TWO HUNDRED TON SIXTEEN-INCH DISAPPEARING GUN FOR THE
PANAMA FORTIFICATIONS.

sent of the Senate he appoints a governor for the term of four years, and without the consent of the Senate he appoints other officials for an indefinite term.   There is no legislature for the zone, but there is a district court with a judge appointed by the President for four years and local courts conducted by justices who are appointees of the governor.

Because of the President's influence in the governing of the Canal Zone it has been called a " crown colony."

142. Other Insular Dependencies. — Like Porto Rico and the Philippines, Guam was acquired in 1899 as a result of the war with Spain.   The Samoan Islands were acquired by treaty in 1900.   Each of these possessions is commanded by a naval officer.

Wake, Midway, Howland, Baker, and Guano islands are claimed by the United States, but as they are totally or practically uninhabited they need no government.

In 1916 the United States purchased the islands of St. Croix, St. Thomas, and St. John from Denmark by treaty for $25,000,000.

BIBLIOGRAPHY

WILLOUGHBY, W. F.   Territories and Dependencies of the United States.   (American State Series.)   1905.
Annual Report of·the Bureau of Insular Affairs.   .

QUESTIONS ON THE TEXT

1. What was the main reason for annexing Hawaii in 1898?

2. The government of Hawaii is somewhat similar to that of what former territories of the United States?

3. Are Hawaiians American citizens?

4. Into what three branches is the Hawaiian government divided?

5. How is the governor of Hawaii chosen?   The Senate?   The House of Representatives?

6. What laws may be enacted by the legislature of Hawaii?

7. By whom is the territory of Hawaii represented in Washington? May he vote?

8. How and when did the United States acquire Alaska?

9. How is the governor of Alaska chosen?   The Senate?   The House of Representatives?

10. In what respect do Alaskan laws differ from Hawaiian laws as to the method of making them?

11. How is Alaska represented in Washington?

12. How and when did the United States acquire Porto Rico?

13. How do Porto Ricans differ from Hawaiians and Alaskans in their relationship to the United States?

14. How is the governor of Porto Rico chosen? The Executive Council? The House of Delegates?

15. How is Porto Rico represented in Washington?

16. How and when did the United States acquire the Philippine Islands?

17. Are Filipinos citizens of the United States?

18. How is the Governor General of the Philippine Islands selected? The Philippine Commission? The Assembly?

19. How are the Philippine Islands represented in Washington?

20. How and when did the United States acquire Panama?

21. How is Panama governed? Why is it called a "crown colony"?

22. What other insular dependencies does the United States own?

23. Name the foreign possessions of the United States in the order of their degree of local self-government.

QUESTIONS FOR DISCUSSION

1. Do you approve of the recent appropriation by Congress of $35,000,000 for the building of a government railroad in Alaska? Why?

2. Do you think Porto Ricans should be given full United States citizenship? Why?

3. Do you think the Filipinos should be given their independence, or do you think the Philippines should become a state of the Union?

4. President Wilson issued an executive order prohibiting the sale of intoxicating liquor in the Canal Zone. Why cannot he issue a similar order for Hawaii?

5. Could the House of Representatives grant cabinet members the right to speak on the floor of the House and to serve on committees?

6. If the question as to the constitutional privileges of a citizen of any of these possessions arises, to what court may the questions in dispute be finally appealed?

7. Prepare a report on any one of these possessions.

CHAPTER XVII

POLITICAL PARTIES AND POLITICS

143. National Parties. — A political party is an organization of many people, united by common principles or a common policy, and having for its immediate end the control of the government through the carrying of elections and the possession of office. A political organization, like any other organization, perpetuates itself by representative men known as *committeemen*.

For each of the national parties there is a *National Committee* composed of one member from each State, chosen at the National Convention every fourth year. The National Committee elects a *National Chairman* for the same period of years, and he is the real party manager.

In each State there is a *State Committee* and a *State Chairman* to coöperate with the National Committee and its chairman. It is the duty of these party representatives to promote harmony, to arouse enthusiasm by speeches and literature, to arrange for the selection of party candidates for public office, to instruct the voters concerning the merits and virtues of their own principles and leaders and the mistakes of their opponents, to enlist new voters such as naturalized foreigners — in short, to capture the government.

An old party may have no principles differing from the opposing party, and may be said to be " looking for an issue." " A party may hold together ' long after its moral life is extinct. . . . Parties go on contending because their members have formed habits of joint action, and have contracted hatreds and prejudices, and also because the leaders find advantage in using these habits and playing on these prejudices. . . . The mill has been constructed and its machinery goes on turning even when there is no grist to grind.'"[1]

However, when a political party with a large membership has been in control for a long period and has had no formidable party to oppose it, sectional or economic differences of opinion tend to "split" it into "factions." During Taft's administration the Republican Party split into two factions, — the "insurgents" and the "standpatters." Their differences of opinion were irreconcilable, and the insurgents, after "bolting" the Republican Convention of 1912, organized the Progressive Party with Roosevelt as its leader.

The immediate end of political parties is the control of the government. This control may be honest or it may be corrupt. If the voter is wide awake the parties out of power will assist him in obtaining good government by exposing any improper acts committed by the party in power and by educating him to an understanding of the reforms advocated by them. Therefore, political parties are useful to democratic government, and as there is no provision for them in the Constitution of the United States they have developed as extra-legal institutions.[2] Laws distinctly recognizing the existence of parties and attempting to regulate their activities are very recent, but State primaries provided by law are gradually displacing the old extra-legal State conventions.

144. Party Platforms. — A party platform is a statement of principles or policies for which the party stands. A national party platform is framed every four years by the Committee on Resolutions at the National Convention of the party. Each party platform contains a somewhat detailed statement of the principles and policies which it advocates, though its statements are not always clear.

[1] Ray, P. Orman, "An Introduction to Political Parties and Practical Politics," page 7.
[2] *Extra-legal* means outside of the law; not illegal or contrary to law, but simply not regulated at all by law.

If the delegates of the convention cannot agree upon specific public questions, ambiguous or non-committal "planks" will be adopted rather than offend any large faction of the party. As platforms are partisan documents and not judicial, their value depends much upon the character of the party leaders and candidates who indorse them. It has been cynically said that platforms are good things to get in and out on, but not to ride on.

In many respects the 1916 Republican and Democratic platforms were alike. Both of these platforms advocated an adequate army and navy and a continued faith in the Monroe Doctrine. They favored rural credit banks, the conservation of natural resources, and the prohibition of child labor. They also recommended woman suffrage by State action.

145. The Republican Platform. — The 1916 platform of the Republican party reaffirmed the party's belief in tariff protection to American industries and advocated a tariff commission. It continued its belief in a subsidy to commercial ships suitable for use in time of war, and in the retention of the Philippine Islands. It favored placing the entire transportation system under Federal control; advocated civil service reform and a budget system; and promised to restore order in Mexico.

The Progressive party, which came into existence in 1912 under the leadership of Theodore Roosevelt, was to a very great extent reabsorbed by the Republican party in 1916 when this favored leader declined its presidential nomination. However, many of the progressive planks in its 1912 platform found their way into the Democratic and Republican platforms of 1916.

146. The Democratic Platform. — The 1916 platform of the Democratic party advocated tariff for revenue — the rate to be determined by a non-partisan commission — and the establishment of a shipping board to encourage and regulate foreign and interstate commerce by water. It favored the reclamation of arid lands and federal aid for the development of roads, rivers, harbors, and inland waterways. It urged the establishment of tuberculosis sanitariums, and promised generous pensions to soldiers and their widows. It recommended a single committee on appropriations as a practical step towards the budget system. It promised a greater degree of self government to the Philippine Islands and a liberal territorial government to Hawaii, Alaska, and Porto Rico. It held that claims of humanity are of greater moment in Mexico than those of property.

147. The Prohibition Platform. — Besides advocating the prohibition of the sale of liquor throughout the United States, the 1916 platform of the Prohibition party favored woman suffrage, uniform marriage and divorce laws, child labor laws, the eight- hour day, old age pensions, and insurance against unemployment. It also favored the erection of public grain elevators and cotton warehouses, and advocated public ownership of all natural monopolies. The party would give the President power to veto single items of appropriation bills; and in times of peace it would employ the army in reclamation plans, in reforesting hills and mountains, in building highways, and in constructing inland waterways, for which adequate industrial wages should be paid. It further favored the initiative, referendum, and recall for States.[1]

148. The Socialist Platform. — The Socialist platform of 1916 was by far the most radical. It favored :

(1) The collective ownership and democratic management of railroads, wire and wireless telegraphs and telephones, express services, steamboat lines, and all other social means of transportation and communication and of all large-scale industries ; and the shortening of the work day in keeping with the increased productiveness of machinery.

(2) The immediate acquirement by the municipalities, the States, or the Federal government, of all grain elevators, stock yards, storage warehouses, and other distributing agencies, "in order to reduce the present extortionate cost of living."

(3) The extension of the public domain to include mines, quarries, oil wells, forests, and water-power.

---

[1] See Sections 156, 168, 169, and 243.

(4) Further consideration and development of natural resources for the use and benefit of all the people :

(a) By scientific forestation and timber protection.

(b) By the reclamation of arid and swamp tracts.

(c) By the storage of flood waters and the utilization of water-power.

(d) By a stoppage of the present extravagant waste of the soil and of the products of mines and oil wells.

(e) By the development of highway and waterway systems.

(5) The collective ownership of land wherever practicable, and in cases where such ownership is impracticable the appropriation by taxation of the rental value of all land held for speculation or exploitation.

(6) The collective ownership and democratic management of the banking and currency system.

(7) The abolition of monopoly ownership of patents and the substitution of collective ownership, with direct rewards to inventors by premiums or royalties.

(8) Government relief of the unemployed by the extension of all useful public works.

(9) Old age pensions.

(10) The adoption of woman suffrage, the initiative, referendum, and recall, and of proportional representation.

(11) The abolition of the Senate and of the veto power of the President.

(12) The abolition of the power of the Supreme Court to declare laws unconstitutional.

(13) Election of all judges for short terms.

(14) Amendment of the Constitution of the United States by a majority of the voters of the country.

(15) A convention for the revision of the Constitution of the United States.

149. The National Convention. — In the early summer of every fourth year each party holds a convention for the purpose of formulating its principles and policies into a party platform, nominating candidates for President and Vice-President, and electing a national committee to represent the party during the following four years. In December or January preceding a presidential election the national committee of each of the national parties meets in Washington and decides upon the time and place to hold the convention.[1] When this is determined the committee sends a call for the National Convention to each State committee, naming the time, place, and number of delegates to which each State and Territory is entitled. For half a century the two leading parties assigned to each State twice as many delegates as the State has representatives and senators in Congress.[2] Each State is entitled to as many alternates as it has delegates, and these serve in the absence of the delegates.

When the call from the national committee is received the State committee calls a State convention for the purpose of selecting four delegates-at-large with alternates and suggesting planks for the national platform. At the same time the State committee notifies each congressional district committee of the State to call a district convention for the purpose of selecting two delegates with alternates.[3] The conventions which

[1] The convention must be held in a city with railroad facilities, hotel accommodations, and auditorium space. In January, 1912, the business men of Baltimore presented to the Democratic National Committee a certified check for $100,000 on the condition that they would select Baltimore for the convention. These business men further offered an auditorium to seat 20,000 and agreed to spend $15,000 for decorations. No other city offered as much and Baltimore was named. St. Louis paid a like sum to have the 1916 convention meet in that city.

[2] The Republican National Committee provided that for the National Convention of 1916 a congressional district should lose one of its delegates if it did not poll a Republican vote of 7500 in 1908 or 1914. The effect of this rule was to reduce the total number of delegates by 89, of which the Southern States lose 79.

Each party assigns delegates to Hawaii, Alaska, District of Columbia, Porto Rico, and the Philippines, but the number assigned by the parties differs. In 1912 the total number of delegates in the Democratic Convention was 1094; in the Republican, 1078.

[3] In some States the State law requires the selection of delegates by a direct

choose these delegates frequently "instruct" them to support a certain candidate for the presidential nomination and to urge that certain policies be included in the party platform.

In the large auditorium decorated with flags, bunting, and pictures of candidates and dead statesmen, the convention is called to order by the chairman of the national committee. After the secretary reads the official call for the convention

Copyright, Underwood & Underwood, N. Y.

THE REPUBLICAN NATIONAL CONVENTION IN CHICAGO.

and prayer is offered, the national chairman names the temporary chairman and other officers whom the national committee has previously selected. Unless there is a factional fight, as there was in 1912 in both parties, these nominees are elected by the convention. The temporary chairman is escorted to the chair and makes a lengthy speech in which he assails the record

primary. In New York and several other States Democratic State conventions choose the entire delegation. At the New York State convention congressional district caucuses are held and nominate to the National Convention the delegates from their district. These nominations are usually ratified by the State convention.

of the opposite party, eulogizes his own party, and pleads for harmony.

Following this speech four committees are formed : (1) Committee on Permanent Organization; (2) Committee on Credentials; (3) Committee on Rules and Order of Business; and (4) Committee on Platform and Resolutions. Each State is entitled to one member on each committee. As the roll of the States is called the chairman of each State delegation announces the members whom the delegation has chosen to represent that State on the respective committees. After these committees are named the first session usually ends.

The second session of the convention is usually devoted to receiving the reports of the committees. The committee on rules and order of business usually recommends the adoption of the rules of the preceding National Convention and of the House of Representatives so far as they are applicable, and recommends a program, or order of business, for the existing convention.

The committee on credentials recommends what delegates shall be seated where there is a split in the party and two sets of delegates claim to be the proper delegates.

The committee on permanent organization nominates a permanent chairman and other permanent officers. When elected, the permanent chairman is escorted to the chair and delivers a long speech outlining the issues of the campaign.

Next, the committee on platform and resolutions presents a platform of which a preliminary draft has been prepared by a party leader previous to the meeting of the convention. The platform is sometimes debated before the convention adopts it.

The next duty of the convention is to nominate the President. The secretary calls the roll of States alphabetically, beginning with Alabama; and as a State is called, its delegates have a right to propose candidates for nomination by long eulogistic speeches. Any number of delegates may second a nomination by similar speeches. After all candidates are placed in nomination the balloting begins. The secretary again calls the roll of the States, and the chairman of each delegation announces the votes for the entire delegation.[1]

In the Republican convention the votes of a bare majority of delegates nominate; in the Democratic the votes of two thirds of the delegates are necessary.[2] In 1912 it was necessary to ballot forty-six times to nominate Woodrow Wilson, although in 1916 he was nominated by the first ballot. The Vice-President is nominated in the same manner as the President.

Thirteen States have recently extended the direct primary to the selection of delegates for national conventions, or else to the instruction of delegates as to whom the majority of the party desires to be nominated.[3]

150. Party Machinery.[4] — Between the nomination of candidates and election day a political campaign must be waged, and for this purpose party organizations are necessary. Party machinery in the form of a national committee, national sub-committees, a congressional campaign committee, State committees, and local committees, is necessary for each party.

The National Committee of each political party consists of

---

[1] The " unit rule " prevails in the Democratic convention but not in the Republican. By the " unit rule " the majority of each State delegation binds the entire delegation. To illustrate, the New York delegation consists of 90 members. If 46 of the 90 delegates favor one candidate the entire 90 votes must be cast for him. The unit rule shows the early State-rights leaning of the Democratic party by recognizing the right of a " sovereign " State to vote as a unit.

[2] The " two-thirds rule " and the " unit rule " are closely bound together. " If the two-thirds rule be abrogated while the unit rule prevails, a few of the large States, though their delegations may be nearly evenly divided, may, by enforcing the unit rule, secure a majority of the convention for a candidate whom only a minority of the delegates really favor. The two-thirds rule lessens the probability of this." — Woodburn, 183.

[3] In Pennsylvania and South Dakota delegates to the National Convention are selected by a direct primary. In Maryland, Illinois, and Michigan a direct primary enables the party voters to express a presidential preference. In Oregon, North Dakota, Wisconsin, New Jersey, Nebraska, California, Ohio, and Massachusetts the delegates are chosen by a direct primary and a presidential preference is expressed at the same direct primary.

[4] The party machinery described in this section applies to the Democratic and Republican parties. That of other parties is very similar.

one member from each State and Territory. The members are chosen at the National Convention by the respective State delegations. At the head of the national committee is the national *chairman*,[1] nominally chosen by the national committee, but really selected by the presidential candidate. He is the campaign manager, "the head master of the machine." For convenience and efficiency the national committee is usually divided into sub-committees, such as an executive committee, a finance committee, a committee in charge of the bureau of speakers, a committee in charge of literary and press matters, and a committee in charge of the distribution of public documents.

The Congressional Campaign Committee, with headquarters in Washington, consists of a representative of each State and Territory selected by a party caucus of its representatives and senators. The purpose of this committee is to secure the election of as many party members as possible. During presidential years the resources of this committee are placed at the disposal of the national committee.

The State Committees vary in composition and powers from State to State. In number they vary from a few to more than a hundred members, and serve terms varying from one to four years. Except in those States where the State convention system has been abolished, the committeemen are selected at the State conventions. In some States the unit of representation is the congressional district, in others the county. Subordinate to State committees are various local committees.

151. Party Finance. — In the Lincoln campaign of 1860 the national committee "campaign fund" was only slightly over $100,000. Following the Civil War campaign funds steadily increased until 1896, when the Republicans alone, it is believed, had a fund of $7,000,000. In 1912 the Democrats expended

---

[1] Second in importance only to the national chairman is the national secretary, who is director at headquarters. He is more familiar with the actual details of the campaign than the chairman, who has largely determined the policy.

over $1,130,000, the Republicans over $1,070,000, and the Progressives over $670,000. These funds are collected by the national chairman, treasurer of the national committee, and the finance sub-committee of the national committee.

The various sources of these funds are : (1) voluntary contributions by loyal supporters, (2) contributions or assessments by candidates, (3) contributions by aspirants for appointive offices, (4) contributions or assessments by office-holders, (5) contributions by contractors for State, county, or city work, and (6) contributions by keepers of gambling houses, saloons, disreputable resorts, and others who violate city ordinances or State laws.

Until recently private corporations contributed large amounts, sometimes as much as $50,000 or $100,000 at a time. But in 1907 Congress passed an act prohibiting contributions by any corporations to any campaign fund used to aid in the election of the President, Vice-President, a Representative or a Senator. By the same law national banks and other federal corporations are forbidden to contribute to any campaign fund.[1]

By acts of Congress, passed 1910 and 1911, a candidate for representative in Congress may not expend more than $5000 and a senator not more than $10,000 [2] towards his election. At presidential and congressional elections the treasurer of the national committee and the treasurer of the congressional committee must report before and after elections the entire " campaign fund " contributed and expended, giving the name of each person contributing as much as $100 and an itemized statement of all expenditures of as much as $10. This report is filed with the clerk of the House of Representatives and is open to the public.

---

[1] Besides this federal law prohibiting corporations from contributing, many States prohibit corporations from contributing to State and local elections. States have various laws limiting the amount of money a candidate may spend and also specifying for what purposes he may spend it.

[2] Postage and a few items such as those which members of Congress obtain free are not included in the $10,000 limit.

A campaign fund may be expended for the maintenance of headquarters, convention halls, club rooms, mass-meetings, parades, and speakers' expenses; in most States for salaries, bulletins, pamphlets, and posters; and in a few States the cost of primaries must be borne by the State committees.   Bribery, or gifts to influence voters, is everywhere illegal.

A law of Congress enacted in 1912 requires newspapers and other periodicals to publish the name or names of persons owning the publication so that it may be known to what extent certain persons or interests are influencing public opinion at election times.   The law also requires publishers to insert the word "Advertisement" at the end of any reading matter for which the publisher receives pay.

BIBLIOGRAPHY

RAY, P. ORMAN. An Introduction to Political Parties and Practical Politics.   1913.
Campaign Text-Book of each Political Party.
The Platform Text-Book, containing all the platforms of all parties.   Price 25 cts.   The Vincent Publishing Co., Omaha, Neb.

QUESTIONS ON THE TEXT

1. What is a political party?
2. What is the National Committee?   Of whom is it composed?
3. How is the National Chairman chosen?   What is his position?
4. What is the duty of the various party representatives?
5. What is meant by party factions?
6. Why must the principles of a new party be emphasized? What holds together an old party?
7. What is the immediate end of a political party?
8. Why are political parties useful to a democratic government?
9. What is a political platform?
10. What is meant by a plank of a party platform?
11. What determines the value of a platform?
12. What was advocated in the Republican platform of 1916? The Democratic?   The Prohibition?   The Socialist?   Discuss the different planks.

13. Describe a National Convention. When does it meet? Who, and what considerations, determine where it will meet?

14. What is accomplished by a National Convention?

15. How many votes of a convention are necessary to nominate a Republican candidate? A Democratic candidate?

16. How are vice-presidential candidates nominated?

17. Describe party machinery and the methods of conducting a campaign.

18. What is the Congressional Campaign Committee?

19. Describe the political organization within a State.

20. Explain how funds are raised for campaign expenses.

21. May corporations contribute money to a political party to influence a federal election?

22. May a candidate for Congress spend as much as he desires towards his election?

23. How can one learn how much money has been expended by a candidate for a federal office?

24. Is it legal in any State to use gifts or bribes to influence voters?

QUESTIONS FOR DISCUSSION

1. Referring to party organization, Mr. C. R. Fish says: " There must be drilling and training, hard work with the awkward squad, and an occasional dress parade. This work requires the work of many men : there must be captains of hundreds and captains of tens, district chiefs and ward heelers. . . ." Explain the meaning of this quotation.

2. Is your State a one-party State? Would government be more efficient if there were two parties of about equal strength?

3. Compare the last platforms of the four leading political parties. Which is the most progressive? Which the least? Which do you favor? Did you inherit your views or do you think for yourself? Compare the last platforms with the most recent preceding ones. (See World Almanac for presidential year.)

4. What are the differences between socialism and anarchism?

5. What is the method of procedure in calling and conducting a caucus or primary in your own State?

6. How are the delegates of the county and State conventions chosen in your own State — in theory and in actual practice?

7. Why is there always a lull in business during a presidential campaign when tariff reduction is an issue?

8. President Roosevelt recommended that campaign expenses be paid by the Federal government. What arguments can be advanced for and against this recommendation?

9. What argument can you advance for and against compulsory voting?

10. Though it is morally just, why is it practically inexpedient to penalize both bribe-giver and bribe-taker?

11. Prepare a report on the election of 1824.

12. Woodrow Wilson, in a message to Congress, advocated the nomination of the presidential and vice-presidential candidates by a direct primary election instead of National Conventions. Why do you favor or oppose this suggestion? Do you think Congress can enact a law creating such a primary, or must the Constitution be amended? (See Art. II. Sec. 1; also Amendments XII, XIV, and XV.)

13. Make an outline of the National, State, and local organization of the Democratic Party.

CHAPTER XVIII

STATE CONSTITUTIONS

152. Origin of State Constitutions. — As the result of the Revolutionary War the thirteen colonies of North America became thirteen independent States. Each had power to enact such laws as it considered wise. As expressed by a meeting of New Hampshire towns: "It is our humble opinion, that when the Declaration of Independence took place, the Colonies were absolutely in a state of nature, and the powers of Government reverted to the people at large." Thus the people of each State had power to create any kind of government they preferred.

Connecticut and Rhode Island found the colonial charters granted to them by Charles II to be so liberal that these charters were sufficient for their purposes. These States merely renounced their allegiance to the King of England and continued to be governed according to the provisions of their charters until 1818 and 1842 respectively. Between 1776 and 1780 all of the other States prepared new documents, known as *constitutions*. In addition to outlining a form of government these documents contained certain rules to which all State legislation must conform.

These original constitutions were framed by State conventions, or congresses, some of which were composed of members of the State assemblies; while others were especially constituted for that purpose. All of our State constitutions now in existence were framed by assemblies representing the people.

Congress never admits a new State into the Union until the

territory desiring to be admitted has framed its constitution. On the admission of some States Congress has passed an act empowering the people of a territory to hold a convention and frame a constitution; on the admission of other States Congress has accepted and confirmed the constitution previously drawn up by a territorial convention.

153. State Constitutions Analyzed. — State constitutions commonly consist of six parts :

(1) A *preamble* stating the general purpose for which the government is organized.

(2) A *Bill of Rights* listing certain rights which must not be infringed upon even by enactments of the legislature.

(3) *Provisions for the organization of the legislative, executive, and judicial departments*, and the powers and duties of each.

(4) *Provisions of a miscellaneous character* treating of such subjects as suffrage and elections, revenues and expenditures, local government, public education, and railroads and other corporations.

(5) *Provisions for future changes* by partial amendment or total revision.

(6) A *schedule* providing for such matters as submitting the new constitution to the voters and putting it into operation without conflicting with the previous constitution.

154. Revision of State Constitutions. — As the provisions of our State constitutions cannot be changed by the State legislatures in the same manner that ordinary laws are changed, special means have developed for altering them when new conditions make it advisable. If the people desire to make many changes in the constitution a *convention* is called to revise the old constitution or to frame a new one. But if only a few portions of the constitution are to be changed, a simpler procedure is followed, known as *partial amendment*.

155. Constitutional Conventions. — A constitutional convention is an assembly of delegates chosen by the voters to revise an old constitution or to frame a new one. In all States except Rhode Island the constitution may be changed by a convention, but in most States it must then be ratified by the voters before it becomes law.

There are usually three popular votes connected with a new or revised constitution : (1) the vote of the people authorizing a convention, (2) the election by the voters of delegates to the convention, and (3) the submission to the people for approval of the constitution framed by the convention.[1]

NEW YORK STATE CAPITOL.

Here the Constitutional Convention recently met. This is the most expensive State Capitol in the United States.

156. Partial Amendment. — In all States except New Hampshire the constitution may be changed by partial amendment, which method is used when only a few alterations are to be

---

[1] Some States dispense with the first vote, others with the third, and Mississippi dispensed with both the first and the third in 1890. On this occasion the legislature of Mississippi provided for an election at which delegates were chosen, and when the delegates had framed a constitution they adopted it without consulting the people.

made. The details of this method are given below in order
that the reader may learn in what manner the constitution of
his State may be amended.

(1) Amendment by an affirmative vote of two successive
legislatures, without being submitted to the voters.[1]

(2) Proposal by the legislature and confirmation by a vote of
the people, but with the final determination left to the
legislature.[2]

(3) Amendment proposed by the legislature, and approved
by the voters, but with the amending process subject
to such restrictions as to make constitutional changes
difficult. Such restrictions are of three kinds:

   (a) Requirement of an affirmative vote by two successive sessions of the legislature for the proposal
of amendments.[3]

   (b) Limitations as to the number, frequency, or
character of proposals.[4]

   (c) Requirement of an affirmative vote by more than
a bare majority of all persons voting upon the
amendment — e.g., by a majority of those who
vote for officers at that election.[5]

(4) Unrestricted proposal of amendments by one legislature
and their adoption by the vote of a majority of the persons voting thereon.[6]

The Initiative. — In addition to the above methods of amending State constitutions a new way has developed since 1902,

[1] Delaware.

[2] Mississippi and South Carolina.

[3] Connecticut, Indiana, Iowa, Massachusetts, Nevada, New Jersey, New
York, North Dakota, Pennsylvania, Rhode Island, Tennessee, Vermont, Virginia, and Wisconsin.

[4] Arkansas, Colorado, Illinois, Indiana, Kansas, Kentucky, Montana, New
Jersey, Pennsylvania, Tennessee, and Vermont.

[5] Alabama, Arkansas, Illinois, Indiana, Minnesota, Nebraska, New Mexico,
Oklahoma, Rhode Island, Tennessee, and Wyoming.

[6] Arizona, California, Florida, Georgia, Idaho, Louisiana, Maine, Maryland, Missouri, Michigan, North Carolina, Ohio, Oregon, South Dakota, Texas,
Utah, Washington, and West Virginia.

and is now practiced by a number of States.[1] This new method
is known as the *Initiative* because the proposed amendment is
initiated by voters. When a prescribed per cent of the legal
voters — *e.g.*, eight per cent in Oregon — desires to have any part
of the constitution changed they sign a petition stating exactly
what change they desire. This proposal is sent to the secretary of state, who places the proposed change upon the ballot
for the next State election. If a majority of the voters cast
their ballots in favor of the change the constitution is thus
amended.

At the November election of 1914 forty-one amendments
were initiated by the voters of nine States as compared with
161 proposed by the legislatures of twenty-four States. Only
seven of the initiated amendments were accepted by the voters,
and eighty-one of those proposed by the legislatures.

157. Present Tendencies. — Our early State constitutions
were very brief, rarely containing more than 5000 words, but
most of the State constitutions of to-day contain from ten to
twenty times as many words as the original documents.

There are two reasons for this increase in length. First,
the government performs so many more functions now than it
did when the first constitutions were adopted. Second, the
members of a constitutional convention now lack confidence
in the ability of the ordinary member of a State legislature
and think it best to include in the constitution itself many
detailed laws which were originally left to be enacted by the
legislature.

The constitution of Oklahoma, one of the most recent, goes
into such minute detail as to enumerate the classes of persons
who are permitted to accept railroad passes, and contains about
50,000 words. Laws which go into great detail need to be
amended frequently, and since 1902 twelve States have adopted
the easier method of amending their constitutions — the
initiative method.

---

[1] For complete list of Initiative States see Section 244.

Those States which have not adopted the new method of amending their constitutions are obliged to resort to the old methods more frequently. Never before 1914 were as many as forty-one amendments initiated by the voters in any one year, nor were as many as 161 ever submitted by the legislatures.

158. Authority of State Constitutions. — The constitution with its amendments constitutes the supreme law of the State, and it overrides any laws enacted by the legislature which conflict therewith. Whenever a legislature passes a law which conflicts with some provision of the constitution the first person who is in any way inconvenienced by the law may refuse to abide by it, and permit some one to sue him because he knows that the court will declare the law null and void, that is, of no force.

For example, a few years ago the legislature of New York State enacted a law providing that any employer whose workmen are injured in certain enumerated dangerous pursuits, such as stone quarrying, must compensate the workmen by a money payment, whether the employer was at fault or not. The first employee who was injured demanded his money. The employer refused to pay him, claiming that the law was contrary to the constitution of the State. The workman sued the employer, but the highest court of the State (Court of Appeals) decided that the law did conflict with the constitution, was thus null and void, and could not be enforced.

The legislature still thought that there should be such a law; therefore two successive sessions proposed an amendment to the constitution and submitted it to the people. The majority of voters cast their ballots in favor of it, and thus changed the constitution so that the next legislature could enact the same workmen's compensation law, for it would no longer conflict with the constitution. The next legislature did pass the law, and to-day the courts enforce it.

159. Relative Rank of Laws. — The following outline shows the relative rank of laws in the United States:

United States Constitution.
   United States statutes and treaties.
      State constitutions.
         State statutes.
            County, town, or city statutes, called county
               "regulations" or "by-laws" and town
               or city "ordinances" or "by-laws."

The Constitution of the United States is the supreme law of the land, and every other law is subordinate to it. If Congress passes any statute which conflicts with the Constitution of the United States or if the President and Senate make any treaty which conflicts with the Constitution of the United States, such statute or treaty will not be enforced by the courts.

Likewise, if a State constitution contains any provision which is contrary to the Constitution of the United States or to a statute of Congress the same cannot be enforced. Furthermore, if a State legislature enacts a statute contrary to the Constitution of the United States, a statute of Congress, or a provision of the State constitution it cannot be enforced. Or if a county board or town or city council passes a by-law contrary to any of the above laws, it is void and the courts will not enforce it.

It is impracticable to write definite laws regulating in detail all possible human actions; so in addition to the above written laws we have a set of rules and principles which are not written in any definite form but are enforced by the government. These rules and principles grew out of custom and court decisions in England during a number of centuries, and because they were uniform throughout all England they were called *common law*.[1] When the American States became independent of England they retained the English common law to supplement their definite written laws.

As each American State has a distinct system of courts the common law rules and principles have become different in

---

[1] Equity is similar to common law, see Sec. 182.

some details in the various States; but as decisions of the courts of each State are known to the judges of the courts of each of the other States these rules and principles remain very much the same throughout the country.[1]

If there is a case in court for which there is no definite written law it must be decided according to the rules of common law. Occasionally a case arises which is unlike any previous case; for instance, a suit growing out of the collision of aeroplanes. There is no express law governing such a collision, but there are rules establishing a standard of care in the case of other classes of vehicles, so the court would apply the general rules and principles of the common law for vehicles to aeroplanes and thus determine the case by analogy.

BIBLIOGRAPHY

DEALEY, JAMES QUAYLE. Growth of American State Constitutions. 1915.

DODD, W. F. The Revision and Amendment of State Constitutions. 1910.

THORPE, FRANCIS NEWTON. Federal and State Constitutions. 7 vols. 1909.

A copy of the State Constitution can usually be obtained gratis from the Secretary of State.

QUESTIONS ON THE TEXT

1. What is a State constitution?

2. Of, what six parts does a State constitution commonly consist?

3. For what purpose is a constitutional convention assembled?

4. What part do the voters usually take in making a new constitution?

5. What is meant by *partial amendment* of a State constitution? Describe in detail how it is accomplished in the State in which you live.

---

[1] Louisiana, which State obtained its system of laws from France, is the only one that did not adopt the common law.

6. What new way of amending constitutions has developed since 1902? Explain this method.

7. What are some of the present tendencies of State constitutions?

8. If you are in any way inconvenienced by an Act of the legislature which is contrary to the constitution, need you abide by it?

9. If a law is declared unconstitutional is there any possibility of making it constitutional?

10. Name the various kinds of laws in the United States according to their relative rank of importance.

QUESTIONS FOR DISCUSSION

1. The members of the English House of Commons are elected for a term not exceeding five years. When the five-year term expired in 1915 the House continued to sit without an election because of the war condition. Could the United States House of Representatives prolong its term of office with the assent of the Senate? (See U. S. Constitution, Art. I, Sec. 2.)

2. Suppose South Carolina should add an amendment to its constitution depriving negroes of the right to vote. Would this be a valid law? (See Amend. XV.)

3. The constitution of New Jersey restricts the right of suffrage to male persons 21 years of age. Could the State legislature enact a law extending suffrage to women in all elections?

4. Women as well as men are permitted to vote in Colorado. Could a constitutional convention or the State legislature permit women to vote for United States congressmen without permitting them to vote for members of the more numerous branch of the State legislature? (See U. S. Constitution, Art. I, Sec. 2.)

5. The constitution of Virginia, until recently amended, provided that all cities of the first class should be governed by a two-body council. Staunton, Virginia, a city of the first class, desired to be governed by a single body commission. Could it be so governed?

6. The legislature of the State of Alabama enacted a law prohibiting saloons anywhere within the State. Could the council of the city of Birmingham license saloons in that city?

7. When and under what circumstances was the constitution of your State adopted? Was it approved by the people? Prepare a brief outline of it showing the main topic of each division and article.

8. The contents of State constitutions are beco
ordinary statutes, and since the method of cha
initiative, is that which is commonly used for
we any longer need. these constitutions? If Sta
abolished would it make the governments more

9. Prepare a brief constitution for a baseball
team.

CHAPTER XIX

STATE LEGISLATURES

160· Structure of State Legislatures. — Every State has a legislative body. In twenty-three of the States this body

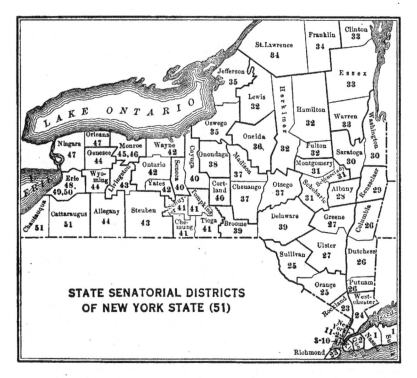

STATE SENATORIAL DISTRICTS
OF NEW YORK STATE (51)

is known as the "Legislature," in twenty as the "General Assembly," in three as the "Legislative Assembly," and in New Hampshire and Massachusetts as the "General Court." In each State the legislative body is composed of two houses —

251

the Senate and House of Representatives. In six States, however, the lower house is known as the "Assembly," and in three as the "House of Delegates."

161. Membership of State Legislatures. — The *Senates* vary in membership from 16 in Nevada to 67 in Minnesota. In some States one senator is elected from each county, but most States are divided into Senatorial Districts of about equal

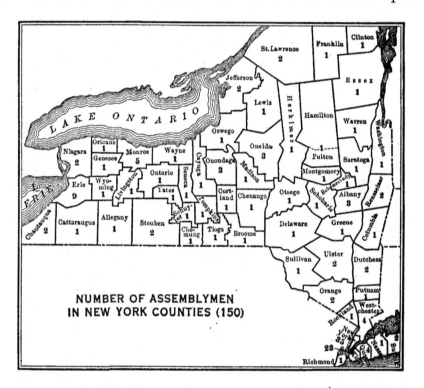

NUMBER OF ASSEMBLYMEN
IN NEW YORK COUNTIES (150)

population. Senators are elected for terms varying from one year in Massachusetts to four in thirty-one of the States.

The membership of the *House of Representatives* varies from 35 in Arizona and in Delaware to 405 in New Hampshire. In some States one or more representatives is elected from each county or each township, whereas other States are divided into House Districts of about equal population.

From time to time the legislatures create new Senate and

House districts which correspond to the changed distribution of population. As the cities grow in population the rural county representatives commonly refuse to increase city representation proportionately for fear that the counties will be controlled by the cities. An especially unfair apportionment is called a "gerrymander." (See Sec. 35.)

In most States any qualified voter is eligible to membership in the Senate or House, but in some States the age qualification for the Senate is higher than that for the House. The members, either by law or custom, usually reside in the districts from which they are elected.

162. Legislative Sessions. — The legislatures of six States meet annually, that of Alabama quadrennially, and those of all other States biennially. Every odd-numbered year forty-one legislatures convene — thirty-nine of them in the month of January. Many State constitutions absolutely limit the sessions to a definite number of days, others allow no compensation after the prescribed number of days. However, there is a tendency to remove the restriction because many of the bills which are rushed through the last days do not receive careful consideration. For any special or urgent purpose the governor may call an extra session.

163. Privileges, Immunities, and Compensation of Members. — State constitutions usually provide that for any speech or debate in either house a member may not be questioned in any other place; and that members are not subject to arrest under any civil process during any legislative session or coming thereto or going therefrom. This latter privilege amounts to scarcely anything to-day, for a member who commits treason, felony, or breach of the peace may be arrested like any other individual.

The salary of members of each house is always the same. In some States it is determined by the legislature, while in others it is prescribed by the constitution. It varies from $3 per diem while in session in Kansas to $3500 per session in Illinois.

STATE LEGISLATURES

STATE	ANN. OR BIEN.	LIMIT OF SESSION	No. OF MEMBERS IN SENATE	No. OF MEMBERS IN HOUSE	TERM OF SENATORS	TERM OF REPRESENTATIVES	SALARY OF MEMBERS	No. OF BILLS INTRODUCED IN ONE YEAR [1]
Alabama . . .	Quad.	50 days	35	106	4	4	$4 per diem	1,311
Arizona . . .	Bien.	60 days	19	35	2	2	$7 per diem	529
Arkansas . . .	Bien.	60 days	35	100	4	2	$6 per diem	743
California . .	Bien.	None	40	80	4	2	$1000 term	3,922
Colorado . . .	Bien.	None	35	65	4	2	$1000 term	1,286
Connecticut . .	Bien.	None	35	258	2	2	$300 ann.	1,751
Delaware . . .	Bien.	60 days	17	35	4	2	$5 per diem	625
Florida . . .	Bien.	60 days	32	75	4	2	$6 per diem	1,492
Georgia . . .	Ann.	50 days	44	186	2	2	$4 per diem	1,297
Idaho . . .	Bien.	60 days	37	65	2	2	$5 per diem	635
Illinois . . .	Bien.	None	51	153	4	2	$3500 ses'n.	1,608
Indiana . . .	Bien.	60 days	50	100	4	2	$6 per diem	1,329
Iowa	Bien.	None	50	108	4	2	$1000 ses'n.	1,264
Kansas . . .	Bien.	50 days	40	125	4	2	$3 per diem	1,773
Kentucky . . .	Bien.	60 days	38	100	4	2	$10 per diem	914
Louisiana . .	Bien.	60 days	38	118	4	4	$5 per diem	1,001
Maine	Bien.	None	31	151	2	2	$400 ann.	1,396
Maryland . . .	Bien.	90 days	27	101	4	2	$5 per diem	1,404
Massachusetts .	Ann.	None	40	240	1	1	$1000 ann.	3,167
Michigan . . .	Bien.	None	32	100	2	2	$800 ses'n.	1,261
Minnesota . .	Bien.	90 days	67	130	4	2	$1000 ses'n.	2,226
Mississippi . .	Bien.	None	45	139	4	4	$500 ses'n.	1,314
Missouri . . .	Bien.	70 days	34	142	4	2	$5 per diem	1,570
Montana . . .	Bién.	60 days	31	85	4	2	$10 per diem	610
Nebraska . . .	Bien.	60 days	33	100	2	2	$600 ann.	1,346
Nevada . . .	Bien.	60 days	16	37	4	2	$10 per diem	480
New Hampshire	Bien.	None	24	405	2	2	$200 ann.	800
New Jersey . .	Ann.	None	21	60	3	1	$500 ann.	1,240
New Mexico . .	Bien.	60 days	24	49	4	2	$5 per diem	512
New York . .	Ann.	None	51	150	2	1	$1500 ann.	4,081
North Carolina	Bien.	60 days	50	120	2	2	$4 per diem	4,308
North Dakota .	Bien.	60 days	49	113	4	2	$5 per diem	889
Ohio	Bien.	None	36	128	2	2	$1000 ann.	978
Oklahoma . .	Bien.	60 days	44	102	4	2	$6 per diem	1,125
Oregon . . .	Bien.	40 days	30	60	4	2	$3 per diem	971
Pennsylvania .	Bien.	None	50	207	4	2	$1500 ses'n.	2,726
Rhode Island .	Ann.	60 days	38	100	2	2	$5 per diem	711
South Carolina.	Ann.	None	45	124	4	2	$200 ann.	752
South Dakota .	Bien.	60 days	45	104	2	2	$5 per diem	902
Tennessee . .	Bien.	75 days	33	99	2	2	$4 per diem	2,742
Texas . . .	Bien.	60 days	31	142	4	2	$5 per diem	1,397
Utah	Bien.	60 days	18	46	4	2	$4 per diem	482
Vermont . . .	Bien.	None	30	246	2	2	$4 per diem	845
Virginia . . .	Bien.	60 days	40	100	4	2	$500 ses'n.	1,600
Washington . .	Bien.	60 days	42	96	4	2	$5 per diem	1,200
West Virginia .	Bien.	45 days	30	94	4	2	$4 per diem	646
Wisconsin . .	Bien.	None	33	100	4	2	$500 ses'n.	1,759
Wyoming . . .	Bien.	40 days	27	57	4	2	$8 per diem	392

[1] Bills introduced: Alabama, 1911; all even year States, 1912; all odd year States, 1913.

164. Powers of State Legislatures. — According to the Tenth Amendment to the Constitution of the United States " the powers not delegated to the United States by the Constitution, nor prohibited by it to the States, are reserved to the States, respectively, or to the people." (See Sec. 24.) State constitutions confer all of this reserved law-making power upon the legislatures, except as to certain specified matters reserved to the voters which may be altered only by changing the constitution.[1]

The legislatures do not attempt to exercise all of their powers, but delegate a portion of them to other local legislative bodies in counties, townships, school districts, cities, and towns or villages. The county board and the city council are examples of minor legislatures which derive all of their powers from general or special laws framed by a legislature, except a few which are bestowed directly through the constitution.

Of course it is impossible to enumerate the powers of the State legislatures because they may enact any laws which are

---

[1] The following restrictions are commonly placed upon State legislatures by State constitutions:

1. The Bill of Rights guarantees freedom of the press and speech, religious liberty, jury trial, right to the writ of habeas corpus, etc., and prohibits the taking of private property for a public purpose without compensation.

2. Other parts of the constitution:

    (a) Prohibit special privileges to corporations.

    (b) Limit State debts and compel regular payment of interest and principal.

    (c) Prescribe qualifications for voters and define terms and duties of certain officers.

    (d) Prescribe certain rules for local government, public education, and public institutions.

    (e) Place certain restrictions upon the passage of special or local laws, that is, laws applying to some particular person, corporation, or locality — township, county, or city. As an illustration of the need of such restrictions, some years ago the legislature of Pennsylvania compelled Philadelphia to build a city hall costing millions of dollars, which was larger and more extensive than the city needed or would have otherwise built.

not denied them by the Constitution or laws of the United States or by the constitutions of the respective States, but examples can be given of subjects concerning which they legislate. Such examples are taxation; civil matters, such as contracts, real and personal property, inheritances, mortgages, corporations, marriage, and divorce; crimes for which fines, imprisonment, or death are imposed; "police regulations," such as

TEXAS STATE CAPITOL AT AUSTIN.

morals, public health, business or professional regulations, or any general welfare rule which restricts a person's inclination to do as he pleases.

165. Organization of State Legislatures. — Each house of the State legislatures commonly has power to select its own officers, except that some States have a lieutenant-governor provided for in the constitution who presides over the upper chamber. (See Sec. 177.) It also determines its own rules of procedure and the qualifications of its members, and by a certain prescribed majority, usually two thirds, may expel members. Legally the speaker of the House and the president or chairman of the Senate, except where there is a lieutenant-governor, are elected by the respective houses over which they preside, but practically they are chosen in a party caucus. (See Sec. 57.)

The officers of each house of the State legislatures are very similar to those of Congress and their duties are about the same. (See Sec. 51.) For instance, the speaker is presiding officer of the House and has power to refer bills to committees, but unlike the speaker of the United States House of Representatives he has power to appoint the committees in nearly all States. Each house has a clerk and a sergeant-at-arms and numerous other officers varying in number from 21 in Delaware to 315 in Missouri.

The committee system in State legislatures is also very similar to that of Congress. (See Sec. 53.) Here also most committee meetings are held in secret and their votes upon measures are not recorded in a majority of the States. It is by these committees that popular measures are so often defeated. For instance, a common method of preventing the passage of a bill is for the speaker to refer it to the Judiciary Committee, claiming it to be of doubtful constitutionality, but really desiring to prevent the bill from coming to a vote. The majority of this committee is naturally composed of friends of the speaker inasmuch as he appoints them, and he can usually count upon them to " pigeon-hole " any such bill and fail to report upon it. Thus it dies and it is buried in the committee. Because of the great number of deserving bills which are buried in this committee it is often spoken of as " the graveyard committee."

Ex-Governor Sulzer of New York, who has had considerable opportunity to observe actual methods of legislation, has said : " The crooked work in legislatures is all, or nearly all, done in committees. People who take an intelligent interest in public affairs think they have made a great step when they have the public watching the legislature. They have, but a greater step will have been made when they have the public keeping the spot light on legislative committees and particularly the chairman. For immediately behind the chairman of the committee will be found the Big Boss."

Professor Paul Reinsch considers the Massachusetts legislature to have reached the highest stage of development. He says, "In that State committee hearings are a very important part of legislative action. Notice of all hearings is given in the public press, and the committee meetings are well attended, not only by people who have an ax to grind, but by citizens of the State who interest themselves in legislative reforms. All testimony brought before the committees is carefully weighed; in fact, the legislature and its committees assume rather a judicial attitude. Petitions are brought before them, testimony is given, arguments are made, and they can generally decide the matter impartially upon the basis of all these considerations."

166. How Bills Become Laws. — *Preparation of Bills.* — The State legislatures may represent the average honesty and intelligence of the people, but few legislators are capable of preparing their bills in unmistakable language or in accordance with superior law.[1] For some years the members of our legislatures drafted their own bills, the lawyer members or some legislative clerk assisting the inexperienced.

After the development of large corporations their lobbyists, or legislative agents, often prepared bills free for members whose acquaintance and good-will they desired. To-day half of the States have trained assistants whose duty it is to put in clear legal form the ideas that members wish to enact into statutes. The assistant is ordinarily connected with a legislative reference bureau.

A *Legislative Reference Bureau* is a library or division of a library especially equipped to assist legislators. Such a

---

[1] *Superior law* means the Constitution of the United States, laws of Congress, treaties, and the State constitution.

bureau collects references, summaries, files, card indexes, court decisions, newspaper clippings, magazine articles, reference books, government reports, bills introduced into other legislative bodies, governors' messages, platforms of political parties, and any other information available for legislators. Since 1890 thirty-odd States have undertaken this work on varying scales, usually in coöperation with the State library.

Introduction of Bills. — Any member of either house may introduce as many bills as he chooses. In introducing bills the members merely file them with the clerk. Some legislatures prohibit the introduction of bills after the legislature has been in session a certain number of days; others require that bills of a local or private character must be announced in the locality to be affected; and others require that local bills receive a two-thirds vote of each house instead of a bare majority, which is sufficient for public bills.

As the passage of a bill through a State legislature is so similar to the procedure of Congress it need not be described here in detail. (See Sec. 55.)

On account of the large number of bills introduced at each session of the State legislature it would be impossible even for the committees to give consideration to all of them. Therefore those bills which are not introduced by prominent members or backed by influencial lobbyists are commonly not seriously considered and are said to be " pigeon-holed." Other bills which the committees do not favor but feel obliged to report upon are often intentionally reported too late to be considered by the houses.

167. Lobbying. — The practice of frequenting lobbies[1] or any other convenient places for the purpose of persuading legislators to vote for or against certain bills is known as *lobbying.* For instance, the Retail Liquor Dealers' Association of a State, the Anti-Saloon League, railroads, and many other

---

[1] A *lobby* is an anteroom or corridor communicating with the main assembly room, or else a part of the room itself to which the public is admitted and which is usually railed off from the part used for the assembly.

organizations interested in legislation — good or bad — send agents to State capitols to frequent the legislative halls for the purpose of influencing legislative votes. All such agents engaged in lobbying at the capitol are known as *lobbyists*.

The State of Wisconsin requires lobbyists to register their names and that of the organization which they represent. The register is open to public inspection. Thus the State is endeavoring to give publicity to the lobbyists who have been responsible for much bad legislation.

168. The Referendum. — In one third of the States the Governor is not the only authority that can prevent a bill which has passed the legislature from becoming law.[1] In these States a device known as the *referendum* permits a small percentage of the voters to require the reference of any act passed by the legislature to all of the voters for approval or rejection. The referendum thus enables the voters to reject undesired legislation.

In November, 1914, the voters of nine States had a total of twenty-seven legislative statutes referred to them by petition, and of these nineteen were rejected by the voters. For instance, the legislature of Missouri passed a law known as the " full crew law " which required railroads to man their trains with more men than the railroad companies thought were necessary. Therefore the railroads had five per cent of the voters in each of two thirds of the congressional districts sign a petition demanding that the statute be referred to the people. It was referred at the November election and rejected by a vote of 324,384 to 159,892.

169. The Initiative. — All of the States which have the State-wide referendum, except Maryland and New Mexico, also have the State-wide *initiative*,[2] which is a device whereby a small percentage of voters may initiate a law and have it referred to all of the voters for their acceptance or rejection. Thus, if a legislature will not enact a law which a certain per

---

[1] For list of Referendum States see section 244.

[2] For a complete list of Initiative States see section 244.

cent of the voters think the majority favor they can have the prescribed per cent sign a petition, and the measure will be referred to the voters at the next election. This is known as *direct legislation* because voters make law directly, not depending upon their legislators.

At the 1914 November election six States voted upon forty-one initiated statutes of which they enacted thirteen into law and rejected twenty-eight. As examples, Oregon abolished capital punishment by means of the initiative, the vote standing 100,552 to 100,395, and Washington State abolished the sale of liquor throughout the State by the same means, the vote being 189,840 to 171,208.

170. Commission Government for States. — Believing that the State legislatures are no longer able to carry out the various duties which new conditions impose upon them, Governor Hodges of Kansas sent a special message to the Kansas legislature on March 10, 1913, containing the following passage:

"In common with a large and growing number of thoughtful people I am persuaded that the instrumentalities for legislation provided for in our State constitution have become antiquated and inefficient. Our system is fashioned after the English parliament, with its two houses based upon the distinction between the nobility and the common people, each House representing the diverse interests of these classes. No such reason exists in this State for a dual legislative system, and even in England at the present time the dual system has been practically abandoned and the upper House shorn of its importance, and I believe that we should now concern ourselves in devising a system for legislating that will give us more efficiency and quicker response to the demands of our economic and social conditions and to the will of the people. . . .

"You senators and representatives cannot but have observed the defects of our present system. In a short session of 50 days you are required to study and pass upon hundreds of measures, and the hurry with which this must be done must of necessity result in a number of more or less crude and ill-digested laws, which often puzzle learned jurists to interpret with anything like satisfaction to themselves or to the public. Hundreds of measures also, embodying important legislation, die on the calendar every two years. After a brief session the

Legislature adjourns, and the business of one coördinate branch of the State government is absolutely abandoned for a whole biennium, unless the Legislature is convoked in an expensive extraordinary session by the governor. It is as if the head of an important department of some big business should give only 50 days every two years to its management.

*   *   *   *   *   *   *   *   *

" For myself, I can see no good reason why this new idea of government by commission should not be adopted for the transaction of the business of the State. Two years ago I suggested a single legislative assembly of thirty members from thirty legislative districts. I am now inclined to believe that this number is too large and that a legislative assembly of .one, or at most two, from each Congressional district would be amply large. My judgment is that the governor should be *ex officio* a member and presiding officer of this assembly, and that it should be permitted to meet in such frequent and regular or adjourned sessions as the exigencies of the public business demand; that their terms of office be for four or six years, and that they be paid salaries sufficient to justify them in devoting their entire time to the public business. Such a legislative assembly would not, I believe, be more expensive than our present system. It would centralize the responsibility and accountability, and under the check of the recall would be quickly responsive to the wishes of the people."[1]

BIBLIOGRAPHY

REINSCH, PAUL S.   American Legislatures and Legislative Methods. 1907.
SHELDON AND KIEGAN.   Legislative Procedure in the Forty-Eight States.   Nebraska Legislative Reference Bureau, Bull. No. 3, 1914.

---

[1] So far the State of Kansas has taken no serious action upon this recommendation, but the question has been voted upon by the people of two other States, Oregon and Oklahoma. In Oregon an initiative amendment to abolish the State senate was defeated by the people at the November election, 1914. In Oklahoma an initiative amendment to establish a one-body legislature of 80 members was voted on at the same time. The vote in favor of the amendment was 94,636, that against it only 71,742, but since 94,636 was not a majority of all the votes cast at that election the amendment was lost because Oklahoma requires a majority of the total number of votes cast at the election to amend its constitution.

QUESTIONS ON THE TEXT

1. By what name is the legislature of the State in which you live known? The upper house? The lower house?

2. How many members are there in the upper house of the legislature of the State in which you live? The lower house?

3. How many senators are elected from the senatorial district in which you live? How many representatives?

4. How often does the legislature meet in the State in which you live? When? Is the length of the session restricted? How may an extra session be called?

5. What special privileges and immunities do State legislators enjoy?

6. What salary do legislators receive in the State in which you live?

7. What restrictions are there upon the legislative powers of the legislature of the State in which you live?

8. What legislative power may counties, townships, and cities exercise?

9. Mention a number of subjects which may be legislated upon by State legislatures.

10. How are the two houses of a State legislature organized and what control have they over their own members?

11. Who is the presiding officer of the lower house in the State in which you reside? Of the upper house? How are they selected? What powers do they have? May they vote?

12. Name some other legislative officers.

13. How are committees chosen? Name several important committees of the legislature of the State in which you live. Do all State legislatures have the same kind of committees?

14. What is the defect of our committee system, according to ex-Governor Sulzer of New York?

15. What is a joint committee?

16. Explain how committee hearings are conducted in Massachusetts.

17. How are bills proposed?

18. What is a legislative reference bureau? Does the State in which you live have one?

19. Who may introduce bills? What restrictions do some legislatures have regarding the introduction of bills?

20. Name the stages through which a bill passes in becoming law.

21. What is meant by *lobbying?* How does Wisconsin regulate the practice of lobbying?

22. Explain the referendum. The initiative. Does the State in which you live have either or both?

23. Explain Governor Hodges' criticism of State legislatures and his proposed remedy for the evils of the present system.

Questions for Discussion

1. Bound the senatorial district in which you live. Who is your State senator?

2. Bound the house district in which you live. Name your representative or your representatives.

3. Has the State in which you live been "gerrymandered" for the advantage of either party, or for the advantage of the rural districts over the cities?

4. If the salary of a State legislator is low it will not prevent candidates who have special interests from seeking election, but what effect does the low salary have upon one who is not backed by any special interests? Will a legislator who receives a low or a high salary be more likely to vote as the people desire?

5. State constitutions commonly restrict the session of State legislatures to 60 days, which means that bills must be passed or rejected because of the calendar rather than after due consideration. Would it not be well for all States to pay their legislators by the year and permit them to prolong the session as long as need be?

6. In the United States there are 48 State legislatures. Do you think this is too many? For instance, if one legislature made laws for all New England, would it not save expense and the confusion resulting from six different sets of laws?

7. Pennsylvania employs 257 legislators divided into a senate and a house, a governor, and a supreme court to provide its laws. The two legislative bodies are supposed to check each other; the governor with his veto checks them both; and the supreme court checks them all by decisions as to the constitutionality of legislative acts. The salary of the legislators alone amounts to about $400,000 annually. According to the recommendations of ex-Governor Hodges of Kansas how might this method of lawmaking be improved?

8. Experienced legislators cannot be elected, but they can be re-elected until they become skilful legislators. What is the inference of this statement?

9. The National Voters League prepares a bulletin, called the "Searchlight on Congress," which gives the votes of each congressman upon all important measures that come up during his term of office. Is there any organization in the State in which you live to inform you as to the record of your State legislators? Should there be?

10. If possible examine a copy of the acts of the legislature and mention a few of the laws passed at its last session. (Any lawyer, court clerk, or justice of the peace should have a copy.)

11. Do you think a legislator should vote according to the will of the majority of his constituents or that he should use his own discretion regardless of their wishes?

12. Why may one fifth of the members voting in either house of the State legislature demand that the vote of each member be recorded in the journal?

13. The constitution of Idaho (Art. V, Sec. 25) requires the judges of her trial courts to report annually to her supreme court such defects and omissions in the State constitution or statutes as they have observed. The supreme court considers these suggestions and makes recommendation to the governor for suitable legislation. Do you favor this practice?

14. Draft a bill in due form for the enactment of any law which you would like to see passed by your State legislature. Be careful to prepare a measure which does not conflict with any higher law. The wording should begin: "Be it enacted by the legislature of the State of ——, that," etc.

CHAPTER XX

STATE GOVERNORS

171. The Office of Governor. — Every State has a governor as its chief executive officer. He is elected by the voters of

GOVERNOR'S MANSION, ANNAPOLIS, MARYLAND.

the State.[1] During colonial days the royal governors did the bidding of the King and often merited the dislike of the people. When the colonists grew weary of British rule their legislatures were able to protect them against despotic acts of the governors.

Thus when they gained their independence they naturally

---

[1] In Mississippi the Governor must receive a majority of the popular votes of the State as in all other States, but in addition to this requirement he must receive a majority of popular votes in more than half of the districts from which representatives are elected for the most numerous branch of the legislature.

STATE GOVERNORS

STATE	CAPITAL	TERM OF SERVICE (years)	SALARY
Alabama	Montgomery	4	$ 5,000 and residence [1]
Arizona	Phœnix	2	4,000
Arkansas	Little Rock	2	4,000 and house rent
California	Sacramento	4	10,000 and residence
Colorado	Denver	2	5,000
Connecticut	Hartford	2	5,000
Delaware	Dover	4	4,000
Florida	Tallahassee	4	6,000 and residence
Georgia	Atlanta	2	5,000 and residence
Idaho	Boise	2	5,000
Illinois	Springfield	4	12,000 and residence
Indiana	Indianapolis	4	8,000
Iowa	Des Moines	2	5,000
Kansas	Topeka	2	5,000 and residence
Kentucky	Frankfort	4	6,500 and residence
Louisiana	Baton Rouge	4	7,500 and residence
Maine	Augusta	2	5,000
Maryland	Annapolis	4	4,500 and residence
Massachusetts	Boston	1	10,000
Michigan	Lansing	2	5,000
Minnesota	St. Paul	2	7,000
Mississippi	Jackson	4	5,000 and residence
Missouri	Jefferson City	4	5,000 and residence
Montana	Helena	4	5,000 and residence
Nebraska	Lincoln	2	2,500 and residence
Nevada	Carson City	4	7,000 and residence
New Hampshire	Concord	2	3,000
New Jersey	Trenton	3	10,000
New Mexico	Sante Fe	5	5,000 and residence
New York	Albany	2	10,000 and residence
North Carolina	Raleigh	4	5,000 and residence
North Dakota	Bismarck	2	5,000 and residence
Ohio	Columbus	2	10,000
Oklahoma	Oklahoma City	4	4,500
Oregon	Salem	4	5,000
Pennsylvania	Harrisburg	4	10,000 and residence
Rhode Island	Providence	2	3,000
South Carolina	Columbia	2	3,000 and residence
South Dakota	Pierre	2	3,000
Tennessee	Nashville	2	4,000 and residence
Texas	Austin	2	4,000 and residence
Utah	Salt Lake City	4	6,000
Vermont	Montpelier	2	2,500
Virginia	Richmond	4	5,000 and residence
Washington	Olympia	4	6,000 and residence
West Virginia	Charleston	4	5,000 and residence
Wisconsin	Madison	2	5,000 and residence
Wyoming	Cheyenne	4	4,000 and residence

[1] Furnishings, heat, and light are usually supplied, and the wages of servants are paid in some States.

regarded governors with suspicion and looked upon the legis-latures as guardians of their liberty. Therefore governors were granted little power in the early constitutions. In addressing the Federal Constitutional Convention of 1787 Madison said, "The executives of the States are in general little more than ciphers; the legislatures are omnipotent."

However, the public have gradually lost confidence in their State legislatures because the character of the legislators has deteriorated. This is due to the fact that the States extended suffrage more rapidly than they educated the voters in the proper use of the ballot. Prejudice against governors has disappeared, and it is realized that it is easier to elect one honest and efficient leader who can be held responsible to the people than it is to elect numerous responsible legislators.

So, recently the governors have been regarded as the guardians of the people's liberty. Such governors as Roosevelt and Hughes of New York, LaFollette of Wisconsin, and Woodrow Wilson of New Jersey, have exalted the office of governor in the public mind; and constitutional changes have increased the legal powers of the occupant.

172. The Governors' Powers. — The powers of a governor are usually classified under three heads: (1) executive powers, such as appointing officers and seeing that the civil and criminal laws of the State are enforced; (2) legislative powers, such as sending messages to the legislature and vetoing objectionable laws; and (3) judicial powers, such as pardoning persons convicted of crime.

173. Executive Powers of the Governor. — A State constitution almost invariably provides that the governor shall take care that the laws of the State are faithfully executed, but to him is never given power for the performance of this duty as is given to the President of the United States. (See Sec. 63.)

Practically all of the most important State officers, such as the secretary of state, attorney general, auditor, and treasurer are elected by the people. Judges are elected by the people in most States. Sheriffs and state's attorneys are elected by the people with few exceptions. Thus, the governor is merely one of a number of officers whom the people elect to enforce the laws, and if the other officers do not perform their duties in an efficient and honest manner the governor is often helpless.

A story is told of a sheriff who permitted a prisoner to be taken from his jail and lynched. The governor wrote a letter to the sheriff repri-manding him for his neglect of duty. The sheriff promptly re-plied by telling the governor to mind his own business; that he was responsible to the people of his county who had elected him and to nobody else. Accord-ing to the law of his State the sheriff was right. It may be said that a governor is the captain of a Ship of State which is navi-gated by a crew that he does not select, and over which he has few powers of command.

Underwood & Underwood, N. Y.

A MOUNTED SQUAD OF PENNSYLVANIA CONSTABULARY.

As commander-in-chief of the State militia the governor has a real power. When a riot occurs, when a prisoner is in dan-ger of being lynched, or when a strike cannot be handled by local officers the governor may call out the militia.

State Police. — A few of the States have regular State police. For example, the governor of Massachusetts has a small body of State police to assist him in the enforcement of the State laws. It acts as a detective force to aid in the suppression of disorder and in the enforcement of criminal laws. It also per-

forms such other functions as the inspection of factories and
the investigation of fires. The governor of Texas has four
companies of Rangers consisting of twenty-two men each to
patrol the border. He appoints their captains and may order
them where needed. The most famous body of State police is
the Pennsylvania Constabulary.

Pennsylvania Constabulary. — The Pennsylvania department
of police, called "the constabulary" (body of constables), was

PENNSYLVANIA CONSTABULARY OFF TO
ANSWER A HURRY CALL.

created by the legisla-
ture in 1906. It con-
sists of a superintendent
and 228 mounted police
and officers, ninety per
cent of whom have
served in the United
States army and pos-
sess excellent discharge
papers. Previous to the
creation of this depart-
ment the governor was
supposed to maintain
peace and order
throughout the entire
State of Pennsylvania
(45,000 square miles)

with no one to assist him but his secretary and stenographer,
as one governor jocularly remarked.

This Pennsylvania police force is divided into four companies, and each occupies a barrack in a different section of
the State. The force not only acts upon the orders of the
governor but coöperates with local peace officers of any community. In general, the duties of the force are to maintain
order in communities where strikes occur; raid disorderly
resorts, gambling houses, and "speak-easies"; pursue criminals; detect "black hand" miscreants; act as game and fish
wardens; and extinguish forest fires. Though these police

ordinarily move about on horseback, they sometimes answer emergency calls in automobiles and often disguise themselves as civilians and as miners.

Appointments. — The power of the governor to make appointments is slightly on the increase, though he usually does not have power to remove most of those whom he appoints; and as the appointments are distributed through his term he is appointing as many officers to serve for his successor as for himself.

174. Legislative Powers of the Governor. — The governor is considered the head of the executive branch of government, yet his legislative powers have increased more rapidly than his executive powers. He has three legislative powers : (1) to send messages to the legislature, (2) to call an extra session of the legislature, and (3) to veto bills passed by the legislature.

Governor's Messages. — The message power has not been used by governors to the extent that the constitutions allow. A weak governor will send a formal message to the legislature when it meets, recommending legislation which the annual reports of the State officers bring to his attention. His message is read to the two houses sitting together, and the various recommendations are distributed to the appropriate legislative committees by the Speaker of the House of Representatives. This is often the end of the matter. The governor has done " his duty " — no more.

A strong governor will send a number of short messages, and " get back of them " — one at a time. In fact, a governor has the right to make his recommendation in the form of a bill if he chooses, but it is wiser to take a number of members into his confidence and have a chairman of a legislative committee introduce a bill containing his ideas.

In 1913 the Illinois House of Representatives adopted a rule providing that a bill which a governor has had introduced shall have precedence in the consideration of the house over all other measures except appropriation bills.

Extra Sessions. — For any reason that a governor thinks suffi-cient he may call an extra session of the legislature. When Roosevelt was governor of New York he recommended a certain tax reform when the legislature was in session. The legis-lature failed to enact it, therefore he called them back in extra session to consider this particular bill. The governor of Colorado called a special session to consider the settlement of large labor strikes. Extra sessions are rather common, especially in Alabama, where the legislature meets in regular session only once in four years.

The Veto. — With the exception of North Carolina all States give the governor power to veto bills passed by the legislature, though such veto may be overridden by a subsequent vote of the legislature.[1] When a bill is sent to the governor for his signature he is allowed a period varying from three to ten days in which to consider it before taking action. In case the governor does not approve of a bill he may veto it in its entirety, but in South Carolina and Washington he is allowed to veto any portion of any bill if he so desires.

In order to check extravagance most of the States allow the governor to veto specific items in a general appropriation bill. However, this power of the governor encourages legislators to vote appropriations in excess of the revenues in order to comply with the wishes of the various institutions seeking State aid, and thus "put it up to the governor" to veto numerous items so that the total amount appropriated will come within the revenues of the State.

175. Judicial Powers of the Governor. — Nearly all of the governors have some power of mercy towards persons accused or convicted of crime. It may be to remit fines, to shorten jail or penitentiary sentences, to pardon a prisoner conditionally or absolutely, to postpone the execution of a death sentence, or

---

[1] In two thirds of the States the legislatures are permitted to override the veto of the governor by the repassage of a vetoed bill with a two-thirds vote in each house. In Delaware, Maryland, and Nebraska a majority of three fifths is required, and in a few States a bare majority is sufficient to overcome his veto.

to change a death sentence to a penitentiary sentence. That is, a governor may have all or some of these powers, but these powers are commonly shared by a State board of pardons. Recently a governor of New York pardoned a prisoner on condition that he would not make capital of his notoriety by posing for motion pictures or on the vaudeville stage.

The primary purpose of the pardoning power is to release prisoners who have been proved innocent after being sentenced ;

A ROOM IN THE WHITE HOUSE.
This scene shows prominent men who attended the First Governors'' Conference.

but one governor pardoned some hundreds of prisoners because he thought the penitentiary as then conducted would do the convicted persons more harm than good, and another pardoned about a thousand because he thought the sentences were out of proportion to the offences. This arbitrary use of the pardon power is dangerous because it encourages the so-called "lynch law." If one man can overturn the opinions of many jurors there is danger that the people will take the enforcement of law into their own hands.

176. Conference of Governors. — In 1908 President Roosevelt called a Conference of Governors at the White House to confer in regard to the conservation of the natural resources of the nation. Since then the governors have held annual conferences at one of the State capitals for the purpose of discussing uniform laws, interstate good-will and the interchange of State experience. The conference is sometimes called the "House of Governors." It has a permanent secretary who is paid by small appropriations made by the various State legislatures.

This conference is of course extra-legal and its actions are not binding upon any State.

177. Executive Officers More or Less Independent of the Governor. — In most States the following offices exist and the officers are more or less independent of the governor:

The Lieutenant-Governor serves when a governor is absent from his State or incapacitated for duty. He is *ex officio* president of the Senate and in most States succeeds to the governorship if for any reason the office becomes vacant.

The Secretary of State is the chief clerk and records the official acts of the governor and legislature, has charge of various State papers and documents, and performs other miscellaneous duties.

The State Comptroller or Auditor has charge of the State finances. He estimates the amount of revenue needed by the State, enforces the collection of taxes, and sees that no money is expended contrary to law.

The State Treasurer receives the State moneys for safe keeping and pays them out only upon warrants (orders) from the comptroller or auditor.

The Attorney-General is the principal law officer of the State. He gives legal advice to the governor and other executive officers, and represents the State in court.

The Superintendent of Public Instruction is the head of the public school system of the State.

Additional officers, such as the following, exist in the several States according to their needs: banking commissioner, insurance commissioner, industrial commissioner, factory commissioner, highway commissioner, health commissioner, public service commissioner, etc., etc.

BIBLIOGRAPHY

FINLEY, JOHN H., and SANDERSON, JOHN F. American Executive and Executive Methods. (American State Series.) 1908.
Proceedings of the Annual Conference of Governors.

QUESTIONS ON THE TEXT

1. By what title is the chief executive officer of each State known?
2. What did Madison mean when he said, "The Executives of the States are in general little more than ciphers; the legislatures are omnipotent"? Does this condition remain true?
3. How do the powers of a governor compare with those of the President?
4. What executive powers has the governor?
5. What is meant by the statement that "a governor is the captain of a Ship of State, which is navigated by a crew that he does not select, and over which he has few powers of command"?
6. Describe the manner in which the State police of several States assist the governor in enforcing the laws. By what name are these police known in Pennsylvania?
7. Is the appointive power of the governor on the increase or decrease?
8. Have the legislative or executive powers of the governor increased more rapidly?
9. Name the three legislative powers of the governor.
10. Explain the use which a strong governor makes of messages.
11. Under what circumstances does a governor call an extra session of the legislature?
12. Under what condition may a bill become law in the State in which you live if vetoed by the governor?
13. What advantage results from the power possessed by most governors to veto specific items in appropriation bills? What unpleasant duty is often shifted from the legislatures to the governor as a result of this power?
14. What judicial powers has a governor?
15. Under what conditions should a governor grant pardons?

Questions for Discussion

1. Who is the governor of the State in which you live? May he succeed himself as governor?

2. In New Jersey no executive officers of the State are elected by the people except the governor. With all the interest centred in the governor it is easy for the people to express intelligent opinions at the polls. Would you favor having the State executive officers appointed by the governor?

3. The People's Power League in Oregon proposed a constitutional amendment giving the governor power to appoint a cabinet consisting of all State executive officers who are now elected and also all sheriffs and district attorneys throughout the State — the latter, however, being subject to a recall by the local electorate. This scheme also provides for a legislature of one house in which the governor and his cabinet have a right to propose their measures and take part in debates. It further proposes that the governor may introduce the appropriation bill which might not be increased by the legislature but might be reduced. What do you consider the merits and demerits of this scheme?

4. Governor Wilson of New Jersey broke all precedents by appearing at legislative hearings and by participating in the meetings of members of the legislature. He urged the passage of "administration bills" and "took the stump" when his measures were not passed. By the force of "pitiless publicity" this independent and courageous governor forced the legislature to give what legislation the people desired. Do you favor this type of governor?

5. New Jersey has no lieutenant-governor. The president of the Senate becomes governor if the elected governor dies or resigns. Does the State in which you live need a lieutenant-governor?

6. What executive officers are elected in the State in which you live besides the governor?

7. In 1913 the Illinois House of Representatives adopted a rule providing that a bill which the governor has had introduced shall have precedence in the consideration of the House over all other measures except appropriation bills. Would you favor similar action by the lower house of the legislature in the State in which you live?

8. Twenty-seven of the States maintain residences for their governors. Is the State in which you live one of them?

9. When a new governor elected on a party platform finds an

organized opposition in the legislature, what steps can he take to carry out the platform pledges?

10. In comparing the executive powers of the governor with those of the President we find the governor at a great disadvantage. The present population of a number of States is greater than that of the Nation when the United States Constitution was framed, and the number of State employees (10,000 in New York State) and of State functions is much greater than those of the Federal government during Washington's administration. What changes would have to be made by your State to give the governor the same control over State administration that the President has over federal administration?

CHAPTER XXI

STATE COURTS

178. Dual System of Courts. — Each of the forty-eight States of the Union has its own system of courts to interpret its laws, apply them to controversies brought into court, and to administer justice. The primary duty of the highest State courts is to interpret the laws and that of the lower courts to apply them to the controversies brought to them for settlement.

Besides these State courts, and independent of them, is a system of federal courts extending throughout the United States. These federal courts have jurisdiction of a limited class of cases enumerated in the Constitution of the United States. (See U. S. Constitution, Art. III, Sec. 2.) The State courts hear all other cases.

179. Organization of State Courts. — The lowest courts of each State are commonly called Justices' Courts. Each township or other local district has at least one such court presided over by a magistrate, usually called the justice of the peace. He generally has jurisdiction[1] over most misdemeanor cases[2] and small controversies between man and man — civil cases[3] — con-

---

[1] Jurisdiction (Lat. *jus* and *dictio*) is the right or power of a court to hear and determine cases brought before it.

[2] Crimes are of two kinds, misdemeanors and felonies. A felony is the greater crime and may be punished by death or imprisonment; a misdemeanor is the lesser crime and is punished by a fine or a relatively short term in jail.

[3] A civil case is a suit brought by one person against another for the enforcement or protection of a private right, or for the prevention or redress of a private wrong. It is distinguished from a criminal case, which is a suit brought by the State against one who is accused of having committed a crime. Officers of the government always prosecute the accused in a criminal case. (See Sec. 184.) In a civil case the counsel (lawyer) must usually be paid by the person who employs him.

cerning money demands (seldom over $50 or $100), the ownership of personal property and wrongs or injuries to property.
He is generally denied jurisdiction to determine questions of
title to real estate, titles to office, torts to the person, and other
like matters of great importance.

Above these local courts are County Courts (called Courts of
Common Pleas, or District Courts in some States) which have
jurisdiction of civil cases involving greater sums, and of major
misdemeanors and minor felonies, or of all felonies. Appeals
from the judgments of the justices of the peace can be taken to
these County Courts unless it is a matter of the most minor
character over which the justice of the peace has final jurisdiction.

In many States Superior Courts exist above the County
Courts. These are commonly called Circuit Courts because
the judge goes on circuit to the county seats of the counties
composing his circuit. In some States these Circuit Courts
take the place of the County Courts. These courts have jurisdiction over civil cases involving unlimited sums and over
major felonies, or all felonies, in many States.

As the capstone to a State's judicial system there is always
one appellate court of last resort, the name of which varies
from State to State. For instance, in some States it is known
as the "Court of Appeals," and in others as the "Supreme
Court of Appeals." This court is appellate because practically
all of its cases are appealed to it from the lower courts, few
if any originating in it.

In addition to the regular State courts just enumerated,
nearly half of the States have a special court for each county
known as the Probate Court (called Orphans' Court or Surro-
gate Court in some States) to probate (prove) wills and qualify
executors to execute the wills, or to appoint administrators to
administer the estates of persons who have died intestate (without a will). In the other States the County Courts usually perform these functions.

Every State provides special courts for its cities, especially

its larger cities, which are known as municipal courts.   There
is usually a Police Court to try persons who have violated city
ordinances or minor criminal laws of the State which would
ordinarily come before a justice of the peace.   There are in
some cities special Civil Courts to hear minor civil cases which
would ordinarily be heard by a justice of the peace.   In a
large city there is one special court, or more, of equal rank

NIGHT COURT FOR WOMEN, NEW YORK CITY.

with a County or a Superior Court from which appeals may be
taken directly to the appellate court of last resort.

A few cities have Domestic Relations Courts to settle family
quarrels, as between man and wife, parents and child, adult
and child.   New York City has a Night Court for women,
where all women arrested on the streets for drunkenness or
other minor offences are tried immediately so as to prevent un-
due publicity.   Women officers are present to whom the guilty,
especially girls, are turned over in the hope of reforming them.

Juvenile Courts to try children have recently been established in many cities. In times past children were tried by the same court as adults, and were sent to the same prisons, where they learned the vices of hardened criminals. To-day these special Juvenile Courts are supposed to be presided over by judges who are especially interested in the welfare of children. Instead of sending a bad or criminal child to the jail or peniten-

JUDGE LINDSEY HOLDING HIS JUVENILE COURT, DENVER, COLORADO.

tiary the judge gives him over to a State reformatory unless he himself can save him by good advice and the help of a probation officer, who watches the children that have been found guilty of minor offences and released on probation (good behavior).

In a very short time one forenoon the judge of a Juvenile Court disposed of the following four cases. No. 1 was a fight between two small colored boys. The mother of the larger boy, being present, was directed to go into an adjoining room and whip her boy in the presence of an officer. No. 2 was a white girl brought by her own parents. The girl, agreeing to do

better, was directed to return to her home and to report weekly
to a woman probation officer. No. 3, a colored girl, who had
previously been on probation, was accused of stealing. She
was turned over to the State Board of Charities and Corrections.
No. 4, a young colored man accused a colored boy of annoying
his " place of business," a shoe-shining stand. Their statements conflicted. When one referred to a reputable witness
they were ordered to return three days later with the witness.

180. State Judges. — State courts are usually conducted by
one judge, except the appellate court of last resort, which consists of three, five, seven, or nine judges, five being the more usual
number. These judges are chosen in one of three ways : elected
by the voters, chosen by the legislature, or appointed by the
governor with the consent of the senate. Their term of office
varies from one year to life or good behavior, the judges of
the higher courts having longer terms than those of the lower
courts. Salaries vary from nothing (merely fees) for justices
of the peace to $17,500 for judges of the New York Supreme
Court in New York County. The principal duty of a judge
is to decide points of law, and also points of fact if there is no
jury, and to issue orders for the enforcement of his decisions.
He often performs other duties, such as appointing certain
local officers, issuing liquor licenses, and serving on local boards.

181. Juries. — A jury is a number of men selected according
to law, and sworn to declare the truth on the evidence laid before them. There are two kinds of juries [1] — the grand jury
and the petit, or trial, jury.

The Grand Jury. — A grand jury is a body of persons summoned into a court to consider the evidence against persons
accused of crimes, and to determine whether the evidence is
sufficient to justify a formal trial for such persons. This jury
consists of twenty-three jurors or less, according to the State
law and the importance of the charges to be investigated. In
most States it consists of more than twelve jurors, of which

[1] The so-called coroner's jury is not a real jury. See Section 191.

at least twelve must agree that an accused person is probably guilty or he cannot be held for trial, but in some States it may consist of as few as six. When the jury consists of as few as six jurors five must agree or the accused cannot be held for trial.

When a grand jury is empaneled (selected) the judge instructs the jurors to find a *true bill of indictment* (charge) against all persons whom the prosecuting attorney brings to their attention and whom they think probably guilty. He further instructs them to bring a *presentment* (accusation) against any person whom they of their own knowledge believe to have violated the criminal laws of the State within their county. They swear or affirm that they will do so, and retire to the jury room where they deliberate in secret. The chairman of the jury, who is appointed by the judge or chosen by themselves, is known as the *foreman.*

The prosecuting attorney for the county brings into the jury room witnesses to testify against the accused and usually questions them himself, but after he retires the jurors may resummon the same witnesses and question them further or may have the court summon other witnesses to testify against the accused. Nobody is allowed in the room with the jurors except the prosecuting attorney, and in some States his stenographer. All are bound to secrecy.

After all witnesses have been summoned and questioned the jurors are left entirely alone to deliberate, and when they have completed their finding they proceed to the court-room and their bill of indictment is read in their presence. The bill is recorded in the clerk's office and the jury is dismissed if the term has expired; or, if the term has not expired, it is adjourned until the court needs it again to investigate other accusations.[1]

---

[1] It is not uncommon for a State to impose upon the grand jury duties other than the consideration of evidence against accused persons. For instance, they may be required to approve the erection of public buildings and bridges in Pennsylvania, fix the tax rate in Georgia, investigate the

In a peace-abiding county one grand jury a year is often found to be sufficient, whereas in counties where large cities are located there must either be a number of grand juries during the year or else the same grand jury must sit from time to time during several months.

The Petit Jury. — A petit or trial jury is a group of persons summoned into court to hear the evidence on both sides of a case and to decide the disputed points of fact, the judge in most States deciding the points of law. This jury tries both civil and criminal cases. Any one may usually demand a jury trial if the question of life, liberty, or property is at stake.

The number of petit jurors is usually twelve, but in a number of States a lesser number is sufficient in civil cases and minor criminal cases. In the court of the justice of the peace six jurors or less is the rule, though in several States this court, too, may have twelve jurors.

In nearly one third of the States an agreement of two thirds, three fourths, or five sixths of the jurors is sufficient for a verdict in civil cases or unimportant criminal cases. In the remaining States a unanimous verdict is required even in unimportant cases.

The Grand Jury and the Petit Jury Compared. — The same courts that have *grand* juries to *accuse* have *petit* juries to *try* the accused. But some courts which do not have grand juries do have petit juries. For instance, in most States Justices' Courts may use petit juries, though they nowhere have grand juries; and courts which have no criminal jurisdiction have no need of grand juries. Appellate courts of last resort do not use either grand or petit juries because they are concerned primarily with points of law which have been appealed to them from the lower courts. A grand jury investigates all indictable offences committed during its existence, and hears only accusations, never defences.

---

sufficiency of the bonds of county officers in Alabama and Tennessee, arrest persons selling liquor contrary to law or arrest intoxicated persons in Vermont.

Selection of Jurors. — In scarcely any two States are jurors selected in exactly the same manner, but in all they are selected in a similar manner. Once a year, or oftener, some county official[1] or special jury commissioners, appointed or elected as the law prescribes, prepares a considerable list of persons who are eligible for jury service. In some States any qualified voter of the county in which the court is sitting is eligible, while in others only tax-payers may serve.

In the former States the names can be obtained from the poll books and in the latter from the tax assessors' books. Persons under twenty-one and those over sixty or seventy years of age, criminals, illiterates, and women are commonly ineligible. In most States other classes of persons, such as State and federal officials, professional men, foremen, firemen, and State militiamen, are not required to serve.

Although a juror receives a small fee for each day he serves, most persons endeavor to avoid jury service. A story is told that in a certain large city every man " with any brains," other than those exempt from jury service, was found to be an honorary member of the State militia, and in another town the voluntary fire company monopolized the "brains" of the town.

The chosen names are written on slips of paper and placed in a locked jury box,[2] which is usually kept in the custody of the clerk of the court. When the court needs a jury the names are drawn from the box by a designated official,[3] and

---

[1] This official is usually the clerk of the court, the sheriff, the judge, or county board of commissioners. In the New England States and Michigan names of jurors are selected by township ("town") officers and sent to a county officer.

[2] In New Jersey the chancellor (highest judge) appoints a jury commissioner for each county who is of the opposite party to the county sheriff. These two are commissioners of juries and they select names of eligible persons as in other States, but instead of putting the names in the jury box they are numbered consecutively from one up, and a piece of metal with a corresponding number is placed in the box instead of the name.

[3] In North Carolina the names must be drawn from the jury box by a child under ten years of age. In many States the clerk or whatever officer draws the names must be blindfolded.

the sheriff is directed to summon such persons by a writ known as a *venire facias.* After eliminating the names of those who, for good reason, cannot serve he makes a list of those who can serve and returns it to the clerk. The list is known as the *panel of veniremen.*

Grand jurors are commonly selected in the same manner as petit jurors, but in some States a separate list of names is prepared from which grand jurors are selected. Jurors for the justices' courts are commonly selected by the justice himself.

Sometimes a judge, at the request of the parties to a suit, directs a special jury to be summoned to hear a controversy of peculiar importance and difficulty. The members of such a jury are more carefully selected and usually receive a larger fee than ordinary jurors, the additional compensation being paid by the parties to the suit.

BIBLIOGRAPHY

BALDWIN, SIMEON E. The American Judiciary. (American State Series.) 1905.

QUESTIONS ON THE TEXT

1. What are the duties of a court?
2. What two systems of courts are there in each State?
3. What classes of cases are brought into the federal courts? Into the State courts?
4. What three grades of State courts are found in every State?
5. What is a probate court?
6. What special courts do cities commonly have?
7. What is a juvenile court?
8. How are State judges chosen? For what terms?
9. Do judges have any duties other than interpreting law and deciding cases?
10. What is a grand jury? What is the petit jury? How many jurors commonly compose each? How does a grand jury differ from a petit jury?
11. Does the highest State court have jury trials?

12. Who serve on juries and how are they chosen?

13. What is meant by a *true bill of indictment?* *Presentment?* *Foreman?*

QUESTIONS FOR DISCUSSION

1. Name the courts in the State in which you live, beginning with the lowest. Tell how the judges for each are chosen. (For the above information consult your State constitution.)

2. Name one or more judges and tell what court each presides over.

3. Is it more important that a legislator, governor, or a judge be chosen for a long term?

4. Why are citizens never justified in resorting to lynch law?

5. "The Constitution of New Hampshire provides that when the governor cannot discharge the duties of his office, the president of the senate shall assume them. During the severe illness of a governor recently the president of the senate hesitated to act in his stead; it was not clear that the situation was grave enough to warrant such a course. Accordingly the attorney-general of the State brought an action against the president of the senate for not doing his duty. The court considered the situation, decided against the president of the senate, and ordered him to become acting governor. Why was this necessary? Was it conducted in a hostile spirit? Wherein did the decision help the State? Wherein did it help the defendant? Wherein may it possibly prove helpful in the future history of the State?" — "Civil Government in the United States," by John Fiske.

6. Most States elect their judges. Why do most students of government think it better to have them appointed by the governor or by the chief justice of the highest court in the State, or elected by the licensed lawyers in the territory in which he serves?

7. Jury service is so burdensome to business men of cities that some young men refuse to register for voting in order that their names may not be as easily obtained for jury service. Would you favor abolishing juries for civil cases and the less important criminal cases? An effort is always made to have jurors who know nothing about the case to be tried. In rural communities such persons are usually those who do not read the papers. Is it probable that such men make the best jurors?

8. In Idaho a prisoner charged with threatening a man with a revolver was tried and found guilty by a jury composed wholly of women. Do you think men should be tried by their peers? Women?

9. Chicago has a "lawyerless court for the poor," which deals with suits where the amount in dispute is less than $35. Officially it is called the "Court of Small Claims." No lawyers are allowed; the judge questions the witnesses on both sides and makes the decision. Would you favor a "lawyerless court" in your city or county?

CHAPTER XXII

CIVIL AND CRIMINAL PROCEDURE

182. Civil Procedure. — A civil suit is one between two persons[1] as distinguished from a criminal case, in which the State is the plaintiff against a person charged with a public offence. There are two kinds of civil procedure — *law* suits and *equity*[2] suits.

For instance, if one owes you a debt, does injury to your person or property, or violates a contract you can sue him at law for money damages; but if you want to restrain persons from committing wrongs you must get an injunction (an equity writ), which will direct the individuals to refrain from doing the wrong, or, if a person who has property in trust for you refuses to pay you the income, you can sue him in equity.

In cases *at law* the judge usually has a jury to decide the facts, and the witnesses usually testify in court; but in *equity*

---

[1] One or both persons may be artificial, *i.e.* a corporation, such as the Pennsylvania Railroad Company or the U. S. Steel Corporation.

[2] *Equity* is a branch of law which developed along-side of common law. Most of the early English law was developed by courts instead of by parliament. The judges of the courts in time became conservative and ceased to create means of obtaining justice as new conditions demanded. They had certain forms, called " court writs," upon which one had to state his case. If he could not state it on one of these forms he could not bring suit in court. Aggrieved persons appealed directly to the king for justice. The appeals became so numerous that the king created a new court, called Chancery Court, to administer justice by deciding in a conscientious and equitable manner cases in which justice could not be obtained at common law. Hence grew up a branch of law known as *equity*, with a distinct set of principles and writs.

The American States retained these two branches of law, but in all States except New Jersey the same judges hear cases both at law and in equity.

cases the judge usually decides the facts himself without a jury, and instead of having the witnesses in court he often appoints a "referee" to hear the evidence and report it to him in writing. The two kinds of suits are illustrated as they would proceed in Virginia, for they would proceed in a similar manner in other States.

Suit at Law. — Suppose Mr. A., a passenger, has received bodily injury from a railroad wreck in Albemarle County, say on the Southern Railroad, and brings suit for $5000 damages.

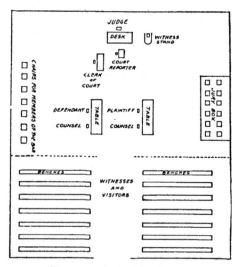

PLAN OF A COURT ROOM.

Here Mr. A. is the *plaintiff* and the Southern Railroad Company the *defendant*. Mr. A. will have his lawyer file his claim against the Southern Railroad Company with the clerk of the court in Albemarle County. The railroad company will deny A.'s right to $5000 damages, by a plea, and will have its lawyer represent it in court.

When the judge holds court in Albemarle County a jury will be empaneled unless the lawyers, known as the counsel for the plaintiff and defendant, are willing to dispense with a jury. The judge also must agree to decide the facts of the case, as well as the law, else the jury cannot be dispensed with. If a jury is empaneled it will decide all disputed facts, as, for example, whether Mr. A. was in fact injured, to what extent injured, and hence how much damages he should receive; whereas the judge will decide all points of law and instruct the jury as to the law.

After the judge instructs the jury as to the law, the counsel for each side argue the facts of the case and the jury retires to the jury room. After deliberation, if the jury can agree upon the amount of damage done Mr. A., it renders a decision, called a *verdict*. If the jurors cannot agree, it is a mis-trial and the case may be tried again. The judge finally gives *judgment* in accordance with the verdict of the jury. In this case if the judgment is in favor of the plaintiff the defendant might appeal the case to the Supreme Court of Appeals, because damages exceeding $300 are involved. Or suppose it accepts the decision but fails to make prompt payment of the damages awarded; then the clerk will issue an execution to the sheriff or a constable directing him to levy execution and sell the personal property of the defendant. If there is no personal property the court may authorize the sale of real estate.

Suit in Equity. — Suppose A., a farmer, has a fresh stream of water running through his farm and by his house, which he uses to water his stock and which his wife uses for washing clothes. B. establishes a large creamery on this stream above the farm of A. The creamery empties greasy water and acids into the stream to such an extent that it produces a stench at the farmer's home, his cattle refuse to drink the water, and the water can no longer be used for washing clothes.

A. will have his attorney file suit with the clerk of the court to enjoin (forbid) B. from emptying the grease and acids into the water, and the clerk will have the sheriff notify B. that suit has been brought. A jury is not needed to decide the facts, and witnesses need not appear in court.[1] A master in chancery, notary public, or justice of the peace gets the counsel for each side together at some convenient time and place to take *depositions* (question and cross-question the witnesses), which a stenographer takes word for word. These depositions are given to the judge, and the counsel for the plaintiff and for the defendant argue the points of law and evidence before the judge in court or in vacation.

---

[1] In some States the evidence would be taken in open court, the lawyers and judge asking questions of the witnesses.

If the judge is not satisfied as to the facts perhaps he will go to the scene, call witnesses before him, or order the master in chancery to make further investigation as to certain facts. With the facts and the law both presented, the judge is prepared to render a decision, called a *decree* in equity cases. If the judge decides that the injury to A. is as claimed he will decree that B. must cease emptying grease and acids into the stream.

The court costs of a civil suit such as witness fees, jury fees, and recording fees are usually placed by the court upon the party losing the case, and sometimes some costs are granted with which to pay lawyers, but each party usually pays his own lawyers.

183. Crimes. — A crime is an act or omission which is prohibited by law as injurious to the public and is punished by the State in a proceeding in its own name or in the name of the people thereof. Crimes may be immoral in themselves, such as murder or burglary, or they may be acts considered as crimes only because they have been prohibited by law, such as exceeding the speed limit in an automobile or failing to remove snow from the sidewalk. Crimes are of two degrees — felonies and misdemeanors.

Felonies are crimes of a more serious character than misdemeanors. They vary so much from State to State that no general definition of them can be given, but in many States all crimes which are punishable by confinement in a State penitentiary or by death are defined as felonies. The following crimes are almost universally classed as felonies.

(1) *Murder in the First Degree* generally means the unlawful intentional and premeditated killing of a human being, or such a killing resulting from the commission or the attempt to commit one of the graver crimes such as arson, burglary, or robbery. Such crimes are punished in thirteen States by death, in twenty-five by death or life imprisonment, in eight by life imprisonment, and in two by life imprisonment or imprisonment for not less than five and fourteen years respectively.

(2) *Murder in the Second Degree* generally means the unlawful intentional killing without premeditation, or such killing as

a result of an attempt to commit some lesser crime. It is punished by imprisonment varying from a minimum of two years in North Carolina to a maximum of life in many States, and even death in several.

(3) *Manslaughter* is the unlawful killing of another without malice. The killing may be voluntary, upon a sudden heat of passion; or it may be involuntary, in the commission of some unlawful act or a lawful act without due caution. Many States divide manslaughter into two degrees. It is punished by imprisonment for a term ordinarily shorter than that for murder in the second degree. Great discretion is given to the jury or judge.

(4) *Arson* is the act of unlawfully and maliciously burning a building. It is more serious if done at night and most serious if an inhabited dwelling is burnt at night.

(5) *Burglary* is the breaking and entering a dwelling house during the night, with the intent to commit a felony therein, whether the felony be actually committed or not. In some States so entering other buildings is burglary. The same offence is called house-breaking if committed during the day.

(6) *Robbery* is the theft of property from the person or in the immediate presence of the victim, accompanied by force or fear.

(7) *Larceny* is simply theft, and *Grand Larceny* is the theft of property above a fixed value, generally from $25 to $50. In a number of States to steal any amount from the person of another without force or fear is considered grand larceny.

Arson, burglary, robbery, grand larceny, assault with intent to kill, bigamy, perjury, forgery, and embezzlement are commonly punished by a considerable term of imprisonment. Burglary and robbery may be punished by death in several States, arson by death in eight States, and rape by death in sixteen Southern States.

Misdemeanors are crimes of a less serious character than felonies and, like felonies, cannot .be defined by any general definition which will apply to all States. For instance, in

Virginia offences which are punishable with death or confinement in the penitentiary are felonies; all other offences are misdemeanors. In the same State the following crimes are misdemeanors and, in general, would be so classed in other States: violation of town or city ordinances, carrying concealed weapons, cruelty to animals, attempting to defraud a hotel keeper, petit larceny, which is a theft less than a grand larceny, setting fire to woods, etc., non-support of wife and minor children, permitting a gambling house on one's premises, libel, assault and battery. The above misdemeanors are punishable by confinement in jail or by fine. But such misdemeanors as drunkenness without disorder, profanity, or unnecessary labor on Sunday are punishable by fine only. In such cases if the person who has been fined cannot or will not pay his fine he may be sent to jail according to the law of many States.

184. Criminal Procedure. — *Arrest of Felons.* — A private individual may arrest a person to prevent the commission of a felony in his presence, or may, without a warrant, arrest a felon whom he has seen commit a felony, or may even arrest one without a warrant on reasonable suspicion of his having committed a felony, provided a felony has been committed.

An officer of the peace (sheriff, constable, police) may do anything a private person may do. He should furthermore pursue a felon who is making his escape though he has not actually seen the crime committed. If the police, constables, or sheriff do not attempt to arrest a felon, the prosecuting attorney will likely take the initiative and have the suspected felon arrested.

Or the injured party or any one knowing of the crime may go to a justice of the peace or some other magistrate who has power to issue a warrant, and by taking oath as to the crime, have a warrant issued for the arrest of some designated person, provided the magistrate is satisfied as to the truth of the complaint. The *warrant* is a written document describing the felon, setting forth the offence, and directing that he be brought before some specified magistrate, usually the one who has issued the warrant. A policeman, constable, sheriff, or any other peace officer may make the arrest ("serve the warrant"), and bring the felon before the proper magistrate for trial. In making the arrest the officer may call upon any persons to assist him, may break into a building, or may kill the felon *if necessary*. By "necessary" is meant self-defence or preventing the escape of one who has committed a felony.

Arrest of Misdemeanants. — A private person may arrest another without a warrant to quell a breach of the peace in his presence, but he may not arrest one to prevent any other misdemeanor; nor may he arrest one for any misdemeanor already committed. A peace officer may arrest without a warrant for a breach of the peace committed in his presence, but for no other misdemeanor. The same magistrates who issue warrants for felons may issue them for misdemeanants, and arrests are made by the same officers in the same manner except that an officer is never justified in killing a misdemeanant fugitive, though of course he has the right of self-defence.

The Commitment. — After the accused is arrested he is brought before the magistrate, usually the justice of the peace, except in cities where there is a special police justice, or in towns in which the mayor has the powers of a justice. If the crime is a misdemeanor the accused is likely tried at once. If the crime is a felony the magistrate gives the accused a preliminary hearing, and when the evidence indicates a probability of guilt the accused is held for the grand jury. If the crime is murder the accused is usually committed to jail, but otherwise, unless his being at large is considered especially dangerous, he is released until the grand jury meets, provided he can give bail.[1]

The Indictment. — The *prosecuting attorney*, called state's attorney or district attorney in some States, investigates the

---

[1] Bail (Old French *bail*=a guardian) is the guarantee that an accused person will appear for trial if allowed to go at large. It is a sum of money, depending upon the character of the charge, and is determined by a judge or special bail officer. The cash, or good security, may be furnished by a friend or by the accused himself if he possesses the amount required.

evidence against such persons as the committing magistrates
have held for the grand jury, or against any other persons
whose probable guilt has been brought to his attention. If he
thinks there is evidence against any such person which will
probably convict, he draws up a *bill of indictment*, a written
document stating the charge, and has witnesses summoned for
the grand jury.

If a certain majority of the grand jury, which majority varies
from State to State, thinks there is sufficient evidence to
warrant a court trial, the foreman writes across the face of the
indictment the words, "a true bill" (of indictment), and the
indicted person must stand trial in court. If the prescribed
majority does not think that the evidence justifies a trial the
words "not a true bill" are used, and the accused is discharged,
if he has already been committed.

The Trial. — The justice's court usually has original jurisdiction in misdemeanor cases, and here the trial is very in-
formal because justices of the peace are not usually lawyers
and must depend upon what untrained minds can glean from a
volume of statutes compiled for their use. With few exceptions an appeal may be taken to the county or superior court
in criminal cases.

In felony cases sent to the county or superior trial court by
the grand jury the prisoner appears in the custody of the
sheriff, deputy-sheriff, or some like officer who perhaps bears a
different title. In misdemeanor cases sent from the grand jury
or appealed from a justice of the peace the prisoner need not
appear in person. He often prefers to leave his case to an
attorney. But a felony case cannot proceed unless the accused
is present.

The prisoner is charged with committing a crime against the
State[1] and is prosecuted by the prosecuting (state's) attorney

---

[1] For a great many acts a person may be proceeded against criminally by
the State because he has disturbed the peace of the community generally,
and also in a civil action by a person because the latter has been injured individually. For instance, if I libel you by an unlawful malicious publication

of the county. The clerk of the court reads the indictment or presentment to the prisoner, who pleads "guilty" or "not guilty." If he pleads guilty, and is of a sound mind, the judge usually pronounces the sentence according to the State law, and the case ends. But if he pleads not guilty he is entitled to a trial by jury if he desires it, and in some States one accused of a felony is obliged to stand trial by jury. If the prisoner cannot afford an attorney the judge appoints a lawyer, commonly a young inexperienced one, to defend him. In most States this attorney is paid a small fee by the State.

There are usually about twice as many persons summoned as are needed for the jury, but when the court meets, the counsel may challenge a certain number, which is limited by law, without giving any cause, and the judge will excuse such veniremen. Then the counsel may challenge any other veniremen for cause, such as relationship to the parties to the suit or some other reason why they might not give an impartial decision; if it is a murder trial, because they do not believe in capital punishment.[1]

If others are challenged, the judge, in some States, may have the sheriff summon by-standers (*talesmen*), whereas in other States a new list must be prepared as the former one was and this procedure must continue until the prescribed number of suitable men are *empaneled,* that is, secured to serve.[2]

---

and thereby injure your good name you can sue me for money damages; if my libeling you causes a breach of the peace I have also committed a crime and may be punished by the officers of the State in the name of the State because the entire State is injured by lawless people who break the peace.

[1] In some States unsatisfactory laws or inefficient judges often permit the lawyers to ask every conceivable question in order to determine whether the jurors hold any opinions which would cause them to be prejudiced in the case. For example, after the Iroquois Theatre fire in Chicago, in which so many people lost their lives, the Theatre Company was being sued, and the counsel for the company asked the prospective jurors such questions as these: "What paper do you read? Do you believe in card playing? Dancing? Theatre going? Have you any prejudices against city people? Have you ever had a friend killed in a fire?"

[2] In the famous Gillooley murder case (1878) in Indiana, 4150 veniremen

After the case is opened the witnesses for the State and for the prisoner are examined and cross-examined, arguments are delivered by the attorneys for each side, and the judge gives the *instructions* to the jury explaining the law governing the case. (In Virginia the instructions precede the arguments.)

The jury then retires to consider the evidence of the case and arrive at a decision. If the jury cannot agree the foreman reports "no agreement": if the requisite number agree, usually all in an important criminal case, he reports "guilty" or "not guilty." If guilty, the jury usually determines the punishment in its verdict,[1] which is read by the clerk of the court, and the judge pronounces the sentence. If the penalty is merely a fine, this is paid to the clerk; if more than a fine the sheriff takes charge of the prisoner, who is taken to jail to serve his term, or until he can be transferred to the penitentiary, executed, or disposed of according to the sentence. If there has been a disagreement ("a hung jury") the case is either set for a new trial or dismissed.

If the verdict has been "guilty," the prisoner may petition for an appeal to a higher court on the ground that the verdict is not according to the law, or to the evidence, or that some error has been committed in the trial. If the appeal is granted and is sustained the higher court will order the lower court to hold a new trial; but if no error is found the appeal is dismissed and the order of the lower court stands.

BIBLIOGRAPHY

Copies of warrants of arrest, indictments, subpoenas, summonses, etc.

QUESTIONS ON THE TEXT

1. What is the difference between a civil suit and a criminal suit?
2. If you sue for a sum of money do you sue *at law* or *in equity?*

were summoned and nine and a half weeks were required to complete the jury. Recently 91 days were required to select a jury in a certain California case.

[1] In many States the judge determines the punishment after the jury has determined the guilt.

3. If you want to prevent the commission of a wrong which cannot be remedied after once committed would you bring suit *at law* or *in equity?*

· 4. Explain just how a suit *at law* proceeds. What do you mean by *plaintiff? Defendant? Verdict? Judgment?*

5. Explain just how a suit *in equity* proceeds. What is a *master in chancery? Decree? What are depositions?*

6. What is a crime? Are all crimes wrong in themselves? If not, why are they considered crimes?

7. Crimes are of what two degrees? What distinguishes them in many States?

8. What is Murder in the First Degree? Murder in the Second Degree? Manslaughter? Arson? Burglary? Robbery? Larceny? Grand Larceny?

9. Who may arrest felons?

10. What is a *warrant?* Is it necessary to have a warrant to arrest a felon? Who serves a warrant? May he call upon by-standers to assist him?

11. May a peace officer without a warrant arrest one who has committed a misdemeanor?

12. Who usually tries a criminal and commits him to jail when he is first arrested?

13. What do you mean by *giving bail?*

14. Who draws up bills of indictment to present to the grand jury?

15. Describe a jury trial.

16. What do you mean by *instructions?*

17. By whom is the law governing a case decided? The facts?

18. What is meant by a "hung jury"?

19. Describe a court in session.

QUESTIONS FOR DISCUSSION

1. In New York City a thief stole a plume worth $57, but proved that it was marked down to $49.50 the day he stole it; hence his offence was merely a misdemeanor, whereas it would have been a felony if he had stolen goods valued for as much as $50. — It pays to know the law. — What crime did this thief commit?

2. In the eighteenth century nearly 200 crimes were punishable by death in England. A death penalty was prescribed for stealing a handkerchief. The people and even the judges ceased believing in the

justice of such laws and did not enforce them. For instance, in one case a man was accused of stealing a sheep. The judge threw the case out of court because it was a ewe that he had stolen, so that he might not have to pronounce a death sentence. Have any of these technicalities of the law come down to us to-day when we do not need them? Why do we not need them to-day?

3. Are crimes prevented more by the severity of punishment or by the certainty of punishment? Would you consider it extravagant for the government to spend $100,000 in order to detect and bring a murderer to justice?

4. In Porto Rico an accused person may choose whether he will be tried by a jury or by a judge. It is said that if he is innocent he always chooses the judge. Explain why.

5. You cannot compel a person accused of a crime to testify against himself according to law. You cannot so much as ask him where he was when the crime was committed. What do you think of this old legal rule? Would you favor compelling the accused to make a statement as to his whereabouts to the justice of the peace before whom he is brought — else assume that he is guilty?

CHAPTER XXIII

COUNTY AND TOWNSHIP GOVERNMENT

I. County System

185. Origin of County Government. — The Southern colonists were agriculturalists living far apart on plantations. A small class of aristocrats owned most of the property and were well educated, but illiterate slaves formed the masses. Under these conditions the people did not develop local self-government as they did in New England, where there was a substantial middle class of towns-people.

Therefore it was necessary to divide the colonies into counties[1] so that the laws might be properly enforced. Thus the county became the most important governmental division of the colony. After the colonies became States the importance of county government continued, and the new States in the Southwest and extreme West copied the Southern county system.[2]

186. Functions of Counties. — A county is a governmental division of a State which administers State laws and such county laws as the State permits the county to enact. These county functions are determined by the State legislature except in regard to those matters for which provision is made by the State constitution. The county is always subject to the will of the State.

In most States it is the duty of the county to preserve

---

[1] The divisions were called *counties* because the divisions of England were so called.

[2] In Louisiana the divisions corresponding to counties are named *parishes*.

peace; administer justice; distribute the property of a deceased person; register titles to land; maintain schools; build and repair roads and bridges; care for the poor; protect the health of the community; collect local, county, and State taxes, and expend the county portion of these taxes in the performance of the county functions just enumerated.[1]

ROAD BUILDING MACHINE ON THE PACIFIC HIGHWAY, OREGON.

187. How County Functions are Performed. — Most county officers are chosen by an election conducted at various voting places throughout the county for short terms — commonly two or four years — but in some States a few officers are chosen by the county board, the State legislature, the governor, the

---

[1] In addition to the usual functions that county governments administer for State governments there are a number of local option State laws which may be accepted for a county by its board of commissioners or board of supervisors.

judge, or otherwise appointed. The officers are not exactly the same in all States, but every county except those in Rhode Island and Georgia has a board which in most States is called the "board of commissioners."

188. The County Board. — In England the counties were administered by the Quarter Sessions Court of the justices of

ROAD BUILDING ON THE PACIFIC HIGHWAY, OREGON.

the peace of the county. Naturally this system was copied in America. In Kentucky, Tennessee, and Arkansas the justices of the peace continue to administer the counties, but since they are elected for definite terms the system is not materially unlike the more recent systems to be described in the next paragraph.

Board of Supervisors. — New York early departed from the system described in the last paragraph by establishing a county

COUNTY BOARDS

STATES	NUMBER OF MEMBERS	CALLED BOARD OF	HOW CHOSEN	TERM IN YEARS
Me.	3	Commissioners	Elected at large	6
New ...shire	3	Commissioners	Elected at large	2
...mont	2	Assistant Judges	Elected at large	2
... and	3	Commissioners	Elected at large	3
...it	3	...ders	By State	4
New York	T'ship	...rs	...ps	2
New ...y	T'ship; 3 to 9	...en Freehol ders	...ps; elected at large	1, 2, 3
...nia	3	...rs	...d at large	4
...ne	3, 7, 10	...rs	E...ed by districts	4
...o	3	...rs	...d at ...ge	2
Ida	3 and 7	...rs and C. ...il	...d by districts	3 and 4
...an	T'ship	Supervisors	El...ted by ...ps	1
Illis	T'ship; 3	Sup. (in 85 G.); o...G. (in 17 G.)	...d by ...ps; elected at large	2, 3
...sin	T'ship	Supervisors	...d by ...ps	1
...ta	5 to 7	...rs	...d by ...ts	4
Iowa	3 to 7	...rs	...d by districts or at large	3
North Dakota	3 or 5	...sioners	Elected by districts	4
South Dakota	3 to 5	...sioners	Elected by districts	4
Nebraska	N.U.	Sup. (in ...e) ; Com. (in some)	Elected by districts or at large	4
...s	3	...rs	El...ed by ...ts	4
...nd	N.U.	...rs	El...ed at l...ge	4
V'gia	Dist.	Supervisors	...d by "...ial Dist ...its"	N.U.
West ...Virginia	3	"...ty Court"	...d at large in most ... ...ts	6

				N. U.
North Carolina	3 or 5	. . . . .	. . . .	2
South Carolina	2 or , T'ship	. . . .	El...ted at large	4
Georgia	1	Ordinary	El...ted at large	2
Fla	5	. . . .	El...ted by districts	4
Ky	3 to 8	"Fiscal Court"	El...ted by	6
Tenn	Dist.	"County Court"	El...ted by	4
Ala	Dist.	" Court of County Commissioners"	Elected by districts	4
Miss	5	Supervisors	El...ted by districts	4
Louisiana	Dist.	Police Jury	El...ted by districts	4
Texas	5	4 . . . jurors and county Judge	El...ted by districts and at large	2
Ark	Dist.	Levying Court and County Judge	El...ted by . . . . districts	2
Missouri	3	Judges of the County Court	2 . . . ted by districts and 1 at large	2 and 4
Ala	3	. . . . jurors	El...ted by . . . . districts	2
New Mexico	3	. . . . jurors	El...ted by districts	2
. . . .	3	Supervisors	El...ted at large	2 and 4
Colo	3	. . . . jurors	El...ted at large	4
Utah	3	. . . . jurors	El...ted at large	2 and 4
Wyo	3	. . . . jurors	El...ted at large	2 and 4
Dakota	3	. . . . jurors	El...ted at large	6
Idaho	3	. . . . jurors	El...ted by . . . . districts	2
Oregon	3	. . . . jurors	El...ted by . . . . districts	2 and 4
Nevada	3	2 . . . jurors and county [Judge]	El...ted at large	4 and 6
California	3, 5, or 7	Supervisors	El...ted by districts or at large	2 and 4
			El...ted by districts	2

Dist. = One (sometimes more) from each district.
T'ship = One from each township, ward, or village.
N. U. = Not uniform.

board consisting of one supervisor elected from each township, and called "board of supervisors." This system, with certain changes, has been adopted by many States in all parts of the country, but especially in the Northwest, where the township system found its way.

Board of Commissioners. — Pennsylvania also departed from the system described above, and provided that each county

COOK COUNTY HOSPITAL IN CHICAGO.

should elect three commissioners at large, that is, from the whole county, to be known as the "board of commissioners." This system has been adopted by most of the States which have not accepted the New York plan. It must be remembered that all of these plans have been greatly modified by the various States, and in a few States the practices of one system have been adopted with the name of the other.

The county board, under whatever name, has often been called the "county legislature" because in nearly all States it has power to determine the county tax rate and to appropriate the money for county purposes when collected. In some States it has power to enact certain ordinances, such as fish and game laws and the granting of bounties for the destruction of certain wild animals; but its duties are primarily to administer State laws within the county. It has charge of county buildings at the county seat (courthouse and jail) and

the poor-house, hospital, work-house, and pest-house, if the county owns such institutions; and it determines the location of all or certain roads and bridges and provides for their maintenance.

In the South and West the county board commonly establishes polling places and provides ballots, and in some States it acts as

MULTNOMAH COUNTY LIBRARY, PORTLAND, OREGON.

a county board for declaring the results of elections. In most States the board appoints a superintendent of the poor, but the other officers whom the board appoints in one State or another are very few.

189. Judicial Officers. — In all parts of the country, even in the New England States, the county is an important unit for judicial purposes. There is a courthouse in every county and a clerk of the court, unless the county clerk acts as clerk of the court, who keeps records of suits brought in the county and of judgments and decrees of the court when the judge has disposed of the cases; but less than half of the States have a

judge for each county.   Instead of a county judge it is more
common to have a "district" or "circuit" judge, who holds
court in several counties according to the needs of the counties
in his "district" or "circuit."

The counties of half the States have probate judges, whose
duty it is to probate (prove) wills; whereas in the other States

ROCKINGHAM COUNTY COURTHOUSE, HARRISONBURG, VIRGINIA.

the regular county judge, county clerk, clerk of the court, or
some other officer probates wills.

Every county, except the five in Rhode Island, has a prosecuting attorney to see that criminals are brought to justice,
though in a few States he, like the judge, serves for two or
more counties and is called the district attorney.   If he serves
for one county he is called the county attorney, State's attorney,
commonwealth attorney, or merely prosecuting attorney.   In
fact, he is sometimes called district attorney though his district
consists of only one large county.

190. The Sheriff. — Every county has a sheriff, and in all States except Rhode Island (where he is chosen by the State legislature) he is elected by the people.[1] His duty is to prevent any breach of the peace ; arrest offenders and place them in the jail, of which he or a deputy appointed by him is keeper ; attend court and carry out its orders, whether it be to notify witnesses or jurors, attend the jury, recover property, collect money, or hang a criminal.

In the performance of these duties he may employ deputies regularly or only in case of emergency ; he may summon to his aid the *posse comitatus* (power of the county), which consists of the able-bodied male citizens of the county, in case of a riot ; and in case of a serious disturbance he may call out the State militia. Special duties are imposed on sheriffs in the different States ; for instance, in some Southern States they act as tax collectors.

191. The Coroner. — In nearly all States the coroner[2] is an officer of the county who holds inquests upon the bodies of persons who are supposed to have died from violent or other unlawful means. He empanels a jury, usually of six bystanders, who inquire from witnesses, or even physicians, chemists, and detectives as to the probable cause of a death which is known to have resulted or supposed to have resulted from an illegal act.

If the jury decides that the deceased person has probably met death unlawfully at the hands of a certain person, the coroner may issue a warrant for the arrest of the accused and commit him to jail to await trial, or he may report the facts to a committing magistrate or the prosecuting attorney as the State law may provide. In Massachusetts instead of a coroner there

---

[1] The word "sheriff" comes from *shire-reeve*, which means "peace officer of the shire," shire being the Anglo-Saxon name for a division of England which became known as county (district of a count) after the Norman Conquest of 1066.

[2] "Coroner" is the modern spelling of the older form *crowner*, who in the time of King Alfred was appointed by the king and was especially the crown officer in the shire (county).

COUNTY OFFICERS AND THEIR TERMS OF OFFICE

States	County Judge	Probate Judge	Prosecuting Attorney	Sheriff	Coroner	Clerk of Court	County Clerk	Register of Deeds	County Auditor	County Assessor	County Treasurer	County Surveyor	Supt. of Schools
Maine		4	2	2	Ua	4	—	4			2		
New Hampshire		Ua	2	2	5a	Ua	—	2	1a		2		
Vermont	2	2s	2	2		Ua	—		2a		2a		
Massachusetts		Ua		5		5	—	5			3		
Rhode Island				3a	3a	3a			2a				3a
Connecticut	6		4a	4	3	1a		3f			2a	4	3a
New York	6	6	3	3	3		3	5s			3		4a
New Jersey	5a	5	5a	3	4		5	4			2	2	2a
Pennsylvania		4s	4	4	2	4	—	4	4		4	2	3al
Delaware			4a	2	2	4	—	2	4		N.U.	2	4a
Ohio	6	4	2	2	2	2		4	2	2	2	4	4
Indiana		4f		2	2	4	2	2	4	4	2	2	4
Michigan		4	2	2	4		4	4f	2f		2		2
Illinois	4	4f	4	4	4		2	2	4f		4	4	4
Wisconsin	4		2	2	2	2	—	2	4		2	2	3a
Minnesota		2	4	4	4	4	—	2	2		4	4	2
Iowa			2	2	2	2	—	4s	2	2	2	2	2
North Dakota	2		2	2	2	2	2	2	2	4m	2	2	2
South Dakota	2		2	2	2	2	2	2		2	2	2	2
Nebraska	2	2	2	2	2a	4m	—		2as		2	2	6al
Kansas		4	4	4	2a	2	8	—		4s	2	4a	4am
Maryland			4	4	2a	6	6	—		4	N.U.	4	4
Virginia			4	4	Ua	6	6	—		4	4		
West Virginia			4	4		6		—					

State													
North Carolina	…	2f	2f	2	2	4	2	…	…	…	…	2m	2	2a
South Carolina	…	4	4	4	4	4	4	…	…	…	2a	…	4
Georgia	4	4s	4s	4	4	4	4s	…	…	4f	4	4	4
Florida	4	4	4	4	4	6	4	…	…	…	…	4	2a
Kentucky	8	4	…	2	4a	6	4a	4	2af	4a	4a	4a	4
Tennessee	…	6	4f	4	4	6	…	…	…	2	2	4	4
Alabama	…	…	…	4	4	4	4	…	…	4	4	4	4a
Mississippi	…	…	…	4	4	…	…	…	…	2a	Ua	2
Louisiana	…	…	…	2	2	…	2	4	2af	4a	4a	2	4a
Texas	2	2	2	4	…	2m	4	…	2	2s
Arkansas	2	2	…	2	2	4	4s	2	4	2	4
Missouri	…	4	2	2	2	4	4	4m	…	4	4	4	2
Oklahoma	2	…	2	4	2	2	2	2	…	2	2	2	2
New Mexico	4	2	…	2	…	2	…	2	2s	…	2	2	2
Arizona	4	…	2	…	2s	2	2	2	2s	2	2	2	2s
Utah	…	…	…	2	4	2	2	2	2	2	2	2	2
Wyoming	…	2	2	2	4	2	2	…	…	4	2	2	2
Montana	…	2	2	2	2	…	2	…	…	2	2	2	2
Idaho	2	2	2	2	2	…	2	…	…	2	2	2	2
Washington	…	2	2f	2	2	…	2	…	2f	2f	2	2	4
Oregon	6	4 and a	2	2	…	…	…	2	2	2m	2m	2m	2
Nevada	…	2	2	4	…	…	2	2	2	4	4	2m	2m
California	4	4	…	4	…	4	4	4s	4s	4	4	4	4

Legend:

Numeral = Term for which officer is elected.
Numeral followed by *a* = officer which … for extn.
Numeral followed by *al* = officer … appointed, and met … this have … indirect method.
Numeral followed by *am* = Officer … which officer is … end in the *few* … officer while others are grouped into larger districts.
N followed by *f* = Term for which officer is … end in *most* … this having such officer.
N followed by *m* = officer for which officer is … end in … this; that is, in all … officer.
Ua = officer … for an … this as to … this; that is, in all … having such officer.
N.U. = Not uniform in the … one … the county officer.
— = Is performed by … officer of a … dist larger (e.g., judicial district) or smaller (e.g., township) than a county, if performed at all.
.... = Duties performed by an officer of a …

is a medical examiner in each county to pass upon unusual deaths. As a knowledge of medicine and pathology is desirable the change made by Massachusetts is a very wise and progressive one.

192. The County Clerk. — In half of the States there is a county clerk. He acts as clerk of the court in some States; prepares election ballots and receives election returns, and issues marriage licenses in others; and audits the county accounts, acts as clerk of the county board, and records documents such as deeds, wills, and mortgages in others. In short, he is assigned various functions of a clerical nature for which there is no specialized officer in the county.

193. The Register of Deeds. — In the more populous States it has been thought expedient to have a special officer to keep the records of such legal documents as deeds and mortgages. It is the duty of the register of deeds to make exact copies of instruments to be recorded and enter them in indexed books where they may easily be found. As one's title to property often depends upon these records it is very important that no mistakes be made.

194. The County Auditor. — Nearly half of the States have a county auditor, whose business it is to go over the accounts of the other officers of the county, prepare statements of county finances, and issue warrants on the treasurer for the expenditure of county money according to the appropriations made by the county board. Until recently the duties of this office were performed in a very loose manner, but the States are gradually enacting laws for State supervision of local finances. For example, some States require uniform accounting, which can easily be examined by a State accountant or even by an educated citizen of the county.

195. The County Treasurer. — In every State except Rhode Island, where township officers have charge of local funds, and in several Southern States, where banks perform the duties of county treasurers, there is a county officer to receive and safeguard the county taxes. In a few States there are tax collectors in addition to the treasurer, and in several Southern States collections are made by the sheriff. The treasurer is always placed under bond to insure the State and county against loss from dishonesty or carelessness. He is usually paid a definite salary, but some are paid wholly by commissions on the money handled by them.

Many county treasurers deposit the county funds in local banks and earn interest for themselves where there is no law requiring them to earn it for the county. In counties containing large cities many thousands of dollars have been made in this way by a single treasurer.

196. The Superintendent of Schools. — In nearly every county outside of New England (where public education is administered by the township) there is a county superintendent of schools. In most States he is elected by the people, but in some he is chosen by the county school board, the State school board, appointed by the governor, or otherwise selected. In most States his duty is to conduct teachers' examinations, visit schools to observe and advise teachers, assist district trustees in the selection of teachers and with other advice, and collect school statistics; and in many States he acts as assistant to the State commissioner of education in a general campaign against illiteracy and indifference to education.

197. Minor County Officers. — Most counties have a surveyor, who surveys land for private owners at their own expense or upon the direction of the court when a dispute in court over a land boundary necessitates it. In some of the more progressive States there is a county engineer instead of a county surveyor, who performs those duties formerly done by the county surveyor; but in addition to this he acts as an engineer in the construction of roads, bridges, drains, and like improvements.

Southern and Western counties have assessors to determine the value of property to be taxed, but in New England and the Central States this function is usually performed by a township officer. Other usual county officers are a health officer or board and a superintendent or overseer of the poor who has charge of the almshouse, poor farm, or hospital of the county.

198. Counties Unimportant in New England. — The county is of little importance in New England except as a district for the administration of justice. No New England State has a county clerk, county superintendent of schools, county surveyor, or county assessor; only two have a county auditor, and only three have a county register of deeds. The duties of these officers are performed by township officers.

II. Township System

199. Origin of Town Government in New England. — The Pilgrims came to Plymouth, Massachusetts, as a congregation, and very soon (1622) they erected on Burial Hill a "meeting-house," which was used both for public worship and for town-meetings. The church and government were practically one: sermons were preached on the' inside to save souls from perdition and a cannon was mounted on the outside to save bodies from the Indians. It was at the meeting-house that the voters met and made their laws directly.

Other congregations from England settled along the coast and established similar governments. As the population of these coast settlements increased, pastors led congregations from them and established towns. The desire to be near the church, the hostility of the savages, the severe climate, and the unsuitableness of the country for large plantations caused the emigrants to settle in compact communities, called "towns."

200. Terms "Town" and "Township" Distinguished. — These communities were called "towns"[1] because they had been so called in England. When it became necessary to survey bound-

---

[1] When a clan of our ancestors in northern Europe or England fixed upon some spot for a permanent residence and built a wall around it, the wall was known as a *tun;* in time the space within the wall was known as a *tun,* or *town.* The settlers were called by the clan name, as for example "the Boerings" or "the Cressings"; and the town would be called *Barrington,* "town of the Boerings," or Cressingham, "home of the Cressings."

aries between the various towns the small irregular patches of land which resulted were properly known as "townships,"[1] but frontier communities are not very discriminating in their terms, and the term "town" was used not only for the cluster of buildings but for the entire township.

In New England to-day "town" means a political subdivision of a county which in other parts of the country is called "township." For the sake of uniformity we shall use the word township when referring to what is called "town" in New England. The early townships were very irregular in shape and contained an average of not more than twenty square miles.

201. Powers of New England Townships. — For many years the New England townships were undisturbed by the king or parliament of England and exercised such powers of government as are now exercised by a State. They waged war against the Indians, established schools, and as late as the Revolutionary War they appropriated money for war supplies; in fact, they created the States which now control them.

To-day they exercise only such powers as the States permit. They have control of most roads, bridges, schools, libraries, poor relief, and taxation for most local purposes. Some townships have charge of such public works and institutions as street pavements, sewers, water-works, electric light plants, public baths, parks, and hospitals. They also have certain powers to enact police ordinances, such as determining whether the township shall license saloons.

The township officers act as agents of the State for an increasing number of functions. They assess and collect State taxes, keep records of vital statistics (births and deaths), and enforce the health laws of the State. Except in one State the township is the usual district from which a representative is elected to the more numerous branch of the State legislature.

---

[1] The word *ship*, as here used, comes from the Anglo-Saxon word *scip*, which means shape, hence township means the shape of the town or the entire bounds of the town.

202. The Town-Meeting. — Township laws have always been made in the town-meeting, which is composed of the male inhabitants twenty-one years of age or over. Any one may introduce motions or take part in the discussions; but only adult males may vote, except that women are allowed to vote on school questions. During the first few years the colonists attempted to hold monthly meetings, but this was found to be a cumbersome way to transact business, and as early as 1635 *selectmen* (officers selected by the people) were chosen to administer the affairs of the township during the interval between the assemblies. Thus the government became less democratic (direct rule of the people) and more republican (indirect rule of the people through representatives).

To-day the regular meetings are usually held in the town-hall once a year, but the selectmen may call special meetings. The first Monday in March is a favorite time to have the meetings, but some are held as early as February or as late as April, and Connecticut prefers October. The general nature of the business to be transacted at a meeting must be announced in a warrant which is posted in the various parts of the township.

The town clerk calls the meeting to order, usually at nine o'clock, and acts as secretary of the meeting. The first business is the election of the presiding officer, called the *moderator*. In many townships some well-respected citizen is elected year after year as a matter of course. The organization being perfected, the principal township officers are nominated from the floor, but the nominations have frequently been arranged by preliminary party meetings, called *caucuses*. Election is by ballot, and the polls remain open several hours, depending upon the population of the township.

The interesting session of a town meeting occurs after the balloting — usually in the afternoon, but in a few larger towns not until evening. Each voter has been furnished a printed report of the expenditures for the previous year, and the selectmen make an oral report of what has been done during the year. It is then that the policy for the next year is to be discussed — the real interest of the meeting.

Nahum Smith may rise and say, "I should like to be informed why the selectmen took the stone from Red Hill quarry instead of Cross Roads quarry, which is nearer?" If there is "a rooster in the bag" he is rather certain to crow. It is difficult for a political boss or ring to prosper under this

TOWN HALL, DOVER, MASSACHUSETTS.

system because any bag containing a rooster must annually or oftener be brought into the presence of the interested parties, and a Nahum Smith is pretty certain to bring at least one crow from the rooster.

Perhaps the cross-questioning of the chairman of the school committee by Jeremy Jones will bring discomfort to the chairman, much to the delight of the boys seated in the rear of the hall. Or perhaps the article under consideration is the purchase of an electric light plant or an automobile chemical engine. Or the younger blood may be advocating a consolidated school or a new high school, which is probably opposed by Aaron, Hiram, and Nahum, who live in the country some distance from the centre where the school would be located.

203. Township Officers. — *Selectmen,* of whom there are three, five, seven, or nine, three being the more usual number, are the principal officers of the township. They are elected by the town-meeting, annually as a rule, but in some Massachusetts townships they are elected for three years, one being elected each year.

They issue warrants for holding regular or special town-meetings, specifying in a general way the subjects which the citizens desire to have acted upon; lay out highways; grant licenses; arrange for elections; have charge of township property; appoint some of the minor officers; and may act as assessors, overseers of the poor, and health officers. It should be borne in mind that they have no power to determine the tax rate or appropriate money, these functions being performed by the town-meeting, and that they have no powers except those conferred by the State or the town-meeting.

The Town Clerk is just as important as the selectmen, and performs many duties which are imposed upon the county clerk outside of New England. He keeps minutes of town-meetings, of meetings of the selectmen, and other town records; he records the vote for State and county officers and issues marriage licenses; and he records births, marriages, and deaths. He is elected by the town-meeting for only a year at a time, but is usually reëlected for a great number of years.

Other Township Officers are the town treasurer, assessors of taxes, overseers of the poor, justices of the peace (so considered in some States), constables, commissioner of roads (under various titles), a school committee (board), and numerous other less important officers. Most of these officers are elected at the annual town-meeting. Not many years ago the township of Middlefield, Massachusetts, had eighty-two voters and eighteen officers.

204. Absence of Townships in the South and West. — In the Southern and Western States townships cannot be said to exist. In some States the counties are subdivided into one or more sets of districts for one or more purposes. They have no township meetings, and districts other than school districts usually have no power of taxation or of owning property, and few, if any, officers independent of county officers. They are simply convenient divisions for performing county functions. Different districts exist for various purposes, such as schools, roads, justice, and elections; and one kind of district commonly overlaps another kind. The name for the more important of these districts varies from State to State.[1]

III. COUNTY-TOWNSHIP SYSTEM

205. Imitation of New England Township Government. — Nowhere outside of New England is township government so important as in those six States, but in the tier of States extending from New York to Nebraska it is of considerable importance. The northern portions of these States were settled largely by emigrants from New England, who were accustomed to township government; but those who settled the southern portions were from Pennsylvania and the States to the south of the Ohio River and were accustomed to county government. Those accustomed to county government had never attended town-meetings but preferred to elect county officers and trust them with all functions of local government.

The result was a compromise. Some functions were assigned to the county and some to the township. In this

---

[1] In North Carolina, South Carolina, Missouri, Arkansas, Montana, and Nevada these districts are called *townships;* in California, *judicial townships;* in Virginia, West Virginia, and Kentucky, *magisterial districts;* in Tennessee, *civil districts;* in Mississippi, *supervisors' districts;* in Georgia, *militia districts;* in Texas, *commissioners' precincts;* in Delaware, *hundreds;* and in the remaining Southern and Western States, *election districts* or *precincts,* except in Louisiana where the parishes (counties) are subdivided into *wards.*

tier of States the State government preceded the township government and created it; hence those democratic elements did not develop as they were found in New England, where the township existed first and created the States.

206. County-Township Conflict in Illinois. — When Illinois was admitted to the Union in 1818 the greater number of her citizens were emigrants from the South, who had settled in the southern part of the State; so the State was divided into counties, which were governed by a small board of county commissioners elected at large according to the Pennsylvania plan.

By 1848 when the second State constitution was framed, New England settlers, or emigrants with New England ideas, had settled in large numbers in the northern part of the State; so in this constitution we find a local option provision which permitted the voters of each county to divide the county into townships whenever the majority should vote in favor thereof. To-day eighty-five of the 102 counties of the State have townships.

207. Township Officers in the Central States. — The New England title of *selectmen* is nowhere found in the Central States. In Pennsylvania, Ohio, Iowa, Minnesota, and the Dakotas their place is taken by a "board of supervisors" or "trustees." In other States there is a well-defined head officer who is assisted, and checked in some matters, by a township board. In New York, Michigan, and Illinois, where this officer is called "supervisor," he is also a member of the county board of supervisors. In Indiana, Missouri, Kansas, and Oklahoma the title of "township trustee" is applied to this officer. The other usual township officers are the clerk, assessor, treasurer, overseer of the poor, overseer of roads, justices of the peace, and constables.

208. Village Government Weakens Township Government. — Townships of the Central States are not only under greater State and county control than New England townships, but as soon as a considerable settlement develops it will obtain a

" village " or " town " charter from the State and then exist as
a separate government, performing all or certain functions
within its boundaries that were formerly performed by the
township. In New England many compactly settled communities which would be incorporated cities in other States
and absolutely independent of the township are there a part
of the township.

IV. Geographical Townships

**209. The Terms " Governmental Township " and " Geographica.
Township " Distinguished.** — In the preceding sections we discussed townships merely as divisions of territory for the purpose of government, and these are known as governmental or
political townships. Divisions of territory for the purpose of
surveys are another kind of townships, and are known as
geographical or congressional townships because they are
merely bounded by imaginary lines drawn upon the earth in
accordance with acts of Congress.

In States where the geographical townships were surveyed
before settlements were made, they were generally used also as
governmental townships; but in some localities natural ob-
stacles, such as rivers and mountains, made them unsuitable for
purposes of government, and separate areas were created for
governmental townships.

210. Conditions Preceding Geographical Townships. — During
the colonial period New England and the Southern States
developed two very different land systems. In the South as
the settlers pushed from Virginia and North Carolina into
Kentucky and Tennessee the pioneer selected a fertile piece
of land where he chose and occupied it. A rude survey was
made by a public surveyor or his inexperienced deputy, the
limits were marked by " blazing " the trees with a hatchet, and
the survey was put on record in the State land office.

Conflicting patents[1] were not infrequently given for the

---

[1] " Patent " as here used means a written title to land granted by the proper
State authority.

same tracts, and this produced no end of law suits. Some of the feuds for which the mountains of eastern Kentucky were once famous are said to have grown out of these disputed land patents and the irregularly shaped pieces of land which lay between the patents. This Southern system, which encouraged initiative and resourcefulness, has been called " indiscriminate location."

In New England the laying out of geographical townships preceded the settlements made during the eighteenth century,

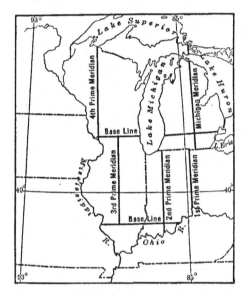

and there could be no title to land outside of townships. Square townships were easier to survey in a systematic way than those of any other shape; hence when the land north of the Ohio River, known as the Northwest Territory, was to be surveyed Thomas Jefferson suggested that it be surveyed into square townships for convenience of description when sold by the government, and to prevent disputes as to title. He also had in mind that they would be of convenient size as governmental townships.

211. Geographical Townships in the West. — When Congress was preparing for the government and settlement of this Northwest Territory, the National Government decided that it should be laid out into townships six miles square.[1] A law of Congress passed in 1785 applied this system of rectangular surveys to all lands belonging to our public domain. This

---

[1] The fact that a six-mile square rather than any other size square was adopted by Congress has no special significance.

" Ordinance of 1785 " was the foundation of the American land system, and its leading principles have continued in operation to the present day.

According to the system gradually perfected, north-and-south and east-and-west lines are established. As starting points certain meridians have been designated as *prime meridians.* There are twenty-four of these, the first being the dividing line between Ohio and Indiana, and the last running a little west of Portland, Oregon.

On each side of the prime meridian are subordinate meridians known as *range lines.* These lines are six miles apart and are numbered east and west from their prime meridian. There must also be a *base line* for each survey following a parallel of latitude, and this crosses the meridians at right angles. There are numerous base lines for surveys in different parts of the country. For example, eleven of them cross the State of Oregon.

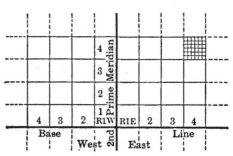

FIGURE 1.

On each side of a base line are subordinate parallels called *township lines*, six miles apart, and numbered north and south from their base line. Thus these range lines and township lines divide the land into townships six miles square.

The map shows the prime meridians and base lines in the States of Ohio, Indiana, and Illinois, that is, in the area between the Ohio and Mississippi rivers. From any prime meridian the tier of townships directly east is called range 1 east (R. 1 E. in Figure 1) and of course other ranges are numbered east and west of that meridian. They are likewise numbered 1, 2, 3, etc. both north and south of the base line. Thus the sectioned township in Figure 1 is township 4 north, range 4 east of the 2d Prime Meridian in the State of Indiana.

6	5	4	3	2	
7	8	9	10	11	12
18	17	16	15	14 .	13
19	20	21	22	23	24
30	29	28	27	26	25
31	32	33	34	35	36

Six Miles Square

FIGURE 2.

This township six miles square is surveyed into thirty-six square miles, which are numbered as shown in Figure 2, and each square mile is called a *section*. Each section is subdivided into rectangular tracts known as halves, quarters, half quarters, and quarter quarters, as shown in Figure 3. Thus if we consider this square mile (Figure 3) as section 1 of Figure 2 we should describe the forty-acre tract starred in Figure 3 as follows: SW¼, NE¼, Sec. 1, T. 4 N., R. 4 E., which means the southwest one quarter of the north east one quarter of section 1, township 4 north of the base line in range 4 east of the 2d Prime Meridian in the State of Indiana. So you can readily see that if this tract is to be sold it is very easy to describe it in the deed of conveyance[1] without the costly aid of private surveyors.

One Square Mile

FIGURE 3.

BIBLIOGRAPHY

FAIRLIE, J. A. Local Government in Counties, Towns, and Villages. (American State Series.) 1906.
Annual Report of the State Highway Commissioner.
The Manual or Legislative Handbook of your State.

QUESTIONS ON THE TEXT

1. Explain how county government originated in America.
2. What functions are performed by county governments?
3. What State first established county " boards of supervisors "? " Boards of commissioners "? How did they differ originally?

---

[1] A deed of conveyance is a contract giving the boundaries of real estate transferred from one person to another.

4. What legislative powers have the county boards? What administrative powers?

5. What judicial officers has a county?

6. What other county officers are there in the State in which you live? For what terms are they selected? What are their duties?

7. What is meant by *posse comitatus*? Of whom does it consist?

8. What officer does Massachusetts have instead of a coroner? Why is the Massachusetts plan preferable to that of most other States?

9. Who grants marriage licenses in the State in which you live? Who records deeds?

10. Explain how the New England town or township originated.

11. What does "town" mean in New England? What does it mean in the South and West?

12. What powers do New England towns possess?

13. Explain the work done by a town-meeting. What is a town "warrant"? What is a moderator? What are the duties of the selectmen?

14. What are the benefits of a New England town-meeting?

15. How are the various town or township officers selected in New England? For what term?

16. By what name are the districts known into which the counties of your state are divided?

17. Explain to what extent the Central States imitated New England township government.

18. Why are townships less important in States having numerous villages than in New England?

19. Describe the county-township conflict in Illinois. In what division of States are counties least important?

20. In your State what title is applied to township officers, such as the "selectmen" in New England?

21. What is meant by a governmental or a geographical township? How did they come into existence, and why are they useful?

22. Explain how a survey of land is described where geographical townships exist.

QUESTIONS FOR DISCUSSION

1. Give the names of as many county officers as you know.

2. Bound the county in which you live.

3. If you had a vote would you vote for a member of the county

board of commissioners or supervisors who favors low taxes or high taxes?

4. Could your county board enact an ordinance requiring all heavy vehicles to have wide tires? If not, what body could give it authority to do so?

5. In Virginia each city of the first class forms a separate county. Should not county and city government be merged so as to save the expense of a double organization?

6. Some Southern counties have dispensed with a county treasurer and the taxes are collected and warrants paid by a designated bank for about half the usual cost. Do you favor this new plan?

7. In California and in Maryland a county may have a charter and govern itself much as a city is governed. That is, a county may have a greater degree of "home rule" than the other counties of the State if the majority vote in favor of a charter. Would you favor a law permitting your county to have a council and a greater degree of "home rule"?

8. Write a county ordinance which you would like your county board to enact. It should begin: "Resolved, that" etc.

9. Does your State have the county system of government, township system, or county-township system? What are the merits of each? Which has the greater educational value? Which is more efficient? Which is more expensive?

10. If you live in a township name as many township officers as you know?

11. May women vote for any township officers? May they serve as township officers? For what offices are they best fitted?

12. The Torrens System of title registration, devised by Sir Robert Torrens for Australia in 1857, has been adopted by a number of American States. It provides for the conveyance of real property by registration and certificate instead of deeds. An officer of the government investigates all the documentary evidence of title, descriptions of boundaries, etc. The owner is furnished a certificate giving details of the title which he has to the property, and a duplicate is filed with the county or township registrar. When the property is sold, the owner merely delivers the certificate to the new owner, and has the fact entered at the registrar's office. This does away with the necessity of repeated title examinations and the cost of having a deed written. Would you favor this system for your State?

CHAPTER XXIV

VILLAGE AND CITY GOVERNMENT

I. VILLAGE GOVERNMENT

212. "Village" Defined. — A village is an organized community whose population is less and whose government is more simple than that of cities in the same State. When enough people collect in a district sufficiently compact to justify such public improvements as sidewalks, street lights, and a public supply of water, a State permits them to form a government separate from that of the township or county in order that they may select officers, collect taxes, and provide these public conveniences within the defined area.

. In the New England States villages have not been created, except in a few cases in Maine, Vermont, and Connecticut, because there the township itself is sufficiently organized to collect taxes and provide these public conveniences.

In the West and South the small incorporated centres of population are called "towns," but in the States east of the Mississippi River which border on Canada they are more generally known as "villages," and in Pennsylvania, New Jersey, and Connecticut the English term "borough" is commonly used. However, for the sake of uniformity, the term "village" will be used to include towns and small boroughs.

213. How Villages are Incorporated. — Each State prescribes under what conditions and in what manner a community may become incorporated as a village. In Alabama 100 inhabitants are all that are necessary, but a minimum of 200 or 300 is a more common requirement. Some States further specify that the required number of inhabitants must reside within a prescribed area — a square mile in New York State.

In some States a community may become an incorporated village by a charter enacted by the State legislature, but the usual procedure is for the inhabitants to present to a designated public officer a petition with a prescribed number of signatures. When this officer is satisfied that the conditions necessary to become a village are fulfilled, he will declare that the people living within a certain surveyed area are incorporated[1] as the village of X and have such powers of self-government as the State has granted to villages. In most States the officer may not declare a village incorporated until the inhabitants have voted in favor of it at an election called by the officer when petitioned to do so by a prescribed number of the inhabitants.

214. Powers of Villages. — The few incorporated villages of New England continue a part of the township for many important purposes, such as roads and schools, but may provide for sidewalks, water, lights, sewers, fire protection, and police protection, independently of the township. In those States which adopted the New England township system the villages remain a part of the township for certain purposes, but are more independent of the township than those in New England.

In certain other States, including New Jersey, Pennsylvania, Wisconsin, Minnesota, and the Dakotas, the villages are entirely independent of the township and have power to perform township functions in addition to the usual village functions. In the South and West villages, called " towns," are usually included in the township, or county district known by some other name, but as these districts are unimportant the village has power to deal with practically all local problems except those attended to directly by the county.

215. The Organization of Village Government. — *The Council.* — Every village has a legislative body usually known as the council or the board of trustees. This body varies in number from three to nine, and is usually elected at large for terms

---

[1] " Incorporated " means created into a legal body (artificial person) by the State. This body may then bring suit in court, borrow money, or enter into other contracts as a natural person may do.

of one or two years. In all States the council has power to
determine the tax rate, within certain limits prescribed by the
State, and to appropriate the money for the various needs of
the village.

Generally it can levy special assessments against persons
whose property borders streets which have been especially
favored by sidewalks or other improvements; but villages
have rather limited power to borrow money, and most villages
must submit the question of a bond issue to the voters. The
power to pass ordinances differs from State to State and often
from village to village as provided by the State. Commonly a
council may choose certain officers and regulate their duties;
pass health and police ordinances on special subjects within
certain limits; determine the license taxes of saloons, peddlers,
public vehicles, and other businesses that are licensed; control streets, bridges, and public grounds; maintain police and
firemen; and control any public services owned by the village,
such as water and light plants.

The Mayor. — The principal executive officer of a village is
usually called "mayor" or "president," and is ordinarily
elected for one or two years. He presides over council meetings, and usually has the rights of a member, but in some
villages he merely casts the deciding vote in case of a tie, and
in very few places does he have the veto power. He enforces
the village ordinances enacted by the council, and in a number
of States he acts as police justice.

Every village has a clerk or recorder, a treasurer or collector,
and a police officer ("constable," "marshal," "sergeant," or
"bailiff"). There are, in many places, a street commissioner,
an assessor, and an attorney or solicitor. . In the West these
officers are usually elected by the voters; in other sections they
are commonly selected by the council or appointed. Some villages have a justice of the peace, and if the village forms a
separate school district it, of course, has school officers. Larger
villages have such officers as health, fire, lighting, sewer, or
cemetery commissioners.

II. City Government

216. Meaning of the Term "City." — A city is a governmental unit created by the State, with more population and more powers than a town or village. Each State determines how many inhabitants a town or community must have to become a city, and what governmental powers it will permit its cities to exercise.

In Kansas a community with as few as 200 inhabitants may become a city, but in New York State 10,000 inhabitants are required. About as many of our forty-eight States will create a city government with less than 2500 inhabitants as require a greater population, but the United States census classifies as cities all incorporated places with as many as 2500 inhabitants.

217. Rapid Growth of Cities. — When the first United States census was taken in 1790 only 123,475 people, or about 3 per cent of the population, dwelt in cities with as many as 8000 inhabitants. New York, Philadelphia, Boston, Baltimore, and Charleston were then the only cities of that size.

Just nine years previous to the taking of this first census Watt had taken out a patent for his double-acting steam engine, which made large scale manufacturing possible. Fulton's steamboat (1806) and Stephenson's locomotive (1829) made easy the transportation of raw materials to the factories and the distribution of the manufactured products from the factories. Thus factories were erected where there was water transportation or rail transportation, and workmen from scattered shops, which were put out of business by the factories, had to move to the factory town and help make it a city.

As a result of the invention of various farming implements less labor was needed for the production of food and other raw material; therefore the excess labor was employed in turning the raw products into luxuries — grains into breakfast cereals, wool and cotton into fine clothes, and iron ore into automobiles. So long as improved machinery and fertilizers continue to reduce the amount of labor necessary to produce the world's food supply, so long will the proportion of people who live in cities probably continue to increase.

The number of cities in the United States with 8000 or more population from decade to decade has been as follows:

DATE	NUMBER OF CITIES	PER CENT OF TOTAL POPULATION	DATE	NUMBER OF CITIES	PER CENT OF TOTAL POPULATION
1790	5	3.1	1860	141	16.1
1800	6	4.0	1870	226	20.9
1810	11	4.9	1880	286	22.6
1820	13	4.9	1890	447	29.0
1830	26	6.7	1900	545	32.9
1840	44	8.5	1910	778	38.8
1850	85	12.5			

This rapid growth of cities is not peculiar to the United States but is world-wide, and is due to industrial conditions. City growth in England and Germany has been even greater than in the United States.

New York, the second largest city in the world, with a population of about 5,000,000, has more Jews than there are in Palestine, more Germans than in any city of Germany except Hamburg and Berlin, more Bohemians than in Prague, and more Italians than in Rome. It has an increase in population of 1,500,000 in ten years, annual expenditure of nearly $200,000,000, and a debt exceeding $1,000,000,000 — or slightly more than that of the United States government.

218. Council-Mayor Type of City Government. — There are three types of city government in the United States — council-mayor, commission, and manager. Of these the council-mayor type is the oldest and as yet the most prevalent. It consists of a council, usually a large one, to make the laws, and a mayor to enforce them.

At one time or another the councils of most of our large cities have been composed of two chambers, a board of aldermen and a common council, but the present tendency is strongly towards a single-chamber council. Of our ten largest cities only Baltimore and Philadelphia retain councils of two chambers, and only nine of our fifty cities with populations exceeding 100,000 have two-chambered councils.[1] Very few small cities have councils composed of two chambers.

Copyright, Underwood & Underwood, N. Y.

THE MUNICIPAL BUILDING, NEW YORK.

The council, elected by the voters of the city for terms varying from one to four years, enacts all city ordinances, determines the tax rate, and appropriates the revenues for city purposes. Committees of the council have some control over the administrative departments, such as the street or police department, but the tendency is to make the head of each department responsible to the mayor.

---

[1] These cities are Philadelphia, Baltimore, Kansas City, Mo., Providence, Louisville, Atlanta, Worcester, Richmond, and Cambridge.

The mayor is elected by the voters of the city for a term varying from one to four years. Under him are the heads of various departments, such as street commissioner and police commissioner. These officers are elected by the voters in some cities, but in most cities they are selected by the council or appointed by the mayor with or without the approval of the council. In some cities the mayor presides at council meetings, and in nearly all cities he can veto ordinances passed by the council, which can then become law only by a larger vote of the council — usually two thirds.

City judges are sometimes appointed by the governor of the State for long terms, but in most cities they are elected by the citizens for a term of only a few years, and those for minor courts are in some cities chosen by the council.

The school affairs of a city are usually entrusted to an independent board ; and in many cities other duties are entrusted to boards more or less independent of the foregoing organization.

The council-mayor type of city government does not work well because no one person is responsible. The government is so complex that the citizens do not understand the working of it; therefore some shrewd person, usually a corrupt politician, by making a practical study of it, makes himself political boss. He receives no salary as boss, but by controlling the elections and filling the offices with his friends he can compel them to spend large amounts of money in a manner which will yield graft for him. For instance, in 1868, when Tweed was boss of New York, a court-house was designed which was to cost $250,000. Three years later more than $8,000,000 had been expended upon the building and it was still unfinished. For thermometers $7500 was charged. Contractors for various parts of the building presented enormous bills and then divided with the boss.

Even if a city avoids a boss it is little better off. The officers are then elected at random and are not likely to work together harmoniously. The mayor will veto the ordinances passed by the council, or the department heads will not enforce them, or the head of the water department will tear up the new paving laid by the street department.

If an individual wants to make complaint of bad service and goes to the head of a department, the citizen will, in all probability, be told that the mayor has not authorized the department to act. He then goes to the mayor and is told that the request is a proper one but that the council failed to vote funds for that particular service. The individual cannot visit a hundred councillors, more or less; therefore the bad service continues bad. Each officer shifts the responsibility to another because no one has power to act.

This jungle-like government has fallen into bad repute, and cities are rapidly abandoning the council-mayor type of government for the commission type. However, of the 778 cities with 8000 or more of population 556 continue to have the council-mayor type of government.

219. Commission Type of City Government. — A commission government is one in which a few elective officers (usually five) exercise all legislative and executive powers and are held responsible to the voters for their proper use. This form of city government was first tried at Galveston, Texas, in 1901, and came by chance. On September 8, 1900, a tidal wave swept over the island city. The bridges connecting the city with the mainland collapsed, buildings fell, the water-works and the lighting plant were destroyed, the wood-block paving floated off in great strips, and about 6000 of the city's 37,000 inhabitants perished.

This city had been extravagantly managed under its council-mayor type of government. Expenditures had regularly exceeded receipts, and the deficit had been made up by selling city bonds, that is, by borrowing. After the flood, persons owning these bonds had so little faith in the government that they were willing to sell them for sixty cents on the dollar. The old inefficient council of twelve men passed resolutions but did little else to restore the city and its credit.

The Deepwater Committee, an organization of substantial business men previously formed to bring about the improvement of the harbor, interested itself and had a new city charter prepared.   They had a member of the State legislature present it to the legislature for adoption.   At the same time the Deepwater Committee issued an address to the people of Galveston, which read, in part:

> "We are asking for a charter placing the entire control of the local government in the hands of five commissioners, designed to benefit the people rather than to provide sinecures (offices with no special duties) for the politicians."

The legislature granted the charter and in September, 1901, a year after the catastrophe, the new government went into operation.

The Galveston Type of Commission Government. — The Galveston government has undergone practically no change during the intervening years except that in 1903 the provision whereby the governor of the State appointed three of the five commissioners was declared to be in conflict with the constitution of the State.   Since that date all five commissioners have been elected; hence the name "commission government" no longer accurately describes the government, because a commissioner is a person appointed.   However, the name "commission government" has persisted, but in all commission cities the commissioners—called *council* in many "commission cities"—are elected.   The provisions of the Galveston charter are:

(1)   Five commissioners elected by the voters of the entire city for terms of two years and a salary of $1200 a year.   (These commissioners are business men and devote only a portion of their time to the city service.)

(2)   Joint power of the commissioners
> (*a*)   to enact all city ordinances, except that bond issues must be submitted to the people for their approval or rejection;
> (*b*)   to grant franchises (permits) for such public services as street railways;

(c) to appoint an expert head and subordinates for each ad-
    ministrative department and dismiss the same with or
    without cause.

(3) Supervision of the city departments distributed among the
commissioners, except the mayor-president, as agreed upon by the
commissioners themselves.

(4) Mayor-president elected by the citizens as one of the five. (He
must be in his office six hours a day; receives $600 extra, or a total
of $1800; has no veto; and is merely first among equals so far as
actual power is concerned, but endeavors to harmonize the work of
the commission, and represents the city at social functions.[1])

Good results from the new form of government were almost
immediate. A sea wall was built, a causeway for vehicles and
for electric and steam railways was constructed to the mainland, and the level of the city was raised.[2] Bonds are again
worth full value, and a proper proportion of the debt has been
paid without increasing the tax rate.

During the decade following the change in the form of
government $136,000 was earned in interest derived from city
deposits. Under the old régime no interest had been required
of the favored bankers. The Galveston plan soon became
famous and spread to other Texas cities.

In 1907 the citizens of Des Moines, Iowa, became dissatisfied
with their council-mayor type of government, and the Commercial Club arranged a debate to discuss the merits of the
commission government as compared with a small council
and strong mayor plan. As the result of the debate a large
majority of the committee of three hundred citizens who had

---

[1] The school board is elected at a special election and is not subordinate to
the commission, but is dependent upon it for appropriations of money. Judges
are likewise selected independently of the commission.

[2] A canal 2½ miles long, 300 feet wide, and 20 feet deep was excavated from
Galveston Bay through the residential section of the city. The houses were
moved to vacant lots. Self-loading, self-propelling, and self-discharging
dredges sucked sand from the bottom of the bay, brought it into the canal
and discharged it through pipe lines, the water draining back into the canal.
When the work was completed the canal was refilled and the houses replaced
on the foundation thus made.

been named as "jurors" decided in favor of the commission plan. The Iowa legislature was appealed to, and enacted a general law allowing any city of a prescribed population to adopt this new plan of government.

The Des Moines Type of Commission Government is practically the Galveston plan with the five additional features:

(1) *The Initiative* — 25 per cent of the voters can propose a city ordinance and have it voted upon at a special election, or 10 per cent of the voters can have an ordinance voted upon at a regular election.

(2) *The Referendum* — 25 per cent of those who voted at the last election can have an ordinance which the commission has passed referred to popular vote for approval or rejection, provided the petition is presented within ten days of the date of its passage.

(3) *The Recall* — 25 per cent of the voters may demand that any one or all of the commissioners again stand for office at a special election called before the expiration of the term.

(4) *Non-Partizan Primaries Followed by Non-Partizan Elections* — Any person may have his name placed upon the primary ballot by presenting a petition containing twenty-five names. The names of candidates are arranged alphabetically with no indications of party. The ten highest are placed upon the ballot for the regular election in the same manner, and the five highest are elected.

(5) *A Civil Service Committee* — A committee of three citizens is appointed by the commission, for a term of six years, to examine employees for subordinate positions. The employees, however, may be removed by the commission.

The advantages of the commission government are: (1) the number to elect is small; (2) they can act promptly; (3) they have full power to act, and cannot shirk their responsibility by referring an aggrieved citizen to some one else; and (4) they are easier to watch than if they were many.

The way to get good government is to give power to a few people and watch those few in order to hold them responsible. A city boss does not steal when he is being watched. The commissioners meet in public, record their votes for the inspection of the public, publish their ordinances in the papers, and issue frequent financial reports.

If they refuse to enact an ordinance which the majority of voters desire, the voters themselves may initiate and pass it (initiative); if the commission passes one which the voters do not want they may have it referred to them and reject it (referendum); if the commissioners are believed to be dishonest or are inefficient a new election may be called and one or all of the commissioners recalled by electing others to take their places (recall). Thus we get government for the people by a few who are responsible to the people.

Of the 778 cities with 8000 or more population 197 have commission government, and the number is rapidly increasing.[1]

220. The Manager Type of City Government. — The manager type of government is really a modification of the commission type. It consists of a council of three or five members, according to the size of the city, who determine the policy, but select a manager to administer the government of the city. The council of five who represent the people are like the directors of a commercial corporation who are selected by the stockholders to determine the business policies, and the city manager selected by the council is like the general manager of a commercial corporation.

In 1907 Staunton, Virginia, the birthplace of Woodrow Wilson, was casting about for a plan of government which would increase the efficiency of its city government, and would have adopted the commission plan had not the constitution of Virginia required all cities of the first class to have a two-chambered council, for Staunton is a city of the first class. However, the city charter permitted the council to appoint new officers, and early in 1908 it appointed a "city manager." The manager was given full charge of the administration of the city, and was allowed to appoint and dismiss heads of departments and other city employees.

The manager of Staunton for the first three years was Mr.

---

[1] Commission cities with more than 100,000 inhabitants are Buffalo, New Orleans, Jersey City, St. Paul (modified form), Portland, Oakland, Birmingham, Memphis, Omaha, Nashville, Lowell, and Spokane.

Ashburner of Richmond, formerly construction engineer for the Chesapeake and Ohio Railroad Company. Through business-like methods he brought about efficient administration for the city. For example, by purchasing supplies for all of the departments he saved a neat sum for the city; he laid granolithic walks at about half their cost when put out at contract under the old system; and by putting meters in all houses the usual shortage of water was overcome. A few other cities have added a manager to their existing form of government.

The first real manager government was organized by Sumter, South Carolina. The Short Ballot Organization, of which Mr. Richard S. Childs of New York is secretary and leading spirit, prepared a model charter which, with a few modifications, Sumter adopted in 1912, after obtaining permission of the State legislature. The first three councilmen were exceptionally capable men, one being a planter, one a banker, and the third a lawyer. They advertised for a manager and chose one from another State. He brought about a number of economies.

An interesting incident is told of how this manager got rid of mistletoe which was killing miles of trees in the streets of the city. It had not been removed previously because of the great cost. The manager knew that mistletoe has a time and place value, so he had a number of workmen cut the mistletoe from the trees and sold it in the North for enough to cover the entire cost of having the trees cleaned.

The new constitution of Ohio permits cities to draft their own charters, and after the flood in the spring of 1913 Dayton elected a charter committee pledged to the manager plan. As Dayton is the only city with more than 100,000 inhabitants that has adopted the manager plan, an outline of its government is most interesting.

The Dayton Type of Manager Government is as follows:

(1) A Commission of five elected from the city at large for a term of four years, partial renewal biennially, on a salary of $1200. Duties: enact ordinances, determine tax rate, make appropriations, and elect a manager and a civil service board.

(2) A Mayor who is the commissioner receiving the greatest vote the year that three are elected. Merely first among equals. Duties: presides at meetings of the commission, is ceremonial head of the city, suits against the city are brought in his name, is agent of the governor in carrying out the State militia law, but has no veto.

(3) A Manager chosen by the commission for an indefinite term. Removed either by commission or by recall of the voters. Salary determined by the commission. Duties: enforces the city ordinances, employs and dismisses department heads, dismisses even civil service employees, advises commission as to needs of city.

(4) Non-Partizan primaries and elections.

(5) Initiative.

(6) Referendum.

(7) Recall of commissioners or manager.

(8) Publicity provisions as in the regular commission plan.

Mr. Waite, the first and present manager of Dayton, was street commissioner of Cincinnati. His salary is $12,500.

The advantages of the manager plan are: (1) The burdensome duties are performed by the manager, therefore a prominent business man can afford to serve as commissioner because he can continue with his regular business. (2) The manager may be chosen from within or without the city. (3) The manager may be chosen without political considerations. Mr. Waite recently said that he does not know the politics of any of his subordinates. (4) Powers and responsibility are centered in one man. "If anything goes wrong you know whom to hang." Either the manager or the three or five commissioners are to blame. In the main, the responsibility is centred in the manager as the commissioners give him great latitude. (5) It makes city governing a profession instead of political graft. For instance, the manager of Staunton received $2500 a year, but was successful and is now manager of Springfield, Ohio, on a salary of $6000.

There are only twenty-five manager cities with as many as 8000 inhabitants,[1] but the number is increasing very rapidly.

[1] The following cities with more than 25,000 inhabitants (census 1910) have the manager type of government: Dayton and Springfield, Ohio; Wheeling,

221. Home Rule for Cities. — A city government has only such powers as the State grants it. These powers are usually enumerated in a charter which contains the name of the city, a description of its boundaries, the form of its organization, and an enumeration of its powers. Until recent years it was the practice in most States for the legislature to grant a separate charter for each city. This procedure occupied much of the time of the legislatures and resulted in a favoritism to certain cities. In time, however, many State legislatures grouped their cities into classes and enacted general uniform laws for the government of all cities of a class.

City inhabitants felt that they should have more control over their own government, and in recent times " home rule " provisions have been placed in the constitutions of a number of States. These provisions allow the people of a city, under certain restrictions, to frame their own charter. Of course these charters must not contain provisions inconsistent with the State laws.

Of the States permitting cities to draft their own " home rule " charters Ohio is the most liberal.[1] The Ohio Constitutional Convention of 1912 gave cities the power either to frame their own charters or to adopt by local referendum any general or special charter laws which the State legislature might pass. The legislature promptly prepared three model charters; one of the council-mayor type, one of the commission type, and one of the manager type. However, most of the larger cities of Ohio prepared their own charters and are now enjoying self-made or " home rule " charters.

222. City Problems. — *City Portals.* — Every city should have a union station for the convenience of the traveling public. One

---

W. Va.; Jackson and Grand Rapids, Mich.; Niagara Falls, Newburg, and Watertown, N. Y.; San Jose, Cal.; and Portsmouth, Va.

[1] The other " home rule " States are California, Colorado, Michigan, Minnesota, Missouri, Oregon, Oklahoma, and Washington. These States, however, lay various troublesome restrictions upon the right of cities to make their own charters, whereas in Ohio the only restriction is the will of the people of the particular city.

of the most attractive and convenient union stations is that at Washington, D. C. For this station about $25,000,000 was expended for the site, approaches, and building. Of this amount the United States Government and the District of Columbia Government contributed about $5,500,000.

Streets. — In the material development of a city the question of street-paving is of first importance. Mr. W. B. Munro[1]

THE UNION STATION, WASHINGTON, D. C.

has summarized the desirability of the various kinds of pavements in the following table:

ECONOMY IN CONSTRUCTION	ECONOMY IN REPAIR	DURABILITY	CLEANLINESS	NOISE-LESSNESS	SAFETY
1st Macadam	Granite	Granite	Asphalt	Wood	Granite
2d Asphalt	Brick	Wood	Brick	Macadam	Macadam
3d Brick	Wood	Brick	Wood	Brick	Brick
4th Wood	Asphalt	Asphalt	Granite	Asphalt	Wood
5th Granite	Macadam	Macadam	Macadam	Granite	Asphalt

[1] "Principles and Methods of Municipal Administration," page 103.

An increasing number of cities light their own streets and furnish electricity and gas to their citizens. In 1912 there were 3659 commercial lighting plants and 1562 municipal plants in the United States, the commercial plants having increased 30 per cent and the municipal plants 91 per cent in ten years.[1]

Nothing mars the beauty of city streets more than billboards. City laws prohibiting billboards on private property have usually been declared unconstitutional because the courts have considered the restriction an unreasonable interference with one's use of his private property. (See U. S. Constitution, Amend. XIV.) The courts do not *yet* consider the unsightliness of billboards to be a sufficient annoyance to compel one to remove them from his private property. However, billboards which might conceal thugs, produce disease, set fire to adjoining property, or blow down and destroy life may be prohibited.

CLEVELAND'S THREE-CENT-FARE TROLLEY CAR.

For instance, New York requires fireproof billboards with secure wind braces and prohibits electric signs which unduly interfere with sleep. Chicago requires billboards to have an open space below them and at the sides. St. Louis limits the area of billboards to 500 square feet, and some cities tax them as real estate.

[1] Zueblin, Charles, "American Municipal Progress," page 68.

Electric Railways. — Scarcely any of the American cities own and operate their own street railways, though some of the subways[1] are built by municipalities. The threat of public ownership in Cleveland brought a three-cent fare to most parts of the city.

Water Systems. — Most. of the larger cities own their water systems, the most interesting of which is the Los Angeles

system. This city brings its water a distance of 250 miles by gravity through concrete and steel conduits and pipes. In constructing this system it was necessary to dig a five-mile tunnel through the mountains and to cross 150 miles of desert. The gravity of the water supplies 120,000 horse power of electrical energy, and in addition to supplying water for the city reclaims nearly 200 square miles of arid land near the city.

Sewage Disposal. — New York and most other cities empty their sewage into nearby streams, though New York is preparing for a more sanitary

THE WATER SUPPLY OF LOS ANGELES SIPHONS ITSELF OVER MOUNTAINS.

method of disposal. Baltimore and New Orleans have very modern disposal systems. The Baltimore system consists of a series of settlement tanks. The water is siphoned from

---

[1] The only American subways for passengers are those of Boston, Greater New York, and Philadelphia. Chicago has a subway for freight.

one tank to another, then flows through a revolving screen, is sprayed into the air by a series of thousands of small fountains, and falls upon beds of stone and sand through which it is filtered. It flows into the Bay as pure as the water in the city reservoirs. As the water falls from the filtration beds into the Bay it is used to generate electricity by which the disposal plant is operated.

Pasadena, being in a dry climate, uses its sewage to water a city farm containing an orange grove, an English walnut orchard, and fields of alfalfa, grain, and hay.

Wharves. — Every city should own its wharves for the encouragement of commerce. San Francisco and New Orleans, the gateways to the Panama Canal, own practically all of their water fronts, and Greater New York now owns 349 of its 577 miles of water front. Los Angeles, a city 21 miles from water, has already acquired four

THE HANDSOMEST POLICEWOMAN IN AMERICA.

Miss Blanche Payson of San Francisco.

miles of water front. On the other hand, the Lake cities own scarcely any of their wharfage; and though the United States has spent $20,000,000 improving and maintaining a 30-foot channel for the harbor of Galveston, the wharves are owned almost entirely by private persons.

The states of Australia own the land 66 feet back from their waterways, hence private persons cannot monopolize the water front as in the United States.

Social Centres. — The importance of parks, playgrounds, recreation piers, public baths, and other social centres are more and more appreciated by cities. Library and school auditoriums are commonly used for public lectures, music, and moving pictures. A few cities maintain public laundries where

FORSYTH DENTAL INFIRMARY, BOSTON.
Here hundreds of children are treated free daily.

a housewife may do her week's washing with the aid of machinery.

Policewomen. — Since 1911, when Los Angeles employed the first policewomen, many cities have employed them, Chicago alone having about thirty policewomen. These officers protect girls from insults by young men who frequent street corners; act as public chaperons at places of amusement which are frequented by women and girls; obtain evidence from women; and attend court when women are testifying. In Los Angeles they enforce the 9 o'clock curfew law for girls under seventeen years of age.

Health Protection. — Most cities have a health board to look after the general health conditions of the city. School children are inspected in nearly all American cities, and in many free treatment is given to the eyes and teeth. Free medical dispensaries are commonly maintained to supply the needs of the poor.

Many cities send health agents into the country for miles around to inspect all dairies and herds from which the city's milk supply is obtained. The milk itself is further inspected

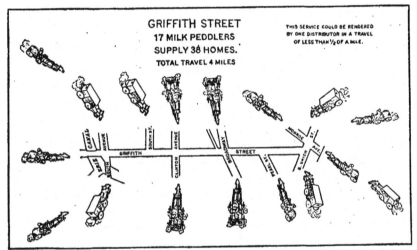

GRIFFITH STREET
17 MILK PEDDLERS
SUPPLY 38 HOMES.
TOTAL TRAVEL 4 MILES

THIS SERVICE COULD BE RENDERED BY ONE DISTRIBUTOR IN A TRAVEL OF LESS THAN ½ OF A MILE.

Courtesy World's Work, Vol. 26.

AN ECONOMIC WASTE IN DISTRIBUTION OF MILK IN ROCHESTER, NEW YORK.

from time to time after it reaches the city. Would it not be well for our cities to distribute their milk supply in order to insure its quality as well as to save the present economic waste in its distribution ?

Cities have various regulations to prevent such diseases as tuberculosis and typhoid fever, but the American cities have not become as efficient as the European cities in reducing the death rate caused by typhoid fever. This is shown in the following table :[1]

---

[1] Munro, W. B., "Principles and Methods of Municipal Administration," page 144. Published 1916.

ANNUAL DEATH-RATE FROM TYPHOID PER 100,000

IN AMERICAN CITIES	RATE PER 100,000	IN EUROPEAN CITIES.	RATE PER 100,000
New York . . .	12	London	5
Philadelphia . :	36	Paris	8
Chicago	15	Berlin.	4
St. Louis	15	Vienna	4
Boston	26	Glasgow	8
Baltimore	31	Hamburg . . .	. 4
Buffalo	21 ·	Munich	3
Cleveland	13	The Hague . . .	1

BIBLIOGRAPHY

BEARD, CHARLES A. Digest of Short Ballot Charters. 1911——.

BRADFORD, ERNEST S. Commission Government in American Cities. (Citizens Library.) 1911.

FAIRLIE, J. A. Local Government in Counties, Towns, and Villages. (American State Series.) 1906.

MUNRO, W. B. The Government of American Cities. 1912.

——. Principles and Methods of Municipal Administration. 1916.

TOULMIN, H. A. The City Manager. 1915.

WILCOX, DELOS F. Great Cities in America. (Citizens Library.) 1910.

ZUEBLIN, CHARLES. American Municipal Progress. 1916.

The charter of your city.

QUESTIONS ON THE TEXT

1. What is a village?

2. In what section of the country are small incorporated centers of population called *towns? Villages? Boroughs?*

3. What is meant by the term *town* in the New England States?

4. How are towns or villages created in the State in which you live? How many inhabitants are necessary?

5. What are the usual powers of towns or villages?

6. By what name is the legislative body of a town or village commonly known? What character of ordinances may it enact?

7. By what title is the principal executive officer of a town usually called?

8. What other officers do towns or villages commonly have?

9. How does a city differ from a town or village?

10. How many inhabitants are necessary for city government?

11. What per cent of the American people lived in cities in 1790? In 1910?

12. What has been the cause of such rapid growth of cities? Is this rapid growth of cities peculiar to the United States?

13. What three types of city government are there in the United States?

14. Is the tendency toward a council of two branches or of one branch?

15. Explain the present organization of the council-mayor government for cities.

16. How is the mayor selected and what are his duties?

17. How is the council selected and what are its duties?

18. Explain why the council-mayor type of city government does not work well and why it is favored by political bosses.

19. Describe the commission type of city government. Explain how it originated in Galveston.

20. Is "commission government" the correct name for this type of government?

21. What do you mean by a *city charter?* (See Sec. 221.) What are the provisions of the Galveston charter?

22. What are some of the benefits derived from this new form of government in Galveston? Tell how it came to be adopted by Des Moines.

23. What five features did Des Moines add to the Galveston plan?

24. Name four advantages of the commission type of government.

25. Describe the manager type of government. Explain how the idea originated in Staunton, Virginia.

26. Explain the working of this type of government in Sumter, South Carolina.

27. Why and when was the manager type adopted in Dayton, Ohio?

28. Explain the Dayton type of manager government.

29. What are the advantages of the manager type of government?

30. What is meant by "home rule" for cities? Why is it important? Which State has the most liberal "home rule" provisions?

31. What material do you consider best for paving a street?

32. Is city ownership or private ownership of electric light plants increasing more rapidly?

33. Could your city prohibit billboards?

34. Describe the Los Angeles water system.

35. Describe the Baltimore filtration plant. The Pasadena system of sewage disposal.

36. Why are wharves so important for a city? Should the wharves be owned by the city or by private persons?

37. What social centers do cities commonly have?

38. How do American cities attempt to guard health? Do they guard it as efficiently as European cities?

QUESTIONS FOR DISCUSSION

1. What offices has your town or village and by whom are they filled?

2. Bound your town or village. Name all the incorporated towns or villages within your county.

3. What county taxes are paid by the residents of your town or village?

4. What is the population of your town or village?

5. Why does your town or village need a government distinct from that of your county?

6. Has your town or city a civic improvement league of any sort? If so, what valuable services does it perform? How can you assist it? Does it improve the school grounds? Does it place waste paper receptacles along the sidewalk? Does it place bulletin boards at certain places along the main streets for posters so that they will not be stuck over buildings, fences, and telephone posts? Does it take part in the social service or moral uplift work? What do *you* propose to do?

7. Would it be wise for your town or village to have a public meeting annually and hear reports from your officers and discuss needed improvements? Also, may not your representative to the State legislature give an account of the most important things done by the legislature for the village, county, or State?

8. What determines the location of cities?

9. Does your State constitution contain any provisions in regard to cities? What are they? Could your town become a city? How?

10. How many cities has your State? What is the population of the largest? Of the one in which you live?

11. Name the principal officers of your city. How are they selected? For what term?

12. The cities of Ohio are allowed to draft their own charters. Do you think every city should be allowed to prepare its own charter?

13. States may enact any laws which do not conflict with federal laws. Why not allow all cities to enact any laws which do not conflict with State laws?

14. Does your city own its water system? Gas system? Electric light system? Street railways? Jitney bus lines? Heating system? If not, why not?

15. By the right of eminent domain many European cities condemn old city blocks, tear down the unsanitary buildings, and put up new ones and rent them at their actual cost. Most American cities do not have this privilege. Should they have it?

16. Buenos Ayres has recently built 10,000 homes for working men. Do you think your city should follow this example if the State law permits?

17. Many cities have ordinances against permitting weeds to grow in vacant lots. Has yours?

18. At the suggestion of the civil service board of Oakland, California, cash prizes are offered to city employees who make valuable suggestions for the betterment of the service in the various departments. Do you favor this scheme for your city?

19. Many Southern cities have segregation ordinances providing that if the majority of persons living in a block are white, no colored persons may move into said block, and *vice versa*. What arguments are there for and against this distinction?

20. What organization is there in your city working for the improvement of its government? If there is none, start one.

21. Harrisonburg, Virginia, a city of 5000, owns a gravity water system which earns $10,000 a year net profit for the city, and an electric power plant on a nearby river which also produces a similar profit for the city. Is there a water power site available near your city or a supply of water which would flow by gravity to the city?

22. The University of Illinois has a Professor of Civic Designing. Is there any plan for the future development of your city? Draw a map of your city as it should be, showing where a town hall, library, high school, fire engine house, post office, court house if a county seat, ball grounds, and tennis courts should be located.

CHAPTER XXV

SUFFRAGE

223. Suffrage and Citizenship Distinguished. — The word *suffrage* comes from the Latin word *suffragium*, and means *a vote*. Suffrage, then, is simply the privilege of voting at elections. *Citizenship* means *membership* in a State. " All persons born or naturalized in the United States, and subject to the jurisdiction thereof, are citizens of the United States and of the State wherein they reside."[1] Infants born in the United States are citizens and are entitled to the privileges of citizens at home and abroad, but they cannot vote.

224. Suffrage Determined by Each State. — So long as a State maintains a republican form of government[2] it may determine what persons are to enjoy the political privilege of voting at both its own and national elections, with two exceptions: (1) that the same persons must be allowed to vote for United States senators and representatives that vote for members of the more numerous branch of the State legislature, and (2) that no person may be deprived of suffrage because of race, color, or previous condition of servitude.[3]

---

[1] United States Constitution, Amendment XIV.

[2] A republican form of government is a representative government, or one in which the people elect their law-makers and other public officers directly or indirectly.

[3] The Fourteenth Amendment to the Constitution of the United States (Sec. 2) provides that any State which denies male citizens twenty-one years of age the privilege of voting, except for crime, shall have its representation in Congress reduced in the proportion which the number of such male citizens shall bear to the whole number of male citizens twenty-one years of age in such State. This provision has never been enforced, but after each decennial census when a reapportionment of representatives is being made, some congressman calls attention to the provision.

In practice the States commonly permit the same voters to participate in all elections, though in a number of States women may vote in school elections only, in a few they may vote on the question of bond issues only, in Illinois they may vote for those officers that are not provided for in the State constitution, and in 1915 the governor of Rhode Island recommended to the legislature that women be permitted to vote for presidential electors only. The Rhode Island legislature voted against the governor's recommendation, but had they chosen to extend to women the right to vote for presidential electors only, they would have acted within their rights.

All of the States agree that no person should have more than one vote, but four persons out of every five have no vote. Some early State constitutions prescribed religious tests as a prerequisite to voting, and most of them limited the privilege to property owners. To-day there are three restrictions on suffrage, or the right to vote, which apply to normal persons in every State and three additional ones in some States.

(1) *Age.* — In no State may a person vote who is less than twenty-one years of age.

(2) *Citizenship.* — In no State may a person vote who is not a citizen of the United States or has not declared his intention to become such.

(3) *Residence.* — In no State may a person vote who has not resided in the State a period prescribed by law.

(4) *Sex.* — In more than half of the States women may not vote in all elections.

(5) *Education.* — In nearly one third of the States a person may not vote who cannot read or write.

(6) *Taxation.* — In a few of the States a person may not vote who has not paid his poll tax.

Such abnormal persons as idiots or insane, paupers supported at public expense, and those who have committed certain crimes are, in nearly all States, denied the right to vote.

225. Suffrage Restriction as to Age. — In no one of the forty-eight States may a person vote who is less than twenty-one years of age. Twenty-one years of age has no special significance. We have simply followed the English law which prescribed this age. In ancient Sparta the age was thirty, while in Athens it was only sixteen. In Germany to-day it is twenty-five, but in Switzerland it is only twenty.

The age prescribed by the American States is no doubt as satisfactory as that prescribed by any of the other countries, but it is merely a rough and ready test. Some boys are more mature mentally at eighteen than others ever become. Maybe civil service examinations will be given to all applicants for the suffrage at some future time.

226. Suffrage Restrictions as to Citizenship. — In seven States aliens may vote in local, State, and national elections, provided they have declared their intention of becoming citizens of the United States by taking out their first naturalization papers.[1] In the other forty-one States suffrage is restricted to citizens of the United States. It should be clearly borne in mind that while only those persons who are citizens of the United States or have declared their intention to become such may vote, nevertheless, four fifths of those who are citizens are not permitted to vote, most of the disfranchised being women and children.

227. Suffrage Restrictions as to Residence. — When a citizen of the United States moves from one State to another he is required to reside in the latter State for a period prescribed by the law of that State, varying from three months in Maine to two years in most of the Southern States,[2] before he can vote

---

[1] These States are Arkansas, Indiana, Kansas, Missouri, Nebraska, South Dakota, and Texas. Eight other States permitted aliens to vote until the last few years.

[2] In Idaho, Indiana, Iowa, Kansas, Michigan, Nebraska, Nevada, New Hampshire, Oregon, and South Dakota a residence of six months is required; in Arizona, Arkansas, California, Colorado, Connecticut, Delaware, Florida, Georgia, Illinois, Kentucky, Maryland, Massachusetts, Minnesota, Missouri, Montana, New Jersey, New Mexico, New York, North Dakota, Ohio, Oklahoma, Pennsylvania, Tennessee, Texas, Utah, Vermont, Washington, West Virginia, Wisconsin, and Wyoming, one year; and in Alabama, Louisiana, Mississippi, North Carolina, Rhode Island, South Carolina, and Virginia, two years.

there, though he is usually permitted to vote in the State from which he has moved, either by law or practice, until he has qualified in the State to which he has moved. If a citizen moves from one part of his State to another he is, in most States, required to reside there for a brief period before he can vote.

228. Suffrage Restrictions as to Sex — Woman Suffrage.— In most of the States women are either wholly or partially excluded from suffrage, but the following States and territory have extended full suffrage to them :

Wyoming	1869	Arizona	1912
Colorado	1893	Kansas	1912
Idaho	1896	Oregon	1912
Utah	1896	Alaska	1913
Washington	1910	Montana	1914
California	1911	Nevada	1914
	New York	1917	

In 1913 the Illinois legislature extended to women the right to vote for presidential electors and all State and local officers not provided for in the State constitution.   In 1917 North Dakota followed the example of Illinois, and four state legislatures extended to women the right to vote for presidential electors only. The same year the legislature of Arkansas extended to women the right to vote at direct primary elections, and as the democratic nomination in the South is usually equivalent to election the women of that State have practically full suffrage.

The woman suffragists are endeavoring to have the Constitution of the United States amended in a way which would compel the States to give the vote to women.   Just as the Fifteenth Amendment of the Constitution provides that no State may deny any citizen of the United States the right to vote " on account of race, color, or previous condition of servitude," the suffragists would have an Eighteenth Amendment to provide that no state may deny any citizen of the United States the right to vote on account of sex.   However, this cannot happen until three fourths of the States are in favor of equal suffrage.

In States where women have full suffrage rights they do not

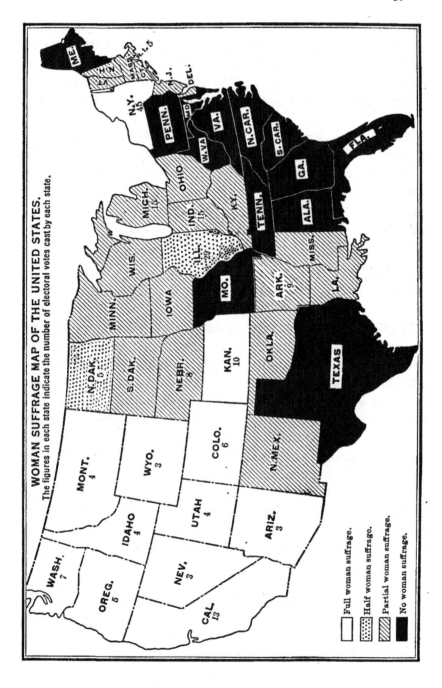

WOMAN SUFFRAGE MAP OF THE UNITED STATES.
The figures in each state indicate the number of electoral votes cast by each state.

Full woman suffrage.
Half woman suffrage.
Partial woman suffrage.
No woman suffrage.

ordinarily vote in such large numbers as men, though the greater number of them do vote. In the presidential election of 1912, when Wilson, Roosevelt, and Taft were candidates, 30 per cent of the total population of the woman suffrage States voted, whereas in the remaining States of the Union only 15 per cent of the total population voted.[1]

Copyright, G. V. Buck, Washington.

WOMAN SUFFRAGISTS PRESENTING THEIR PETITION TO CONGRESS.

229. Arguments in Favor of Woman Suffrage. — The following arguments in favor of woman suffrage are representative of those advanced by suffragists:[2]

---

[1] The fact that twice as great a proportion of the people of the woman suffrage States voted as those of the States without woman suffrage might seem to indicate that all the women of the equal suffrage States voted; however, when we consider that there is a larger proportion of men in the western suffrage States than in the non-suffrage States of the East, and that many colored men of the South do not vote, we must conclude that a greater proportion of men than women voted in the suffrage States even at this interesting election.

[2] A *suffragist* is one who favors equal suffrage and may be either a man or

(1) *Women need the ballot because of new industrial conditions.* The discovery of steam power and electricity and the invention of machinery have shifted the production of most articles of food and clothing from the home to the factory; hence women are forced to work in factories, stores, and offices. Her new experiences prepare her for the use of the ballot, and in 1916 the five leading parties favored granting it.

A Suffragette Speaking to Wall Street Men.

(2) *The minds of men and women differ only slightly by nature,* says Bergson, the French philosopher.

(3) *When women are given the ballot they take more interest in civic duties than in idle pastimes.*

(4) *More girls than boys are being educated.* In 1914, for instance, 106,805 girls and 74,104 boys graduated from public and private high schools in the United States.

(5) *Persons who train citizens should understand the political*

---

a woman ; a *suffragette* is a woman who actively advocates equal suffrage for her sex.

duties of citizens.   In 1913 there were 501,014 female and only 143,924 male teachers in public and private schools of all kinds in the United States.

(6) *Both by nature and by necessity women have better moral habits than men* and their votes would therefore improve moral legislation.

(7) *The most dignified way for women to influence legislation is by the secret ballot.*   Without equal suffrage a woman who works for legislative reforms must go to the legislative halls and impress her views upon the legislators by "lobbying."

230. **Arguments Opposed to Woman Suffrage.** — The following arguments opposed to woman suffrage are representative :

(1) *The growth of civilization is marked by an increasing specialization and division of . labor.* Woman suffrage would therefore be a step backward.

Copyright, Underwood & Underwood, N. Y.

FORTY THOUSAND WOMAN SUFFRA-GISTS PARADING ON FIFTH AVENUE, NEW YORK.

(2) *Women are represented already by their husbands, fathers, and brothers.*

(3) *If laws are unjust they can be corrected by woman's indirect influence.*

(4) *Men know more about business than women.*   A city or state is a big business concern ; and men, by the nature of their occupations, are better fitted to govern them.

(5) *Equal suffrage would double election expenses.*

(6) *It is not quantity but quality of votes that is needed.*

(7) *More bad women than good women would vote.*

(8) *Women have an influence because they are non-partizan.*
They, like men, cease to be non-partizan when they become
voters.

(9) *If women vote they must be prepared to hold elective offices.*
As soon as women want laws enforced which men do not want,
women themselves must take charge of the enforcement.

(10) *Women cannot fight, and therefore should not vote.*

(11) *Woman suffrage is a step toward feminism.* By feminism is meant the new radical ideas advocated by many women
which tend to give them a more independent position.

(12) *States without woman suffrage have enacted as much social
legislation as those with woman suffrage.* New England has as
much social legislation benefiting women and children as the
Western Suffrage States.

(13) *The majority of women do not want suffrage.* The question should be decided in each State by the votes of women
themselves.

231. Educational Restrictions on Suffrage. — Some sort of
educational test is now required in one third of the States.[1] In
some it is merely ability to read; in others, to read and write;
and in still others, to read, write, and understand a passage
from the Constitution. The first educational test was adopted
by Connecticut in 1855 during the Know Nothing agitation
against foreign immigrants. Massachusetts followed in 1857,
Wyoming in 1889, and Maine in 1891. Since that date most
of the Southern States have adopted educational tests. In the
Northern States the tests do not extend beyond the ability to
read and write. In some of the Southern States the understanding clauses were added.[2]

---

[1] The following States have the educational test in some form: Connecti-
cut (1855 and 1897), Massachusetts (1857), Wyoming (1889), Mississippi (1890),
Maine (1891), California (1894), South Carolina (1895), Washington (1896),
Delaware (1897), Louisiana (1898), Alabama (1901), Virginia (1902), North
Carolina (1902), New Hampshire (1903), Georgia (1908), and Oklahoma (1910).

[2] The Virginia educational test is as follows: Every person unless physically unable, "makes application to register in his own handwriting, without
aid, suggestions, or memorandum, in the presence of the registration officers,

" Grandfather Clauses " were inserted in the constitutions of most Southern States. These clauses provided that persons who voted before the Civil War and their male descendants may vote without taking the educational tests. These exceptions however were all abolished by 1915 when the last, that of Oklahoma, was declared to be in conflict with Amendment XV of the Constitution of the United States.

Ideal Educational Test. — Justice would seem to demand that every adult citizen of the United States — whether man or woman, white or colored — should have the right to vote, provided such citizen is sufficiently intelligent and has not forfeited the right by misconduct, such as crime. The most practical way of testing intelligence is by a civil service examination conducted under the direction of an impartial civil service board. Such an examination would not be unlike the State examinations given by the Board of Regency for New York State. This need be given only once, provided the applicant passes the first time, and as the voter registers anew he could simply present his certificate.

The questions of such an examination should concern government and should not be made difficult enough to exclude an unreasonable number. Nor should any questions be asked which are not taught in free public schools. Every intelligent and energetic person should be encouraged to vote, and not discouraged.

232. Tax Restrictions on Suffrage. — In a number of Southern States suffrage is restricted to those who have paid a small annual poll tax. This tax varies from one to two dollars.

For instance, in Virginia one cannot vote unless he has per-

stating thereon his name, age, date and place of birth, residence, and occupation at the time and for two years next preceding, and whether he has previously voted, and, if so, the State, county, and precinct in which he voted last; and . . . answers on oath any and all questions affecting his qualifications as an elector, submitted to him by the officers of registration, which questions, and his answers thereto, shall be reduced to writing, certified by the said officers, and preserved as a part of their official records." This registration is permanent so long as the person registered remains in the same precinct.

sonally paid his $1.50 poll tax six months previous to the regular election. Moreover, this tax must be paid for the past three years. That is, if one fails to pay this tax for three years he must pay $4.50 six months before the regular election. The voter is required to pay this tax six months before the election so that the candidates for office will not have been nominated. Thus the politicians are not so likely to give voters money with which to pay this tax. The payment of this tax is strictly enforced. If it is not paid at the end of three years real estate can be sold to pay it if the man owns any.

A poll tax is not very just because the poor man must pay as much as the millionaire. In the South its purpose was to discourage from voting the negroes who had passed the educational test. In practice it keeps a great many whites from voting, some worthy and many worthless ones.

BIBLIOGRAPHY

Literature issued by the National American Woman Suffrage Association, New York City.

Literature issued by the Man-Suffrage Association Opposed to Political Suffrage for Women, New York City.

See bibliography at the end of Chapter XXIX for further references.

QUESTIONS ON THE TEXT

1. What is meant by the word *suffrage?* By the word *citizenship?*
2. Is suffrage determined by the United States or by the States?
3. What restrictions are placed upon the regulation of suffrage by the Constitution of the United States?
4. Could any State permit women to vote for presidential electors but for no other officers?
5. What three restrictions does every State place upon suffrage? What three additional ones do some States impose? What abnormal persons are excluded from suffrage in nearly all States?
6. Has the requirement that an American voter must be 21 years of age any special significance?
7. Do any States permit aliens to vote? Under what condition?

8. How many years must one reside in the State in which you live before he may vote?

9. How many States have full woman suffrage? Half? Partial?

10. How are the suffragists endeavoring to have suffrage extended to all women throughout the United States?

11. Distinguish between the words *suffragist* and *suffragette*.

12. What are the arguments in favor of woman suffrage? Opposed to it?

13. What kind of educational tests do a number of States have?

14. What is meant by "grandfather" clauses?

15. What would be an ideal educational test for suffrage?

16. What tax restrictions do some States have on suffrage?

17. Explain the Virginia law.

Questions for Discussion

1. Should voting be viewed as a right, privilege, or duty.?

2. Under what conditions may a Chinese woman vote for United States senators and representatives in some States? (See U. S. Constitution, Amend. XIV, Sec. 1; Art. I, Sec. 2; Amend. XVII; Amend. XV.)

3. Under what conditions may a Chinese woman vote for the President? (Art. II, Sec. 1, Cl. 2.)

4. If the women in an equal suffrage State should disfranchise the men what effect would it have upon the State's representation in Congress? (Amend. XIV, Sec. 2.)

5. Can you advance any good argument against the following statement? "Every law-abiding adult citizen — man or woman, white or colored — should be permitted to vote if such person passes an examination which shows that he has a graded school education and average intelligence."

6. Suffragists argue that woman suffrage has spread to adjacent States, for there the people naturally know most about how it works. Do you accept this argument, or can you advance some theory why a solid mass of States have adopted it?

7. The full suffrage States have 908 State legislators; ten of these are women. Do you favor electing women to legislative bodies?

8. The anti-suffragists argue that the bad women cannot work in the open to prevent reform legislation which the women now advocate, but if women were enfranchised they would cast a secret ballot

against reforms, as this would require no energy or publicity. Do you think there is anything in this argument?

9. In the eighth assembly district of New York City only 42 out of 13,662 families own their own homes, and of these 42 homes all but 14 are mortgaged. Is this population likely conservative or radical in voting? Does this mean that all but the 14 families should be disfranchised? (See Sec. 4.)

10. It is the ideal of every good citizen to leave the world a little better than he found it. Intelligent voting is one way to attain this ideal. Are you preparing to be a good citizen? How?

CHAPTER XXVI

NOMINATIONS AND ELECTIONS

233. Registration. — In order to determine whether all persons who claim the right to vote are really entitled to vote, and to identify individuals in communities where residents are not personally known to one another, nearly all the States require each voter to "register" his name, address, age, length of residence, and other facts pertaining to his qualifications as a voter with a registration officer or board provided for each voting-place.

All States, except Arkansas, where the constitution provides that registration shall not be a prerequisite to voting, require registration in some form in order to prevent double voting and other election frauds. In rural districts where the voters are well acquainted with one another one registration is sufficient so long as the voter remains in the same voting district, but two thirds of the States require voters to register each year that an election is held.

For instance, in New York the voter must sign his name in the registration book and on election day he must again sign his name so that the election officers may compare the two signatures. Where there is annual registration the party "machines" see to it that their regular party men register, but independent voters and many travelling men often fail to register and hence lose their vote. However, for cities, this practice involves less evil than would result from permanent registration, which is necessarily very inaccurate.

234. Political Parties. — From the beginning of our governments men have held different opinions on matters of government; so they have formed themselves into political groups, known as political parties, for the purpose of electing officers who will carry on the governments in accordance with their views.

The national party organization performs a useful purpose by organizing the people who hold similar views to support candidates who promise to carry out these views if elected. But the county and State committees of the national parties also work for the election of members of their parties to the county and State offices, and this practice is harmful.

By means of clubs, parades, bands of music, and speakers who play upon the prejudices of the people, politicians induce weak-minded persons to work for a Democrat " right or wrong," or a Republican " right or wrong." It makes no difference whether a member of a county board of commissioners is a Democrat or a Republican, or whether a State legislator is a Democrat or a Republican. It does matter whether the county commissioner believes in good roads and good schools or whether the State legislator believes in a good State university or whether he is for or against the continuance of open saloons.

An intelligent man should not be fooled into supporting a candidate for a local or State office because he is a Democrat or a Republican.

235. — Nominating Methods. — Very soon after the establishment of the United States it became customary for political parties to nominate a candidate for their support at the election. In the United States there are at present five different methods of nominating candidates for elective offices.

1. Self-announcement.
2. Caucus or primary.
3. Delegate convention.
4. Direct primary election.
5. Petition.

Self-announcement, or self-nomination, is very rare, and indicates either little competition within the party or a dissatisfied candidate whom the party has refused to indorse as its regular candidate. Some Southern and Western States provide for printing the names of self-announced candidates upon the ballots.

The "caucus" [1] is the New England name for a local mass-meeting of party voters, and "primary" [2] is the name applied to the same in the Middle or Western States. The caucus, or primary, selects candidates for town, ward, or precinct offices, and members of the town, ward, or precinct party committee. It also selects delegates to county and other nominating conventions.

The caucus has generally proved unsatisfactory because it is easily manipulated by machine politicians, especially in cities, and it is there that half the American population live. The unregulated caucus has often been called on short notice to meet in an inadequate hall at an inconvenient time, and then "packed" with foreigners or "repeaters" hired by the "ring." As this uninviting caucus frequently ended in a "free for all" it is not strange that good citizens have considered it not only useless but even dangerous to attend.

The delegate convention has been in common use since 1840 for selecting county, State, and National candidates. The delegate convention for a county or city is a meeting of delegates from the various election districts of the county or wards of the city. These are chosen by mass-meetings, called caucuses or primaries, held in each district or ward. ✔

· The delegate convention for the State is a meeting of delegates from the counties and cities, commonly chosen at the county or city conventions. The National Convention has been described at some length in Chapter XVII. As the delegates have been selected directly or indirectly by caucuses, the evils of the caucus have also been the evils of the convention. [3] For

---

[1] The term "caucus" used in this sense must not be confused with the legislative caucus, which is a secret meeting of legislators of a particular party to decide upon united action against the opposing party on the floor of the legislative hall.

[2] The term "primary" as here used must not be confused with the term "direct primary," or "direct primary elections," which is a recent substitution for the delegate convention.

[3] By controlling the primary-caucuses the machine politicians had the following candidates selected as delegates for a Cook County convention which

this reason conventions are rapidly giving way to direct primary elections.

The direct primary election is conducted with some of the safeguards accompanying a regular election, such as registration, secret voting, and penalties against bribery. Each party prints upon its ballot the members of its party who desire to be party candidates at the regular election, and the person receiving the greatest number of the party votes is nominated.

Nomination by petition means that candidates are placed in nomination by petitions signed by a certain number of voters and filed with some specified officer. This entitles the candidate to have his name printed upon the official ballot. This method practically eliminates national politics from local elections and is well suited to cities, where national political parties should play no part.

236. The Direct Primary. — In thirty-odd States the direct primary method is used to nominate local, county, and State officers, and representatives to Congress; and in some States it is used for senators.[1] The direct primary systems generally have the following points in common:

---

was held in Chicago in 1896: keepers of houses of ill fame, 2; ex-prize-fighters, 11; had been on trial for murder, 17; had served sentences in the penitentiary, 46; had been in jail, 84; no occupation, 71; political employees, 148; saloon keepers, 265. The total number of delegates was 723.

[1] In the following thirty-eight States the direct primary has been adopted either by law or by party rules:

Alabama	Maine	Oklahoma
Arizona	Massachusetts	Oregon
Arkansas	Michigan	Pennsylvania
California	Minnesota	South Carolina
Colorado	Missouri	South Dakota
Florida	Montana	Tennessee
Georgia	Nebraska	Texas
Idaho	Nevada	Vermont
Illinois	New Hampshire	Virginia
Iowa	New Jersey	Washington
Kansas	New York	Wisconsin
Kentucky	North Dakota	Wyoming
Louisiana	Ohio	

1. Different parties hold primaries at the same time and place.

2. Australian secret ballot is used.

3. Ballots are printed at public expense.

4. Names are presented by petitions and are printed in alphabetical order.

5. Regular election officials preside and are paid from public funds.

6. Polls are open during specified hours.

7. Plurality vote nominates.

8. Corrupt practices acts for elections apply to primaries.

9. Members of party committees are selected at the primary.

10. Party membership is determined (*a*) by an intention to support generally at the next election the nominees of such a party; or (*b*) by the party the voter supported at the last election; or (*c*) by answering any questions the party pre-. scribes, as is done in the South in order to keep negroes from participating in Democratic primaries.

When party membership is determined by test *a*, *b*, or *c*, in number 10 above, the primary is called a "closed primary" because it is closed against any persons who will not announce their party preference. In most States primaries are closed, but they are objectionable because there the voters must make known their party preference, which thus defeats the principle of the secret ballot. It also works against independent voting.

Wisconsin has the "open primary," which is open to all voters without registering their party preference. The voter is given a separate primary ballot for each party. He votes one and deposits the others in a box for unmarked ballots. The open primary is less objectionable than the closed, but it has one objection — it allows the leaders of the majority party, especially in large cities, to direct a number of their dishonest followers to vote the ballot of the opposite party and on it to support candidates for nomination who will be friendly to the majority's interests, and thus rob the minority party of its real leader.

The following Republican primary ticket for New Jersey was used for a "closed primary." Each person who voted the Republican primary ticket the previous year (1913) was permitted to vote this ticket (1914). If he voted a Democratic ticket the year before (1913) he was obliged to vote the Democratic primary ticket in 1914. If a person who voted the Democratic ticket in 1913 turned Republican in 1914 he could not vote in the 1914 primary, but had to wait until 1915 to vote the Republican primary ticket.

The direct primary system has not proved a panacea for all the ills of the convention system, but it offers an *opportunity* to defeat a conspicuously unfit candidate or to nominate one conspicuously well fitted. It is "an opportunity, not a cure"; it "puts it up to the voters." No primary or election machinery takes the place of intelligence and public spirit, but the direct primary places the responsibility for good government upon the voter.

237. Elections. — *When Held.* — Most States hold their elections for the selection of State officers at the same time that presidential electors and United States senators and representatives are chosen — Tuesday after the first Monday in November of even-numbered years. However, Georgia, Indiana, Kentucky, Maryland, and Mississippi hold State elections in November of odd-numbered years; and Massachusetts,

New York, and New Jersey elect certain state officers annually.

A few States hold their elections earlier than November. City elections are commonly held earlier in the year. When State elections are held at a different time from the national elections the voters pay more attention to State issues, and are not so likely to vote a straight Democratic or Republican ticket as they are during the excitement of a national campaign.

How Held. — For each voting district or precinct into which the county or city is divided, the county clerk, city clerk, board of election commissioners, or some designated officer provides a polling place, equipped with booths, a ballot-box, poll books, tickets, and in some States a flag. On election day the polls are open during prescribed hours — commonly from 6 A.M. to 6 P.M., but sometimes longer.

Each polling place is in charge of judges of election, whose duty it is to pass upon the qualifications of the voters, and clerks to assist them. They open and close the polls, count the ballots, and certify the results to the proper officials (*e.g.*, county board of elections or county clerk). A " watcher " from each political party is permitted to be present at the voting place to challenge any person whom he does not believe to be qualified to vote, and to see that the votes are fairly counted.

238. Australian Method of Voting. — The Australians devised a secret method of voting, which found its way to the United States through England. In 1888 the Kentucky legislature adopted it for municipal elections in Louisville, and the following year Massachusetts adopted it for all elections.

The Australian method of voting is as follows: The voter enters a room in which no one is allowed except election officers, " watchers," and perhaps a policeman. He gives his name and if it is found on the registration book he is given a ballot, which he carries into a canvas booth about three feet square. After marking the ballot he folds it, comes from the booth, and gives it to a judge of election, who tears off the top of the ballot containing the number, and he or the voter deposits it in an election box made of wood, metal, or glass in the presence of the other. The ballots have been printed at public expense, and no ballot may be taken from the voting place. In some States a "sample ballot," printed on colored paper, is mailed to each voter before the election day, but this, of course, cannot be voted.

Between 1888 and 1910 all but two States, Georgia and South Carolina, adopted this method of voting, though the details vary from State to State.

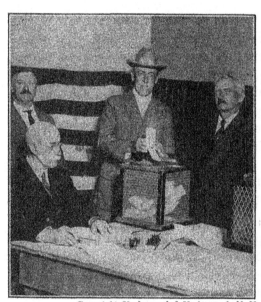

Copyright, Underwood & Underwood, N. Y.

PRESIDENT WILSON VOTING IN PRINCETON, NEW JERSEY.

Voting machines have proved undesirable because they encourage the voting of a "straight ticket," but the use of them continues in some States.

239. Origin of Ballots in the States.— For many years our voting was *viva voce* (by living voice). The voter came to the polling place and announced publicly the names of the candidates for whom he voted. This method encouraged vote-buying and intimidation. When a vote was bought "the goods were delivered" in the buyer's presence. A voter was often influenced to vote against his better judgment because he would get the ill will of an acquaintance if he voted against him, or of the community if he supported the unpopular candidate, or of his employer if he voted contrary to the employer's interest. The States gradually abandoned *viva*

voce voting, but it continued in the South until after the Civil War.

Unofficial written ballots were at first substituted for the *viva voce* method, each voter preparing his own ballot. Then the candidates began to print their own ballots; and finally the political party had ballots printed — each party having ballots of a different color. Thus the new method was just as public as the old. A vote buyer, friend, or employer, could know how you voted from the color of your ballot or could see you deposit the ballot which he had prepared for you.

240. Ballots Now in Use. — While all but two of the States have followed the general feature of the Australian plan and have made elections secret, only fourteen now use the true Australian ballot, but the number is increasing. The Australian ballot

places the names of the candidates of all parties for a given office in alphabetical order, giving each candidate's party affiliation after his name as shown in the ballot above.

In twenty-seven States the Party Column ballot is still in use. On such a ballot all the names of the candidates of one party for the various offices are arranged in a vertical column under the party's name, usually with a circle at the top in which the voter by placing a cross mark therein may vote for all of the candidates of that party — "a straight ticket." This arrangement works in the interest of a strongly organized corrupt party because an ignorant voter can vote the ticket with almost as much ease as an intelligent one. It is gradually giving way to the Australian ballot which requires a degree of intelligence and education to vote.

241. The Short Ballot Movement. — *The Usual American Ballot is too Long.* — The names of so many candidates appear on the ballot that it is impossible for the voter to know the qualifications of many of them. At the November election, 1914, the voters of Omaha, Nebraska, voted three tickets, one of which was eight feet in length and contained more than 200 names.

A Long Ballot Leads to Blind Voting. — Several years ago immediately after an election figures were collected from the most independent Assembly District in Brooklyn, New York, which showed that 87 per cent of the voters did not know the name of the State treasurer just elected. When the names of candidates for scores of offices appear on a ballot practically all voters cast a straight ticket.

Blind Voting Leads to Government by Politicians. — Because of the scores of officers to be voted for about nine tenths of the voters vote blindly, that is, vote a straight ticket, thus practically ratifying the "appointments" made by the other tenth — the politicians. Hence most of our officers are practically appointed by politicians.

The National Short Ballot Organization, of which Woodrow Wilson is president,[1] is educating the American people to the fact that most officers — especially unimportant ones — are actually chosen by politicians, whereas the people imagine that they are electing them. This organization advocates the election of important officers for long terms. It would allow these

---

[1] Mr. Richard S. Childs, secretary and treasurer of this organization, is its chief promoter. By writing to him (383 Fourth Avenue, New York) you can obtain literature regarding its work.

few to appoint the others. For instance, the State governor, State legislator, county commissioner, city councilor or commissioner, and mayor could be elected. The other State officers could then be chosen by the governor, county officers by the county board of commissioners, and city officers by a small council or commission, or by the mayor. This would center the authority and responsibility in a few officers, who could be more easily watched by the voters.

The present method of electing officers is a puzzle, the intricacies of which are understood only by politicians. Those who favor the short ballot would make the election process so simple that even the voter might understand it and be able to know something about those for whom he is to vote. The short ballot system would produce a democracy *in fact* instead of a democracy *in theory*. At present we are a *democracy in theory* — a *politicians' oligarchy in fact.*

"For Experts Only."

242. Short Ballots. — No State has yet reduced the number of elective officers to the extent advocated by the National Short Ballot Organization, but the organization has shown the folly of the present long ballots, and the States are beginning to reduce the number of elective officers. However, most cities of the commission type and of the commission-manager type, and a number of the council-mayor type, have adopted the short ballot.

It would be impossible to show a typical long ballot here, as the page would not contain it. The city ballots on the following pages illustrate three advanced types of short ballots.

BIRMINGHAM'S NON-PARTIZAN
SHORT BALLOT

OFFICIAL BALLOT

Regular Municipal Election

City of Birmingham, Alabama

September 21st, 1914

Make a Cross Mark (X) before or after
the name of the Candidate you wish
to vote for.

**For Commissioner for the term of
three years.**

JONES, HARRY

WEATHERLY, JAMES M.

    In 1914 Birmingham was governed by three commissioners,
one elected each year for a term of three years. Nominations
were made by petition, and no party indication is shown on
the ballot. For the 1914 election there were only two candidates nominated for the commissionership.[1]

---

[1] If no candidate receives a majority of all the votes cast, a supplemental
election is held a week later, at which election the two highest are voted upon.

CLEVELAND'S NON-PARTIZAN PREFERENTIAL
SHORT BALLOT

FOR MAYOR (One to be Elected)	First Choice	Second Choice	Other Choices
JOS. E. ROBB			
NEWTON D. BAKER			
HARRY L. DAVIS			
WARD 24 FOR COUNCIL (One to be Elected)	First Choice	Second Choice	Other Choices
HARRY B. HOENER			
CHARLES A. LEISHER			
FELIX J. O'NEIL			
GEO. A. REYNOLDS			
LOUIS G. SPROUL			
CARL F. WETZEL			
M. C YEAGLE			
H. A. CUMMINGS			
ROBERT FOSTER			

Cleveland has a new home rule charter. At her last city election there were but two officers for each voter to help elect — the mayor and one councilman from his ward. Candidates are nominated by petition, and each candidate's name appears first on a portion of the ballots. There is no party indication on the ballot. Voters may express more than one choice if they like. If no candidate receives a majority of first choices, the second preferences are added to the first, and so on until some candidate receives a majority.

ASHTABULA'S NON-PARTIZAN PREFERENTIAL PROPORTIONAL
REPRESENTATION SHORT BALLOT AS MARKED BY A VOTER

MUNICIPAL TICKET

DIRECTIONS TO VOTERS		For Members of Council
		FRED A. BRIGGS
		JOHN CARLSON
		M. R. COOK
		NICK CORRADO
	5	ROBT. W. EARLYWINE
		JAMES H. FLOWER
		C. O. GUDMUNDSON
	3	J. J. HOGAN
	1	ROBERT LAMPELA
		GEORGE H. LOOSE
	2	J. H. McCLURE
		E. R. McCUNE
		ARTHUR RINTO
	4	E. N. TILTON

DIRECTIONS TO VOTERS

Put the figure 1 opposite the name of your first choice for the Council. If you want to express also second, third, and other preferences, do so by putting the figure 2 opposite the name of your second choice, the figure 3 opposite the name of your third choice, and so on. You may express thus as many preferences as you please. This ballot will not be counted for your second choice unless it is found that it cannot help your first; it will not be counted for your third choice unless it is found that it cannot help either your first or your second; etc. The more choices you express, the surer you are to make your ballot count for one of the candidates you favor.

A ballot is spoiled if the figure 1 is put opposite more than one name. If you spoil this ballot, tear it across once, return it to the election officer in charge of the ballots, and get another from him.

Ashtabula, Ohio, has a home rule charter of the commission-manager type. The Ashtabula commission consists of seven members elected at large. Candidates are nominated by petition and no party name appears on the ballot. Each voter need vote for only one candidate, but may express additional preferences if he likes, as did the voter who marked the accompanying ballot. When the ballots are counted the candidate receiving the least number of first choices is eliminated and the ballots which express a first choice for him are redistributed according to the second choice expressed thereon.

This process of elimination is continued until there are but seven candidates left, and these are considered elected. Thus, if one seventh of all the voters favor one candidate he is certain of election. This system gives what is known as proportional representation, *i.e.* each group of people has a chance to be represented on the council in proportion to its voting strength.

243. The Recall. — When the people elect very few officers and trust everything to them it seems advisable to be able to remove those who do not give satisfaction. Therefore twelve States [1] and over two hundred cities, principally of the commission and commission-manager types, reserve the right to remove such officers.

Whenever a prescribed number of voters, the number varying from State to State, become sufficiently dissatisfied with an officer to petition for a new election the officer whom they wish to remove must again stand for election. If the officer receives more votes than any other person who has offered himself as a candidate he remains in office, but if he receives less than any other candidate he is removed from office; that is, he is recalled by the people.

244. Direct Legislation. — The idea of the short ballot movement is to reduce the number of elective officers so that the voters may know the qualifications of those whom they elect. If these few officers pass improper laws the *Referendum* (see Sec. 168) enables the voters to prevent the final enactment of such laws. If they refuse to enact laws desired by the people

---

[1] For complete list of Recall States see Section 244.

the voters themselves may enact them by means of the *Initiative* (see Secs. 156 and 169). Or if the officers prove incompetent or dishonest they may be removed by the *Recall* (see Sec. 243).

PROGRESS OF THE INITIATIVE, REFERENDUM AND RECALL

Percentages in this table refer to voters required on petitions

WHERE ADOPTED	WHEN	STATUTORY INITIATIVE	CONSTITUTIONAL INITIATIVE	REFERENDUM	RECALL
So. Dakota	1898	5 %; indirect [1]		5 %	
Utah	1900	([2])		([2])	
Oregon	1902	8 %; direct	8 %; direct	5 %	25 %
Nevada	1904, 1912	10 % 1912; indirect	10 % 1912; indirect	10 % 1904	25 % 1912
Montana	1906	8 %; direct		5 %	
Oklahoma	1907	8 %; direct	15 %; direct	5 %	
Maine	1908	12,000 voters		10,000 voters	
Missouri	1908	5 %; direct	5 %; direct	5 %	
Michigan	1908, 1913	8 % 1913; indirect	20% 1908 10% 1913; direct		25 % 1913
Arkansas	1910	8 %; direct	8%; direct	5 %	Carried but killed by Supreme Court
Colorado	1910	8 %; direct	8 %; direct	5 %	25 %
Arizona	1911	10 %; direct	15 %; direct	5 %	25 %
New Mexico	1911			10 %	
California	1911	5 %; indirect 8 %; direct	8 %; direct	5 %	12 % state 20 % local
Ohio	1912	3 %; indirect 6 %; direct	10 %; direct	6 %	
Nebraska	1912	10 %; direct	15 %; direct	10 %	
Washington	1912	10 %; direct and indirect		6 %	25 % state 35 % local
Idaho	1912		([2])		
No. Dakota	1914	10 %; direct	25 %; [4] indirect	10 %	
Kansas	1914				10, 15, 25 %
Louisiana	1914				25 %
Maryland	1915			10,000 voters [3]	

[1] "Indirect" means that opportunity must first be given for action by the legislature on initiated measures.

[2] Initiative and Referendum amendments were adopted by the voters of Utah in 1900 and of Idaho in 1912, but in both cases without a self-enacting clause. Each has remained a dead letter for lack of action by the legislature; hence they are omitted from the above table.

[3] Laws for any one county or Baltimore city may be referred to the voters thereof on a 10 % petition.

[4] Petition to be signed by 25 % of the voters in each of not less than one half of the counties of the State.

MUNICIPAL: The Initiative, Referendum, and Recall have been incorporated more or less completely in the charters of over 300 cities and towns in the United States and are in successful operation. Many such municipalities

This direct action on the part of the people demands enlightenment on the part of the voters, and for this purpose many of the States which have adopted the Initiative and Referendum send a pamphlet to each voter before an election giving in a condensed form the strongest arguments on each side of every question referred to them. Thus with this publicity the people are prepared to vote upon the various issues with a degree of enlightenment.

If too many measures are submitted to the people, the voters are just as burdened as when they have too many officers to elect. President Wilson feels that these safeguards should be considered merely as "a gun behind the door" to be used only in cases of emergency.

BIBLIOGRAPHY

CHILDS, R. S. Short Ballot Principles. 1911.

JONES, CHESTER LLOYD. Readings on Parties and Elections in the United States. 1912.

KALES, ALBERT M. Unpopular Government in the United States. 1914.

RAY, P. ORMAN. An Introduction to Political Parties and Practical Politics. 1913.

Bulletins and Publications of the National Short Ballot Organization, 383 Fourth Avenue, New York.

Election Laws of your State.

Sample Ballots.

QUESTIONS ON THE TEXT

1. What is meant by registration? How often need one register in the State in which you live? Explain just how one registers.

2. What useful service is performed by political parties?

3. How do political parties induce weak-minded persons to vote a straight ticket?

4. Name five different methods of nominating candidates.

---

are not in the above mentioned Initiative and Referendum States, the Initiative, Referendum, and Recall having been granted by the legislatures by means of general laws or special charters.

By courtesy of *Equity*.

5. Describe a delegate convention.

6. Describe a direct primary election.

7. What is meant by nomination by petition?

8. What is meant by the "closed" primary? By the "open" primary? What advantages and disadvantages has each?

9. Is the direct primary "an opportunity" or a "cure" of election evils? Explain.

10. When are most elections held for choosing State officers? Federal officers? City officers?

11. Explain just how an election is held — officers, place, equipment, ballots, booths, poll books, time of day, "watcher."

12. Explain the Australian method of voting and tell just how it was introduced into the United States.

13. Why are voting machines undesirable?

14. Explain why secret voting has taken the place of the *viva voce* method.

15. Describe an Australian ballot.

16. Should the names of candidates be arranged on the ballot in party columns or alphabetically?

17. What is meant by the short ballot movement? Give the arguments in favor of short ballots.

18. Explain how city officers are elected in Birmingham? In Cleveland? In Ashtabula?

19. What is meant by the *Recall*?

20. What is meant by *direct legislation*? Does Woodrow Wilson favor it?

QUESTIONS FOR DISCUSSION

1. What provision is made in your State constitution in regard to State elections?

2. Upon what date is your State election held? City election? National election? County election? Why should National, State, and local elections be held on different dates?

3. Obtain a copy of the last ballot voted at your home and compare it with those printed in this chapter. Which do you consider the better?

4. Have your father, or your brother, who votes make a list of the National, State, county, township, city or village, and school officers elected by the people in your State If they cannot do this do you not think that it is a strong indication that more officers are being

elected than the voters are capable of electing wisely? Which of them do you think should be appointed?

5. Explain the following quotation, which favors a "short ballot": "We cannot make the voters all go into politics, but by a drastic reduction in the number of elective officers we can make politics come to the voters."

6. Nicholas Longworth when congratulated on his election to Congress is reported to have said: "Election! I wasn't elected; I was appointed." What is the significance of this remark?

7. The New Jersey election law enacted under the influence of Woodrow Wilson provides that a State convention of each party shall be held annually to adopt a party platform. The convention is composed of forty candidates nominated at the party primary for the offices of assemblymen or State senators, hold-over senators, members of the State committee, and the governor, or the candidate for governor.the autumn when a new governor is to be elected. Would you favor this arrangement for your State? Why?

8. Mr. C. L. Gruber explains the word "government" in the following words: "The word 'government' is derived from the French *gouverner*, from the Latin *guberno*, which was borrowed by the Romans from the Greek *kybernao*, a word meaning 'to steer a ship.' We therefore sometimes speak of the government as the 'ship of state.' The idea of general welfare and great vigilance is therefore embodied in the etymology of the word, since the interests of him who steers the ship are but the interests of every one on board. The safety of the vessel depends upon the skill and watchfulness of the man at the helm." Prepare an argument on the subject, "Eternal vigilance is the price of liberty."

CHAPTER XXVII

STATE FINANCE

245. The Taxing Power of a State. — Taxes are charges imposed by a·legislative body upon persons or property to raise money for public purposes. With the following exceptions, a State legislature may impose taxes of any kind and any amount, or may give permission to the legislative bodies of counties, townships, towns, or cities to do the same.

(1) *Taxes must be for a public purpose.* Exactly what is meant by a "public purpose" cannot be defined, but must be decided by the courts whenever taxpayers feel that they are being taxed for a private purpose and carry their complaints into court.

Some years ago Topeka, with permission of the legislature of Kansas, agreed to pay a sum of money to a manufacturing concern if it would locate its iron works in that city. The factory was so located, but when taxes were assessed for the payment of this sum of money certain taxpayers brought their complaint to court, and, after several appeals, the Supreme Court of the United States decided that taxes could not be collected for this private purpose. .

On the other hand railroads may receive aid from a State, county, or city, unless the State constitution prohibits it, because the public generally have such a direct interest in the transportation of commodities and the circulation of business that the whole community is benefited.

(2) *Taxes must operate uniformly upon those subject to them.* The assessment of all persons and property within a class or district selected for taxation must be according to a uniform rule. For instance, when a citizen of New York State

384

inherits property worth more than $5000 he must pay a State tax varying from 1 per cent to 8 per cent, depending upon the amount inherited and the degree of relationship. This tax operates uniformly because all who fall within the same class are taxed alike.

(3) *The classification of property for taxation must be reasonable.* For instance, it was declared reasonable for Louisiana to impose a license tax upon manufacturers of sugar, at the same time exempting from its operation those who refined the products of their own plantations. But you could not thus tax Jews, Germans, Negroes, Republicans, or Catholics who manufacture sugar and exempt all others, because the classification would be unreasonable.

(4) *Either the person or the property taxed must be within the jurisdiction of the government levying the tax.* For instance, a citizen of Wisconsin who owns property in Iowa must pay a tax on his property where it is located in Iowa, but in Wisconsin, where he lives, he must pay a tax on the income from his Iowa property if the income is great enough to be assessed according to the Wisconsin income tax law.[1]

(5) *In the assessment and collection of a tax certain guarantees against injustice to individuals must be provided.* For instance, if property worth $10,000 is assessed for $15,000, the owner has the right to go before some tax revision board or court and have the mistake corrected.

(6) *A State may not tax the agencies by means of which the federal government is enabled to exercise its functions.* The

---

[1] The city of Charleston, South Carolina, borrowed money by issuing bonds which paid 6 % interest. Afterward it attempted to tax these bonds whether they were held by citizens of Charleston or persons living outside the State, the city treasurer being directed to deduct 5 % of the interest before sending it to the owners of the bonds. Those living outside the State went to court, and the Supreme Court of the United States decided that the city could not thus tax persons living outside the State. The city government did not have jurisdiction either of the persons or the bonds (property) ; hence to keep back a part of the interest was breaking the contract with the persons who lent money from outside the State.   (U. S. Constitution, Art. I, Sec. 10.)

power to tax is the power to destroy, and if States could tax the agencies of the federal government they might destroy these agencies. To illustrate, a State may not tax federal government bonds or the incomes therefrom, salaries of federal officers or the public money in its treasuries, or discriminate in any way against patented articles.

(7) *A State may not, without the consent of Congress, tax imports or exports to or from the United States.*[1] About two thirds of the imports of the United States come through the port of New York. If New York State could tax these imports, most of which are intended for other States, she would really be levying a tax upon other States. The same would be true if she could tax Western wheat which is shipped abroad from the port of New York.

(8) *A State may not tax interstate commerce as such.* If a State could tax interstate commerce it might interfere with the right of the United States to regulate it. For instance, logs owned by one Coe were floating down a river from Maine to New Hampshire. When the river froze they were within the town of Errol, which town attempted to tax them. The Supreme Court of the United States prohibited it, as it would have been a tax upon interstate commerce.

A State may not place a license tax on drummers who sell commodities to be sent from another State, but may tax peddlers who carry the commodities with them or get their supplies from commodities already in the State, provided, of course, that they are not discriminated against because of the fact that they sell goods brought from without the State.

(9) *A State may not, without the consent of Congress, lay any duty on tonnage.* Tonnage means a vessel's internal cubic capacity in tons of one hundred cubic feet each. A State may tax a vessel as ordinary property, but may not tax it on the basis of tonnage.

---

[1] A State may impose small fees sufficient to cover the cost of enforcing its inspection laws.

(10) *State constitutions place a few restrictions upon their legislative bodies.* For instance, the Oklahoma constitution limits
the tax rate for the State, counties, townships, cities, towns, or
school districts to a prescribed number of mills on the dollar.
The constitutions also exempt from taxation certain classes of
property, such as churches, schools, and burial grounds.

246. Different Kinds of State and Local Taxes. — The revenues
for the forty-eight States in 1913 [1] were derived from the
following sources:

State Taxes:

General Property Taxes	$139,750,303
Special Property Taxes	67,675,933
Business Taxes	53,642,322
Interest and Rents	21,300,430
Liquor Licenses	20,992,857
Other Business Licenses	8,589,208
Special Assessments and Charges for Outlays	6,454,807
Non-business License Taxes	6,450,932
Subventions and Grants	3,190,750
Poll Taxes	2,965,069
Earnings of Public Service Enterprises	1,715,422
Fines, Forfeits, and Escheats	1,428,011
Donations and Gifts	434,526
Miscellaneous	32,994,761
Total	$367,585,331

County Taxes:

General Property Taxes	$282,077,069
Subventions and Grants	23,682,813
Special Assessments and Charges for Outlays	9,323,078
Liquor Licenses	6,577,556
Poll Taxes	5,817,855
Interest and Rents	5,531,485
Fines, Forfeits, and Escheats	3,531,537
Non-business License Taxes	1,703,316

[1] For further details as to the revenues of the respective States see "National and State Revenues and Expenditures 1913 and 1903," Bureau of the Census, 1914.

Business Licenses (other than liquor) . . .	1,474,255
Special Property Taxes	805,419
Earnings of Public Service Enterprises . . .	413,329
Donations and Gifts	283,233
Highway Privileges	164,768
Business Taxes	92,866
Miscellaneous	28,564,467
Total	$370,043,046

Incorporated Villages, Towns and Cities of 2500 and over:

General Property Taxes	$661,144,096
Earnings of Public Service Enterprises . . .	120,182,809
Special Assessments and Charges for Outlays	97,440,808
Liquor Licenses	51,946,576
Subventions and Grants	51,498,823
Interests and Rents	35,561,915
Special Property Taxes	15,478,766
Highway Privileges	13,521,183
Business Licenses (other than liquor) . . .	12,265,342
Fines, Forfeits, and Escheats	6,717,873
Donations and Gifts	4,971,296
Non-business License Taxes	4,791,654
Poll Taxes	3,629,553
Business Taxes	3,289,709
Miscellaneous	25,832,348
Total	$1,108,272,751

General Property Taxes, which constitute more than half of all State and local revenue, consist of taxes on realty and personalty. Realty is land and permanent improvements thereon, and personalty is movables, such as cattle, money, or shares of stock. In 1913 every State except Connecticut and Delaware collected property taxes, and the local governments of all forty-eight States collected such taxes also, but the rate of levy varied from 4 cents to $2.70 on the hundred dollars worth of property.

Special Property Taxes consist of inheritance taxes, taxes on capital stock of various corporations, investments, mortgages, etc.

Business Taxes consist of taxes on insurance companies;[1] taxes on

---

[1] In 1913 taxes on insurance companies amounted to $17,554,971. Arizona and Arkansas are the only States which do not report an insurance tax, but

the gross earnings of express, telegraph and telephone, sewing machine, mining, oil, railway, car, and other companies, and building and loan associations; taxes on savings banks; and income taxes. Five States collected income taxes,[1] but the greatest amount collected was $160,978 by Wisconsin.

Interest and Rents consist of interest on money deposited in banks, and rents from such sources as public school lands and public works belonging to a State or city but operated by a renter.

Liquor Licenses are usually definite sums levied by a State and by a city, but not so generally by counties — e.g., a State saloon license may be $500 and a city license $1000. This is in addition to the United States license of $25 and a tax of $1.10 a gallon on whiskey and $1.50 a barrel on beer.

Other Business Licenses are such charges as are levied for conducting a store or a billiard table.

Special Assessments and Charges for Outlays constitute collections made for drainage, maintenance of levees, fire protection in forests; or collections made by Massachusetts from the cities and towns by reason of the metropolitan park, sewer, and water loans, and loans for State highways, armories, etc.

Non-business License Taxes include hunting, fishing, and automobile licenses. For instance, the State of New York derived a million and a half dollars from automobile licenses in 1915.

Subventions and Grants represent amounts received from the National government in aid of agriculture, education, experiment stations, and highway construction and maintenance.

Poll Taxes mean capitation taxes, a levy of say $1 annually against male adults. Only about one fourth of the States or localities have this tax.

Earnings of Public Service Enterprises are from such items as the following: by California from docks and wharves of San Francisco, by Connecticut from a toll bridge, by Maryland from hay scales and wharves, by Massachusetts from a water-supply system, by New York and Ohio from the State canals, by North Dakota from the State hail insurance business, by Oregon from a portage railway, and by South Carolina

---

the tax produced as much as $1,000,000 in New York, Pennsylvania, Ohio, and Massachusetts only.

[1] North Carolina, Oklahoma, South Carolina, Virginia, and Wisconsin collected income taxes. These State taxes were, of course, in addition to the United States income tax.

from the State insurance business and the county dispensaries; by cities from various enterprises such as water, light, and gas plants.

Fines, Forfeits, and Escheats refer to fines for crimes, property forfeited for the nonfulfilment of duties attached therewith, and property reverting to the State when one dies without heirs or a will.

Donations and Gifts refer to gifts for endowment funds for schools, etc., money for libraries, and the like.

247. The General Property Tax. — *Assessment.* — Each local governmental division — city, town, or township [1] — has one or more tax assessors to determine the value of property which is subject to taxation. In case of personalty this is done each year, but in some States realty is assessed at longer intervals — *e.g.*, every five years in Virginia — but, of course, taxed each year. Assessors are expected to visit property and have the owner fill in a tax form. In practice they commonly assess one's property as it was assessed the previous year, and thus avoid the trouble and duty of visiting the property. The valuation put upon property by these assessors is usually accepted as the basis for county and State taxation.

Suppose your home in a certain township has been assessed $10,000, and suppose the township tax rate is 8 mills on the dollar, the county rate 7 mills, and the State rate 5 mills, or a total of 20 mills. Then your taxes will be 10,000 times 20 mills (2 cents), which is $200. If this home is in a city you will ordinarily pay city, county, and State taxes, but no township taxes. If the city rate is 10 mills, you would pay .022 times $10,000, or $220.

Equalization. — If your property is assessed higher than a neighbor's property of equal value usually there is a means of having the injustice corrected. You may complain to an appeal tax court, to the county board of commissioners, or to a local board of equalization, as the law provides. Many States have county boards of equalization to come into a township

---

[1] In a few States the county is the smallest local division for purposes of assessment.

and raise or lower the assessment on all real estate in that township if it has been improperly assessed.

In some States there is also a State board of equalization to see that the property is assessed alike in the different counties. States without such boards often have property in one part of the State — *e.g.*, in a large city — assessed at its full value, whereas in another part of the State — *e.g.*, rural counties — it is assessed at only half of its value. This means that the city people are paying twice as much State tax as justice demands.

Collection. — State, county, and local taxes are usually collected by the same officials. After the taxes are assessed tax bills are prepared. In some States they are mailed to the taxpayers; but in others the taxpayer must come to the county treasurer or township officer who collects taxes, to learn the amount of his taxes.

Delinquency. — If taxes are not paid by a prescribed date a certain per cent is added. The property upon which the tax is levied is then said to be delinquent, and if the tax remains unpaid for a certain length of time the property is sold, perhaps at auction. If it brings more than enough to pay the taxes, added per cent, and costs, the former owner receives what is left.

Exemption. — State constitutions commonly enumerate certain kinds of property which the legislative body may not tax. Schools, free libraries, churches, and government property are good examples of property usually exempt from taxation.

248. Inheritance Taxes. — In 1903 the States derived $6,000,-000 from inheritance taxes; in 1913 they derived $17,000,000. In 1913 New York State alone derived over $4,000,000 from this tax, and in some years it amounts to much more. (See Sec. 45.)

This New York law exempts parents, husband, wife, child, descendants, brother, sister, son-in-law, daughter-in-law, or adopted child to $5000. On the excess of $5000 the rate is 1 per cent up to $50,000; 2 per cent from $50,000 to $250,000; 3 per cent from $250,000 to $1,000,000; 4 per cent for all over

$1,000,000. Persons other than those enumerated are exempt from the tax on the first $1000 only; but instead of paying 1 per cent, 2 per cent, 3 per cent, or 4 per cent on the amounts in excess, they must pay 5 per cent, 6 per cent, 7 per cent, or 8 per cent. This method of assessing higher rates on large estates than on small is known as progressive taxation.

Every State except Arizona and Arkansas reported the collection of inheritance taxes in 1913, but in many States the amount was small. Some States, Virginia for instance, exempt all lineal ancestors or lineal descendants, husband or wife, brother or sister, and levy 5 per cent on others. Money is seldom inherited by others, and the Virginia tax for 1913 was only $253,000.

249. How Revenue is Expended. — After revenue is collected, and the local division, the county, and the States have each received their proper share, the respective treasurers are not permitted to pay it out until a proper warrant is presented. After the State legislature appropriates its revenue, the State comptroller or auditor issues warrants to persons entitled to the money, as he is directed to do by the legislative acts appropriating the money.

After the county board appropriates the county money the county treasurer pays it out when a warrant signed by the county auditor, or some other designated person, is presented. In cities and towns the council appropriates the revenue, and some designated officer or officers sign the warrants to be cashed by the treasurer.

BIBLIOGRAPHY

Annual Report of the State Treasurer.
Annual Report of the State Auditor.

QUESTIONS ON THE TEXT

1. What are taxes?
2. What ten restrictions are there upon a State's power to impose taxes? Explain each restriction carefully.

3. Name the principal sources from which States derive their revenue.

4. What is the general property tax? Special property tax? Business tax? Poll tax?

5. How are general property taxes assessed?

6. What do you mean by a board of equalization?

7. How are taxes collected?

8. What is meant by delinquent taxes?

9. What classes of property are usually exempt from taxation?

10. What is an inheritance tax?

11. What is meant by progressive inheritance taxes?

12. Explain the use of warrants in the expenditure of revenue.

QUESTIONS FOR DISCUSSION

1. What provisions are made in your State constitution regarding taxation?

2. How many mills on the dollar is property taxed for State purposes in your State? For county purposes? For village or city purposes if you live in such place?

3. Does your State have a capitation tax? If so, how much is it and who must pay it?

4. Does your State have an inheritance tax? If so, what would be the net proceeds of an inheritance of $100,000?

5. Figure the approximate amount of taxes paid by some person of average means.

6. How much does your State contribute towards the support of the National government, assuming that it contributes in proportion to its population? Considering the objects taxed by the National government do you believe that your State pays as much per capita as other States? Is the per capita amount paid to the National government more or less than the per capita amount paid to the State government?

7. If your property is assessed higher than your neighbor's what redress do you have?

CHAPTER XXVIII

PUBLIC EDUCATION

250. Growth of Elementary Education. — Public free schools were established in several of the New England States as early as the seventeenth century, shortly after their settle-

CORRIDOR, WEBSTER SCHOOL, ST. LOUIS.
Lessons in art and nature study.

ment; but even there interest in education declined during the next century.

It is doubtful whether previous to the Revolutionary War as many as one half of all the white persons throughout the thirteen colonies could read and write. Most children depended upon the little instruction that their parents could give them at home, and the boys were given the preference because it was not considered that girls needed much schooling to prepare them for household duties. It was not until the nineteenth century that a systematic effort was made to educate the masses of people throughout the country.

In 1838 Horace Mann, first secretary of the Massachusetts State Board of Education, aroused great interest in public

PENNY LUNCH IN A CHICAGO SCHOOL.

school education throughout the North. In the South there were no successful efforts to establish systems of public free schools until after the Civil War. As late as 1880 seventeen per cent of the individuals over ten years of age in the United States were illiterate — that is, could not write. By 1910 the number had been reduced to seven per cent. There should be no illiterate adults except those who are mentally unable to learn — less then one per cent.

Compulsory Education. — In 1914 over 19,000,000 pupils were enrolled in elementary schools[1] — principally public free

---

[1] Elementary schools ordinarily include the first eight grades which a child is supposed to pass through between the ages of six and fourteen. The first

schools — but unfortunately less than half of those that enter the first grade continue through the eighth grade. However, all of the States north and west of Maryland, Virginia, Tennessee, Arkansas, and Texas have compulsory education throughout the State; and Maryland, Virginia, North Carolina, Tennessee, Arkansas, and Louisiana have compulsory education in portions of their territory.

In some States compulsory education laws require children to attend school until they are twelve years of age, and in others they must remain in school until they are fourteen.

GARY-PLAN CLASS IN MENTAL ARITHMETIC.

Parents who do not send their children to school in compliance with the law may be fined from $5.00 to $50.00 for each offence according to the penalty imposed by the respective States.

251. Year-Round Schools. — During the summer months young pupils forget much that they have learned during the previous school year; therefore some schools are running the year round, pupils being permitted to take three or four twelve-week terms. Thus a pupil can gain one school year every third year.

Superintendent William A. Wirt, of Gary, Indiana, feeling that the chore time of the farm boy has become the "street and alley time" of the city boy, keeps the pupils at school eight hours a day instead of six. Half of this time is spent in their classrooms, the other half on the playgrounds, in the

four grades are commonly known as primary grades, the fifth and sixth as intermediate grades, and the seventh and eighth as grammar grades.

STUDYING MUSIC APPRECIATION WITH THE VICTOR.
SEATTLE, WASHINGTON.

HIGH SCHOOL AND STADIUM, TACOMA, WASHINGTON.

school gardens, in the manual training department, in the laboratory, in the assembly hall, or taking observation excursions. Thus two sets of classes can recite in the same rooms, the pupils having every other hour in the classroom. Hence the children are kept profitably occupied without growing weary of continuous hours in the classrooms.

252. Growth of Secondary Education. — Until about 1850 only the few persons who could afford an education at a private

REDONDO, CALIFORNIA, UNION HIGH SCHOOL.
This high school is supported by a community of five thousand. There are two hundred day and two hundred and fifty evening students.

academy could hope for schooling extending much beyond the three R's. Public high schools began to spring up about 1850 in most of the large Northern cities, and gradually spread to the Southern cities after the Civil War, but it is only very recently that they have been established in the small towns and districts of the South.

In 1914 there were 1,373,661 students in secondary schools, of whom all but about 150,000 were in public high schools. Of these 56 per cent were girls and 44 per cent boys. The fact that only about 39 per cent of those who enter the high schools graduate is regrettable.

CIVIC AUDITORIUM IN REDONDO UNION HIGH SCHOOL.
This auditorium is used as a community social centre.   Seating capacity 1000.

SINGING WITH THE VICTOR.   SOUTH HIGH SCHOOL, MINNEAPOLIS.

253. Growth of Higher Education. — Nine colleges which continue to exist[1] were established under church influence before the Revolutionary War and were assisted by the colonial treasuries. Since the Revolutionary War schools of higher education have increased to the number of 567 so-called colleges, universities, and technical schools, with more than 200,000 students — 64 per cent men and 36 per cent women.

States and cities support and control 93 of these 567 schools, and 41 of the 93 are State universities. All of the State

HOME ECONOMICS EXHIBIT CAR, CORNELL UNIVERSITY.

universities are coeducational except those of Virginia, Georgia, and Florida; and in all tuition is practically free to residents of the State. From time to time the United States has given to State universities a total of more than 3,000,000 acres of land.

Agricultural Colleges. — Since 1862 the Federal government has granted to the States more than 11,000,000 acres of land for the establishment of colleges for the study of agriculture,

---

[1] Harvard (1636), William and Mary (1693), Yale (1701), Princeton (1746), Kings, now Columbia (1754), University of Pennsylvania (1759, reorganized 1779), Brown (1764), Rutgers (1766), and Dartmouth (1769).

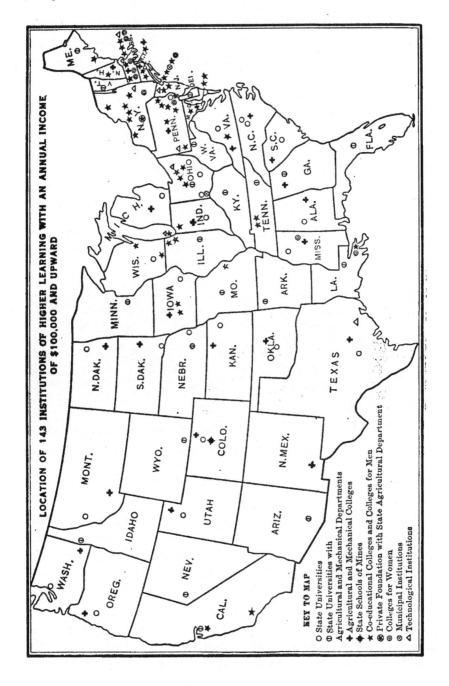

LOCATION OF 143 INSTITUTIONS OF HIGHER LEARNING WITH AN ANNUAL INCOME OF $100,000 AND UPWARD

KEY TO MAP

O State Universities
⊖ State Universities with Agricultural and Mechanical Departments
✚ Agricultural and Mechanical Colleges
★ State Schools of Mines
✦ Co-educational Colleges and Colleges for Men
⊗ Private Foundation with State Agricultural Department
◉ Colleges for Women
⊘ Municipal Institutions
◁ Technological Institutions

the sciences, and military tactics; and now it annually appropriates $75,000 to aid each State in the support of such school, $30,000 for an agricultural experiment station, and $10,000 for coöperative agricultural extension work, plus a much larger sum on condition that the State give an equal amount.

254. Administration of Public Schools. — Each State has its own system of public schools; and hence the administration is not exactly the same in any two. Certain central control is reserved by the State governments, but the regulation of school

Tent for Home Economics Travelling Exhibit, University of Texas.

affairs is left chiefly to the local governments — districts, townships, counties, and cities.

Under the *district system*, which originated in New England, each school is controlled by the patrons residing in the district from which the school is attended. This system is inefficient and is being replaced by a system with a much larger unit, such as the township. The *township system* places all the schools within its limits under one authority, usually a small board chosen by the voters. This system encourages the establishment of union high schools with free transportation for pupils who live at a considerable distance from the school.

The *county system*, with county officials in control, prevails in the South, but there is always some smaller school division subject to county control. Large cities and many smaller ones have a *city school system* independent of the township or county. The city board of education is usually chosen by the voters.

State Supervision. — Each State has a superintendent of education, and about three-fourths of them have State boards of

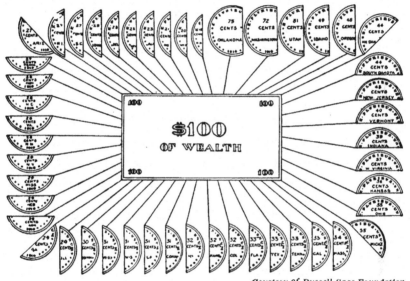

Courtesy of Russell Sage Foundation

For Every $100 of Wealth Each State Contributed the Above Amount in 1910.

education. In thirty-five States the superintendents are elected, but the boards are selected by various methods. The superintendent, or the board working through a superintendent, supervises the State system in accordance with the general school laws of the State.

255. School Revenue. — The annual cost of education in the United States in all kinds and grades of schools is about three-quarters of a billion dollars. In 1912 the revenue of the State common school systems was $469,110,642, of which $346,897,587 was derived from local taxes or appropriations (county, township, district, or city), $75,813,595 from State taxes or appropriations, $15,239,234 from permanent school funds and rents of school lands given to the States by Congress from time to time (132,000,000 acres in all), and $31,160,229 from other sources.

It might seem that $750,000,000 is a liberal amount to spend for educational purposes in one year, but those who think themselves burdened by school taxes should consider that more than three times as much is spent annually on alcoholic drinks. The relative amounts expended for alcohol and for education would seem to indicate that America's thirst for alcohol is three times as strong as her thirst for knowledge. Fortunately the use of alcohol as a beverage is on the decrease and the support of education is on the increase.

256. Apportionment of School Funds. — After school taxes have been collected by the State or county the money must be distributed among the townships or other school districts to supplement their local taxes in the support of their schools. There are various bases for the distribution of these funds,[1] but the best is that used by New Jersey in apportioning the county school funds. The sum of $200 is apportioned to a school for each teacher employed and the remainder of the fund is apportioned on the basis of aggregate days of attendance. This method of apportionment induces the local school board to have a sufficient number of teachers, to encourage a large attendance, and to have a long term.

257. Importance of Industrial Education. — To-day most products can be manufactured by means of complex machines; but it is necessary to have skilled labor to make, manipulate, and care for these machines. Thus it is necessary that the States educate their industrial classes for the duties which they are obliged to perform to meet the competition of the day.

[1] These various bases are: (1) Taxes-Where-Paid-Basis, (2) Total Population Basis, (3) School Population Basis, (4) Average Daily Attendance Basis, (5) Aggregate Days Attendance Basis, (6) Teachers Employed Basis, and (7) Combined Basis of Apportionment.

If Germans are industrially trained, and they are, and Americans remain untrained, the Americans must do the menial labor while the Germans do the skilled labor, for which the pay is always greater. Instead of merely attempting to force up wages of the untrained, which is impossible beyond a certain point, the States or cities should see to it that the real earning capacity of their citizens is increased by industrial education.

258. Industrial Training in Cities. — Less than half of our boys complete the eighth grade, and in a number of industrial cities, such as Bridgeport, Richmond, and Birmingham, less than one-fourth go beyond the sixth grade. Thus the systematic training of most boys ceases at the age of twelve or fourteen either because they do not care for or cannot afford such schooling as is offered; hence the great need of· to-day is to make

Courtesy of Pratt Institute.

TRADE DRESSMAKING TAUGHT IN PRATT INSTITUTE, BROOKLYN, NEW YORK.

possible industrial training for these boys. Many cities have night schools for boys who work during the day, but industrial subjects are not usually offered.

In Massachusetts any local school board may establish an industrial school with thorough technical courses, and may secure State aid covering one-half the cost. At Worcester apprentice boys in the machine trade spend four hours weekly in the school taking courses in English, shop computations, drawing, and shop practice. The classes are held during the working day.

At Fitchburg, Massachusetts, a number of the manufacturers of the city have agreed to coöperate with the high school by allowing the students of the industrial department to alternate weekly between the factories and the school. An employer takes two boys for each job and thus has one to work all the while. Each Saturday morning the boy who has been in school that week goes to the factory to get hold of the job on which his mate is working, and is thus ready to continue the work on Monday morning when the mate goes to school.

By this arrangement a boy can pay his expenses while getting an education. The practical experience in the shop shows him just what he needs to study in school and the schooling increases his efficiency and wages.

The University of Cincinnati School of Engineering has a somewhat similar arrangement with the shops of that city and vicinity. The students alternate between the school and the shops, spending two weeks in the school and two in the shops, but under the supervision of their teachers and for regular wages. The class work includes a discussion of the principles which the students have put into practice in actual shops.

259. Industrial Training in the Country. — For the same reason that cities need trade continuation schools — to increase the efficiency and earning power of city artisans — the country districts need agricultural schools and farm demonstration extension courses. Dr. Knapp, who did so much for the encouragement of agriculture, estimates that there is a possible 800 per cent increase in the productive power of the farm laborer in the average Southern State, distributed as follows:

300 per cent to the use of better mules and farm machinery;

200 per cent to the production of more and better stock;

150 per cent to a rotation of crops and better tillage;

50 per cent to better drainage;

50 per cent to seed of higher vitality, thoroughbred, and carefully selected;

50 per cent to the abundant use of legumes and the use of more economic plants for feeding stock.

In some agricultural sections the average annual earnings of individuals engaged in agriculture is only $150, whereas it is

$1000 in Iowa. It is obvious that no substantial improvement in local education can come until the farmers are taught methods which will enable them to provide themselves with larger incomes.

260. Agricultural High Schools. — In various parts of the country, especially in the South, efforts are being made to establish high schools in rural parts of the States, where boys and girls may be taught to farm in a more profitable manner than has been done by their fathers. In some States, counties are permitted and encouraged to establish agricultural high schools, often with State aid; in others the State establishes one agricultural high school in each congressional district, while localities sometimes maintain such schools at local expense.

The Farragut School of Concord, Tennessee, is a good illustration of an agricultural high school, supported by the community, which meets the needs of the majority of people. "Several years ago this school was reorganized with a view to making it a part of the life of the people it serves. Six years ago the building was destroyed by fire, but it was immediately replaced by the people of the community at a cost of about $12,000. A complete water system has since been incorporated, which cost a little less than $3000, making the initial cost of the school property, including 12 acres of land, about $17,000.

"The school stands in the open country, about one and a half miles from Concord, a village of about 300 inhabitants. The school building is a two-story brick structure, with basement. The high school occupies the second floor and has a laboratory on the first floor. The other rooms on the first floor are occupied by the elementary school. One half the basement contains the home economics room, a lunch room, and a toilet for the girls; in the other half are found the manual training room and the boys' lunch room and toilet room.

"The building was made as attractive as possible and at the same time thoroughly practical. The water system, which adds very much both to the convenience and sanitary conditions, was secured in the following manner: The water from a

large spring about 1200 feet distant is pumped into two large
tanks in the attic of the building by a No. 40 double-acting
rifle ram, with a capacity of 3600 gallons per day. The ram
is driven by creek water, but delivers only spring water to the
tank. From the tanks the water is conveyed to all parts of
the building, to the principal's home, and to the barn. Drinking fountains are located in the halls and lunch rooms, and
wash bowls and sinks and laboratories. Shower baths are in-
stalled in both the boys' and girls' toilet rooms. The waste
water from the showers, sinks, and fountains is carried by a
tile sewer directly to the creek. The sewer pipe leading from
the closets empties into a four-compartment septic tank, which
is 15 feet long, 9 feet wide, and 7 feet deep. The tank over-
flows clear and odorless into the creek.

"Six acres are devoted to buildings, playgrounds, etc. The
other six acres are used for demonstration purposes and for
growing feed for the stock. One man is employed the year
round as janitor and farm laborer. A four-year rotation of
crops is used, and fertilizer demonstrations are in progress.
Other land is devoted to general farm crops, so grouped as to
get two crops per year. One crop is harvested, the other being
turned under to improve soil, which was very poor when the
school took charge of it.

"Another prominent feature of the agricultural course is
that of seed selection and seed testing. A flock of Plymouth
Rock chickens is maintained and used in teaching animal
husbandry. In the course in domestic economy the girls give
as much study to the feeding of man as the boys in agriculture
give to the feeding of live stock.

"An interesting feature of the school work is the moonlight
social, which is held the last Friday night before each full
moon. This is an effort to help solve the social problem of the
rural community. The program varies from meeting to meeting, but always there is a talk on a subject of general interest
pertaining to some phase of farm life. There is always plenty
of music, and after the regular program, which lasts about one

hour, the evening is given over to social converse. These meetings are well attended. The big meeting of the year is on Commencement Day, with an all-day program, including a basket dinner. In the forenoon the graduating class read their essays and receive their diplomas. After dinner opportunity is offered to study the demonstrations and general farm work. The commencement address is given at 2 o'clock and there is a baseball game at 3:30. At 8 o'clock a two-hour drama is given by the high school students." [1]

261. Agricultural Demonstration. — In many agricultural counties, especially in the South, a practical farmer who understands the theory of farming is employed to demonstrate to any farmer who will follow his directions how to care for a certain plot of ground according to the most improved methods. The farmer so employed is called the " county demonstrator," and commonly the State and United States agricultural departments bear one half the cost of the demonstrator, the county bearing the other half.[2]

262. Boys' Corn Clubs. — The county demonstrators also aid members of boys' corn clubs. A boys' corn club consists of a group of boys varying in number from 25 to 100, and ranging in age from 10 to 18. They cultivate both corn and cotton, corn being preferred. As a rule each boy cultivates one acre on his father's farm. The county superintendent of education is usually in charge.

Local, county, and State prizes are given, and the topmost boys are usually sent to Washington to meet the Secretary of Agriculture and to shake hands with the President. The club enrollment is now 100,000. The average number of bushels of corn grown by members of the boys' clubs, and on similar lands by the average farmer in twelve Southern States from 1908 to 1913 was as follows : [3]

[1] Quoted from " U. S. Bureau of Education," Bulletin, No. 5, 1913, page 63.
[2] The Rockefeller General Education Board has given large sums of money through the U. S. Agricultural Department for this work.
[3] The General Education Board, 1902–1914, page 60.

State	Average Yield on Boy's Acre	Average Yield on Similar Lands
Alabama	62.3	17.2
Arkansas	49.5	22.
Florida	38.58	8.
Georgia	56.4	14.
Louisiana	55.32	20.24
Mississippi	66.3	18.
North Carolina	62.8	20.
Oklahoma	48.	22.63
South Carolina	68.79	18.5
Tennessee	91.46	35.5
Texas	38.	24.
Virginia	59.5	20.

263. Girls' Canning Clubs. — Similar to the boys' corn clubs are the girls' canning clubs. Each girl takes one tenth of an acre, and is taught how to select the seed, to plant, cultivate, and perfect the growth of the tomato plant. Inexpensive canning outfits which can be set up out of doors — in the orchard or garden — are obtained by each girl or by a small club. Commonly the girls meet at their various homes, bringing the raw vegetables or fruit with them. The girls are instructed by a county domestic science demonstrator or by some local teacher or well-informed person who understands practical and scientific canning.

In 1913 there were 30,000 members of the girls' canning clubs in fourteen States. The average net profit made by the girls reporting in twelve States has been $21.98 a season; and a girl in Lincoln County, Mississippi, earned a net profit just under $100 on her 950 cans of tomatoes.

264. Rank of States Educationally. — The following table, prepared by the Russell Sage Foundation, gives the approximate rank of each of the 48 States in ten specified educational features for the year 1910. Whose duty is it to see that your State makes a better showing in 1920?

THE TESTS OF EFFICIENCY

APPROXIMATE RANK OF EACH OF THE 48 STATES IN 10 SPECIFIED EDUCATIONAL FEATURES, 1910

GENERAL RANK	STATE	RANK IN									
		Children in School	School Plant	Expense per Child	School Days per Child	School Year	Attendance	Expenditure and Wealth	Daily Cost	High Schools	Salaries
1	Wash.. .	9	6	1	10	12	20	2	3	3	6
2	Mass. . .	8	1	4	1	3	2	15	19	1	4
3	N. Y. . .	17	2	3	3	2	6	33	14	10	3
4	Cal. . .	36	3	2	14	8	10	16	7	2	1
5	Conn. . .	3	4	10	2	5	12	23	28	15	12
6	Ohio . .	7	9	9	6	16	13	13	18	12	15
7	N. J. . .	26	11	11	11	7	16	8	16	22	5
8	Ill. . . .	14	7	8	8	15	11	28	13	20	11
9	Colo. . .	4	10	7	22	24	39	20	6	14	8
10	Ind. . .	22	12	24	20	28	4	10	15	6	16
11	R. I. . .	19	5	16	4	1	14	40	25	5	9
12	Vt.. . .	1	15	14	5	22	9	9	24	17	43
13	N. H. . .	11	8	21	13	20	7	34	20	4	35
14	Utah . .	21	16	18	17	19	15	3	17	28	10
15	Oreg. . .	37	18	15	23	34	1	5	11	8	17
16	Mont.. .	6	13	6	15	6	45	37	10	27	7
17	Mich.. .	25	17	25	7	14	3	14	30	13	20
18	N. Dak. .	12	20	12	27	27	36	6	4	29	32
19	Idaho . .	10	19	20	31	35	31	4	8	34	14
20	Minn.. .	33	22	19	24	26	5	27	12	21	19
21	Iowa . .	5	23	23	12	13	22	42	22	9	38
22	Me.. . .	2	24	28	9	23	17	21	32	11	45
23	Pa.. . .	30	14	26	16	17	8	38	23	24	13
24	Kans.. .	18	29	29	18	21	18	12	29	19	25
25	Nebr.. .	20	21	27	19	10	29	31	21	16	28
26	S. Dak. .	32	32	22	28	18	42	7	9	23	34
27	Nev.. .	47	26	5	37	29	19	44	1	7	21
28	Wis. . .	35	27	30	21	9	27	25	31	18	22
29	Wyo.. .	24	31	17	26	31	30	47	5	30	24
30	Ariz.. .	13	28	13	34	37	38	39	2	31	2
31	Okla.. .	16	35	32	36	32	34	1	33	38	29
32	Mo. . .	31	30	31	25	25	25	32	27	26	23
33	W. Va. .	28	34	33	32	38	28	11	34	46	36
34	Fla. . .	15	37	36	35	45	23	19	36	37	41
35	Del. . .	38	33	34	30	11	43	43	37	25	27
36	Md. . .	41	39	35	29	4	47	46	38	33	18
37	Tenn.. .	23	41	43	33	40	24	17	45	43	39
38	Tex. . .	46	36	39	42	39	33	18	39	32	30
39	La.. . .	48	40	38	46	36	26	25	35	40	26
40	N. Mex. .	40	25	37	48	48	32	48	26	35	31
41	Va.. . .	44	42		40	33	35	35	42	36	42
42	Ky. . .	39	38		41	41	40	22	40	42	33
43	Ark. . .	34	43		43	44	37	30	41	45	40
44	Ga. . .	42	45		38	30	46	29	46	39	44
45	Miss. . .	29	48		39	42	48	26	44	44	47
46	N. C. . .	27	46		44	47	41	36	47	47	48
47	S. C. . .	43	47	41	45	46	21	41	48	48	46
48	Ala. . .	45	44	46	47	43	44	45	43	41	37

The foregoing table can be better understood if illustrated in detail by the State of Washington, whose general rank is first. In proportion of children in school she ranks 9th; in value of school property divided by the number of pupils, 6th; in amount expended on each child, 1st; in the average number of days 'of attendance, 10th; in length of school year, 12th; in regularity of attendance, 20th; in amount of money expended on public education in proportion to the total wealth of the State, 2d; in daily cost per child, 3d; in the proportion that high school pupils bear to elementary school pupils, 3d; and in average annual salaries, 6th.

BIBLIOGRAPHY

HACKETT, WALLACE E. Vocational Training in the United States. A Summary. Published by the Board of School Directors, Reading, Penna.

LEAVITT, FRANK MITCHELL. Some Examples of Industrial Education. 1912.

—— Prevocational Education in the Public Schools. 1915.

MUNROE, PAUL. A Cyclopedia of Education. 5 vols. 1911–1913.

RICHARDS, C. R. Special Report of the United States Bureau of Education on Industrial Training.

Annual Report of the United States Commissioner of Education.

Bulletins of the Bureau of Education, Washington.

Annual Report of the State Superintendent of Education.

A Summary of School Laws. (Usually distributed by the State Superintendent.)

QUESTIONS ON THE TEXT

1. To what extent were the American people educated previous to the Revolutionary War?

2. Who aroused great interest in public school education throughout the North in 1838?

3. When were public free schools established in the South?

4. What is meant by *elementary* schools? *Primary* schools? *Grammar* schools? *Secondary* schools? *Higher* education?

5. What proportion of pupils complete the eighth grade throughout the United States?

6. How are compulsory attendance laws enforced where they exist?

7. When did public high schools develop in the United States?

8. How many colleges were established in the United States before the Revolutionary War?

9. How many colleges are there to-day in the United States? How many students are enrolled? What proportion are women?

10. Name some of the universities whose annual incomes exceed $100,000.

11. Explain how the United States has aided higher education in the States.

12. How many colleges and universities with incomes exceeding $100,000 are located in the State in which you live?

13. Name four systems for administering public schools. Describe each.

14. From what sources is public school revenue derived?

15. Is the amount of money spent on public education as much as should be spent?

16. Does the State in which you live spend as much on education per capita as other progressive States? Does it spend as much in proportion to its wealth?

17. What are the seven different bases for the distribution of school funds?

18. Why is it so important that the States furnish industrial education?

19. Explain how industrial education is taught at the Fitchburg (Mass.) High School. At the University of Cincinnati.

20. Explain how farms can be made more productive.

21. Describe the Farragut School of Concord, Tennessee, and tell how it is conducted.

22. Explain how agriculture is taught by " county demonstrators."

23. Describe Boys' Corn Clubs.

24. Describe Girls' Canning Clubs.

25. According to the Russell Sage Foundation report what is the general rank of the State in which you live?

QUESTIONS FOR DISCUSSION

1. What provisions does the constitution of your State make regarding education?

2. Does your State have compulsory education? Is the compulsory

education law enforced in your community? If not, by what means do you think it could be enforced?

3. Nineteen out of every twenty-one counties in Wyoming have women as superintendents of schools. In what respect do you think the women are especially equipped for this work?

4. The Manual Arts High School of Los Angeles, California, has a student government organization, which includes all the students and the faculty. Its officers are chosen from the student body, with the exception of the auditor and the treasurer, who are appointed by the principal; the treasurer being under $2000 bond. The government of the school is practically in the hands of the students, but the principal has a right to interfere when he deems it necessary. Courts are held, where offenders who plead "not guilty" are tried. Counsel represents both sides and a student jury gives decisions. Laws may be established by initiative and referendum, and the recall may be invoked against any elected officer. The organization transacts $50,000 worth of business a year, the profit going into the treasury of the school. The book exchange, school printing plant, and cafeteria are among the enterprises. Prepare a constitution for the government of your school.

5. In many States textbooks are furnished free, in others the pupils have to buy them, and in a few the State buys them and rents them to the pupils for a nominal sum. What do you consider the merits and demerits of each of the systems?

6. Has your school a good library of reference books, such as dictionaries, encyclopædias, and atlases? Has your Board of Trustees or your Civic League ever been requested to procure these student utensils?

7. Is there not some philanthropist in your county who would give $50,000 to build a county library as a lasting monument to himself if he were only impressed with the need of it? If a $50,000 library were offered, do you think your county would sustain it? Each school in the county could be a branch library for getting the books into the hands of pupils and patrons.

8. Does your school get circulating books from the State library?

9. Virginia schools of higher rank draw from the State treasury annually a sum of money equal to one per cent of the school annuity in addition to the regular annuity. This money is used as a loan fund for deserving scholars, who may receive sums not exceding $100 each for any one session to supplement what they can earn. Upon this loan

the students pay 4 per cent interest. The New York State Department of Education awards every year 750 scholarships, each of which entitles the holder to $100 a year for a period of four years. A list of the names of all pupils residing in each county who are entitled to college entrance diplomas is arranged in order of merit and the scholarships are awarded in that order. Five scholarships are awarded each county annually for each assembly district therein. Which of these plans do you think the better?

10. Has your school a baseball diamond? Basket ball court? Volley ball court? Tennis court? Plenty of swings? If not, is there not some boy or girl in the school with leadership enough to "start something"?

11. Mr. Edison has prepared moving picture films for use in schools, ranging from "the dog barks" and "the dog runs" or the daily life of a fly for the kindergarten up to illustrations for the department of physics. Can you not interest your Civic League in a moving picture machine for your school?

12. The Board of Education of Brooklyn, New York, adopted a plan to establish penny savings banks in the public schools of that city. Do you think this was a good thing? Do you think it will tend to induce public school children to be frugal and thrifty?

13. In many schools it is customary for either the class in government or the graduating class of high schools to take a trip to Washington to see Congress in session and visit the various departments, the Library of Congress, Mt. Vernon, and other places of interest. The cost is usually defrayed by a class entertainment. The other three classes assist with the entertainment as they, too, look forward to the trip. Could the graduates of the several high schools in your county arrange to take this trip together?

14. Could your city give a summer course in toy-making? The toys could be made and sold by the boys and girls and in this way they would get a practical idea of the manufacturing business.

15. Every child in Wisconsin between fourteen and sixteen years of age who, under a special permit, enters upon some useful employment, must go to an industrial, commercial, or evening school for five hours each week. The employer continues the wages during these hours, the attendance upon school being for such hours and at such places as the local Board of Education prescribes. What is the importance of this Wisconsin law? Should your State have a similar one?

16. The University of Wisconsin can tell a farmer the best way

to blast and pull stumps. This university receives liberal support from the State. Is your State university so practical as this?

17. " At a public meeting called to discuss school taxes the following argument is advanced in an effort to reduce school taxes: (a) The State and local governments are overburdened with school charges, — ' schooling ' is a matter for those who can afford it, — let every one take as much as he can pay for in private institutions ; (b) there are too many ' fads ' in education. Let every one be given the good old-fashioned ' three R's ' without the many additional ' trimmings' that have been loaded on to our school system, — if the old system were maintained, school expenses would be materially reduced. What would be your attitude toward each of these arguments and how would you express it ? " — *The New American Government and its Work, by James T. Young.*

CHAPTER XXIX

SOCIAL LEGISLATION

265. Introduction. — There are numerous organizations[1] promoting legislation for various social reforms, but there are three problems that deserve special attention because they have been subjects of much recent legislation. These are (1) care of mental defectives, (2) regulation of liquor traffic, and (3) conservation of health.

266. Care of Mental Defectives. — Mental defectives who are classed as insane and confined to hospitals for the insane should be distinguished from feeble-minded persons, or those who are unable to compete on equal terms with their normal fellows. While insanity is a disease which is often cured, feeble-mindedness seems to be a permanent condition which cannot be cured.

Insane in Hospitals. — In 1880 only 40,000 persons, or 81 for each 100,000 of population, were supported by the States in institutions for the insane. On January 1, 1910, 187,000 persons were supported by the States in hospitals for the insane, or 204 for each 100,000 of population. Insanity has not increased to so great an extent as these figures would in-

---

[1] Some of the more important of these organizations are: Anti-Saloon League of America, Woman's Christian Temperance Union, World's Purity Federation, International Reform Bureau, American Civic Association, National Committee for Mental Hygiene, National Reform Association, National Probation Association, League for World Peace, Carnegie Endowment for International Peace, American Peace and Arbitration League, American Peace Society.

Those desiring literature from the above organizations may obtain the address of the secretary from the World Almanac or some similar year book.

417

dicate, because a larger proportion of insane persons were cared for in institutions in 1910 than in 1880, but the real increase of insanity is great, and the prevention of insanity and treat- ment of insane persons is one of our greatest problems.

The Feeble-Minded. — Feeble-mindedness is a state of mental defect, existing from birth or from an early age, rendering persons thus affected incapable of performing their duties as members of society in the position of life to which they are born. A feeble-minded person whose mental age does not sur- pass two years is known as an *idiot;* one whose mental age is between three and seven years is called an *imbecile;* and one whose mental age is between seven and twelve is technically known as a *moron.*

The education of imbeciles and morons should be apart from other children. They do not develop initiative, and have weak will power, but can be taught to lead a useful life within an institution and they can be happiest there because occupied at such tasks as they can perform.

In 1910, 20,000 feeble-minded persons were in special in- stitutions, 13,000 in almshouses, and several hundred thousand at large. The greater portion of these are morons and could be nearly self-supporting in institutions, and much happier there among others of their kind than at large.

All but eleven States have laws against the marriage of insane persons, and about the same number prohibit the marriage of idiots; a smaller number prohibit the marriage of imbeciles; and only nine States prohibit the marriage of all feeble-minded persons, thus including the morons,[1] though several other States, such as Michigan and New Jersey, pro- hibit the marriage of morons if they have been in institutions for the feeble-minded.

Not only will the increased proportion of feeble-minded persons injure our race, but they contribute a large proportion of our criminals, paupers, and drunkards; hence all States

---

[1] These States are Connecticut, Indiana, Kansas, Minnesota, Nebraska, North Dakota, Pennsylvania, Washington, and Wisconsin.

should have rigid laws to prevent the marriage of feeble-minded persons.

267. Abolition of the Saloon. — *The License System.* — Before the Civil War liquor was sold at grocery stores at about the same price that is now paid for cider. From the time of the Civil War until the adoption of national prohibition the United States government imposed a tax on liquor ranging as high as several dollars a gallon. In addition to this federal tax on liquor, the United States, the States, and the cities each imposed a license tax ranging from $25 to more than $1000 upon every saloon.

The license system lessened the number of saloons and the amount of liquor sold, and produced revenue for the National, State, and city governments. But the license system made the government a partner in the evils of the traffic and gave a certain respectability to the liquor business. Moreover, the high license tended to put saloons into the hands of a few wealthy men who used their money to secure the election of public officials that were favorable to the liquor business, thus having a corrupting influence upon the National, State, and city officials.

The Dispensary System. — Under the dispensary plan the government had a monopoly of the liquor business, and all liquor was sold in original packages by local dispensers. For a few years the State of South Carolina purchased all liquor sold in the State, put it in bottles in Columbia, and sold it at State dispensaries in the towns and cities of the State. The dispensaries were open only in day time, no liquor could be drunk on the premises, and the profit went to the State.

This system was an improvement over ordinary saloons, but corruption found its way to those in charge of the system; and though many of the evils of the open saloon were checked, the evils of liquor continued. The legislature abolished the State dispensary and permitted each county to vote whether it would have a county dispensary or county prohibition. In 1915, when the State adopted State-wide prohibition, twenty-nine counties were already in the dry column and only fifteen had county dispensaries. In a few other States cities or towns were permitted to have dispensaries.

Local Option. — By local option was meant the right of the people within a certain locality to decide by election whether or not they would permit the sale of liquor within the local area. The area within which the people could vote varied from State to State. It was the county, township, town (village), or city, or even wards of a city.

Before the sentiment against saloons became strong in cities, local option usually applied to townships, towns, and villages, the "drys" hoping to carry elections in the rural townships and towns. If the "drys" succeeded at this, they urged the State legislature to permit county option instead of township option, expecting the voters of the county outside of the city to cast enough votes to overcome the "wet" votes of the city.

State-wide Prohibition. — State-wide prohibition meant the prohibition of the sale of liquor anywhere within the State unless it was at certain drug stores, where it was sold for medical purposes under strict safeguards. The majority of States had State-wide prohibition when national prohibition was adopted.

Nation-wide Prohibition. — In January, 1919, the Eighteenth Amendment to the Constitution of the United States was ratified. It provides that after one year from its ratification the manufacture, sale, or transportation of intoxicating liquors within, the importation thereof into, or the exportation thereof from the United States and all territory subject to the jurisdiction thereof, for beverage purposes, is prohibited.

Both Congress and the State legislatures are given power to enforce prohibition by appropriate legislation. For some years the United States and the States will need special officers to enforce the prohibition laws in those communities where the " dry " sentiment is not strong. "Moonshiners" will try to evade the laws and some persons will endeavor to produce intoxicating drinks in their homes.

World-wide Prohibition. — Where local option existed, some liquor was smuggled in from nearby communities. Where State-wide prohibition existed, some liquor was smuggled in from nearby States. Now, under nation-wide prohibition, the problem of preventing the smuggling in of liquor by land, water, and air, still remains. In fact, rapid communication and transportation have made the world so small that we are obliged to become our brothers' keepers.

How the Saloon Was Abolished. — The Prohibition Party was organized in 1872, and has kept prohibition as a political issue constantly before the people. Six years later the Woman's Christian Temperance Union was founded with Frances E. Willard as its secretary. This society secured legislation requiring the scientific study of the effects of alcohol upon the human body in the public schools of practically all the States.

The Anti-Saloon League of America was organized in 1893, and soon a branch was operating in each State. This league represented the church organized against the saloon. In 1899 the league established legislative offices in Washington, D. C. Later it established the American Issue Publishing Company at Westerville, Ohio, which circulated more than 250,000,000 pages of literature a year.

This league worked through a national superintendent and State, district, and special superintendents. For example, a special superintendent was sent to Oklahoma to see that the State entered the Union with prohibition. Twelve of their best men were sent to Maine when the State-wide question was re-submitted.

As a result of this efficient organization, prohibition legislation made rapid progress. The Anti-canteen Law was enacted by Congress in 1901. An act prohibiting C.O.D. shipments of liquor from one State to another followed. In 1913 the Webb-Kenyon Act permitted a prohibition State to forbid the shipment of liquor into the State. The District of Columbia entered the "dry" column in 1917 by act of Congress. Prohibition as a war measure followed in 1919. In January, 1919, the amendment providing for permanent nation-wide prohibition was ratified, to become effective in January, 1920. Thus culminated another great reform.

268. Conservation of Health. — When people believed that disease was a "humor" in the blood they waited until the malady appeared and cured it with medicines — or at least tried to cure it. But now that we know most of our prevalent diseases to be caused by bacilli (germs), we know it is possible to prevent them if the bacilli are kept from our systems.

For instance, if the germs causing the hookworm disease had been understood in the United States before Doctor Stiles of the United States Public Health Service identified them in 1902 and not allowed to spread, the millions of victims of the disease would have escaped. Fortunately this disease can now be easily prevented or cured, and State and county health boards are coöperating with public schools to eradicate it. Again, if we have the water and milk free from typhoid bacilli, and screen against the flies which carry these germs, we are not likely to contract typhoid fever. But individuals living in cities, especially, cannot know whether the water and milk supplies are pure or whether the hotels are sanitary. The State and cities must have officers to inspect the milk supply,

water·supply, food supplies, hotels, and restaurants. Whereas
in the past it has been the duty of the family physician to *cure*
diseases, in the future it should be the duty of the public medical official to *prevent* diseases by proper sanitary precautions.

States and cities should maintain laboratories for the examination of water, milk, and other foods; should have an
annual examination of school children and even of adults.;

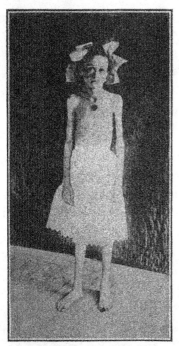 

A SIXTEEN-YEAR-OLD VICTIM
OF THE HOOKWORM DISEASE.

THE SAME GIRL AFTER TREAT-
MENT FOR HOOKWORM.

should enforce vaccination; should inspect meat shops, soda
fountains, hotels, tenements, factories, and the premises of
residences; should disinfect places where contagious diseases
have existed; should establish and maintain pest-houses, sana-
toriums for consumptives, and recreation grounds for all persons.

Citizens are slow to realize that it is cheaper to pay taxes
for the prevention of disease than to pay doctors' bills and

RECREATION GROUNDS, WORCESTER, MASS.
Swings properly arranged.

hospital bills for their cure. A few people can buy milk from the high price dairymen, buy spring water, screen premises, and go to great expense to protect themselves; but most people cannot afford such protection, and therefore contract diseases, menacing the health of all.

A PLAYGROUND ON THE ROOF OF A NEW YORK CITY SCHOOL.

Sanitation to be of any great value must be practiced throughout the city. Mayor Preston, of Baltimore, recently waged a war on the mosquito. Inspectors were employed to go from house to house to locate places where mosquitoes might breed. Behold, in the Mayor's own yard was found a jar containing water in which mosquitoes could multiply. He paid his fine cheerfully, but the incident goes to show that the sanitation of a city, or State, cannot be left to individuals. It is too natural for one to be a bit negligent — to forget.

BIBLIOGRAPHY

Annual Proceedings of the National Conference of Charities and Corrections.

The Survey — A magazine in the interest of social legislation.

Anti-Saloon League Year Book. Published by the Anti-Saloon League of America, Westerville, Ohio. Price 25 cents.

QUESTIONS ON THE TEXT

1. What is meant by " social reforms " as used in this chapter?
2. How are the States taking care of their insane?
3. What do the States do for their feeble-minded persons? What three kinds of feeble-minded persons are there?
4. Do most States permit weak-minded persons to marry? Should they?
5. Explain how liquor is taxed under the license system?
6. Describe the government dispensary plan for conducting the liquor business. Has it proved a success?
7. Explain what is meant by *local option* in relation to the liquor problem. How many States have adopted local option?
8. What is meant by State-wide prohibition? How many States have adopted it?
9. What is the ultimate aim of persons who are opposed to the liquor traffic? How could their desire be accomplished?
10. How has the theory as to the causes of disease changed in recent years?
11. How does the State protect the health of its citizens? How do cities?
12. Under present conditions could the spread of disease be prevented without the aid of government?

QUESTIONS FOR DISCUSSION

1. The united charities associations of many cities have a card index of all deserving and all undeserving poor or street beggars. Any individual can obtain a little folder containing letters of introduction to the association; and if he gives such a letter to a beggar, he knows that the latter will be cared for by the association. Should you give what you have for charities to the unknown beggars or to the association? Is there a State or local officer to whom you can refer beggars for help and employment?

2. Doctor Carl Kelsey has grouped the causes of poverty into three main classes:

1. *Environmental:*
   a. Adverse physical environment: polar regions, tropics, deserts, swamps.
   b. Disasters: flood, earthquake, fire, famine.
2. *Personal:*
   a. Physical defects: feeble-mindedness, insanity, blindness.
   b. Moral defects: dishonesty, laziness, shiftlessness, etc.
   c. Intemperance.
   d. Licentiousness.
   e. Sickness.
   f. Accident.
3. *Social:*
   a. Industrial changes affecting the worker: changes of location of trade, inventions, strikes.
   b. Exploitation.
   c. Race prejudice.
   d. Sickness, death, desertion, crime of natural supporter.
   e. Defective sanitation.
   f. Defective educational system.
   g. Bad social environment.
   h. War.
   i. Unwise philanthropy.

What are the chief causes of poverty in your immediate neighborhood? Which of these numerous causes enumerated are secondary to some primary trait of character or habit: for instance, lack of foresight and frugality? Drunkenness? Lack of religious or moral training?

3. Why is it unwise for a child to have much money to spend?

4. Is your State penitentiary primarily a place to detain criminals or a place to reform them? Which should it be?

5. Warden P. E. Thomas has established a "home rule" system among prisoners of the Ohio prison. Seven men have been selected from various sections of the prison to act as the prison council and meet with the warden every Monday morning to discuss the affairs of the prison. Their powers are merely advisory. Do you think this warden is helping to solve the criminal problem?

6. The warden of the Colorado State prison has organized a convict band. Do you think he is helping to solve the criminal problem?

7. How many of the conditions mentioned below have you observed?

"Intemperance cuts down youth in its vigor, manhood in its strength, and age in its weakness. It breaks the father's heart, bereaves the doting mother, extinguishes natural affections, erases conjugal love, blots out filial attachments, blights parental hope, and brings down mourning age in sorrow to the grave. It produces weakness, not strength; sickness, not health; death, not life. It makes wives widows, children orphans, fathers fiends, and all of them paupers and beggars. It feeds rheumatism, nurses gout, welcomes epidemics, invites cholera, imports pestilence, and embraces consumption. It covers the land with idleness, misery, and crime. It fills your jails, supplies your almshouses, and demands your asylums. It engenders controversies, fosters quarrels, and cherishes riots. It crowds your penitentiaries, and furnishes victims to your scaffolds. It is the lifeblood of the gambler, the element of the burglar, the prop of the highwayman, and the support of the midnight incendiary. . It countenances the liar, respects the thief, esteems the blasphemer. It violates obligations, reverences frauds, and honors infamy. It defames benevolence, hates love, scorns virtue, and slanders innocence. It incites the father to butcher his helpless offspring, and helps the husband to massacre his wife, and the child to grind the parricidal axe. It burns up men, consumes women, detests life, curses God, and despises heaven. It suborns witnesses, nurses perjury, defiles the jury-box, and stains the judicial ermine. It degrades the citizen, debases the legislator, dishonors the statesman, and disarms the patriot. It brings shame, not honor; terror, not safety; despair, not hope; misery, not happiness. And with the malevolence of a fiend, it calmly surveys its frightful desolation, and unsatisfied with its havoc, it poisons felicity, kills peace, ruins morals, blights confidence, slays reputation, and wipes out national honors."

APPENDIX I

CONSTITUTION OF THE UNITED STATES
(ANNOTATED)

PREAMBLE[1]

WE, the people of the United States, in order to form a more perfect Union, establish justice, insure domestic tranquillity, provide for the common defence, promote the general welfare, and secure the blessings of liberty to ourselves and our posterity, do ordain and establish this Constitution for the United States of America.

ARTICLE I

LEGISLATIVE DEPARTMENT

Section 1. Two Houses

1. All legislative powers herein granted shall be vested in a Congress of the United States, which shall consist of a Senate and House of Representatives.

Section 2. House of Representatives

1. The House of Representatives shall be composed of members chosen every second year by the people of the several states, and the electors in each state shall have the qualifications requisite for electors of the most numerous branch of the state legislature.[2]

2. No person shall be a Representative who shall not have attained to the age of twenty-five years, and been seven years a citizen of the

---

[1] The Preamble is an introduction to the main subject, but is no part of it. It grants no powers, but assists in interpreting the various clauses that follow by indicating the intentions of the framers of the Constitution.

[2] " Electors " means voters.

United States, and who shall not, when elected, be an inhabitant of that state in which he shall be chosen.[8]

3. Representatives and direct taxes shall be apportioned among the several states which may be included within this Union, according to their respective numbers, which shall be determined by adding to the whole number of free persons, including those bound to service for a term of years, and excluding Indians not taxed, *three-fifths of all other persons.*[4]   The actual enumeration shall be made within three years after the first meeting of the Congress of the United States, and within every subsequent term of ten years, in such manner as they shall by law direct.   The number of Representatives shall not exceed one for every thirty thousand, but each state shall have at least one Representative; and, until such enumeration shall be made, the state of New Hampshire shall be entitled to choose three, Massachusetts eight, Rhode Island and Providence Plantations one, Connecticut five, New York six, New Jersey four, Pennsylvania eight, Delaware one, Maryland six, Virginia ten, North Carolina five, South Carolina five, and Georgia three.

4. When vacancies happen in the representation from any state, the executive authority thereof shall issue writs of election to fill such vacancies.

5. The House of Representatives shall choose their Speaker and other officers; and shall have the sole power of impeachment.

Section 3. Senate

1. The Senate of the United States shall be composed of two Senators from each state [chosen by the legislature thereof] [5] for six years; and each Senator shall have one vote.

2. Immediately after they shall be assembled in consequence of the first election, they shall be divided, as equally as may be, into three classes.   The seats of the senators of the first class shall be vacated at the expiration of the second year; of the second class, at the expiration of the fourth year; and of the third class, at the expiration of the sixth year; so that one-third may be chosen every

---

[8] The first woman representative, Miss Rankin, was elected from Montana in 1916.

[4] The clause in italics is superseded by the Thirteenth and Fourteenth Amendments.

[5] See Seventeenth Amendment.

second year; [and if vacancies happen by resignation, or otherwise, during the recess of the legislature of any state, the executive thereof may make temporary appointments until the next meeting of the legislature, which shall then fill such vacancies.][5]

3. No person shall be a Senator who shall not have attained to the age of thirty years, and been nine years a citizen of the United States, who shall not, when elected, be an inhabitant of that state for which he shall be chosen.

4. The Vice-President of the United States shall be President of the Senate, but shall have no vote, unless they be equally divided.

5. The Senate shall choose their other officers, and also a President *pro tempore*, in the absence of the Vice-President, or when he shall exercise the office of President of the United States.

6. The Senate shall have the sole power to try all impeachments. When sitting for that purpose, they shall be on oath or affirmation. When the President of the United States is tried, the Chief Justice shall preside ; and no person shall be convicted without the concurrence of two-thirds of the members present.[6]

7. Judgment in cases of impeachment shall not extend further than to removal from office, and disqualification to hold and enjoy any office of honor, trust, or profit, under the United States ; but the party convicted shall, nevertheless, be liable and subject to indictment, trial, judgment, and punishment, according to law.

Section 4.   Elections and Meetings of Congress

1. The times, places, and manner, of holding elections for Senators and Representatives, shall be prescribed in each state by the legislature thereof : but the Congress may at any time, by law, make or alter such regulations, except as to the places of choosing Senators.[7]

2. The Congress shall assemble at least once in every year, and such meeting shall be on the first Monday in December, unless they shall by law appoint a different day.

---

[6] " Two thirds of the members present" must be at least two thirds of a quorum. There are now 96 senators ; 49 is a quorum, hence 33 could convict.
[7] In 1842 Congress provided that representatives should be elected from districts. In 1872 Congress provided that representatives should be elected on the Tuesday after the first Monday in November of every even year. Maine, the only exception to this rule, elects in the late summer, and its election is viewed as a political barometer.

Section 5. Powers and Duties of the Houses

1. Each House shall be the judge of the elections, returns, and qualifications of its own members,[8] and a majority of each shall constitute a quorum to do business; but a smaller number may adjourn from day to day, and may be authorized to compel the attendance of absent members, in such manner, and under such penalties, as each House may provide.

2. Each House may determine the rules of the proceedings, punish its members for disorderly behavior, and, with the concurrence of two-thirds, expel a member.   .

3. Each House shall keep a journal of its proceedings, and, from time to time, publish the same, excepting such parts as may, in their judgment, require secrecy; and the yeas and nays of the members of either House, on any question, shall, at the desire of one-fifth of those present, be entered on the journal.

4. Neither House, during the session of Congress, shall, without the consent of the other, adjourn for more than three days, nor to any other place than that in which the two Houses shall be sitting.

Section 6. Privileges of and Prohibitions upon Members

1. The Senators and Representatives shall receive a compensation for their services, to be ascertained by law, and paid out of the treasury of the United States. They shall, in all cases, except treason, felony, and breach of the peace,[9] be privileged from arrest during their attendance at the session of their respective Houses, and in going to, and returning from, the same; and for any speech or debate in either House, they shall not be questioned in any other place.[10]

2. No Senator or Representative shall, during the time for which he was elected, be appointed to any civil office under the authority of the United States, which shall have been created, or the emoluments

---

[8] This provision permits either House to exclude a member-elect by a majority vote. See sections 35 and 36 of the text.

[9] *Treason* is defined in Art. 3, Sec. 3.

Felony is defined is section 183 of the text.

Breach of the peace means any indictable offence less than treason or felony; hence the exemption from arrest is now of little importance.

[10] The privilege of speech or debate does not extend to the outside publication of libelous matter spoken in Congress.

whereof shall have been increased during such time ;[11] and no person, holding any office under the United States, shall be a member of either House during his continuance in office.

Section 7.   Revenue Bills: President's Veto

1. All bills for raising revenue shall originate in the House of Representatives; but the Senate may propose or concur with amendments as on other bills.

2. Every bill which shall have passed the House of Representatives and the Senate, shall, before it become a law, be presented to the President of the United States; if he approve, he shall sign it, but if not, he shall return it, with his objections, to that House in which it shall have originated, who shall enter the objections at large on their journal, and proceed to reconsider it.[12] If, after such reconsideration, two-thirds of that House shall agree to pass the bill, it shall be sent, together with the objections, to the other House, by which it shall likewise be reconsidered, and, if approved by two-thirds of that House, it shall become a law. But in all such cases the votes of both Houses shall be determined by yeas and nays, and the names of the persons voting for and against the bill shall be entered on the journal of each House respectively. If any bill shall not be returned by the President within ten days (Sundays excepted) after it shall have been presented to him, the same shall be a law, in like manner as if he had signed it, unless the Congress, by their adjournment, prevent its return, in which case it shall not be a law.

3. Every order, resolution,[13] or vote, to which the concurrence of

---

[11] After President Taft had selected Senator Knox to be Secretary of State it was discovered that during the latter's term as senator the salaries of cabinet officers had been increased. The objection was removed by an act of Congress reducing the salary of the Secretary of State to its former figure.

[12] Particular items of bills cannot be vetoed by the President, which fact is very unfortunate.

[13] "Every ... resolution ... to which the concurrence of the Senate and the House of Representatives may be necessary," means every resolution which has the effect and force of law. There are two kinds of resolution, "joint" and "concurrent."

A joint resolution is, in general, the same as a bill with the exception of the different wording of the enacting clause; hence must be signed by the President, except that an amendment to the Constitution is proposed by a joint resolution which need not be signed by the President because it has not the effect of law; it is merely a proposal of a law to the States.

the Senate and House of Representatives may be necessary (except on a question of adjournment), shall be presented to the President of the United States; and before the same shall take effect, shall be approved by him, or, being disapproved by him, shall be repassed by two-thirds of the Senate and House of Representatives, according to the rules and limitations prescribed in the case of a bill.

Section 8. Legislative Powers of Congress

The Congress shall have power:

1. To lay and collect taxes, duties, imposts, and excises,[14] to pay the debts, and provide for the common defence and general welfare, of the United States; but all duties, imposts, and excises, shall be uniform throughout the United States:

2. To borrow money on the credit of the United States:

3. To regulate commerce with foreign nations, and among the several states, and with the Indian tribes:

4. To establish a uniform rule of naturalization, and uniform laws on the subject of bankruptcies,[15] throughout the United States:

5. To coin money, regulate the value thereof, and of foreign coin, and fix the standard of weights and measures:

6. To provide for the punishment of counterfeiting the securities and current coin of the United States:

A concurrent resolution does not have the effect of law; it is merely an expression of the will of Congress on some particular subject, such as adjournment beyond three days, or an expression of sympathy, so does not need the approval of the President.

[14] For the meaning of these terms see section 45 of the text.

[15] *Bankruptcy* means the inability of a person to pay all of his debts; but by turning over what property he has to be distributed proportionately among his creditors, he is released from his ordinary debts. Congress has not exercised its power over bankruptcy continuously. The present federal bankruptcy law was passed in 1898. According to this law there is voluntary and involuntary bankruptcy. Any debtor may become a voluntary bankrupt by filing a petition setting forth the fact that he is unable to pay his debts, and that he is willing to surrender all of his property to his creditors. Any person or corporation (except laborers, farmers, and national banks) indebted to the amount of $1000 may be declared an involuntary bankrupt by a federal District Court if he in any way attempts to defraud his creditors, or if he admits, in writing, his inability to pay his debts and willingness to be adjudged a bankrupt.

7. To establish post-offices and post-roads:[16]

8. To promote the progress of science and useful arts,[17] by securing, for limited times, to authors and inventors, the exclusive right to their respective writings and discoveries:

9. To constitute tribunals inferior to the Supreme Court:

10. To define and punish piracies and felonies, committed on the high seas, and offences against the law of nations:

11. To declare war, grant letters of marque and reprisal,[18] and make rules concerning captures on land and water:

12. To raise and support armies; but no appropriation of money to that use shall be for a longer term than two years:

13. To provide and maintain a navy:

14. To make rules for the government and regulation of the land and naval forces:

15. To provide for calling forth the militia to execute the laws of the Union, suppress insurrections, and repel invasions:

16. To provide for organizing, arming, and disciplining the militia, and for governing such part of them as may be employed in the service of the United States, reserving to the states respectively the appointment of the officers, and the authority of training the militia, according to the discipline prescribed by Congress:

17. To exercise exclusive legislation in all cases whatsoever, over such district (not exceeding ten miles square) as may, by cession of particular states, and the acceptance of Congress, become the seat of the government of the United States, and to exercise like authority over all places, purchased by the consent of the legislature of the state in which the same shall be, for the erection of forts, magazines, arsenals, dock-yards, and other needful buildings: — And

[16] "Post" is the French word *poste* meaning "mail"; and "post-roads" mean mail-routes, such as turnpikes, railroads, rivers, city streets, mountain paths, etc.

[17] This clause refers to copyrights and patents. (See sections 47, 99, and notes to section 120.)

[18] *Marque* is a French word meaning "boundary." "Reprisal" is from the French word *représaille*, which means retaliation. Hence, originally letters of "marque and reprisal" were licenses to cross the boundaries into the enemies' country, and capture or destroy goods. As used here it means a commission authorizing private citizens to fit out vessels (privateers) to capture or destroy in time of war. No privateers were commissioned either during the Civil War or during the Spanish-American War.

18. To make all laws which shall be necessary and proper [19] for carrying into execution the foregoing powers, and all other powers vested by this Constitution in the government of the United States, or in any department or officer thereof.

Section 9. Prohibitions upon the United States

1. The migration or importation of such persons, as any of the states, now existing, shall think proper to admit, shall not be prohibited by the Congress prior to the year one thousand eight hundred and eight; but a tax or duty may be imposed on such importation, not exceeding ten dollars for each person.

2. The privilege of the writ of *habeas corpus* [20] shall not be suspended, unless when, in cases of rebellion or invasion, the public safety may require it.

3. No bill of attainder, or *ex post facto* law,[21] shall be passed.

4. No capitation, or other direct tax, shall be laid, unless in proportion to the *census* or enumeration hereinbefore directed to be taken.[22]

5. No tax or duty shall be laid on articles exported from any state.

6. No preference shall be given by any regulation of commerce or revenue to the ports of one state over those of another; nor shall vessels bound to, or from, one state, be obliged to enter, clear, or pay duties, in another.

7. No money shall be drawn from the treasury, but in consequence of appropriations made by law; and a regular statement and account of the receipts and expenditures of all public money shall be published from time to time.

8. No title of nobility shall be granted by the United States; and no person holding any office of profit or trust under them shall, with-

---

[19] *Necessary* does not mean absolutely or indispensably necessary, but merely appropriate. This so-called *necessary and proper clause* is also known as the elastic clause, because it has made it possible for the courts to stretch the meaning of other clauses of the Constitution. See section 48 of the text.

[20] A *writ of habeas corpus* is directed by a judge to any person detaining another, demanding that person to produce the body of the person detained in order to determine whether such person is rightfully or wrongfully detained. Such person may be a prisoner in jail, an inmate of an insane asylum, a nun in a convent, or any person detained contrary to law.

[21] A *bill of attainder* is a legislative act which inflicts punishment without a judicial trial. See Art. I, Sec. 10; see also Art. III, Sec. 3, Cl. 2.
For the meaning of *ex post facto* see section 128 of the text.

[22] See Amendment XVI. Also see section 44 of the text.

out the consent of the Congress, accept of any present, emolument, office, or title, of any kind whatever, from any king, prince, or foreign state.

Section 10. Prohibitions upon the States

1. No state shall enter into any treaty, alliance, or confederation; grant letters of marque and reprisal; coin money; emit bills of credit; [23] make anything but gold and silver coin a tender in payment of debts; pass any bill of attainder, *ex post !facto* law, or law impairing the obligation of contracts, or grant any title of nobility.

2. No state shall, without the consent of the Congress, lay any imposts or duties on imports or exports, except what may be absolutely necessary for executing its inspection laws; and the net produce of all duties and imposts, laid by any state on imports or exports, shall be for the use of the treasury of the United States; and all such laws shall be subject to the revision and control of the Congress. No state shall, without the consent of Congress, lay any duty of tonnage,[24] keep troops, or ships of war, in time of peace, enter into any agreement or compact with another state, or with a foreign power, or engage in war, unless actually invaded, or in such imminent danger as will not admit of delay.

ARTICLE II

EXECUTIVE DEPARTMENT: THE PRESIDENT AND VICE-PRESIDENT

Section 1. Term: Election: Qualifications: Salary: Oath of Office

1. The Executive power shall be vested in a President of the United States of America. He shall hold his office during the term of four years, and together with the Vice-President, chosen for the same term, be elected as follows:

2. Each state shall appoint, in such manner as the legislature thereof may direct, a number of Electors, equal to the whole number of Senators and Representatives, to which the state may be entitled in

---

[23] *Bills of credit* mean paper money.

[24] *Tonnage* is a vessel's internal cubical capacity in tons of one hundred cubic feet each. *Tonnage duties* are duties upon vessels in proportion to their capacity.

the Congress; but no Senator or Representative, or person holding an office of trust or profit, under the United States, shall be appointed an Elector.

3. [The Electors shall meet in their respective states, and vote by ballot for two persons, of whom one, at least, shall not be an inhabitant of the same state with themselves. And they shall make a list of all the persons voted for, and of the number of votes for each; which list they shall sign and certify, and transmit, sealed, to the seat of the Government of the United States, directed to the President of the Senate. The President of the Senate shall, in the presence of the Senate and House of Representatives, open all the certificates, and the votes shall then be counted. The person having the greatest number of votes shall be the President, if such number be a majority of the whole number of Electors appointed; and if there be more than one, who have such majority, and have an equal number of votes, then the House of Representatives shall immediately choose, by ballot, one of them for President; and if no person have a majority, then, from the five highest on the list, the said House shall, in like manner, choose the President. But in choosing the President, the votes shall be taken by states, the representation from each state having one vote; a quorum for this purpose shall consist of a member or members from two-thirds of the states, and a majority of all the states shall be necessary to a choice. In every case, after the choice of the President, the person having the greatest number of votes of the Electors shall be the Vice-President. But if there should remain two or more who have equal votes, the Senate shall choose from them, by ballot, the Vice-President.][25]

4. The Congress may determine the time of choosing the Electors, and the day on which they shall give their votes; which day shall be the same throughout the United States.[26]

5. No person, except a natural-born citizen, or a citizen of the United States at the time of the adoption of this Constitution, shall be eligible to the office of President; neither shall any person be eligible to that office, who shall not have attained to the age of thirty-five years, and been fourteen years a resident within the United States.

6. In case of the removal of the President from office, or of his death, resignation, or inability to discharge the powers and duties of the said office, the same shall devolve on the Vice-President, and the Congress may by law provide for the case of removal, death, resigna-

---

[25] This paragraph has been superseded by Amendment XII.
[26] For the time of choosing electors see section 59 of the text.

tion or inability, both of the President and Vice-President, declaring what officer shall then act as President, and such officer shall act accordingly, until the disability be removed, or a President shall be elected.[27]

7. The President shall, at stated times, receive for his services a compensation, which shall neither be increased nor diminished during the period for which he shall have been elected, and he shall not receive, within that period, any other emolument from the United States, or any of them.

8. Before he enter on the execution of his office, he shall take the following oath or affirmation:

9. "I do solemnly swear (or affirm), that I will faithfully execute the office of President of the United States, and will, to the best of my ability, preserve, protect, and defend the Constitution of the United States."

Section 2.   President's Executive Powers

1. The President shall be Commander-in-Chief of the army and navy of the United States, and of the militia of the several states, when called into the actual service of the United States; he may require the opinion, in writing, of the principal officer in each of the executive departments upon any subject relating to the duties of their respective offices,[28] and he shall have power to grant reprieves and pardons[29] for offences against the United States, except in cases of impeachment.

2. He shall have power, by and with the advice and consent of the Senate, to make treaties, provided two-thirds of the Senators present concur; and he shall nominate, and, by and with the advice and consent of the Senate, shall appoint ambassadors, other public ministers, and consuls, judges of the Supreme Court, and all other officers of the United States whose appointments are not herein otherwise provided for, and which shall be established by law;[30] but the Congress may by law vest the appointment of such inferior officers, as they think proper, in the President alone, in the courts of law, or in the heads of departments.

---

[27] For the order of succession to the presidency see section 61 of the text.

[28] This clause is the only authority for the President's Cabinet.   There is no law of Congress that makes a department head a member of the Cabinet.

[29] For the pardoning power of the President see section 69 of the text.

[30] For the President's power to remove officers see section 64 of the text.

3. The President shall have power to fill up all vacancies that may happen during the recess of the Senate, by granting commissions which shall expire at the end of their next session.

Section 3. President's Executive Powers (*continued*)

1. He shall, from time to time, give to the Congress information of the state of the Union, and recommend to their consideration such measures as he shall judge necessary and expedient; he may, on extraordinary occasions, convene both Houses, or either of them, and in case of disagreement between them, with respect to the time of adjournment, he may adjourn them to such time as he shall think proper; he shall receive ambassadors and other public ministers; he shall take care that the laws be faithfully executed, and shall commission all the officers of the United States.

Section 4. Impeachment

1. The President, Vice-President, and all civil officers [31] of the United States, shall be removed from office on impeachment for, and conviction of, treason, bribery, or other high crimes and misdemeanors. [32]

ARTICLE III

JUDICIAL DEPARTMENT

Section 1. Courts : Terms of Office

1. The judicial power of the United States shall be vested in one Supreme Court, and in such inferior courts as the Congress may from time to time ordain and establish. The judges, both of the Supreme and inferior courts, shall hold their offices during good behavior, and shall, at stated times, receive for their services a compensation which shall not be diminished during their continuance in office.

---

[31] *Civil Officers* subject to impeachment include all officers of the United States who hold their appointments from the National government, high or low, whose duties are executive or judicial. Officers in the army or navy are not civil officers; neither are senators and representatives officers in this sense, nor can they be impeached, but this would be useless as either House can expel a member by a two-thirds vote.

[32] A majority of the House of Representatives may impeach any civil officer of the United States whom they consider morally unfit for his position.

Section 2. Jurisdiction

1. The judicial power shall extend to all cases, in law and equity,[33] arising under this Constitution, the laws of the United States, and treaties made, or which shall be made, under their authority; to all cases affecting ambassadors, other public ministers, and consuls; to all cases of admiralty and maritime jurisdiction;[34] to controversies to which the United States shall be a party; to controversies between two or more states, between a state and citizens of another state,[35] between citizens of different states, between citizens of the same state claiming lands under grants of different states, and between a state, or the citizens thereof, and foreign states, citizens, or subjects.

2. In all cases affecting ambassadors, other public ministers and consuls, and those in which a state shall be a party, the Supreme Court shall have original jurisdiction.[36] In all the other cases before mentioned, the Supreme Court shall have appellate jurisdiction, both as to law and fact, with such exceptions and under such regulations as the Congress shall make.

3. The trial of all crimes, except in cases of impeachment, shall be by jury;[37] and such trial shall be held in the state where the said crimes shall have been committed;[38] but when not committed within any state the trial shall be at such place or places as the Congress may by law have directed.

Section 3. Treason

1. Treason against the United States shall consist only in levying war against them, or in adhering to their enemies, giving them aid

---

[33] For the meaning of *Equity* see note to section 182 of the text.

[34] *Admiralty jurisdiction* includes cases of prizes seized in time of war, and crimes, torts, etc. in time of peace, which occur on the high seas or navigable waters. *Maritime jurisdiction* has reference to contracts, claims, etc. that are connected with maritime operations — *e.g.*, a contract on land for ship supplies. Admiralty jurisdiction is given by the locality of the act; maritime, by the character of the act.

[35] This clause was modified by the Eleventh Amendment.

[36] *Original jurisdiction* means the right of hearing and determining a case in the first instance. *Appellate jurisdiction* means the right to hear cases appealed from inferior courts.

[37] Jury trials are guaranteed in federal courts only. States could abolish jury trials if they should desire to do so.

[38] If a crime is committed on the sea the accused is tried by the United States District Court of the district where the prisoner is landed.

and comfort. No person shall be convicted of treason unless on the testimony of two witnesses to the same overt act, or on confession in open court.

2. The Congress shall have power to declare the punishment of treason, but no attainder of treason shall work corruption of blood or forfeiture, except during the life of the person attainted.[89]

ARTICLE IV

RELATIONS OF STATES

Section 1. Public Records

1. Full faith and credit shall be given in each state to the public acts, records, and judicial proceedings of every other state. And the Congress may, by general laws, prescribe the manner in which such acts, records, and proceedings shall be proved, and the effect thereof.

Section 2. Rights in One State of Citizens of Another

1. The citizens of each state shall be entitled to all privileges and immunities [40] of citizens in the several states.

2. A person charged in any state with treason, felony, or other crime, who shall flee from justice, and be found in another state, shall, on demand of the executive authority of the state from which he fled, be delivered up, to be removed to the state having jurisdiction of the crime.

3. No person held to service [41] or labor in one state, under the laws thereof, escaping into another, shall, in consequence of any law or regulation therein, be discharged from such service or labor, but shall

---

[89] During the Civil War an act was passed by Congress according to which all Confederate army or navy officers should forfeit their property. A certain piece of real estate in Virginia belonging to a Confederate naval officer, Forrest by name, was seized by the government and sold by legal proceedings to one Buntley. Buntley sold it to Bigelow. After the death of Forrest his son and rightful heir claimed it, and obtained it because treason cannot "work corruption of blood or forfeiture except during the life of the person attainted." See Art. I, Sec. IX, Cl. 3.

[40] For *privileges* and *immunities* see note on Fourteenth Amendment.

[41] *Person held to service* means slave; hence this clause has no significance now.

be delivered up on claim of the party to whom such service or labor may be due.

Section 3. New States : Territories

1. New states may be admitted by the Congress into this Union; but no new state shall be formed or erected within the jurisdiction of any other state, nor any state be formed by the junction of two or more states, or parts of states, without the consent of the legislatures of the states concerned as well as of the Congress.

2. The Congress shall have power to dispose of and make all needful rules and regulations respecting the territory or other property belonging to the United States; and nothing in this Constitution shall be so construed as to prejudice any claims of the United States, or of any particular state.

Section 4. Protection Afforded to States by the Nation

1. The United States shall guarantee to every state in this Union a republican form of government, and shall protect each of them against invasion; and on application of the legislature, or of the executive (when the legislature cannot be convened), against domestic violence.

ARTICLE V

AMENDMENT

1. The Congress, whenever two-thirds of both Houses shall deem it necessary, shall propose amendments to this Constitution, or, on the application of the legislatures of two-thirds of the several states, shall call a convention for proposing amendments, which, in either case, shall be valid, to all intents and purposes, as part of this Constitution, when ratified by the legislatures of three-fourths of the several states, or by conventions in three-fourths thereof, as the one or the other mode of ratification may be proposed by the Congress : provided that no amendment which may be made prior to the year one thousand eight hundred and eight shall in any manner affect the first and fourth clauses in the ninth section of the first Article; and that no state, without its consent, shall be deprived of its equal suffrage in the Senate.

ARTICLE VI

NATIONAL DEBTS: SUPREMACY OF NATIONAL LAW: OATH

1. All debts contracted and engagements entered into, before the adoption of this Constitution, shall be as valid against the United States under this Constitution as under the Confederation.

2. This Constitution, and the laws of the United States which shall be made in pursuance thereof, and all treaties made, or which shall be made, under the authority of the United States, shall be the supreme law of the land; [42] and the judges in every state shall be bound thereby, anything in the constitution or laws of any state to the contrary notwithstanding.

3. The Senators and Representatives before mentioned, and the members of the several state legislatures, and all executive and judicial officers, both of the United States and of the several states, shall be bound, by oath or affirmation, to support this Constitution; but no religious test shall ever be required as a qualification to any office or public trust under the United States.

ARTICLE VII

ESTABLISHMENT OF CONSTITUTION

1. The ratification of the conventions of nine states shall be sufficient for the establishment of this Constitution between the states so ratifying the same.

[Constitution ratified by States, 1787–1790.]

---

[42] If a federal law and treaty conflict, the courts accept the one most recently passed or ratified. A State law always yields to a treaty.

AMENDMENTS

ARTICLE I [43]

FREEDOM OF RELIGION, OF SPEECH, AND OF THE PRESS: RIGHT OF PETITION

Congress shall make no law respecting an establishment of religion, or prohibiting the free exercise thereof; or abridging the freedom of speech, or of the press; or the right of the people peaceably to assemble, and to petition the government for a redress of grievances.

ARTICLE II [43]

RIGHT TO KEEP ARMS

A well-regulated militia being necessary to the security of a free state, the right of the people to keep and bear arms shall not be infringed.[44]

ARTICLE III [43]

QUARTERING OF SOLDIERS IN PRIVATE HOUSES

No soldier shall, in time of peace, be quartered in any house, without the consent of the owner; nor, in time of war, but in a manner to be prescribed by law.

ARTICLE IV [43]

SEARCH WARRANTS

The right of the people to be secure in their persons, houses, papers, and effects, against unreasonable searches and seizures, shall not be

---

[43] The first ten amendments are restrictions upon the National government only. (See section 129 of the text.) They were adopted in 1791.

[44] As this Amendment restricts Congress only, a State may restrict the use of arms as it sees fit — e. g., to militia authorized by it. A State may prohibit the carrying of arms by such orgnizations as the Knights of Columbus or the Masons. Many States prohibit the carrying of concealed weapons, or even the possession of pistols, dirks, etc.

violated; and no warrants shall issue, but upon probable cause, supported by oath or affirmation, and particularly describing the place to be searched, and the persons or things to be seized.[45]

ARTICLE V [45]

CRIMINAL PROCEEDINGS

No person shall be held to answer for a capital, or otherwise infamous, crime, unless on a presentment or indictment of a grand jury, except in cases arising in the land or naval forces, or in the militia, when in actual service, in time of war, or public danger; nor shall any person be subject, for the same offence, to be twice put in jeopardy of life or limb; nor shall be compelled, in any criminal case, to be a witness against himself; nor be deprived of life, liberty, or property, without due process of law; [46] nor shall private property be taken for public use, without just compensation.[47]

ARTICLE VI [48]

CRIMINAL PROCEEDINGS (continued)

In all criminal prosecutions, the accused shall enjoy the right to a speedy and public trial, by an impartial jury of the state and district wherein the crime shall have been committed, which district shall have been previously ascertained by law; and to be informed of the nature and cause of the accusation; to be confronted with the witnesses against him; to have compulsory process for obtaining witnesses in his favor; and to have the assistance of counsel for his defence.

---

[45] Congress cannot authorize the opening of first class mail except by a warrant issued by a court. The warrant must describe the mail to be opened.

[46] *Due process of law* means the law of the land, both written and unwritten (principles known to courts). In brief, *due process of law* is what the majority of the Supreme Court of the United States thinks the law of the land to be. See section 128 of the text.

[47] While this restriction applies only to the National government, the Fourteenth Amendment extends a portion of it to the States. See Amendment XIV, Sec. 1.

ARTICLE VII[48]

JURY TRIAL IN CIVIL CASES

In suits at common law, where the value in controversy shall exceed twenty dollars, the right of trial by jury shall be preserved; and no fact, tried by a jury, shall be otherwise re-examined in any court of the United States than according to the rules of the common law.

ARTICLE VIII[48]

EXCESSIVE PUNISHMENTS

Excessive bail shall not be required, nor excessive fines imposed, nor cruel and unusual punishments inflicted.

ARTICLE IX[48]

UNENUMERATED RIGHTS OF THE PEOPLE

The enumeration in the Constitution of certain rights shall not be construed to deny or disparage others retained by the people.

ARTICLE X[48]

POWERS RESERVED TO STATES

The powers not delegated to the United States by the Constitution, nor prohibited by it to the states, are reserved to the states respectively, or to the people.

ARTICLE XI[48]

SUITS AGAINST STATES

The judicial power of the United States shall not be construed to extend to any suit in law or equity, commenced or prosecuted against one of the United States by citizens of another state, or by citizens or subjects of any foreign state.[49]

---

[48] This amendment was adopted in 1798.

[49] Officers of a State can be sued in some cases, which practically amounts to a suit against a State.

ARTICLE XII [50]

ELECTION OF PRESIDENT AND VICE-PRESIDENT

1. The Electors shall meet in their respective states, and vote by ballot for President and Vice-President, one of whom, at least, shall not be an inhabitant of the same state with themselves; they shall name in their ballots the person voted for as President, and in distinct ballots the person voted for as Vice-President; and they shall make distinct lists of all persons voted for as President, and of all persons voted for as Vice-President, and of the number of votes for each, which lists they shall sign, and certify, and transmit, sealed, to the seat of the Government of the United States, directed to the President of the Senate; the President of the Senate shall, in the presence of the Senate and the House of Representatives, open all the certificates, and the votes shall then be counted; the person having the greatest number of votes for President shall be the President, if such number be a majority of the whole number of Electors appointed; and if no person have such a majority, then, from the persons having the highest numbers, not exceeding three, on the list of those voted for as President, the House of Representatives shall choose immediately, by ballot, the President. But in choosing the President, the votes shall be taken by states, the representation from each state having one vote; a quorum for this purpose shall consist of a member or members from two-thirds of the states, and a majority of all the states shall be necessary to a choice. And if the House of Representatives shall not choose a President, whenever the right of choice shall devolve upon them, before the fourth day of March next following, then the Vice-President shall act as President, as in case of the death, or other constitutional disability, of the President.

2. The person having the greatest number of votes as Vice-President, shall be the Vice-President, if such number be a majority of the whole number of Electors appointed; and if no person have a majority, then, from the two highest numbers on the list, the Senate shall choose the Vice-President; a quorum for the purpose shall consist of two-thirds of the whole number of Senators; a majority of the whole number shall be necessary to a choice.

3. But no person constitutionally ineligible to the office of President shall be eligible to that of Vice-President of the United States.

---

[50] This amendment was adopted in 1804 and supersedes Art. II, Sec. 1.

ARTICLE XIII [51]

SLAVERY

Section 1. Abolition of Slavery

Neither slavery nor involuntary servitude, except as a punishment for crime, whereof the party shall have been duly convicted, shall exist within the United States, or any place subject to their jurisdiction.

Section 2. Power of Congress

Congress shall have power to enforce this article by appropriate legislation.

ARTICLE XIV [52]

CIVIL RIGHTS: APPORTIONMENT OF REPRESENTATIVES: POLITICAL DISABILITIES: PUBLIC DEBT

Section 1. Civil Rights

All persons born or naturalized in the United States, and subject to the jurisdiction thereof, are citizens of the United States and of the state wherein they reside.[53] No state shall make or enforce any law which shall abridge the privileges or immunities of citizens[54] of the United States; nor shall any state deprive any person of life, liberty, or property, without due process of law, nor deny to any person within its jurisdiction the equal protection of the laws.

---

[51] This amendment was adopted in 1865.

[52] This amendment was adopted in 1868.

[53] By defining *citizenship* it is made clear that negroes are citizens.

And subject to the jurisdiction thereof would exclude children of diplomatic representatives of a foreign state and children born to alien enemies in hostile occupation.

[54] *Privileges and immunities* have never been defined, but the courts have named many things which are and are not a denial of such privileges and immunities. For example, it is not a denial to prohibit marriage between whites and blacks; nor to provide separate schools for these races; nor to provide separate coaches for the races; nor to close business places during certain hours or on Sunday. It is a denial for a State to prohibit the employment of a particular nationality; or to pass an act excluding persons from jury service because of their color or race.

Section 2. Apportionment of Representatives

Representatives shall be apportioned among the several states accord- ᐧ ing to their respective numbers, counting the whole number of persons in each state, excluding Indians not taxed. But when the right to vote at any election for the choice of electors for President and Vice-President of the United States, Representatives in Congress, the executive and judicial officers of a state, or the members of the legislature thereof, is denied to any of the male inhabitants of such state, being twenty-one years of age, and citizens of the United States, or in any way abridged, except for participation in rebellion or other crime, the basis of representation therein shall be reduced in the proportion which the number of such male citizens shall bear to the whole number of male citizens twenty-one years of age in such state.

Section 3. Political Disabilities

No person shall be a Senator or Representative in Congress, or elector of President and Vice-President, or hold any office, civil or military, under the United States, or under any state, who, having previously taken an oath, as a member of Congress, or as an officer of ᐧ the United States, or as a member of any state legislature, or as an executive or judicial officer of any state, to support the Constitution of the United States, shall have engaged in insurrection or rebellion against the same, or given aid or comfort to the enemies thereof. But Congress may, by a vote of two-thirds of each House, remove such disability.

Section 4. Public Debt

The validity of the public debt of the United States, authorized by law, including debts incurred for payment of pensions and bounties for services in suppressing insurrection or rebellion, shall not be questioned. But neither the United States nor any state shall assume or pay any debt or obligation incurred in aid of insurrection or rebellion against the United States, or any claim for the loss or emancipation of any slave; but all such debts, obligations, and claims shall be held illegal and void.

Section 5. Powers of Congress

The Congress shall have power to enforce, by appropriate legislation, the provisions of this article.

ARTICLE XV [55]

RIGHT OF SUFFRAGE

Section 1. Right of Negro to Vote

The right of citizens of the United States to vote shall not be denied or abridged by the United States or by any state on account of race, color, or previous condition of servitude.

Section 2. Power of Congress

The Congress shall have power to enforce this article by appropriate legislation.

ARTICLE XVI [56]

INCOME TAX

The Congress shall have power to lay and collect taxes on incomes, from whatever source derived, without apportionment among the several states, and without regard to any census or enumeration.

ARTICLE XVII [57]

SENATE: ELECTION: VACANCIES

The Senate of the United States shall be composed of two Senators from each state, elected by the people thereof, for six years; and each Senator shall have one vote. The electors in each state shall have the qualifications requisite for electors of the most numerous branch of the state legislatures.

When vacancies happen in the representation of any state in the Senate, the executive authority of such state shall issue writs of election to fill such vacancies : Provided, That the legislature of any state may empower the executive thereof to make temporary appointment until the people fill the vacancies by election as the legislature may direct. [57]

This amendment shall not be so construed as to affect the election or term of any Senator chosen before it becomes valid as part of the Constitution.

---

[55] This amendment was adopted in 1870. It was passed to secure negro suffrage and to prevent negroes from being disfranchised.

[56] Amendment XVI was adopted in 1913. It modifies Art. 1, Sec. 9, Cl. 4.

[57] This amendment was adopted in 1913. It modifies Art. 1, Sec. 3, Cls. 1 and 2.

ARTICLE XVIII

NATIONAL PROHIBITION

SECTION 1 — After one year from the ratification of this article the manufacture, sale or transportation of intoxicating liquors within, the importation thereof into, or the exportation thereof from the United States and all territory subject to the jurisdiction thereof for beverage purposes is hereby prohibited.

SECTION 2 — The Congress and the several states shall have concurrent power to enforce this article by appropriate legislation.

SECTION 3 — This article shall be inoperative unless it shall have been ratified as an amendment to the Constitution by the Legislatures of the several states, as provided in the Constitution, within seven years of the date of the submission hereof to the states by Congress.

APPENDIX II

SUGGESTIONS

It is recommended that the teacher read *The Teaching of Civics*, by Mabel Hill, published by Houghton Mifflin Company, New York, 1914. Price 60 cents.

All students should read the Constitution of the United States (Appendix 1) before studying Chapter IV of this text.

A study of local conditions will make the course more practical. For instance, students may be assigned papers on the following subjects concerning the county: history, natural resources, character of population, wealth, domestic animals, livestock products, production of crop wealth, organizations and coöperative enterprises, rural credits, markets, improved public highways, railway facilities, schools, public health and sanitation, churches and Sunday schools, and the farm home. See Syllabus of Home-County Club Studies, The University of North Carolina Record, No. 121, September, 1914. Extension Series No. 9.

Interest in the course will be greatly stimulated if a trip to Washington, to your State capital, to your county courthouse, to the city hall, or to any nearby public institution can be arranged.

Each student should be encouraged to read such books as :

Uncle Sam's Modern Miracles, by W. A. Du Puy. Frederick A. Stokes, New York City, 1914. Price $1.25.

The American Government, by F. J. Haskin. J. B. Lippincott Company, Philadelphia, 1912. Price, $1.00.

Each student should be encouraged to subscribe to a weekly magazine of political events such as:

The Literary Digest, New York City ($3.00).

Current Events, Springfield, Mass. (40 cents).

These magazines usually give club rates at about half price.

The following reference books should be in the school library:

Cyclopedia of American Government, by McLaughlin and Hart. D. Appleton and Company. New York, 1914. 3 vols. Price $22.50.

The American Year Book, a record of events and progress. D. Appleton and Company, New York. Price $3.50.

The World Almanac, Press Publishing Company, New York. Price 25 cents. Postage 10 cents.

The Manual, Legislative Hand Book, or *Blue Book* of your State. This manual contains such valuable information as the State constitutions, list of State and local officers, and election returns. It can usually be obtained free from the Secretary of your State.

The Congressional Directory, which contains a short biography of each congressman, a list of congressional committees, maps of States showing congressional districts, and a list of the administrative departments and bureaus and the duties of the officers thereof. A free copy can be had through your congressman.

The Statistical Abstract of the United States. Issued annually by the Department of Commerce, Washington, D. C. Free through congressman.

Reader's Guide to Periodical Literature. This index will be useful only in case your library contains bound volumes of magazines.

The American Political Science Review, Chester Lloyd Jones, University of Wisconsin, Madison, Wis. Price $3.00 per year.

The National Municipal Review, Philadelphia, Pa. Price $5 per year. This will be useful to city schools.

The teacher should have one of the following text-books to use as a hand-book in connection with this course:

American Government and Politics, by Charles A. Beard. Macmillan, New York, New and Revised Edition, 1914. Price $2.10.

The New American Government and its Work, by James T. Young. Macmillan, New York. 1915. Price $2.25.

APPENDIX III

GOVERNMENT PRINTING OFFICE

SUPERINTENDENT OF DOCUMENTS
WASHINGTON

PUBLIC DOCUMENTS

Every American should be interested in the publications that emanate from this Office, for public documents are the history of the country. While a small proportion of the issues might be obtained without cost through the friendship of public men, by far the larger part must be purchased, and nearly everyone interested in the literature of the United States prefers to pay for what he desires, rather than to be under obligation for small favors. Because of this it may be desirable to give the widest possible publicity to the fact that public documents can be purchased from the Superintendent of Documents, Government Printing Office, at a nominal cost. Price lists, indicating the subjects covered, may be obtained free, upon application in person or by mail. Among them are the following:[1]

---

[1] Lists 1 to 9, 12 to 14, etc. are omitted because they are out of print.

The character of the price lists may be better understood by an illustration. Price List 45, entitled Public Roads Office, lists about one hundred reports, bulletins, and circulars, which sell for five or ten cents each. The following titles are typical: Construction of macadam roads; Sand-clay and earth roads in the Middle West; Dust prevention and road preservation; Bitumens and their essential constituents for road construction and maintenance; Examination and classification of rocks for road building, including physical properties of rocks with reference to their mineral composition and structure; Road-making material in Arkansas; Public roads of Alabama (and each of the other states); Laws of certain states relating to the use of wide tires; Notes on the use of convicts in connection with road building; Descriptive catalog of road model exhibit; Proceedings of National Good Roads Convention; and Historical and technical papers on road building in the United States.

PRICE LISTS

10. Laws of the United States.
11. Food and diet.
15. Geological Survey publications.
16. Farmers' bulletins, Reports, and Yearbooks of the Agriculture Department.
18. Engineering: Mechanics.
19. Army and Navy.
20. Lands.
21. Fishes.
24. Indians.
25. Transportation, publications of Interstate Commerce Commission, and other documents on roads, railroads, inland waterways, and shipping.
28. Finance.
31. Education.
32. Noncontiguous territory and Cuba.
33. Labor questions.
35. Geography and explorations.
36. Periodicals published by various Government bureaus.
37. Tariff.
38. Animal Industry.
40. Chemistry Bureau, publications on chemical analysis of food and drugs.

41. Entomology Bureau, publications on insects.
42. Experiment Stations Office, publications on farmers' institutes and extension work, and nutrition, drainage and irrigation investigations.
43. Forest Service, publications on trees, lumber, wood preservation, and forest management.
44. Plant life.
45. Public Roads Office.
46. Soils.
47. Crop statistics, Agriculture Department.
48. Weather Bureau.
50. American history.
51. Health and hygiene.
53. Maps published by various Government bureaus.
54. Political economy.
55. National Museum publications.
56. Smithsonian Institution publications.
57. Astronomical papers.

List of Library of Congress publications.

The foregoing by no means embrace all the subjects treated in public documents. If you fail to see here what you want, send your inquiries to the —

SUPERINTENDENT OF DOCUMENTS,
GOVERNMENT PRINTING OFFICE,
WASHINGTON, D. C.

INDEX

References are to pages

4 INDEX

References are to pages

References are to pages

References are to pages

References are to pages

References are to pages

Monopolies, 24; ownership of natural monopolies advocated, 230. *See* Trusts.

Montana, constitutional amendment process, 244 note; legislature, 254; governor, 267; board of commissioners, 305; county officers, 311; townships, 319 note; suffrage restrictions, 354 note; woman suffrage, 355; direct primary, 368 note; initiative and referendum, 380; educational rank, 411.

Morals, protection to, 9.

Municipal government. *See* City government.

Municipal ownership, 343–347.

Murder, defined, 292.

National Advisory Board, 165 (7).

National banks, 183.

National conventions, 231–235; choice of delegates, 232; representation reduced, 232 note; meeting of, 233; reports of committees, 234; nomination of President, 234, 235.

National museum. 190.

National Voters' League, 67 (7), 101, 265 (9).

Naturalization, power of Congress over, 42, 434, 449; defined, 80; Bureau of, 175.

Naval Academy at Annapolis, 157.

Naval War College, 158.

Navy, cost of establishment, 141, 156; cost of vessels, 165 (4); number and kinds of vessels, 158; Secretary of, 156; General Board, 158; personnel of the, 157; constitutional provision, 435.

Navy Department, 156–158.

Nebraska, constitutional amendment process, 244 note; legislature, 254; governor, 267; board of supervisors, 304; board of commissioners, 304; county officers, 310; suffrage restrictions, 354 note; direct primary, 368 note; initiative and referendum, 380; educational rank. 411.

"Necessary and proper" clause, 42, 50, 82, 436.

Negro suffrage, 352, 361, 451.

Nevada, constitutional amendment process, 244 note; legislature, 254; governor, 267; board of commissioners, 305; county officers, 311; townships, 219 note; suffrage restrictions, 354 note; woman suffrage, 355; direct primary, 368 note; initiative, referendum, and recall, 380; educational rank, 411.

New Hampshire, colonial government in, 28; ratified federal constitution, 37 note; constitutional amendment process, 243; legislature, 251, 254; governor, 267; board of commissioners, 304; county officers, 310; suffrage restrictions, 354 note, 360 note; direct primary, 368 note; educational rank, 411.

New Jersey, colonial government in, 29, 30; plan of union, 35; ratified federal constitution, 37 note; constitutional amendment process, 244 note; legislature, 254; governor, 267, 276 (4); chosen freeholders, 304; county officers, 310; boroughs, 327; suffrage restrictions, 354 note; direct primary, 368 note; party convention, 383 (7); jury commissioner, 285 note; equity courts, 289 note; educational rank, 411.

New Mexico, constitutional amendment process, 244 note; legislature, 254; governor, 267; board of commissioners, 305; county officers, 311; suffrage restrictions, 354 note; referendum, 380; educational rank, 411.

New York, colonial government in, 28–30; taxes, 33; tariff, 33; ratified federal constitution, 37 note; constitutional amendment process, 244 note; senatorial districts, 251; assembly districts, 252; legislature, 246, 254; governor, 267; salary of judges, 282; board of supervisors, 303, 304; county officers, 310; villages, 327; suffrage restrictions, 354 note; registration in, 365; direct primary, 368 note; inheritance tax,

14   INDEX

References are to pages

Prohibition party, platform, 230, 358.
Property, defined, 207 note; taxes, 387, 388; general tax, 390, 391; constitutional provisions, 446, 449.
Proportional representation, 231.
Proprietary colonies, 29.
Public debt, interest on federal, 141; restrictions on State, 255 note.
Public education, 394–412. *See* Education.
Public Health Service, United States, 5–7, 136 note.
Public lands, sale of, 137.
Public ownership, advocated, 230, 231
Public schools, administration of, 402; appointment of funds, 404; revenue for, 430. *See pp.* 394–412.
Pure food, power of Congress concerning, 74, 87 (14).

Qualifications of federal officers: representatives, 60, 65; senators, 61, 65; President, 104, 122; Vice-president, 120, 123; constitutional provisions, 429, 431, 432, 438, 444, 448, 451.
Qualifications on suffrage, 352–362.
Quarantine, 6, 7, 70, 136 note, 171.
Quorums of Congress, 432, 448.

Race, suffrage restriction prohibited, 352, 361, 451.
Railroads, federal regulation of, 72–75, 87 (13), 183; federal ownership advocated, 230. *See* Interstate Commision.
Recall, of State officers, 379, 380; of city officers, 337, 340, 379; advocated by political parties, 230, 231; progress of, 380.
Reclamation bureau, 168. *See* Irrigation.
Reference bureau, legislative, 258, 259.
Referendum, advocated by political parties, 230, 231; in States, 260, 379, 380; in cities, 260, 337, 340; progress of, 380.

Register of deeds, 310–312.
Registration of voters, 365.
Removal, power of, by President, 113; in Congress, 61, 430, 431, 432, 438, 439, 440.
Republic, 25.
Republican form of government, 24, 25, 443.
Republican party, 228; platform, 229, 358; finance, 237.
Religious liberty, 210, 255, 444, 445.
Representation, in Congress, 430, 450; in Senate, 443; proportional, advocated, 231.
Representatives. *See* House of Representatives.
Resolutions, joint, 118, note, 433; concurrent, 433, 434.
Revenue, federal, 137–142; bills, 65, 94, 433; internal, 137, 138; disbursement of, 141.
Revenue, State, sources of, 387; expenditure of, 392; school, 403.
Revision of federal constitution, 48, 443; of State constitutions, 242–245.
River and harbor improvements, power of Congress over, 82; legislation, 98; advocated, 229.
Rhode Island, colonial government in, 29, 30; ratified federal constitution, 37 note; colonial charter, 241; constitutional amendment process, 244 note; legislature, 254; governor, 267; sheriff, 309; county officers, 310; suffrage restrictions, 354 note; educational rank, 411.
Roads, models of, 11; national aid, 13, 87 (12); advocated, 229, 230.
Robbery, 293.
Royal colonies, 28.
Rules of procedure, in Congress, 91, 92, 432.
Rural free delivery, 16, 162, 165 (8).

Schools, 8; elementary, 8, 398; high, 8, 398; county superintendent of, 310, 311, 313; year-round, 396; administration of public, 402; revenue for, 403; apportionment of funds,

References are to pages

References are to pages

References are to pages

ical, 321, 324; officers of, 318; trustees, 320; New England system, 328; powers granted to, 255; powers of New England, 315; county conflict, 320.

Treason, defined, 432, 440, 411, 442.

Treasurer, of the United States, 141, 145; of the States, 268, 274; of the counties, 310–312.

Treasury, federal department of, 136–147; secretary of, 136, 185, 186.

Treaties, federal power over, 42, 114, 439; ratification of, 63, 65; federal jurisdiction over, 193, 441; relative rank of, 247, 444; States' powers to make, prohibited, 437.

Trial, by jury, 296, 441, 441 note, 446, 447.

Trusts, law against, 74, 188; meaning of, 74 note. *See* Monopolies.

Trustees, township, 320.

Two-thirds rule, 235.

Underwood-Simmons bill traced, 95–97.

Unemployed, insurance against, 230; relief of, advocated, 231 (8); aid to, 174.

Unit-rule, 235.

United States Courts, 193–202.

Universities, State, 400.

Utah, constitutional amendment process, 244 note; legislature, 254; governor, 267; board of commissioners, 305; county officers, 311; suffrage restrictions, 354 note; woman suffrage, 355; initiative and referendum, 380; educational rank, 411; eight-hour law, 207.

Verdict, 291.

Vermont, constitutional amendment process, 244 note; legislature, 254; governor, 267; extra duties of grand jury, 284 note; assistant judges, 304; county officers, 310; villages, 327; suffrage restrictions, 354 note; direct primary, 368 note; educational rank, 411.

Veto, President's, 47, 118, 230, 231,

433; governor's, 272; mayor's, 329, 333, 336, 340.

Vice-President, nomination of, 120; qualifications, election, salary, and term, 65, 120; president of senate, 65; constitutional provisions, 431, 433, 437, 438, 440, 448.

Villages, government of, 320, 327–329; powers delegated to, 255; taxes of, 388.

Virginia, colonial government in, 28, 29; tariff, 34; plan of union, 35; ratified federal constitution, 37 note; religious liberty in, 210; freedom of speech and of the press in, 211; constitutional amendment process, 244 note; legislature, 254; governor, 267; board of supervisors, 304; county officers, 310; magisterial districts, 319 note; cities 326 (5); suffrage restrictions, 354 note; 360 note; educational test, 360 note; direct primary, 368 note; inheritance tax, 392; educational rank, 411; student loan fund, 414 (9).

Volunteers, army, 155.

Vote of two thirds, 431–433, 439, 443.

Votes, for president, table of, 106.

Voter's League, National, 67 (7), 101, 265 (9).

Voting, in Congress, 102 (3); viva voce, 372; by ballots, 373; by Australian method, 371.

War, 42; powers of Congress over, 81, 435, 437, 441; cost of, 156.

War College, Army, 151–154.

War department, 151–156; secretary of, 151; cost of military establishment, 141. *See also* Army.

Washington, constitutional amendment process, 244 note; legislature, 254; governor, 267, 272; board of commissioners, 305; county officers, 311; suffrage restrictions, 354 note; 360 note; woman suffrage, 355; direct primary, 368 note; initiative, referendum, and recall, 380; educational rank, 411.

References are to pages

ADVERTISEMENTS

The Ancient World. Revised Edition

By Professor WILLIS MASON WEST, of the University of Minnesota

PART ONE, Greece and the East. 12mo, cloth, 324 pages.
PART TWO, Rome and the West. 12mo, cloth, 371 pages.
COMPLETE EDITION. 12mo, cloth, 681 pages.

THE New Ancient World is well within the scope of the abilities of the youngest students in high schools and academies. Its style is simple, direct, vivid, and interesting, and never fails to impress even the most immature reader, who carries away from a study of this book a series of striking pictures of ancient life.

The author emphasizes the unity in historical development; he shows that national life, like individual life, has continuous growth and development, and that a knowledge of the past explains the present. Every experiment in government in ancient times has its lesson; and in the hands of Professor West history becomes an instrument for teaching the duties of modern citizenship.

(1) Most stress is laid on those periods and those persons who contributed most to the development of civilization.

(2) Space is found for the exciting and the picturesque whenever it is matter of historical importance. Narrative and biography abound.

(3) Little weight is given to the legendary periods of Greek and Roman history, and the space thus gained is devoted to the wide-reaching Hellenic world after Alexander, and to the Roman Empire which had so deep an influence on later history.

(4) In every paragraph the leading idea is brought out by italics, and illuminating quotations introduce many chapters.

(5) The book teaches the use of a library by giving specific references to topics for reports.

(6) There are forty-six maps and plans, which are made the basis of study, suggested by questions given in the text. There are also one hundred eighty-one illustrations taken from authentic sources.

The Modern World

By Professor W. M. WEST, 12mo, cloth, 794 pages.

THIS volume, intended as a companion to the author's *Ancient World*, is a revision of his *Modern History*.

As in the Ancient World, there has been a determined effort to make a simple history that can be easily understood by pupils in the early years of the High School. Interesting phases of history are given prominence, difficult ideas have been avoided, the language throughout is simple.

One new feature of the Modern World is five preliminary chapters, giving an outline of history from prehistoric times to the accession of Charlemagne. These chapters serve as an excellent review for a course in Ancient History, or even make it possible to use the Modern World to cover the general history of the world.

The book contains nearly two hundred handsome illustrations and is provided with fifty-three maps, all but five of which are colored.

Like the Modern History the book gives especial prominence to the period since the French Revolution. The author treats with comparative briefness many phases of the history of the Middle Ages in order to gain adequate space for the marvellous nineteenth century, and so for an intelligent introduction to the twentieth.

American Government

By DR. FRANK ABBOTT MAGRUDER, 12mo, cloth, 488 pages.

THE economic element in government is emphasized throughout this book. It has a thorough treatment, not only of theoretical government, but especially of practical politics, caucuses, marking ballots, registration.

The enormous influence of the judiciary is made clear, and it is shown how, through interpretation, they often legislate. It contains a frank discussion of the weaknesses of our government, as well as of its strong points.

American History and Government

By Professor WILLIS MASON WEST. With maps and illustrations. 12mo, cloth, 814 pages.

THIS volume fuses the study of American history with the study of our political institutions in their practical workings — each group of institutions being taken up for complete study where it may best be understood as a product of progressive history. Large place is given to economic and industrial development, as the main explanation of political growth, with clear consciousness of the constant interaction between these mighty forces.

Aside from this combination of "History" and "Civics," the book is unique in three great features: (1) the large place given to the influence of the West; (2) the attention given to the deeply significant labor movements of 1825–1840; (3) and the story of the recent Progressive movement. Indeed, a fourth of the space is given to the last forty years.

The common delusion of a golden age of democracy in the days of Jefferson or of John Winthrop is firmly exposed and corrected, and the student is surely and skilfully led to look forward, not backward. The tremendous problems of to-day, too, are put forward with no shading of their difficulties. The book is in no sense a special plea; but it is written in a sincere conviction that a fair presentation of American history must give to American youth a robust and aggressive faith in democracy.

A Source Book in American History

By Professor WILLIS MASON WEST. 12mo, cloth, 608 pages.

THIS is a companion volume to *American History and Government*. It contains much material never before accessible to young students. No extract has been selected unless it has some definite articulation with the purpose of the main text.

History of England

By CHARLES M. ANDREWS, Farnam Professor of History in Yale University. With Maps, Tables, and numerous Illustrations. 12mo, cloth, 608 pages.

AN important feature of this history is the definite method of presentation. At the beginning of each period the author briefly outlines the character and the tendencies of the time. He then elaborates this outline, and before leaving the subject summarizes it in a few brief sentences.

The book teaches that the achievements of the English people have been solid and enduring, not dramatic and sensational, and concern the more peaceful aspects of human existence — government, legislation, agriculture, industry, commerce, and finance — quite as much as the stirring scenes of land battles and sea fights. To quote the author: "History to-day has got rid of much of the stage thunder that passed current in the older narratives. It points to the industry that underlies wealth, and to the wealth that makes military success possible. It lays stress upon the national or social conditions that render the great statute or legislative act necessary, and upon the pressure of food or population and the spurring of religious conviction that urge men to brave the sea and undertake colonization. It calls attention to the deep significance of peasants' rebellions, religious revivals, and industrial revolutions in preparing the way for the rise of democracy and the transformation of the social life of a nation."

The book contains seventeen maps; a large number of genealogical tables; seventy-four well-executed illustrations taken from authentic sources; a facsimile of a section of the Magna Carta; and reproductions of drawings on early manuscripts.

A carefully selected list of books that will be useful in any school library, a detailed chronological table, and bibliographies covering the best and most recent works, add to the usefulness of the history.

The book has numerous foot-notes which refer definitely to original sources by volume and page number.

A Short History of England

By CHARLES M. ANDREWS, Farnam Professor of History in Yale University. With Maps, Tables, and numerous Illustrations. 12mo, cloth, 473 pages.

THIS history of England aims to present within the compass of about 400 pages the main features of England's story from earliest times to the present day. The book traces in rapid survey the development of the people and institutions of England from Anglo-Saxon times to the close of the year 1911, and shows by what steps the primitive organization of a semi-tribal people has been transformed into the highly complicated political and social structure of the United Kingdom and the British Empire. It retains on a smaller scale the essential characteristics of the larger work by the same author, with some additions, chiefly of a geographical and biographical character, and many omissions of details.

The author tells a clear and simple story, avoiding technical expressions and yet passing over no important feature of the history that is necessary for the proper understanding of the subject.

The aim of the book is to be instructive as well as interesting. The narrative is made as continuous as possible, that the pupil may follow in unbroken sequence the thread of the story. It is accompanied with a large number of newly selected illustrations and an ample supply of maps and chronological tables. The elaborate bibliographies contained in the larger work have been omitted and only a small but selective list of the best books in brief form has been retained   The history has been brought down to date in matters of scholarship as well as chronology, and contains many views and statements not to be found in the larger work   It is designed as a text-book for half-year, or elementary courses, but it might well be used by any reader desiring a brief and suggestive account of the main features of England's history.

History of the United States

By the late CHARLES K. ADAMS, and Professor W. P. TRENT, of Columbia University. 12mo, cloth, 630 pages.

THE authors have laid the stress on the two crises of American history — the Revolutionary War and the Civil War. They have treated both these periods very fully, and have endeavored in the case of the first to present the side of Great Britain with fairness, while, at the same time, bringing out the necessity of the struggle, and the bravery and wisdom of the American patriots. In dealing with the period of the Civil War they have aimed to give the Southern side with sympathy and, while upholding the cause of the Union, have sought to avoid recrimination, and to give each side credit for its sincerity and bravery. The other periods of our history have not been unduly subordinated to the great crises, but have been so treated as to lead up to them. The process of the making of the Constitution and the various developments in its interpretation have been fully studied. While emphasis has necessarily been laid on the political and military features of our history, the social, industrial, scientific, and literary development of the country has been given due space.

The following are some of the special features of the book:

Thirty-six maps, of which nineteen are colored.

Two hundred and three illustrations, reproduced from authentic sources. Especial care has been taken to include the best possible portraits of eminent men. Some of these were taken from private collections and have not been published before.

A full chronological table

Foot-notes which describe the lives of persons mentioned in the text, in order that the narrative shall not be interrupted at the appearance of each new name.

The great development of the United States during the past decade makes it imperative that an adequate history be kept up to date. The present edition covers the period to March, 1913, and contains a full account of the chief events of President Taft's administration.

CPSIA information can be obtained
at www.ICGtesting.com
Printed in the USA
BVOW10s1054111217
502490BV00016B/718/P